COMMENTS ABOUT
STORIES OF FAITH AND COURAGE FROM THE VIETNAM WAR:

I've long considered Larkin Spivey a mentor, warrior, leader, and friend. His thoughtful devotional, *Battlefields & Blessings: Stories of Faith and Courage from the Vietnam War*, links moments in time with timeless wisdom. This collection is "a gift a day"—recounting Vietnam experiences that connect and acknowledge all who have had the privilege of serving this great Nation.

—**General Peter Pace,** USMC (Retired) 16th Chairman of the Joint Chiefs of Staff

This book will feed your heart, your soul, and your faith. If I were going to take just one book into battle with me this would be the one I would put into my duffle bag. The stories are uplifting and sacred. Larkin Spivey has the spiritual pulse of combat.

—**William McDonald,** Vietnam veteran, founder of the Military Writers Society of America, and author of *A Spirtiual Warrior's Journey*

Larkin Spivey has given us the greater context of faith, of our Lord's presence—especially IN the darkness . . . even when we are half-way around the world, even when we find our bed in the hell of war. His daily devotion approach, like a "time-release" medication for the soul, enables one to view combat experiences in color and not simply black-and-white.

—**Ray W. Stubbe,** Vietnam veteran, Khe Sanh Chaplain, founder of Khe Sanh Veterans Inc., and author of *Valley of Decision*

The 365 devotionals in this book are as life changing as the 365 days of a GI's tour of duty in Vietnam.

—**Charles W. Sasser,** author of *Predator, Hill 488, Encyclopedia of Navy Seals, God in the Foxhole,* and many other military books

Larkin Spivey uses scripture and war experiences to make a spiritual connection between the human heart and God. This book provides an effective tool for anyone who wants to relate scripture to real life experience. It also offers an avenue of reconciliation for troubled warriors of every conflict.

—**Ron Rayner,** Chaplain, Khe Sanh Veterans, career fire fighter

Stories of Faith and Courage from the Vietnam War is an inspiring devotional that defines the meaning of duty, honor, country, faith, and war. It will change the way every reader views this conflict and is a must read for veterans of this and every other war.

—**Brigadier General Chalmers R. "Hap" Carr,** U.S. Air Force (Retired) and past Chairman of the Clemson University Corps

Larkin Spivey has done a great job of revealing truths, not only about the Vietnam war, but about all war. Puts you right in the action and lets you know Who really is in charge.

> —**Charlie Campbell,** Vietnam veteran and Master Gunnery Sergeant, USMC (Retired).

COMMENTS ABOUT OTHER BOOKS BY LARKIN SPIVEY:

Highly recommended for any Christian military person or veteran who considers prayer, spirituality, and God important parts of his or her life. Also for their loved ones, or simply Christians in general.

> — **Rob Ballister,** lead reviewer, Military Writers Society of America

An amazing compilation of real-life stories brilliantly edited. *Stories of Faith and Courage from World War II* makes a perfect gift for veterans of any war or their family members. This is a book that should be in every church and school library in America and on the required reading list of every serious history student.

> — **Richard R. Blake,** Top 500 reviewer, Amazon.com

Battlefields and Blessings: Stories of Faith and Courage from World War II by Larkin Spivey is a must read for anyone who loves history and is looking for a way to invigorate one's daily devotions. Very readable and intriguing.

> — **Deborah A. Hodge,** adjunct history instructor, University of Tennessee, Martin, TN

"Larkin Spivey knows the Lord and he knows war. The stories he recounts in *Battlefields & Blessings* are memorable and moving, and the accompanying devotional points and Scripture passages are nothing short of inspiring. It's a unique, meaningful work that will inform and bless the reader at home or in the office

> — **Rod Gragg,** author of *Covered with Glory* and other military histories

From a time period that spans the Revolutionary War through the Cuban Missile Crisis, Spivey uncovered . . . fascinating details that lead to the inescapable conclusion that God's hand influenced the cause of freedom during danger ous and pivotal junctures in our nation's history.

> — *National Review*

God in the Trenches is a timely and helpful reminder of how God has watched over America's destiny in previous wars, and inspires trust that He will do so in this one as well.

— The late **Reverend Peter Marshall,** author of *The Light and the Glory, From Sea to Shining Sea,* and *Sounding Forth the Trumpet*

Larkin Spivey has added another important work to the library of the pensive warrior who might be searching for a deeper understanding of his service in the profession of arms.

— *Marine Corps Gazette*

He documents so well critical junctures in our military history when we could have perished as a nation but for the active intervention of God.

— The late **Dr. D. James Kennedy,** former president, Coral Ridge Ministries

Larkin Spivey presents a fascinating story of how God has intervened at critical moments of war to turn the tide. This book should inspire the faith of every American!

— **Luis Palau,** international evangelist

We've always felt it in our hearts—now here's the evidence. Given our nation's current military conflict, his revelations couldn't come at a better time.

— **Conservative Book Club**

Larkin Spivey draws out of history God's purpose for America in an appealing and intriguing way.

— **Maj. Gen. John Grinalds,** past president, The Citadel

This is a wonderful and powerful book! I was truly blessed by having the opportunity to read it.

— **Tim Burgan,** Cornerstone Television

Every American should read *Miracles of the American Revolution.* It will grip your soul!

— **Chuck Crismier,** Save America Ministries

This book is great! It's the best 'little' history book that I've read in my life.

— **John Dayl,** KXAM Radio

ALSO BY LARKIN SPIVEY

God in the Trenches

Miracles of the American Revolution

Battlefields & Blessings: Stories of Faith and Courage from World War II
(Military Writers Society of America Silver Medal Award Winner)

Stories OF Faith AND Courage
FROM THE
VIETNAM WAR

LARKIN SPIVEY

GOD & COUNTRY
PRESS

Print Edition: ISBN 978-0-89957-019-8
EPUB Edition: ISBN 978-1-61715-067-8
Mobi Edition: ISBN 978-1-61715-069-2
e-PDF Edition: ISBN 978-1-61715-229-0

First printing, June 2011

Cover designed by Mike Meyers at Meyers Design, Houston, TX

Interior design and typesetting by Reider Publishing Services, West Hollywood, CA

Edited and proofread by Jocelyn Green, Rich Cairnes, and Rick Steele

Maps by Bowring Cartographic, 258 North Park Dr., Arlington, VA 22203. www.sitemaps.com

Printed in Canada
18 17 16 15 14 13 12 11 –T– 7 6 5 4 3 2 1

Contents

Maps

Acknowledgments

I AM GRATEFUL to my fellow Vietnam veterans who gave their time and emotional energy to relive moments from their past, some of which were painful. Their stories have been inspirational to me, as I hope they will be to readers. I am especially thankful to the Khe Sanh veterans who have shared their experiences in a unique magazine titled *Red Clay.* Tom Eichler, the editor, has graciously given me permission to use many of these amazing stories from an important campaign of the war with which I was involved.

I also need to acknowledge every Army, Navy, and Air Force veteran who might conclude I have overemphasized Marine Corps participation in this war. I have tried to be fair and balanced, but have to admit that, as a Marine, I have more contacts, sources, and firsthand knowledge of this part of the war. To be clear, I publicly affirm my undying admiration for every soldier, sailor, and airman who served. I hope their stories are adequately represented in these pages.

I appreciate the many editorial contributions to this book made by Jocelyn Green, a great freelance writer, editor, author of *Faith Deployed: Daily Encouragement for Military Wives,* and co-author of another book in the Battlefields & Blessings series: *Stories of Faith and Courage from the War in Iraq & Afghanistan.* I also thank my priest and pastor, the Reverend Rob Sturdy, for his continuing spiritual guidance and for his specific counsel regarding this work. My wife and partner, Lani, has contributed immensely to the spiritual direction of this and my other books, as well as my life.

Foremost, I acknowledge my Lord and Savior, Jesus Christ, whom I have tried to keep at the center of my life and every page of this book. I am thankful to Rick Steele, Dale Anderson, Trevor Overcash, John Fallahee, and all the staff at AMG Publishers who daily devote their exceptional professionalism and vision in service to the same cause.

Note about photo credits: The vast majority of photographs in this book have specific credits. If no credit is given for a particular photo, it is either mine or permission was given by the person in the photo.

Introduction

ON JULY 23, 1967, I walked across the red-dust-blown tarmac of the Da Nang airstrip to catch my PanAm charter flight home. At the top of the ramp I paused briefly to breathe the tropical air and scan the far-off jungle-covered mountains where men were still fighting. I said a silent prayer of thanks that I had made it and wondered again why some hadn't. Once again, no answer came to me. My uneasy standoff with God continued, as I pondered the friends and fellow Marines lost on those distant hills. I continued to struggle with the randomness of death and God's apparent absence from those battlefields. There was not even a glimmer of thought at that time or for decades after that he might have somehow played a role in the decisions I made, or that he had saved lives, including my own.

My previous book (on World War II) was about a simpler and more spiritual era in American history. During that period there seemed to be more evidence of faith in the lives of servicemen and women, their families at home, and our national leaders. Unfortunately for the men who went to Vietnam, the times were more complicated and less spiritual. They had to fight a controversial war and then return home to a rapidly changing culture that seemed to be turning away from God. Writing this book has been an amazing journey, taking me back to that time and my issues with God—and the emptiness of what was then my own skeptical nature.

This book is a daily devotional designed to show the role of faith in the Vietnam War. During the course of my research, I made some interesting discoveries. Some young soldiers and Marines went to this war with a deep spiritual connection to God that played an important role in their experience during and after the war. On the other hand, there were many others who went with little or no faith and had negative experiences that caused them to turn away from God. I was surprised and gratified to find that many of these veterans eventually returned to God or later found him for the first time. Amazingly, these men have found a deeper relationship to God than many of their fellow citizens who never seriously questioned their own faith.

My secondary purpose in writing this book is to correct some of the history written about the war and to provide a more complete image of the veterans who fought it. These subjects are addressed in the monthly summaries explaining the different phases of the war and in many of the daily devotions themselves. I hope to convince every veteran this was a war the United States needed to fight. Their long struggle was an important part of the Cold War, and they can be proud that their heroic effort in Vietnam contributed to America's ultimate victory over a system of government that never had an elected Congress, free press, or antiwar movement of any kind.

Unfortunately, the antiwar agenda in the United States has lived on after the war, seeking to portray the great men and women who went to fight it as victims rather than as heroes. Independent research confirms my own observations that the vast majority of Vietnam veterans returned home to become well-adjusted and productive citizens. They are proud of their military service, but don't feel their lives were defined by it. They are heroes in every sense of the word and the greatest part of their own unique generation.

This description of the average Vietnam veteran is not meant to ignore or belittle the men who saw the kind of action during the war that caused significant problems afterward. Post-traumatic stress disorder is a real medical condition many have been treated for, and has left some needing help who don't even know it. I hope veterans with issues of depression or repressed anger and guilt recognize themselves in some of the stories told in this book and are motivated to seek the treatment they need.

Although I left Vietnam a religious skeptic, I am gratified to report that many years later the spiritual void in my life was filled by Jesus Christ. I am now proud to serve in his great army and to carry on the mission of glorifying him. If there are fellow Vietnam veterans reading this who have not found peace in their lives, I hope they will be moved by these stories to seek a new life in the one place where peace is guaranteed—the person of Jesus Christ.

Glossary

APC—armored personnel carrier

ARVN—Army of the Republic of Vietnam (South Vietnam)

Arc Light—B-52 strike

CO—commanding officer

DMZ—Demilitarized Zone

DoD—Department of Defense

Dustoff—medical evacuation helicopter or mission

FAC—forward air controller

FMF—Fleet Marine Force

FO—forward observer (artillery)

Grunt—infantryman

Huey—a UH-series utility helicopter, manufactured by Bell

In country—in Vietnam, as opposed to being "in the world" (anyplace else)

LZ—landing zone

LP—listening post

LRRP—long-range reconnaissance patrol

MACV—Military Assistance Command Vietnam

Medevac—medical evacuation, usually by helicopter of same name

MIA—missing in action

mm—millimeter, as in "7.62-mm ammunition"

NCO—noncommissioned officer

NVA—North Vietnamese Army, also PAVN (People's Army of Vietnam)

PTSD—post-traumatic stress disorder

P-38—can opener issued with C-rations

RPG—rocket-propelled grenade (Soviet-made)

RVN—Republic of Vietnam (South Vietnam)

R&R—rest and relaxation (or recreation)

Seabees—Navy construction engineers, from Construction Battalion (C.B.)

Tet—Vietnamese Lunar New Year holiday period

VC—Viet Cong, also known as "Victor Charlie," or "Charlie"

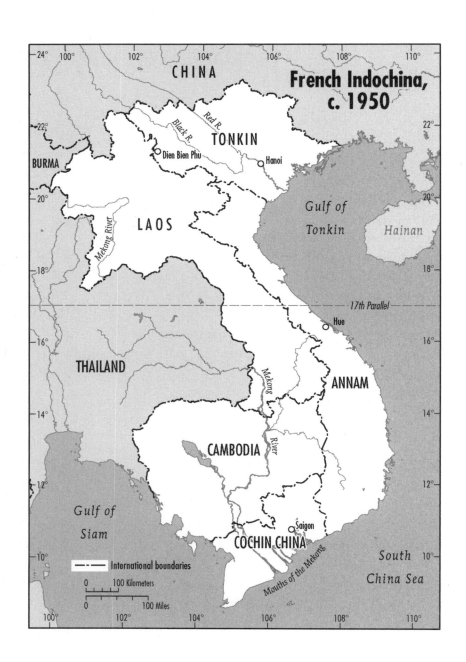

French Indochina,
c. 1950

CHINA

Red R.

Black R.

TONKIN

Dien Bien Phu

Hanoi

BURMA

LAOS

Mekong River

Gulf of
Tonkin

Hainan

17th Parallel

Hue

THAILAND

Mekong

ANNAM

CAMBODIA

River

Saigon

Gulf of
Siam

COCHIN CHINA

Mouths of the Mekong

South
China Sea

International boundaries

0   100 Kilometers

0   100 Miles

HISTORY OF CONFLICT

WHEN WORLD WAR II ended with the surrender of Germany and Japan in 1945, the world seemed finally and blessedly at peace. Unfortunately, this was not the case for long, as the United States and the Soviet Union, the two emerging superpowers, soon became engaged in a deadly struggle for global military and diplomatic primacy. Due to the possibility of nuclear confrontation resulting from the growth of both countries' nuclear arsenals, this third world war, or "Cold War," was waged in a series of regional confrontations and proxy wars fought on a limited scale.

As early as 1947, the United States began actively opposing further Communist expansion in Europe and Asia by supporting other nations fighting Communist takeovers. Conflicts flared in Greece, Burma, Malaya, the Philippines, Indonesia, and Indochina. In 1949 China fell into Communist hands, and the next year, with full Soviet and Chinese backing, the North Korean army aggressively invaded South Korea. This precipitated direct United States involvement in a larger, but still limited, conventional war, eventually involving China as well. Reluctant as always to allow the war to escalate, the United States refrained from crossing the Yalu River into China and eventually settled for a peace agreement leaving North and South Korea in roughly the same configuration that existed before the war.

As these events were unfolding after World War II, a Communist-controlled group in Indochina known as the Vietminh (also "Viet Minh") moved into the vacuum left by the defeated Japanese and seized power. When France attempted to reimpose its prewar colonial authority over the region, war broke out in 1946. The Vietminh, led by Ho Chi Minh, managed to survive in this struggle until the Communists took over China in 1949, giving the Vietminh an important ally to the north and a decisive advantage over the French.

The Vietminh achieved final victory over France in 1954 by defeating the French Army at a remote location west of Hanoi called Dien Bien Phu. The war was formally concluded by an international conference that divided Indochina into three states: Vietnam, Laos, and Cambodia—with Vietnam partitioned at the 17th parallel between Communist and non-Communist zones. During a period in 1954–55 when free movement was allowed, more than a million Vietnamese, mostly Catholic, moved from North Vietnam to South Vietnam. Although unification under Communist control always remained the long-term goal of North Vietnam, this effort was put on hold temporarily to enable consolidation of power and "land reform" in the areas already under Communist control.

So-called land reform in North Vietnam went forward in the 1950s on the model used in the Soviet Union and China that had produced millions of deaths. Under a 1953 "Population Classification Decree," the population was grouped into five categories, from landlord down to agricultural worker. Thousands of Vietnamese citizens were either imprisoned or summarily executed for being in the wrong class.[1] Popular revolts against these measures were put down with overwhelming military force.

With the end of the Korean War and increasing Communist activity in South Vietnam, the United States finally began to focus its attention on Indochina. It had little option at first, other than lending support to the newly constituted government of South Vietnam, beset with problems establishing its own viability. Nevertheless, by the early 1960s the entire region finally took center stage in the worldwide superpower struggle.

My Country Needed Me

IN MARCH 1966 W. D. Ehrhart was a senior in high school when he began having serious thoughts about delaying his plans for college and, instead, serving his country. Speaking about the experience of many in his generation, he recounted:

> As a ten-year-old, I had cowered beneath my desk at school during nuclear bomb drills, waiting for the Russians to attack us. Over the next few years, the U.S.S.R. and its evil minions had built the Berlin Wall, spawned Communist insurgency in Laos, and tried to put nuclear missiles in Cuba. I had watched on television as Soviet premier Nikita Khrushchev pounded his shoe on the podium at the United Nations General Assembly, shouting, "We will bury you!"
>
> [President] Kennedy had said we would bear any burden and pay any price to prevent that from happening. And then Kennedy was dead. I'd written on the cover of my school notebook [his] clarion call: "Ask not what your country can do for you; ask what you can do for your country."[2]

When the battles in the Ia Drang Valley confirmed the presence of North Vietnamese regular army troops fighting in South Vietnam, Ehrhart finally made up his mind about his immediate future: *"College could wait. My country needed me now. I would join the Marines."*[3]

> Blessed is the nation whose God is the Lord, the people he chose for his inheritance.
> ~Psalm 33:12

Seven months later this young man arrived in Vietnam, where he served a yearlong tour with 1st Battalion, 1st Marines, was wounded in action, and rose to the rank of sergeant. There his idealism came face-to-face with the harsh reality of war. His story illustrates the attitude of countless young men and women of his generation who went to war with a desire to do the right thing for their own nation and a foreign country struggling for freedom.

The war was controversial, as some others have been, but this man's motives for going were pure. It is my belief that his nation's motives were equally pure. Preventing the establishment of another repressive Communist regime was a simple and worthy goal. I pray that every man and woman who served in Vietnam shares this confidence. They fought a difficult war for a good reason. God bless each and every one for his or her faithful service.

Endless Tunnel

IN THE early 1950s, French commandos of the Composite Airborne Commando Group, known as the G.C.M.A., operated deep in Vietminh-controlled territory. French officers and NCOs worked with bands of tribesmen to fight an unpublicized guerrilla war against the Vietnamese Communists. Once committed, these troops were seldom brought out of the fight:

> What a wretched man I am! Who will rescue me from this body of death? Thanks be to God— through Jesus Christ our Lord! Through Christ Jesus the law of the Spirit of life set me free from the law of sin and death.
> ~Romans 7:24, 25; 8:2

(An) important psychological factor for the French members of the G.C.M.A. was the "endless tunnel" aspect of the whole operation. To train a man for guerrilla work was long and tedious. If he managed to stay alive for more than a year in his assignment, he usually had learned at least one, or even several, mountain dialects perfectly and had physically adapted to the murderous climate and the food and the way of life in the jungle. The man had become irreplaceable because of his specialized knowledge, and the better he was the more certain he could be that he would be sent out again and again until his luck ran out, his health broke, or his mind cracked up. There was no magical "fifty missions" to look forward to, no end to the ordeal in sight beyond the end of the war itself.[4]

If there is a peacetime equivalent to this kind of "endless tunnel," it would be addiction. Alcohol and other drugs enslave many to a lifestyle from which there seems to be no release. The apostle Paul described the spiritual effect of the addictive lifestyle. He said drunkenness and debauchery are *"acts of the sinful nature,"* and warned, *"Those who live like this will not inherit the kingdom of God"* (Galatians 5:19, 21). He also offered the way out of this condition, now an integral component of the "Twelve Steps" of Alcoholics Anonymous and other recovery programs. A "greater power" is needed to change the addict's mind-set.

The only power capable of such a change is our Lord and Savior, Jesus Christ, who seeks to set us all free from every condition separating us from the Father. Jesus said, *"He has sent me to proclaim freedom for the prisoners and recovery of sight for the blind, to release the oppressed"* (Luke 4:18). He is the light at the end of every tunnel, even the ones that seem "endless" to us.

Hook-and-Ladder

TO TRAIN and entertain their T'ai tribesmen, one group of French commandos used motion pictures. Just about any subject was acceptable. One of the most popular ever was an American film about a volunteer fire department in a small town in Illinois. The tribesmen had seen aircraft and jeeps, but nothing like these vehicles:

> *They had never seen anything like the hook-and-ladder assemblies shown in the film. Neither had they ever seen flat land with no mountains on the horizon, or asphalted and straight roads. The hook-and-ladder rig swaying at 60 mph through the Illinois countryside became probably the greatest film success the T'ai hills had ever seen and for days on end, tribesmen would filter in even from the surrounding Communist-held areas to see the "big American car on the straight road."*[5]

In some remote Vietnamese mountain village an Illinois fire department still has friends who will forever think of America as a place of hook-and-ladder fire trucks careening down paved roads.

Our understanding of God is roughly on a par with these T'ai tribesmen's understanding of America. Neither they nor we barely scratch the surface. We see the majesty of his creation and can only wonder at his power and purpose. We feel love for our children, and yet we can hardly conceive of the love he has for us. We are blessed to have his Holy Word and the opportunity to spend a lifetime seeking a better understanding and a closer relationship with him. Our greatest blessing is the hope of an eternity in his presence and the opportunity to perfect our knowledge of his character.

> For we know in part and we prophesy in part, but when perfection comes, the imperfect disappears . . . Now we see but a poor reflection as in a mirror; then we shall see face to face. Now I know in part; then I shall know fully, even as I am fully known.
> ~1 Corinthians 13:9, 10, 12

Shame

IN HIS CLASSIC little volume, *Corps Values,* Zell Miller wrote a thought-provoking piece on the subject of shame, drawing on the time-honored method of the Marine Corps DI (Drill Instructor). When one of Miller's fellow recruits made the mistake of calling his weapon a "gun," the DI didn't hesitate. He had the recruit strip naked, grab his M-1 rifle and run up and down the squad bay shouting, *"This is my rifle!"*[6] In a later era, I witnessed the same drama played out at Officer Candidates School, with only one difference: The victim wore clothes. DIs have found many other ways to use shame in teaching recruits the Marine way of doing things.

(U. S. Marine Corps)

In the modern world of behavioral science, shame and guilt have fallen into disfavor. We are now counseled to get over our guilt and to focus on the positive. I have no problem with this in general and agree most people are best motivated by positive goals and reinforcement of good behaviors.

I do have a problem with dispensing entirely with the guilt. I believe we have a conscience for a purpose. If I feel guilty for overreacting toward my wife, that is usually a good sign. Maybe I will reassess my behavior before repeating it. If a child is ashamed of poor grades when he or she could have done better, maybe that will also lead to better performance later. We can all feel less guilt about guilt.

The ultimate purpose of guilt is to convince us that, as humans, we need help justifying ourselves before God. All fall short of his expectations, either by what we do or what we fail to do. Firmly convicted of this fact, we can clearly see the hopelessness of our eternal condition without the means of salvation God has provided for us.

> Here is a trustworthy saying that deserves full acceptance: Christ Jesus came into the world to save sinners—of whom I am the worst. But for that very reason I was shown mercy so that in me, the worst of sinners, Christ Jesus might display his unlimited patience as an example for those who would believe on him and receive eternal life.
> ~1 Timothy 1:15, 16

Vietnamese soldiers in helicopter. (National Archives)

French troops on tank. (U. S. Army)

A View from France

IN 1967 Canon Jean-Marie Aubert, a French priest, wrote a carefully reasoned essay on his perspective of the Vietnam War. He put the war in a larger context, relating it to the two major opposing worldviews: those of the free world and the Communist bloc. With the specter of the two superpowers' nuclear weapons hanging over this larger conflict, Aubert considered Vietnam to be an issue of *world* peace.

> For he himself is our peace, who has made the two one and has destroyed the barrier, the dividing wall of hostility.
> ~Ephesians 2:14

The French priest then turned to those most directly affected by the hostilities, the Vietnamese people themselves. For their sake, he called for an immediate cessation of hostilities. However, having made this plea, he explained that a cease-fire would not be the ultimate solution. He reiterated the words of the Vatican Council: *"Peace is not the pure absence of war,"* and acknowledged the difficulties that lay ahead: *"It is really too simple, when thousands of miles away, to militate for the immediate withdrawal of American troops from Vietnam; even if their presence leaves us skeptical and is somewhat improper, what other presence would follow it?"*[7] The French priest at least voiced some degree of caution about the long-term effect of a Communist takeover of South Vietnam. He also acknowledged his own country's role in the conflict: *"We Frenchmen cannot consider ourselves strangers in this debate either; we cannot forget our own original responsibilities."*[8]

In concluding his essay, Aubert wisely turned to God for the ultimate answer about peace in Vietnam and the world:

> *If it is the love of Christ that moves our hearts, and if we have faith in the omnipotence of our Father, then, faced with the challenge that the world throws down to us . . . we can only prostrate ourselves at the foot of the Cross and raise our ardent prayer to heaven.*[9]

The Totalitarian Idea

DAVID HOROWITZ was a left-wing activist during the 1960s and editor of *Ramparts*, a monthly magazine associated with the New Left. His schoolteacher parents were members of the Communist Party, and for many years Horowitz considered himself a Marxist. Over a period of years, however, seeds of doubt in his socialist faith began to grow, leading him on a long and complex journey toward the other end of the political spectrum. With the insight of an insider, he later examined the roots of his earlier faith:

> Thomas said to him, "Lord, we don't know where you are going, so how can we know the way?" Jesus answered, "I am the way and the truth and the life. No one comes to the Father except through me."
> ~John 14:5, 6

Totalitarianism is the possession of reality by a political Idea—the Idea of the socialist kingdom of heaven on earth, the redemption of humanity by political force. To radical believers this Idea is so beautiful it is like God himself. It provides the meaning of a radical life. It is the solution that makes everything possible; it is the end that justifies the regrettable means. Belief in the kingdom of socialist heaven is the faith that transforms vice into virtue, lies into truth, and evil into good. For in the revolutionary religion the Way, the Truth, and the Life of salvation lie not with God above, but with men below . . . There is no mystery in the transformation of socialist paradise into Communist hell: liberation theology is a Satanic creed. Totalitarianism is the crushing of ordinary, intractable, human reality by a political Idea.[10]

It has always been clear that Communists were suspicious of any belief system that would detract from their own authority. However, Horowitz shows that their antipathy toward God goes even deeper. The "totalitarian Idea" itself is god. The Idea itself is the reason for being and the way to salvation.

To most people I know, the fallacy of this system of thought is obvious. What is not obvious is the extent to which we all attach ourselves to ideas and activities that give meaning to our lives. Careers, politics, charitable causes, even our families, are all important concerns. However, these concerns are meaningful only as they relate to God and *his* kingdom. God is our ultimate reality, never to be superseded by human causes or ideas.

Sister Mary

THE SISTERS of Charity ran an orphanage near the town of Vinh Long, about eighty miles southwest of Saigon. A reporter stopped there to visit with the staff and was introduced to Sister Mary. She made a lasting impression:

> *Sister Mary was tall, ruddy of face, keen of eye, stern of jaw, and with a smile warm enough to light up an arctic igloo. She took me around the orphanage and showed me the various activities the orphans—many of them grown teen-age girls—were taking part in. No make-work operation this! The girls were busily washing and ironing the uniforms for the helicopter base nearby, for which the orphanage received a generous remuneration from the officers and men involved, which was used to help pay the bills. There were classes in sewing, cooking, English, religion and the general studies that American youngsters receive in school— but tailored to fit the needs of the Vietnamese. The sisters teaching the classes were serious and so were the students. You can't fake this kind of thing.*[11]

Unfortunately, this orphanage was closed by the Communists when they took over in 1975, one of many properties appropriated by the government, *"to transform society toward socialism."*[12] By then the hardworking sisters had been with the children for more than thirty years serving their needs. Under difficult conditions, in a foreign land, these nuns did God's work faithfully and selflessly. They exemplified a great biblical teaching: *"Religion that God our Father accepts as pure and faultless is this: to look after orphans and widows in their distress and to keep oneself from being polluted by the world"* (James 1:27). The dedication of true religious professionals such as these women is inspiring to us who have so much untapped potential for service in his kingdom and who risk so much less.

> Whoever wants to save his life will lose it, but whoever loses his life for me will find it.
> ~ Matthew 16:25

The Golden Rule of Combat

MILITARY HISTORIANS have pointed out an important difference between Vietnam and previous wars. Basically, the war in Vietnam involved smaller units operating independently for long periods of time, unlike World War II and Korea, where many units were on line in large-scale offensive and defensive campaigns. Many Vietnam veterans think this difference caused closer bonds among their ranks. This would of course be a difficult proposition to verify.

Even though each war is different, there have always been certain similarities in the relationships between individual soldiers. One Vietnam veteran might have been speaking for all combat veterans when he wrote:

> *Trust formed the cornerstone for these special relationships and here we are referring to the ultimate form of trust—that of entrusting others with your life. In combat one has to trust that each member of the team will act to protect the others from harm. In other words, the members of a team acted as guardian angels for each other and their golden rule was "not to let your buddies down." This unmatched level of trust between team members was always present and not just during a firefight, but also when patrolling, on guard duty, on ambush operations and while conducting combat assaults. While trust was the cornerstone for these special relationships, it also fostered the development of close friendships between team members and the willingness to take risks and act bravely to protect your buddies.*[13]

> This is love: not that we loved God, but that he loved us and sent his Son as an atoning sacrifice for our sins. Dear friends, since God so loved us, we also ought to love one another.
> ~1 John 4:10, 11

As Christians fight the good fight and share the gospel message with the world, we have access to the same kind of trust relationship with every other believer. Christ has already set the ultimate example of sacrifice—giving himself on the cross for us. Although few will ever be called upon to die for him, we nevertheless share a common mission to live for him and to endure whatever hardship comes—for his sake and for each other. Christians have the same golden rule of combat as soldiers: We never want to let our "buddies" down, or, above all, the One who sacrificed everything for us.

My Kingdom

THE REVEREND Eugene Carson Blake was General Secretary of the World Council of Churches in 1967 when he gave an address on the topic of "Ecumenism and Peace." His remarks were critical of the United States and its policies in Vietnam. They were also thought-provoking in their presentation of the uniquely Christian view of the world:

> *It is not the Christian faith that man is able even by his obedience to establish the Kingdom of God on earth . . . this growing ecumenical consensus I have been describing is based not upon a utopian view of man or history but rather upon faith in God whose son died upon a cross for man's eternal salvation. A Christian view never belittles the fact of human sin and selfishness. A Christian view believes obedience is always more important than success. A Christian view is always based ultimately on what God will do rather than what man can do. The cross is at the heart of the Christian faith. History, in a Christian understanding, is not an automatic triumph of man's development but the arena of God's action of redemption. Christian life is caught up in faith, hope, and love.*[14]

Regardless of one's views on war, these comments are a useful reminder of the difference between God's kingdom and the kingdoms of this world. History, from a human perspective, is the unfolding of time and human activity, toward what most hope will be a better condition. From God's perspective, history is the arena in which he carries out his own purpose for the redemption of mankind. Jesus Christ is the centerpiece of his plan. In the words of the great theologian

> Jesus said, "My kingdom is not of this world. If it were, my servants would fight to prevent my arrest." ~John 18:36

Dietrich Bonhoeffer, *"The way of Jesus Christ . . . leads not from the world to God but from God to the world."*[15] Our divine purpose as human beings is to respond to this call by accepting the incredible gift God offers. It is not up to us to establish heaven on earth. Our proper role as human beings is to seek him and become part of *his* kingdom.

Faith and Fear

RONALD HALL was the bishop of the Anglican Diocese of Hong Kong for more than thirty years until his retirement in 1966. He later gave a unique perspective on the Vietnam War and on the general problem of human conflict. He cited fear as the underlying cause of war and strife at the personal *and* the international level. He used Jesus' words as his text: *"You of little faith, why are you so afraid?"* (Matthew 8:26).

> I have chosen you and have not rejected you. So do not fear, for I am with you; do not be dismayed, for I am your God. I will strengthen you and help you; I will uphold you with my righteous right hand.
> ~Isaiah 41:9, 10

It has been said that our Lord saw fear as the opposite of faith. This is because faith for him was trust, *implicit trust in God. Our rather unfortunate word, "belief," which we use too often for "faith," has as its natural opposite "doubt" or "unbelief." So today we give much time to considering unbelief and doubt, while fear gets far too little attention. But fear is the great enemy of civilization. Fear is more insidious than unbelief. It has more power over individuals, governments, and nations than any amount of unbelief and secularism.*[16] *One single thought of love lifted towards God in truth is worth more than the most resounding action."*[17]

The Reverend Hall saw fear as the great enemy of peace. Even though a basic human instinct important for survival, it can and must be subjected to careful scrutiny. We need to act on well-founded information and not on imaginary fears. When we learn more about our "enemies," we usually fear them less.

Unfortunately, fear is most likely to appear when trust is lacking, and trust often seems in short supply in our secular world. Christians have much to contribute in this area. We know that building trust with others entails risks, and we take these risks willingly to build stronger relationships inside and outside our churches. We may keep our guard up, but, until proven wrong, we have faith in the good intentions of others. Even when others do not have such good intentions, we know that Jesus instructed, *"Pray for those who persecute you"* (Matthew 5:44).

Role Models

GEORGE CADWALADER was a hero of two wars. His first was Vietnam, where he was a Marine captain and wounded so severely by a land mine he could not return to combat. He went to war a second time in a career helping hard-core delinquent boys find better lives.

> Now that I, your Lord and Teacher, have washed your feet, you also should wash one another's feet. I have set you an example that you should do as I have done for you. ~John 13:14, 15

In 1973 he started a school on Penikese Island at a remote location off the coast of Massachusetts. It was his vision to change the lives of young men by using the Marine Corps boot camp model. He had never forgotten a specific incident during his time at Officer Candidates School in Quantico. There was a weak member of his platoon who was driven mercilessly by the staff to either "shape up or ship out." On one forced march this young man finally came to the end of his ordeal and dropped beside the road. Realizing it was over for him, the drill instructor knelt down and said quietly, *"You done real good, son. You gave it all you got, an' there ain't many of us as can say that."*[18] Thanks to one encouraging word, this young man left Quantico with his pride intact.

As he was organizing his school, Cadwalader found that the Department of Youth Services wanted him to hire professionally trained clinicians and psychology majors. He never believed, however, that a severely delinquent young person would respond to a therapist trying to persuade him to feel better about himself. He held to his vision and sought out the kind of men who could be taskmasters and encouragers at the same time. Instead of counselors, he wanted "role models."[19]

This phrase has stuck in my mind ever since. I believe it applies in many areas of our lives. Very few of us need therapy, but we all need role models. There are times we need one for ourselves, and there are times we can be one for someone else. A friend I admire has "adopted" an elementary school boy through a local reading program. While teaching this boy to read, he is giving him an even more precious gift: the model of a Christian man serving others in the world.

I Put My Boots On

EVERYONE GROANED as the General Quarters alarm sounded. The sailors were too exhausted for another exercise. Mike Murphy got dressed, but decided to forego his boots, wearing only his shower shoes as he hurried toward his battle station. He soon learned, however, that this was not a drill. As he ran through the ship, he saw blood on the deck and smoke filling the main passageway. Nearby, a faulty rocket

USS Coral Sea (U. S. Navy)

had fired off in the Weapons Department, punching a hole in the steel bulkhead, wounding several crewmen, and starting electrical fires in several compartments.

For the next ten hours the crew of the *USS Coral Sea* worked feverishly to extinguish the fires and repair the damage to the ship. During the ordeal Murphy thought to himself:

> *The ship is on fire, people are injured, and I'm wearing my damn shower shoes. . . . For the next ten hours I sit and look at the blood on my feet and wonder whose blood it is. I also worry about what will happen if I have to get out over burning steel decks wearing rubber shower shoes. I worry a lot and swear that it will never happen again. Ever.*[20]

Gradually this scene of destruction was restored to normal. Many crewmen had to brave two hundred fifty degree temperatures to fight the fires and keep the engine room functioning. Murphy learned a lesson that would stay with him. He said, *"For the next ten years or so, as soon as I would get out of bed I would put my shoes on. To this day I will not leave the house barefoot. Some fears die hard."*[21]

Unfortunately, most of us seem to learn best the hard way. We don't learn from the mistakes of others—we have to make our own. It is said what doesn't kill us makes us stronger. We can only hope we are learning our lessons and getting stronger as we overcome our difficulties. We know we're going to make mistakes, and we can only pray that God will redeem them and be with us during those times when the "alarm" sounds for real.

> For the Lord loves the just and will not forsake his faithful ones. They will be protected forever.
> ~Psalm 37:28

15

Military Axioms

BY DEFINITION, an *axiom* is a "truth assumed to be self-evident," or a fundamental theorem that doesn't have to be proven. With this in mind, many Vietnam veterans have contributed to a growing list of *military* axioms, depicting simple truths from that war:[22]

The enemy diversion you are ignoring is the main attack.
If the enemy is within range, then so are you.
Friendly fire—isn't.
If it's stupid and works, then it ain't stupid.
The easy way is always mined.
Incoming fire has the right of way.
Teamwork is essential. It gives the enemy other people to shoot at.
Never draw fire—it irritates everyone around you.
No combat-ready unit has ever passed an inspection.
No inspection-ready unit has ever passed combat.
When in doubt, empty your magazine (don't leave any ammunition unused).
In war, important things are simple and all simple things are hard.
Never share a foxhole with anyone braver than you.
No operations plan survives first contact intact.
Murphy was a grunt.
Mines are equal opportunity weapons.
It's not the one with your name on it—it's the round addressed "to whom it may concern" you have to think about.
Anything you do can get you shot, including nothing.

This list seems to grow, as new iterations appear on veterans' web sites. A comparable list of *scriptural* truths would be about as long as the Bible itself. At the top of such a list would be the most fundamental, simple, and easily understood *biblical* axiom of all:

> For God so loved the world that he gave his one and only Son, that whoever believes in him shall not perish but have eternal life. ~John 3:16

The Doll

SOON AFTER arriving in Vietnam, a soldier discovered what he thought would be a good souvenir for home—a little Vietnamese doll. She was about eighteen inches tall with long black hair and native silk costume, and extremely "well-proportioned." He made a big mistake sending one of these dolls to his girlfriend back home. Her scathing response caught him by surprise:

> I had no idea the girls in Viet Nam looked like that! I always thought they were supposed to be, well sort of skinny, and now that I think of it, how did you have time to shop around for things like that? You wrote that you spend all your time shoveling dirt into sacks and if you think that I am going to keep that thing on the TV set to remind me during commercials of the good times you might be having without me, you better think again.[23]

Most men are clueless when it comes to gifts for women, experiencing a feeling of dread as birthdays and anniversaries approach. My wife still ridicules me for giving her a dictionary for Christmas while we were dating. I have learned slowly and painfully that this is one area of life where the Golden Rule does not apply.

In his book *The Five Love Languages*, Gary Chapman goes even further in cautioning us about the Golden Rule in love and marriage. He contends each of us, man or woman, needs love in a particular form: words of affirmation, quality time, receiving gifts, acts of service, or physical touch. It is up to each person in a relationship to understand the other well enough to know what love language is most important to that person, and to focus on it. The mistake we make is to give only what we like, expecting this to satisfy the other. To love another person, we need to understand them well enough to know what *they* need. This kind of understanding takes time and patience. We have to resolve to "do unto others" not what *we* want, but what *they* want done unto them.

> How much better to get wisdom than gold, to choose understanding rather than silver! ... Understanding is a fountain of life to those who have it. ~Proverbs 16:16, 22

Reflections of a Vietnamese

NGUYEN BA CHUNG was six years old when his family left their village near Hanoi in 1955, fleeing the Communist government in the North. He never forgot the trauma of the exodus. His family were not rich, but they owned enough land to find themselves on the wrong side of the Communist land reform campaign. Even though they had fought with the Communists against the French, they were subject to imprisonment or even execution for being identified with the wrong class.

> You will hear of wars and rumors of wars, but see to it that you are not alarmed. Such things must happen, but the end is still to come . . . He who stands firm to the end will be saved.
> ~Matthew 24:6, 13

Chung settled with his family in Saigon, where he lived and grew up during the Vietnam War. As he described it, every aspect of his life was touched by the war—*"personal, communal, philosophical, political, religious, and cultural."*[24] Chung is now a writer and poet of note in Vietnam. He is philosophical about the war and has his own unique perspective on those who fought it:

> *I believe the U.S. had noble aims in Vietnam—freedom and democracy. Yet the foundation of the U.S. efforts in South Vietnam was a nation-building program, as if Vietnam were some kind of recently discovered Paleolithic tribe. Because it aligned itself with a group of Vietnamese who carried heavy colonial baggage . . . it could not succeed.*
>
> *Similarly, Ho Chi Minh had all the righteous causes—independence, unification, and social justice . . . but Ho and his revolutionaries had to ally themselves with Communism, a doctrine whose basic features—class warfare, dictatorship of the proletariat, and utopia—ran against the very grain of Vietnamese culture, a culture that had endured for thousands of years.*[25]

Chung now writes eloquently about the durability of Vietnamese culture despite its chaotic history. He gives us hope that our important values and beliefs will always survive the malpractices of big government, public education, political correctness, economic hard times, and even the tragedy of war.

Ultimate Reality

IN AN ELOQUENT 1967 address, Dr. Martin Luther King Jr. painted what is arguably a one-sided picture of America's role and intentions in the Vietnam War. However, he also went on to broaden the scope of his remarks to the larger problems of poverty and discontent in the world. He lamented that many had been driven to feel that only Marxism had the revolutionary spirit to bring change, observing that, *"Communism is a judgment against our failure to make democracy real and follow through on the revolutions that we initiated. Our only hope today lies in our ability to recapture the revolutionary spirit . . ."*[26]

Dr. Martin Luther King (Library of Congress)

Dr. King then explained the key ingredient to what he considered a true revolution in human affairs: an all-embracing and unconditional love among all men. He acknowledged that many would consider this a weak position, but went on to show why it will always be the strongest position possible:

When I speak of love I am not speaking of some sentimental and weak response. I am speaking of that force which all of the great religions have seen as the supreme unifying principle of life. Love is somehow the key that unlocks the door that leads to ultimate reality. This Hindu-Moslem-Christian-Jewish-Buddhist belief about ultimate reality is beautifully summed up in the first epistle of St John.[27]

The Scripture passage referred to by Dr. King gives an exalted vision of the power of love and its importance as God's greatest command to his people:

Dear friends, let us love one another, for love comes from God. Everyone who loves has been born of God and knows God. Whoever does not love does not know God, because God is love. No one has ever seen God; but if we love one another, God lives in us and his love is made complete in us. ~1 John 4:7, 8, 12

Let It Go

MANY MONTAGNARD tribesmen of Vietnam's Central Highlands held the belief that family members had to remain together and could not be separated under any condition. This belief ran counter to good medical practice when a father took his sick son out of the Kontum hospital. American medics were unable to convince the father to return his son for treatment, and finally appealed to the village priest:

> At the priest's urging, the father brought his son to the Medical Aid Station at Highlander Heights for a thorough examination, where the doctors of Company C, 4th Medical Battalion determined that the boy had spinal meningitis and should be returned to the hospital. Finally, the father was convinced that the best thing would be to return his son to the hospital.[28]

We are appalled at the idea of superstition interfering with medical treatment. We would condemn any parent who refused help for a child because of a religious belief. On the other hand, we all know some who are so prejudiced against religion that they can't see the spiritual nature of many of their own problems. One of the most common "tribal beliefs" of our modern culture is that we are the masters of our fate. When someone with this view encounters a problem they can't solve, self-doubt and guilt are inevitable. I know from experience religious skeptics are the victims of their own superstitious belief that they have complete control over their lives.

Times come in life when we have to face the fact that there are problems we can't solve and which may, in fact, have no solution. We know we don't have all the answers and need a strength and wisdom beyond ourselves. God is the only source of this kind of support. He wants us to lift these concerns to him and to lean on him for assurance he is in charge. We will not always understand the outcome, but we will always have peace knowing his will is being accomplished.

> This is the will of him who sent me, that I shall lose none of all that he has given me, but raise them up at the last day. For my Father's will is that everyone who looks to the Son and believes in him shall have eternal life. ~John 6:39, 40

The Pope Arrives

IN THE HUMOR section of the 173rd Airborne Brigade Web site there is a story about a pope who arrived expectantly at the gates of heaven late one night. He was surprised to note a certain military tone in the operation of the heavenly reception center. The orderly on duty checked his roster and found no pope on the list, and so sent him to an upper bunk in the holding barracks, promising to sort it out later. The pope went quietly, but slept fitfully. The story continues:

The next morning he awakens to sounds of cheering and clapping. He goes to the window and sees a shiny convertible coming down from the golden headquarters building on the hill. The sidewalks are lined with angels cheering and throwing confetti. In the back seat of the convertible is an old paratrooper, his jump wings shining on his chest, a cigar in his mouth, a can of beer in one hand and his other arm around a beautiful blonde angel.

This upsets the pope greatly and he runs down to the gate and says, "Explain this to me. Here I am, the recently deceased pope, and I have spent sixty-three years doing godly deeds on Earth and am here in an open squad bay, and I see this old paratrooper that I know has committed every sin known to man, staying in the mansion on the hill and getting a hero's welcome. How can this be?"

St. Peter calmly looks up and says, "We get popes every now and then, at least one every twenty or thirty years, but this is the first paratrooper we've ever had."[29]

I don't want to offend Catholics with this little story, and it would probably be just as good with any well-known religious figure. This is just the way I found it, written by an unknown Airborne humorist. Amazingly, it accurately illustrates one of Jesus' important biblical teachings. When the Jewish religious authorities began to notice that Jesus was spending a lot of time with various unsavory characters, such as prostitutes and tax collectors (and even soldiers), they challenged him about it. Jesus responded by telling them a story about a shepherd who was overjoyed when he found his one lost sheep. He then very pointedly explained the meaning of the story to the Pharisees:

> I tell you that in the same way there will be more rejoicing in heaven over one sinner who repents than over ninety-nine righteous persons who do not need to repent.
> ~Luke 15:7

Men, Women, and Others

IN THE mid-1960s, racial segregation still existed in many small towns in Texas. Don Poss was assigned to Bergstrom Air Force Base and was a member of an honor guard that traveled throughout the state, participating in funerals for soldiers killed in Vietnam. The honor guard had several black members, and, needless to say, some of the soldiers being buried were black as well. The U.S. military was not discriminating about who was being sent to war, nor the Viet Cong about who was being killed.

Because some restaurants *did* discriminate, the sergeant in charge of the group made a habit of going ahead, ostensibly to *"see if they could handle a busload of hungry airmen."*[30] He was actually checking to see if they would serve the black airmen in the group. Frequently, he was turned away. In most places they went, the restrooms and water fountains were still labeled *Men, Women,* and *Others.*

> Get rid of all bitterness, rage and anger . . . Be kind and compassionate to one another, forgiving each other, just as in Christ God forgave you.
> ~Ephesians 4:31, 32

One day the sergeant was refused service several times in a row. Two black airmen, realizing the situation, told him to go ahead and have everyone eat; they would wait in the bus. Every other man, however, refused to go in. They would eat together or not at all. One of the airmen who had a guitar composed a song that night that he called, "Heaven's Gates: Men, Women, and Others." Everyone laughed and sang the song about the quandary certain people would have approaching heaven and not knowing which gate to use. Poss said, *"I don't remember where we ended up that night on the way back to base, but I do remember how proud I felt of the American Airmen I served with."*[31]

As the civil rights movement grew in intensity, the U.S. military establishment had its share of racial tension. Nevertheless, as military men and women lived and worked together, they led the way throughout this era in breaking down racial barriers. It is a task that should continue to challenge each of us today.

President Kennedy

IT WAS the coldest day of my life. On January 20, 1961, I stood in formation with other Citadel cadets on a freshly snow-plowed side street of Washington, D.C., waiting to march in the inaugural parade of John F. Kennedy. As we stomped our feet to ward off the extreme cold, we heard the voice of the new president over a distant loudspeaker calling a new generation of Americans to service and sacrifice. Over the next decade, countless young men and women would answer that call:

> Then your light will break forth like the dawn, and your healing will quickly appear; then your righteousness will go before you, and the glory of the LORD will be your rear guard. Then you will call, and the LORD will answer; you will cry for help, and he will say: Here am I.
> ~Isaiah 58:8, 9

I have sworn before you and Almighty God the same solemn oath our forebears prescribed nearly a century and three quarters ago.

The world is very different now. For man holds in his mortal hands the power to abolish all forms of human poverty and all forms of human life. And yet the same revolutionary beliefs for which our forebears fought are still at issue around the globe—the belief that the rights of man come not from the generosity of the state, but from the hand of God . . .

Let every nation know, whether it wishes us well or ill, that we shall pay any price, bear any burden, meet any hardship, support any friend, oppose any foe, in order to assure the survival and the success of liberty . . .

In the long history of the world, only a few generations have been granted the role of defending freedom in its hour of maximum danger. I do not shrink from this responsibility—I welcome it. I do not believe that any of us would exchange places with any other people or any other generation. The energy, the faith, the devotion which we bring to this endeavor will light our country and all who serve it—and the glow from that fire can truly light the world.

And so, my fellow Americans: ask not what your country can do for you—ask what you can do for your country . . .

With a good conscience our only sure reward, with history the final judge of our deeds, let us go forth to lead the land we love, asking His blessing and His help, but knowing that here on earth God's work must truly be our own.[32]

Friend or Foe

IT WAS a very unusual mission. A Navy captain had to be airlifted alone into a small village near Can Tho for some kind of secret meeting. The village was located in a sparsely populated area where few Americans had been. Little was known about the extent of enemy activity there. Robert Conover and his helicopter crew drew the assignment.

The young pilot's unease grew as he dropped the Huey onto a small mound on one end of a rice paddy dike about two hundred yards from the captain's destination. He had to sit patiently on the small pad, intently scanning the village for any sign of unusual activity. As he waited, he observed a young girl leave one of the huts and start across the dikes toward him, further putting his nerves on edge: *"Scenes from my 'in country' orientation ten months before whirled through my head. 'Don't trust children,' I was told. Chills ran down my back."*[33]

As the girl came nearer, Conover could see she was about five years old. One hand was behind her back. Her bare feet brought her closer and closer. The tension was almost unbearable as she finally stopped a few feet away, paused, and stared at the American. Conover described what happened then:

> *Suddenly, her right hand moved up to the side of her face, her fingers pressed against her forehead. She had come to give me a salute. Her hand fell back to her side, she spun around, and started back. Through watery, squinted eyes I watched her retreat. She never looked back. She never knew the impact of her visit. She did not see the flood of emotion, from a young Army officer, who had never been so honored.*[34]

Whenever we make a gesture of reaching out to someone else, we run a risk of rejection or ridicule. It may be that such a gesture is just outside our comfort zone. But we would do well to remember the power we have to touch someone else's life with a small show of interest or appreciation. Jesus himself gave us the ultimate example of how to honor someone else in an unexpected way:

> Now that I, your Lord and Teacher, have washed your feet, you also should wash one another's feet. I have set you an example that you should do as I have done for you. ~John 13:14, 15

South Vietnamese troops advance in attack. (National Archives)

Vietnamese parachute drop in Tay Ninh Province. (National Archives)

The Hand of Faith

JIM HUTCHENS was a decorated combat chaplain who served heroically with the 173rd Airborne Brigade in Vietnam. His military career and spiritual journey had begun ten years earlier at Fort Campbell, Kentucky, as an enlisted soldier and religious skeptic. Raised in a nominally Christian home where no one talked about their faith, he had grown up with many questions and few satisfactory answers.

> For it is by grace you have been saved, through faith—and this not from yourselves, it the gift of God—not by works, so that no one can boast. ~Ephesians 2:8, 9

On the day Hutchens met Chaplain Burton Hatch, his life began to change. The chaplain sat down beside him that day and began to carefully and confidently respond to his questions. Inspired by this man's knowledge, Hutchens found a Bible and began to read and question him further. Over several months the two men spent a lot of time together, until the day came when it all suddenly "snapped into focus":

> *"You know, Jim," Chaplain Hatch said, "we have been discussing spiritual things for some time now. We've talked about Jesus Christ and what He has done for us. Let me ask you this, Jim: Have you ever personally placed your faith in Christ?"*
>
> *I picked up the key word and asked, "What do you mean by faith?"*
>
> *The chaplain's reply was a startling unfolding of the fountain of truth.*
>
> *"Jim," he said, taking a quarter from his pocket, "I'm going to give you this quarter. Do you believe me?"*
>
> *"Yes sir," I replied. "If you say you'll give it to me, I believe you will."*
>
> *"But," he continued, "how can you know for sure I'll give it to you?"*
>
> *"Well, I guess I would have to take your word for it, sir, and then reach out and take it."*
>
> *"Then do it!" he told me.*
>
> *As I reached out to take the quarter he grasped my hand in his and said softly, "Jim, that is the hand of faith."*
>
> *Suddenly it all became clear. I could have sat there "believing" for a lifetime, but if I had never reached out and taken the quarter offered to me it would never have been mine. What had been so nebulous before finally began to take shape.*[35]

God Invaded My Life

AFTER THE young enlisted man accepted the quarter and, with it, a new understanding of faith, Chaplain Burton Hatch returned to his original question: *"Now let me ask you again, Jim. Have you ever placed your faith in Jesus Christ as your Savior?"* Jim Hutchens replied, *"No, I guess I haven't."*[36]

The chaplain then asked if he would like to, and Jim said he would. The two men bowed their heads, and the chaplain suggested Jim ask Jesus Christ to come into his heart and into his life. Hutchens responded, later recalling:

> *With a simple prayer I did just that, and nothing has been quite the same since that day.*
>
> *A spiritual dimension had been added to my life. By a miracle, which I'll never fully understand, God invaded my life and became a reality to me through the person of the Lord Jesus Christ. The Bible became a new book because I began to understand its message. I read books Chaplain Hatch gave me which taught me basic truths of the Bible. Being linked to God through Christ affected every area of my life, supplying the meaning and purpose I had previously sought in vain.*[37]

We hear the phrase "born again" used loosely to describe an extremely dedicated or even pushy Christian. We have here, however, a perfect illustration of the true meaning of the phrase. Even though we are alive physically, we are dead spiritually until Jesus Christ comes into our hearts. In him, our spiritual beings come into existence for the first time and dwell within us. I have friends who have no recollection of not having this relationship with Jesus. Others, like myself and Jim Hutchens, discovered this profound mystery much later. For some of us, the obstacles to grace were almost insurmountable. In the end, however, the first and lasting step of faith is as simple as reaching out and taking hold of a quarter.

> Jesus answered, "I tell you the truth, no one can enter the kingdom of God unless he is born of water and the Spirit. Flesh gives birth to flesh, but the Spirit gives birth to spirit. You should not be surprised at my saying, 'You must be born again.'" ~John 3:5–7

My Life Began

THE MORTAR attack started at about 4:00 a.m. Incoming shells began exploding throughout the Dak To Special Forces camp as the American and Montagnard soldiers scrambled for their bunkers. Allen Clark remained in the open, directing fire to illuminate the perimeter and interdict the enemy fire. Suddenly a tremendous jolt knocked Clark forward and onto his stomach. A mortar round had detonated about eighteen inches behind him. He knew instantly he was badly hit.

Allen Clark in hospital.

As the mortars continued falling all around, several soldiers helped him to the medical bunker where a corpsman did what he could to deal with the disastrous wounds to Clark's lower legs. It would be hours before the wounded man could be airlifted to a hospital. A long, painful series of surgeries would follow, during which he would lose both legs below the knee.

For his actions that night Allen Clark received the Silver Star and Purple Heart medals. Many years later he would look on that night as the turning point of his life:

> *Had I returned home physically whole, I am not sure that I would have ever attained the spiritual growth that I have attained as a wounded veteran. I know now that nothing happens to God's children without His permission, and it is often through adversity, hardship, and challenges that many of us develop our faith and spiritual awareness. I began a journey in Dak To in 1967 that would continue for many decades of my life. In some ways, my life and what God wanted me to do with it began in Dak To, on June 17, 1967.*[38]

Consider it pure joy, my brothers, whenever you face trials of many kinds, because you know that the testing of your faith develops perseverance. Perseverance must finish its work so that you may be mature and complete, not lacking anything. ~James 1:2–4

With this kind of faith and trust in God, we will not only survive the catastrophes in our lives, we will eventually see them as blessings. Allen Clark and other great Christians bear witness to how God uses hard times to strengthen us and to give us a powerful message to help others.

God Meets Us Where We Are

DURING HIS early life, Allen Clark went through the religious motions, attending church irregularly and praying only when he needed something. Even though the frequency of his prayers temporarily increased while in Vietnam, he never had a meaningful relationship with God.

Under the influence of his wife and friends, he began attending a nondenominational, evangelical church, where he was greatly impressed with the pastor. One sermon in particular made an indelible impression on Clark and played a big part in changing his life. The pastor said, *"The real war in this world is the war between good and evil—Satan and the Lord. They are fighting for the very heart and souls of all people."*[39] This image of spiritual warfare struck deeply into the heart of a wounded soldier listening intently. Clark explained:

> Once, having been asked by the Pharisees when the kingdom of God would come, Jesus replied, "The kingdom of God does not come with your careful observation, nor will people say, 'Here it is,' or 'There it is,' because the kingdom of God is within you. ~Luke 17:20, 21

God meets us where we are and brings people into our lives that can help us understand. He met me where I was when he inspired Pastor Getz to preach on spiritual warfare. I had dedicated myself to being an American soldier, I knew military tactics and strategy, and I understood warfare. Now I had new wars to wage and new battles to fight. I felt as if I was preparing myself to be a soldier in another army.[40]

In thinking about how God came to him, Clark thought of how Jesus talked to Peter, a fisherman, and offered to make him a fisher of men—and how he allowed Thomas, the doubter, to feel his wounds. I was also stimulated to think about Christ coming into my life despite a mature and long-standing skepticism. God presented me with the image of a child and the childlike wonder that can accept a simple truth in spite of complicated doubts. God not only meets us where we are, but sometimes uses us to be there for someone else. We never know when our own story will be the key to another's understanding.

The Prayer Worked

LIFE SEEMED to reach a point where it was on an even keel for Allen Clark. His physical wounds and many of his emotional scars healed, and he mastered the use of his prosthetic legs. Most importantly, he continued to grow in his relationship with God. Unfortunately, in spite of this progress, he was not immune to marital problems. He was plagued by guilt—his wife, Jackie, had never forgiven him for volunteering for duty in Vietnam.

> If you, then, though you are evil, know how to give good gifts to your children, how much more will your Father in heaven give good gifts to those who ask him!
> ~Matthew 7:11

As the situation grew worse and they became separated, he sought the advice of his pastor. Through this spiritual mentor he learned a great lesson in the power of prayer:

Together we prayed a prayer related to Matthew 9:38 regarding the sending of laborers of the harvest: "Pray ye therefore the LORD of the harvest, that he will send forth labourers into his harvest" (KJV). Obviously, this is meant for people to go forth and tell others the Lord's message, but we appropriated this idea. We prayed in agreement that something she would hear, read, see, or experience would convince her finally to forgive me for that life-changing decision made so very long ago.[41]

The prayer worked. Two weeks later Jackie called to say she had watched a television program on forgiveness and been reminded she would not be forgiven if she did not forgive others. She told him she had finally been able to forgive him for volunteering for Vietnam. Clark later said, *"What a relief and closure that was for me. In addition I got to see the PUSH formula (Pray Until Something Happens) actually work firsthand."*[42]

It is awesome to contemplate the nearness of God, and his power to do great things in our lives when we ask and when it is his will to do so. As his children we can be confident he will give us what we need, when we need it.

Battle Plan

TO HEAL from his wounds, Allen Clark had to dedicate himself to a lot of hard work. Just as it took long hours of patient and painful exertion to master the use of prosthetic legs, it took a dedicated effort to learn what he needed to heal his mind and spirit. He came to look at his afflictions as a profound "dis-ease," fueled by anger and past mistakes. With Jesus Christ in his heart, he was able to admit this anger and these mistakes, and was able finally to come to grips with his problems.

With Jesus as his focus, Clark developed a "battle plan" to give others the benefit of some of the important lessons he learned during his painful journey. His plan consists of action steps, such as confession, daily prayer, obedience to God's direction, forgiving others, putting on God's armor, and others. As I was reading and thinking about his advice, I was most moved by the action step titled "Fear Not!"

Come to me, all you who are weary and burdened, and I will give you rest. Take my yoke upon you and learn from me, for I am gentle and humble in heart, and you will find rest for your souls. For my yoke is easy and my burden is light.
~Matthew 11:28–30

But seek first his kingdom and his righteousness, and all these things will be given to you as well. Therefore do not worry about tomorrow, for tomorrow will worry about itself.
~Matthew 6:33, 34

Many of us worry constantly, and most of us worry too much. Worry induces stress and strain, that is, dis-ease. The words "fear not" appear approximately 350 times in God's Word! If He thought it that important to repeat that phrase more than any other in His Word, then we should heed His caution and act in faith by casting all worries upon Him. Next, there is power in action. Write the things that worry you on a sheet of paper, pray to turn them over to the Lord, and then burn the paper. Or kneel at the altar of your church during an altar call and symbolically lay them on the altar as you pray to turn them over to the Father. Lay them at His feet, at the foot of His throne, and tell Him that you can't handle them alone. You will be given such a peace that you will know that He is in control and carrying your burden for you.[43]

Allen Clark addressing veterans.

God's Work

THERE IS an apocryphal story about an atheist college professor who decided to prove to his class once and for all there was no God. With the class assembled, he looked up at the ceiling and said rather loudly, *"God, if you're there, I'll give you five minutes to knock me off this podium!"*

In the silence that followed, you could hear a pin drop. The seconds and minutes ticked by, and the professor again announced, *"God, I'm still waiting."*

As the time ticked down, a former Marine sergeant, new to the class, walked down to the front of the room and delivered a swift but powerful uppercut to the professor's jaw, sending him sprawling to the floor.

The class stared in amazement as the professor staggered to his feet. Standing up, he addressed the offending student, saying, *"What is wrong with you? Why did you do that?"*

The young man replied, *"God was busy. He sent the Marines."*

> The body is a unit, though it is made up of many parts; and though all its parts are many, they form one body. So it is with Christ . . . Now you are the body of Christ, and each one of you is a part of it.
> ~1 Corinthians 12:12, 27

We of course don't know if God would actually send anyone to do this job, even if we agree that it needed doing. A lot of prayerful discernment is always needed to understand God's will or what to do about it. It is very true, however, that God does work in the world through people. St. Teresa of Avila (1515–82) expressed this truth eloquently:

> *Christ has no body but yours,*
> *No hands, no feet on earth but yours,*
> *Yours are the eyes with which he looks*
> *Compassion on this world,*
> *Yours are the feet with which he walks to do good,*
> *Yours are the hands, with which he blesses all the world.*[44]

Moment by Moment

JERRY BOYKIN was destined to be a great U.S. Army general when he reported to Ranger School in 1971. He had been an honor graduate at Virginia Tech, played varsity football on scholarship, and served as a member of the Corps of Cadets. He had proved to be an outstanding Army officer and was physically and mentally prepared to excel at Ranger School. He was also a Christian and kept his New Testament close at hand.

> Come to me, all you who are weary and burdened, and I will give you rest. Take my yoke upon you and learn from me, for I am gentle and humble in heart, and you will find rest for your souls. For my yoke is easy and my burden is light.
> ~Matthew 11:28–30

Amazingly, Boykin met his first serious defeat on a Ranger School patrol in the mountains of North Georgia. After two days on a mission without sleep, he was stumbling along in the middle of the column when someone yelled, *"Boykin!"* The instructor looked at him and said, *"You are now the patrol leader. You have thirty minutes to brief your team and move out."*[45] Unfortunately, he had not taken the warning seriously that any man could be placed in charge of a mission at any time. In his first assignment as patrol leader, he failed miserably.

This failure was not only a wake-up call for Boykin professionally, it was also a wake-up call spiritually:

> Up until that point, I trusted God mainly with my spiritual well-being, the security of my eternal soul—"fire insurance," as the old joke goes. For everything else, I now realized, I had been depending on myself, on my own mental abilities, my athleticism, my determination. But when I failed that patrol, I suddenly understood I had been relying too much on myself and not enough on God. For me, that was the beginning of a life lived relying on God moment by moment.[46]

When I became a Christian, I thought I had passed the reins of my life to God. Unfortunately, I have made a habit of trying to take them back. Some of us seem to be programmed to always 'take responsibility' and to fall back on our own resources. We forget that God waits to share our burdens and, at times, lift them from us completely.

Christian Soldiers

ONE MORNING a soldier walked into Lieutenant Jerry Boykin's office with a question. He asked how you could be in a job where you *go out and kill people?* Boykin was surprised by the question and had to admit he didn't have a good answer. He realized he needed some help.

Soon after this conversation, the lieutenant met with his pastor, the Reverend Bob Jones (not related to the university), and presented him with the question. The pastor replied, *"Life is all about warfare. Life is a battle, a spiritual battle. And, at the root of every war, there is a spiritual battle."*[47] He discussed Communism and the atheism at the heart of its ideology. In contrast, he talked about America:

> The LORD foils the plans of the nations; he thwarts the purposes of the peoples. But the plans of the Lord stand firm forever, the purposes of his heart through all generations. Blessed is the nation whose God is the LORD.
> ~Psalm 33:10–12

> *What you need to understand is that God ordained this nation to be a place where people could worship freely, and a place where other nations could look and see that the foundation of that freedom is the belief that it is God who grants freedom to all men. He's called this country to be a light in a world of darkness. And He didn't create a country where believers could have freedom with the expectation that unbelievers would defend it. It's not only right for Christians to defend this nation, it's their responsibility.*[48]

I believe this minister's words are true. Our nation was founded on this statement from the Declaration of Independence: *"All men are created equal . . . they are endowed by their Creator with certain unalienable Rights."* When our Founding Fathers cut the ties of royal authority, they looked intentionally to God as the true Source of their authority. I believe that God blessed this new nation and has protected it often during its history.

However, these past events don't guarantee God's continued blessing. When Abraham Lincoln was asked if God was on the side of the North in the Civil War, he wisely replied, *"Sir, my concern is not whether God is on our side; my greatest concern is to be on God's side."*[49] We must pray that America remains a beacon of freedom to its citizens and the rest of the world.

The Flame

LIEUTENANT Jason Redman was seriously wounded in 2007 while serving in Iraq. While recovering he wrote a moving tribute to America and all her sons and daughters who have gone to war through the years. He stated the cause shared by the citizens and veterans of today, calling on each to carry some part of the flame that makes America great:

> You are the light of the world. A city on a hill cannot be hidden. Neither do people light a lamp and put it under a bowl. Instead they put it on its stand, and it gives light to everyone in the house. In the same way, let your light shine before men, that they may see your good deeds and praise your Father in heaven.
> ~Matthew 5:14–16

> *Ronald Reagan talked of the city on a hill, a shining beacon to the world. I like to think of that city as being lit by a flame. It's up to all of us, in everything we do, to support that flame and ensure it burns brightly at all times. Soldiers have carried it with them crossing the beaches of Normandy, on Iwo Jima, in Korea and the jungles of Vietnam.*
>
> *Every American citizen is entrusted with a small part of this flame. Many Americans feed their flame and ensure it burns brightly for all to see. Thankfully, there are those of us who wear the uniform who are also entrusted with a part of the flame—to ensure the torch of Freedom always burns.*[50]

(National Park Service)

The analogy of American freedom as a beacon of light to the world comes from Jesus' Sermon on the Mount. Jesus used this image to illustrate the greatest light ever known to man: the saving grace of Almighty God. Throughout his ministry on Earth he shared this light with his followers and challenged them to share it with others. In the same way, he challenges his followers today. The ultimate selfish act would be to receive the gift of salvation and to then keep it to ourselves. This is the flame we must keep alive at all cost.

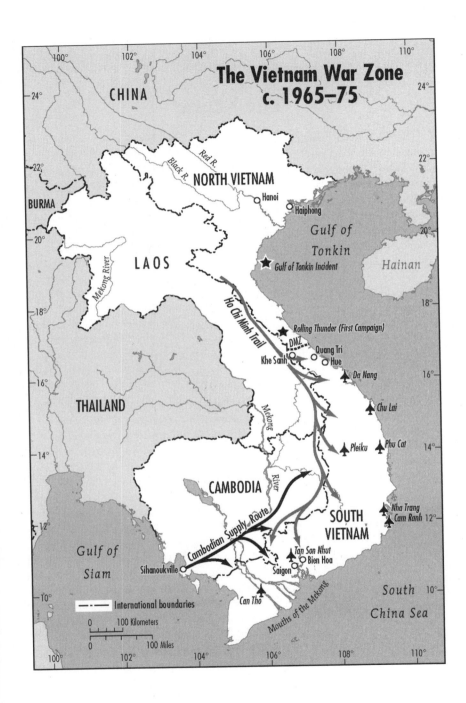

The Vietnam War Zone
c. 1965–75

CHINA

Red R.

Black R.

NORTH VIETNAM

Hanoi

Haiphong

Gulf of
Tonkin

Hainan

BURMA

LAOS

Mekong River

★ Gulf of Tonkin Incident

Ho Chi Minh Trail

★ Rolling Thunder (First Campaign)

DMZ

Khe Sanh

Quang Tri
Hue

Da Nang

Chu Lai

THAILAND

Mekong

Pleiku

Phu Cat

CAMBODIA

River

Nha Trang
Cam Ranh

SOUTH
VIETNAM

Cambodian Supply Route

Tan Son Nhut
Bien Hoa

Gulf of
Siam

Sihanoukville

Saigon

South
China Sea

International boundaries

Can Tho

Mouths of the Mekong

0   100 Kilometers

0   100 Miles

U.S. COMMITMENT

NGO DINH DIEM became prime minister of South Vietnam in 1954. His anti-French and anti-Communist credentials made him one of the few politicians who seemed capable of bringing order to the new government. During the late 1950s Diem struggled to consolidate his power as he fought to suppress a variety of paramilitary religious sects and the remnants of the Communist-dominated Vietminh, now referred to as the Viet Cong, or "Vietnamese Communists."

After a period of consolidation, the Communist government of North Vietnam focused its full attention on South Vietnam, with the aim of unifying the entire country under Communist rule. In 1959, Group 559 was formed to infiltrate South Vietnam through Laos and Cambodia with troops and weapons. The Viet Cong not only had the full backing of North Vietnam, but of the other Soviet bloc countries as well. China began pouring vast quantities of materiel into North Vietnam and by 1963 had supplied 270,000 guns, 200 million bullets, more than 10,000 artillery pieces with more than one million artillery shells, 28 ships, and more than 1,000 trucks.[51] With this support, the Hanoi-controlled Viet Cong guerrilla forces made steady progress extending their domination over many areas of South Vietnam. By 1961 about 4,000 South Vietnamese village and provincial governmental officials were being assassinated each year.

In 1961 several hundred U.S. military advisors were helping the Diem government train their armed forces to combat the growing invasion and insurgency. That year, after the Bay of Pigs debacle in Cuba and construction of the Berlin Wall, the newly elected Kennedy administration decided a firm show of resolve in Vietnam was needed. The Military Assistance Command, Vietnam (MACV), was created, headquartered in Saigon, with a large increase in U.S. military advisors to aid the struggling nation. By the end of 1963 15,000 American soldiers were assigned to MACV. In that year also, the Diem government was overthrown by a military coup.

In 1964 an incident off the coast of North Vietnam between North Vietnamese gunboats and the U.S. ships *Maddox* and *Turner Joy* caused the U.S. Congress to pass the Gulf of Tonkin Resolution. President Johnson was given authority to "respond instantly with the use of appropriate force to repel any unprovoked attack against the armed forces of the United States."[52] With this authority, President Johnson moved to expand the war effort cautiously, trying to support a fragile South Vietnamese government in order to prevent a complete Communist takeover.

The United States started Operation Rolling Thunder in early 1965 under the assumption that an intense bombing campaign would convince the Viet Cong and North Vietnamese to discontinue their military activity and to come to the negotiating table. Air strikes on northern South Vietnam and southern North Vietnam were flown from Navy aircraft carriers and from air bases in Thailand and South Vietnam. Direct American involvement in the ground war began in March 1965, when two battalions of U.S. Marines landed at Da Nang to protect the airbase there.

The air campaign would continue for years, but would never achieve its aim of bringing an end to the Communists' efforts to subdue South Vietnam. Instead, the American troop commitment would grow exponentially to not only secure the air bases, but to take the war to the Viet Cong and growing numbers of regular North Vietnamese Army (NVA) units entering the country through Laos and Cambodia.

Darkness

THE SPECIAL FORCES camp at Duc Co was manned by a few Green Beret troops, several hundred South Vietnamese soldiers, and a small artillery unit. It was located about six miles from the Cambodian border and far from other friendly forces. Life in the remote outpost was always tense, but especially so at night:

> As the last helicopter fades into an unidentifiable dot and the sun kisses the sky its golden goodbye, you know you're in for another long night at Duc Co. Though the night has fallen, work has not ceased. For Duc Co and the men of A Battery, Duc Co is a synonym for work, 24 hours a day. The Duc Co world is a small one. Bunkers, homes, fortresses and recreation rooms are all one [and] the same. Last night PFC Baker was bitten by a rat. The night before was scorpions' night. What will tonight bring? Sunrise is a pleasant sight. For a new day brings relief not only from the things that kill in the night and bite in the dark, but also offers the hope of some mail from home.[53]

And God said, "Let there be light," and there was light. God saw that the light was good, and he separated the light from the darkness. ~Genesis 1:3, 4

The throne of God and of the Lamb will be in the city, and his servants will serve him. They will see his face, and his name will be on their foreheads. There will be no more night. They will not need the light of a lamp or the light of the sun, for the Lord God will give them light. ~Revelation 22:3–5

Fortunately, most of us associate darkness with rest. We get our much-needed sleep at night and know we couldn't do without it. We also know, however, that nighttime can be a time of fear—fear of the unknown and the unexpected. Bad things stalk the darkness, whether insects, enemy soldiers, drunk drivers, or drug dealers. There is nothing worse for a parent than a late-night phone call.

Interestingly, the opening verses of the Bible describe the prevalence of darkness in the universe until the moment God introduced light. He then separated the light from the darkness, creating, in effect, day and night. In the last verses of Revelation, we learn that, when the end time comes, darkness will be finally and totally eliminated. Evil will be purged and, with it, fear of the unknown and unexpected. We are promised we will live then in the pure light of God's eternal love. This is an amazing promise and a spectacular future we cannot even fully comprehend.

Unsung Heroes

LADY BORTON served as a volunteer with a civilian relief agency during the Vietnam War. Working in and around Quang Ngai, she was constantly in rural areas and talking in Vietnamese with the local villagers. She learned things American military leaders, GIs, and journalists never did—including the hidden roles of Vietnamese women in the war:

> A wife of noble character who can find? She is worth far more than rubies. She speaks with wisdom, and faithful instruction is on her tongue. She watches over the affairs of her household and does not eat the bread of idleness. Her children arise and call her blessed; her husband also, and he praises her.
> ~Proverbs 31:10, 26–28

Later that afternoon, I swung by the American army compound to pick up the mail, entering the base as the Vietnamese cleaning women left it. The maids flirted unabashedly as the MPs checked their empty baskets for contraband. What fools those MPs are, I thought. Doesn't it occur to them that the contraband these women carry is information hidden inside their heads? Don't the MPs realize that their flirtatious cleaning maids probably pace off warehouse measurements while they sweep, memorize shipments they unload, and note details of any unusual activity? In the years since, I've checked out my guesses, and learned that I was right. Women formed the core of the North Vietnamese/Viet Cong spy, liaison, and distribution networks. Yet even today, more than twenty years after the war's end, their contribution remains largely unrecognized.[54]

It is not unusual for women to go unrecognized for their contributions, even though more and more in our modern culture earn accolades in government, business, medicine, and practically every other field of endeavor. To their credit, these women make great contributions to society and deserve the visibility they earn.

Still, there are certain women who go unnoticed and unrecognized who would not want it any other way. These are the unsung heroes of our day—those women who quietly oversee the physical and emotional well-being of their families, who raise loving children, who love and support their husbands. Many of these women work outside the home due to necessity. Many remain in the home full-time, consciously deciding to forego additional income for the sake of time with their children. In either case, their families come first, and their rewards can't be quantified. God bless these women who quietly and faithfully fulfill the most important role of this—and every—age.

The Word

MY INTRODUCTION to the Fleet Marine Force was at Camp Lejeune, North Carolina, where I joined 1st Battalion, 8th Marines, in March 1963. At that time the separate battalions went through their training cycles while rotating duty as an alert unit for contingencies around the globe. Depending on the location of the trouble spot, we were issued special clothing, equipment, and maps. Many times while on alert we were told to pack and unpack, load up on trucks and unload, travel to Moorhead City to embark on ships, and then turn around and return. During one of these frustrating periods, I first heard the famous Marine Corps paraphrase of Scripture that states, *"In the beginning was the word—and then the word was changed."*

Marine units on Okinawa went through that same turmoil in 1965 as tension was mounting in Vietnam. A member of 3rd Battalion, 3rd Marines, described how "the word was changed" at that time:

> In the beginning was the Word, and the Word was with God, and the Word was God. He was with God in the beginning. Through him all things were made; without him nothing was made that has been made. In him was life, and that life was the light of men. The light shines in the darkness, but the darkness has not understood it . . . The Word became flesh and made his dwelling among us. We have seen his glory, the glory of the One and Only, who came from the Father, full of grace and truth. ~John 1:1–5, 14

Around April 15th, we were told to get our laundry out of the shops and to take our combat boots to the base cobblers for better soles and heels as we would need them in Vietnam. We were issued mimeographed copies of Vietnamese words and phrases. Our seabags were packed and unpacked all this time through March and April. I believe that we started to mount out like eight times, three times for cold-weather training and five times for Vietnam.[55]

Individual Marines and soldiers have always been frustrated trying to comply with instructions from higher authority while adjusting to constant changes. Fortunately, in the spiritual realm, there has been one defining truth passed down through history that has not changed and never will change. That is the gospel message of Jesus Christ as eloquently set forth in the New Testament book of John.

The Enemies of Peace

WRITING TO his home church, a soldier serving in Vietnam expressed his conflicting thoughts about the nature and purpose of the war and urged his friends to continue praying for peace. He quoted a prayer that was especially meaningful to him, given by the pastor of the Central Presbyterian Church in New York City:

> *Our Father, our hearts are saddened and our spirits are in anguish for we continue to kill those whom we should be healing. We know that the enemies of peace are in all men, avarice, fear, enmity, anger and pride. We know that the first casualty of war is truth, and yet we debate in ignorance the rightness or wrongness of our cause. Help us rise above our petty truths and national interests. May we know Thy will for all men and all nations. Save us from the brink of this man-made Hell of destruction. As we pray for peace, show us what you would have us to be and do.*[56]

I am less ambiguous about the nature and purpose of the war. However, I believe there is a cautionary note in this prayer worth considering. We may believe our cause is right, and we may have ample evidence others are acting wrongly. However, it is always good to question our own motives, realizing the truth of the statement, *"The enemies of peace are in all men."* Christians, by definition, understand they are fallen human beings in need of forgiveness and reconciliation with God. The *"fear, avarice, enmity, anger, and pride"* in each of us is the complete explanation for the conflict we see at all levels of human activity, whether personal or international.

> If we claim to be without sin, we deceive ourselves and the truth is not in us. If we confess our sins, he is faithful and just and will forgive us our sins and purify us from all unrighteousness. ~1 John 1:8, 9

Any time we find ourselves in conflict with others, we should examine our own conscience first and recognize our own shortcomings. When we confess our own sins and seek God's forgiveness, we have addressed the only problem in this world for which we can truly access the solution.

Danger or Not

AFTER A month of hard and incessant combat training in the jungle terrain of Okinawa, the men of 3rd Battalion, 7th Marines, finally embarked on the USS *Iwo Jima*. Within two days they were peering out at the silhouette of the Vietnam coastline. Mike Malsbary knew this was the real thing when the supply section started issuing ammunition, hand grenades, and mortar rounds. Soon he stood waiting his turn to take his first helicopter ride:

> There is a time for everything,
> and a season for every activity under heaven:
> . . . a time to scatter stones and a time to gather them,
> a time to embrace and a time to refrain, . . .
> a time to keep and a time to throw away,
> a time to tear and a time to mend,
> a time to be silent and a time to speak.
> ~Ecclesiastes 3:1, 5–7

"Go! Go! Go! Go!" the loadmaster shouted as the Marines double-timed across the flight deck in their full olive combat gear. Soon two platoons, then three were airborne, and the Marines aboard, their ears popping in the blast of cool refreshing air of increasing altitude, viewed swirling glimpses at the great waiting leviathan of emerald and red, and rock and scrub, and reddish earth passing across the open hatchway of the UH-34s. The Marines . . . felt conflicting notions tugging at their guts as they gazed at the chalky green mountains and ridge lines looming above them. Much like sailors and soldiers of yesteryear who after being at sea for weeks or months they welcomed a change, a commitment, the lack of ambiguity, danger or not.[57]

All the military services seem to have a way of conducting endless drills and repetitive training to the point where the troops will face anything just to get on with the main event, whatever it is. Even though it often takes mere minutes to realize that real danger is worse than imaginary fears, there is an almost universal desire to "get the show on the road," rather than wait and prepare.

The veterans know better. The older but wiser ones know there is no such thing as too much training. One more first aid class may save a life later. Field stripping a weapon one more time in the dark may make a difference when it counts. There is a time for everything.

In God's service, there is definitely a time for study, prayer, and preparation. These times of reflection prepare us for our work in the world. We want to be ready when we have an opportunity to share our witness with another, gently, but compellingly, explaining the gospel.

Special Forces camp in the Central Highlands. (National Archives)

5th Infantry Division soldier prepares defenses. (National Archives)

Counting the Cost

IN APRIL 1967 the congregation of Washington National Cathedral heard a thought-provoking sermon on the Vietnam War given by Dr. Paul Ramsey, a Methodist layman and professor of religion at Princeton University. His text was from Luke, chapter 14, in which Jesus described a king on the verge of war and how he would surely count the cost before going out to meet the enemy. Dr. Ramsey asserted that the national leaders of the United States were obligated to do the same.

Dr. Ramsey cited his own support for the war against North Vietnamese infiltration of the South, but it was his opinion that bombing the infrastructure of the North was unjustified. His main thrust, however, was to lament the fact that there was no outrage left for anyone opposing the war to challenge *how* the war was being fought:

> The kingdom of heaven is like treasure hidden in a field. When a man found it, he hid it again, and then in his joy went and sold all he had and bought that field. Again, the kingdom of heaven is like a merchant looking for fine pearls. When he found one of great value, he went away and sold everything he had and bought it. ~Matthew 13:44–46

> *By this time we were a people spent, well spent—poorly spent, in outrageous protests over the war. The vocal opinion coming from church and academic circles had already exhausted itself in an indiscriminate use of moral language, crying "murder" and "immoral" and "intrinsically wrong."*[58]

Dr. Ramsey used Jesus' parable of the king to illustrate the obligation of leaders to count the cost of their actions and to make prudent decisions. At the same time he was also counseling those opposing these leaders to count the cost of *their own* actions, and to choose their battles more wisely.

There is, of course, another and extremely higher purpose behind Jesus' use of this parable. He wanted every man and woman to count the cost of following him: *"In the same way, any of you who does not give up everything he has cannot be my disciple"* (Luke 14:33). The kingdom of God is not just worth *a lot*; it is worth *everything*.

Genuine Love

CHAPLAIN PETER BAKKER arrived in Vietnam with the 1st Marine Aircraft Wing in June 1965. Working with aviation units and local villagers around the bases at Da Nang and Chu Lai, he was soon involved in an intense ministry. In one of his reports he pointed out it was relatively easy to find the *"material, money, mortar, and mechanics"* he had to have to help people in need. However, to change the hearts of these people, the most important thing of all was in short supply. In his opinion, *"The item which was desperately needed in Vietnam was genuine love."*[59]

> This is how we know what love is: Jesus Christ laid down his life for us. And we ought to lay down our lives for our brothers . . . Dear children, let us not love with words or tongue but with actions and in truth.
> ~1 John 3:16, 18

To illustrate his point, he told the story of John and Simone Haywood, missionary friends who had come to the Da Nang area to start a facility to care for the lepers of Vietnam. Shortly before the birth of their first child, Haywood had to travel to Hue to complete arrangements for a chicken farm he was building for the lepers. En route, his vehicle was caught in an ambush, and he was killed by a Viet Cong rifleman.

The Marine Corps offered Simone an escort to accompany her home to bury her husband, but she replied, *"Thank you very much. Your kind offer is appreciated, but I will bury my husband here in Vietnam. I will have my baby here in Vietnam, and with God's help, I will serve the lepers of Vietnam."*[60] Crowds of Vietnamese attended the funeral where a ribbon lay across the grave with the words, *"To Saint John Haywood."* The chaplain concluded the story with this comment: *"This young man was loved by the Vietnamese because he loved them and was willing to lay down his life for them. His wife is also loved by these wonderful people. With a labor of love such as this, the love of God is communicated."*[61]

East Is East

DURING 1965 two Navy Mobile Construction Battalions (MCBs) were operating in the Da Nang area. These talented men, called "Seabees," have deployed with their heavy equipment and worked side-by-side with Marine units since World War II. They build everything. At Da Nang, they were busy constructing the airstrip, port facility, roads, water systems, defensive positions, and more. They also gave many off-duty hours to local civic action programs, working on schools and orphanages, building playgrounds, and remodeling buildings. There were some inevitable problems understanding the local people, which one officer described:

> The purposes of a man's heart are deep waters, but a man of understanding draws them out... Ears that hear and eyes that see—the LORD has made them both.
> ~Proverbs 20:5, 12

> *The Oriental philosophy of life and the acceptance of different-system values are the hardest things for our men to understand about the Vietnamese. They cannot understand the slow pace and seeming lack of concern for time, life and progress, and the unimportance of the central government since their loyalty may not go past their father or the village chief.*[62]

These comments remind me of the often-quoted Kipling verse, *"East is East, West is West, and never the twain shall meet."* I have heard this line used to justify the impossibility of understanding the "Oriental mind" or anyone of a culture different from our own. The complete poem is not so pessimistic, however, and, in fact, paints an entirely different picture:

> *Oh, East is East, and West is West, and never the twain shall meet,*
> *Till Earth and Sky stand presently at God's great Judgment Seat;*
> *But there is neither East nor West, Border, nor Breed, nor Birth,*
> *When two strong men stand face to face, tho' they come from the ends of the earth!*[63]

There are very real differences between cultures, races, religions, age groups, and the sexes. Our daily challenge as Christians is to bridge these gaps. We do this as we lose ourselves in relationship to others and seek to identify with God's interest in them. What could God's plan be for this person? Do I have a role in helping? What do I need to know? When we shift the focus from ourselves and make a prayerful effort to understand someone else, we are truly doing God's work in the world.

You Could Never Ignore the Smells

TONY BLAKE went aboard ship in Sydney Harbor. The passage to Vietnam was filled with fitness training and long periods of contemplation over what lay ahead. On the morning live ammunition was passed out, the young Australian knew the time had finally come. He and the rest of his unit went ashore in landing craft and then boarded trucks for their final destination: Nui Dat. Someone commented, *"Three hundred sixty-five days and a wakey (Aussie for 'wake-up') to go."*[64]

Blake was soon absorbed in the sights and smells of Vietnam. An intensely green landscape unfolded as far as he could see. Farmers working in the fields were wearing

> For we are to God the aroma of Christ among those who are being saved and those who are perishing. To the one we are the smell of death; to the other, the fragrance of life. And who is equal to such a task?
> ~2 Corinthians 2:15, 16

black pajamas and conical hats, just like in the training films. They passed old French forts from a bygone era. The sights were interesting, but the smells were almost overpowering:

> *Much of the area at Nui Dat was built under rubber trees. The tropical atmosphere of mildew at the Dat attacked clothes, tents, paper. The smells of the place included the blend of the fetid vegetation in the rubber plantations, the hint of village sewage, dried fish, a cocktail of the sump oil used to lay dust on the roads of the Dat, body odors, cordite after a fire mission, and tangible humidity. A powerful mix that took some time to get used to, although you could never totally ignore the smells.*[65]

Our sense of smell is vital to how we perceive the world around us. What we see and touch are usually particular to each of us, but an odor completely permeates an area and affects everyone in its path. In an interesting biblical passage the apostle Paul likens the gospel of Christ to the *"fragrance of the knowledge of [God]"* (2 Corinthians 2:14). He also describes Christians as *"the aroma of Christ"* (v. 15). This imagery paints a vivid picture of our role as Christians. By taking Christ's message of love and forgiveness wherever we go, we can change the atmosphere and bring a new aroma to the people in our path. They will react in different ways, but they will not be able to ignore a fragrance that fills the air around them.

What Can They Do to You?

PRIVATE FIRST CLASS Bob Neener was with 2nd Battalion, 9th Marines, one of the first units deployed to Vietnam in 1965. Neener and his squad were assigned to support an ARVN outpost guarding a bridge over the Song Yen River. One night the young Marine was invited to join the Vietnamese soldiers for a little social hour. After too many rounds of rum, he stumbled back to his own area to discover he was missing his .45 caliber pistol. Enraged and drunk, he pulled the pin on a hand grenade and charged back into the Vietnamese camp. After a brief shouting match his friends restrained him. In the aftermath, Neener found himself with the live grenade in his hand. After a futile search for the pin, he yelled, *"Fire in the hole,"* and threw it into the nearby elephant grass. The explosion brought an immediate visit from his platoon sergeant and a court martial.

> Do not be anxious about anything, but in everything, by prayer and petition, with thanksgiving, present your requests to God. And the peace of God, which transcends all understanding, will guard your hearts and your minds in Christ Jesus. ~Philippians 4:6, 7

The next day Neener stood outside the commanding officer's tent facing charges for being drunk on duty and losing government property. Beside him was another Marine named Jerry Lee Roberts, also charged with drunkenness. Neener, now sober and feeling miserable, was scared to death and voiced his concern to his fellow Marine. Roberts turned to him and said, *"Don't worry. What's the worst they can do to you? They can't send you to Vietnam."*[66]

So was coined a phrase that was destined to live on. Years later, Marines were still saying to themselves, *"What can they do to me? Send me to Vietnam?"*

Looking at the worst-case scenario is often an effective way to relieve anxiety. If we can live with the worst case, we should be at peace with all the lesser possibilities. And how bad can even the worst case be when Jesus Christ is with and within us? He wants us to live without worry so he can help us avoid the only scenario with truly disastrous and eternal consequences—separation from our Father in heaven.

Reincarnation

ON HIS first tour of duty in Vietnam Major Norman Schwarzkopf was assigned to the Vietnamese Airborne Brigade as an advisor. He found the unit full of battle-hardened veterans from past campaigns against the Communists. The officers and troops generally seemed to appreciate him being there, although he was reminded frequently this was *their* war.

One night he was sharing a bottle of cognac with one of his unit commanders named Major Hao. After a few drinks, Hao grinned and asked if Schwarzkopf knew he was a Buddhist. Puzzled by the question, the American replied that he did. Major Hao then commented, *"Well, when I am reincarnated, I want to come back as an American advisor. You have the perfect setup! When we win a battle, the advisor gets a medal. When we lose, the [Vietnamese] commander gets the blame."*[67]

> And I saw the dead, great and small, standing before the throne, and books were opened. Another book was opened, which is the book of life. The dead were judged according to what they had done as recorded in the books . . . If anyone's name was not found written in the book of life, he was thrown into the lake of fire. ~Revelation 20:12, 15

Such tongue-in-cheek references to reincarnation are often heard in our own culture. This concept is a serious conviction in some Eastern and New Age religions and has made subtle inroads into Western consciousness as an attractive alternative to the idea of a final judgment. Reincarnation offers another chance to "get it right." Some people make jokes about it, and some take it much more seriously. We all would do well to realize the risk posed by this idea. Even for a nonreligious person, it would seem unwise to bet on second chances. We need to get it right the first time. Every human being will be in for an eventual rude awakening without an effective advocate before God.

"Can Do" Attitude

MAX DUNKS reported to 3rd Marines in late 1965 fresh out of Chaplain School and with no prior military experience. It wasn't easy for him, but he gradually learned how to work within the military framework. He learned the chain of command and how various staff agencies functioned together and how each commander seemed to have his own way of doing things. As he figured out the details, he also learned some lessons that would stay with him for life:

I will never leave you nor forsake you . . . Have I not commanded you? Be strong and courageous. Do not be terrified; do not be discouraged, for the LORD your God will be with you wherever you go. ~Joshua 1:5, 9

> Frustration was always just around the corner, and I often came face to face with it. I expected, and adjusted to it. Last of all I learned that one needs to have a positive, aggressive attitude toward his goals in South Vietnam. The "can do" attitude prevails among the Marines, and Navy Chaplains serving with the Marines are out of place if they do not have this attitude.[68]

Christians are sometimes stereotyped as being mild-mannered and passive. Although Jesus gave us a lasting example of service-oriented humility, he was nevertheless a man of action. He had a message and boldly proclaimed it. John Eldredge, in his best-selling book *Wild at Heart*, also tries to paint a more dynamic picture of Christian service:

> We don't need accountability groups; we need fellow warriors, someone to fight alongside, someone to watch our back. The whole crisis of masculinity today has come because we no longer have a warrior culture, a place for men to learn to fight like men. We don't need a gathering of Really Nice Guys; we need a gathering of Really Dangerous Men. It's a long-standing truth that there is never a more devoted group of men than those who have fought alongside one another, the men of your squadron, the guys in your foxhole. It will never be a large group, but we don't need a large group. We need a band of brothers.[69]

Eldredge implores Christian men to find their warrior hearts and to be courageous for God: "*That is why God created you—to be his intimate ally, to join him in the Great Battle. You have a specific place in the line, a mission God made for you.*"[70]

God Is Real to Them

TOM COLLINS was the ideal Marine chaplain. He had been an all-star varsity basketball player and high jumper at the University of South Carolina and had more than five years' experience as a Baptist minister before he was commissioned in the Navy in 1961. He was the kind of man young Marines could respect and look up to for guidance.

> We put no stumbling block in anyone's path, so that our ministry will not be discredited. Rather, as servants of God we commend ourselves in every way: in great endurance; in troubles, hardships and distresses; in beatings, imprisonments and riots; in hard work, sleepless nights and hunger; in purity, understanding, patience and kindness; in the Holy Spirit and in sincere love. ~
> 2 Corinthians 6:3–6

In Vietnam, Collins served with 1st Battalion, 9th Marines, defending Hill 55, south of Da Nang. He had to travel by helicopter, jeep, and tank, and on foot to reach the line companies in their forward positions. He held ten to twelve religious services and four or five memorial services each week. Casualties in the unit were heavy due to encounters with VC and land mines. Although he had his share of close calls, he was concerned about "his" Marines and the dangers they faced:

> *I can hardly afford to worry about myself when I watch these young 19-year-old Marines walk out on night patrols trying to set up an ambush. They know what fear is—but they're a brave bunch of young men . . . The religious spirit is high—and services on the front line are very well attended. No one likes to think that he might be killed, yet these guys realize that "some of 'em" will not return. God is very real to these men.*[71]

God was real to many Marines in Vietnam due to men of God such as Tom Collins, who lived with them, struggled with them to endure, and shared their fears. Collins carried the Word of God to men who sometimes rejected it but often needed it desperately. During those times, he was there.

Tom Collins baptizing a Marine

Valentine's Day

VALENTINE'S DAY had an unusual significance to Sergeant Edmund Sheldon. On that day in 1968 a VC mortar round landed five feet from his tent and completely destroyed it. It so happened he was not in the tent at that moment. Sixteen years earlier, his unit in Korea had been hit by enemy mortar fire on February 14, marking the start of a four-day battle. "Happy Valentine's Day" has had a special meaning to this soldier ever since these events.

This day, of course, has an entirely different meaning to most of us. Valentine's Day, as we now know it, is a celebration of love, with vestiges of both Christian and ancient Roman tradition:

> Love is patient, love is kind. It does not envy, it does not boast, it is not proud. It is not rude, it is not self-seeking, it is not easily angered, it keeps no record of wrongs. Love does not delight in evil but rejoices with the truth. It always protects, always trusts, always hopes, always perseveres. ~1 Corinthians 13:4–7

One legend contends that Valentine was a priest who served during the third century in Rome. When Emperor Claudius II decided that single men made better soldiers than those with wives and families, he outlawed marriage for young men—his crop of potential soldiers. Valentine, realizing the injustice of the decree, defied Claudius and continued to perform marriages for young lovers in secret. When Valentine's actions were discovered, Claudius ordered that he be put to death.[72]

Pope Gelasius declared February 14 St. Valentine's Day around AD 498. Ever since then, the day has become ever more associated with romantic love and the exchange of affectionate notes, letters and gifts.

Although some of us have a certain cynicism about the blatant commercialism of all our holidays, including this one, Valentine's Day still presents a golden opportunity to focus our attention on the ones we love. If cards and flowers advance certain romantic relationships, that's a good thing. If well-established couples rekindle a spark, that is even better. I believe that God smiles in heaven when a man and woman nourish the love that brought them together and, in the process, nourish and strengthen their families.

To Die

EDDIE BEESLEY was a good Marine. He made corporal and fire team leader by the time he had a month left on his tour in Vietnam. He didn't think he should be walking point that day, but the lieutenant had specifically called for him to be there for this patrol. Moving through a hedgerow, he spotted a land mine on the ground beside a recently dug hole. He never saw the one that detonated beneath his feet.

PFC Eddie Beesley
USMC

The explosion threw Beesley into the air and over the twelve-foot-high hedgerow. He landed hard on his back and lay there in a confused but conscious state. He looked down, and his legs were a mess of burnt trousers, torn flesh, and jagged bones. His feet were gone. In that instant, the pain hit him, as he almost passed out from the smell of gunpowder and burnt flesh and the sight of his own wounds. He described his thoughts in that moment:

> *"I am dying! I don't want to die! I'm not ready to die!"*
> *I was losing it—going into shock.*
> *I tried to remember the 23rd Psalm, but I couldn't put the words together in sequence. I gave up in frustration and panic overwhelmed me.*
> *"God, please don't let me die in this awful place."*
> *Deep down inside me, a voice said, "Suck it up, Marine. This is what it's all about—to do or die. It's gut-check time.*[73]

Time seemed to stand still as the corpsman worked on Eddie Beesley's wounds. He felt himself drifting toward unconsciousness again and again, but kept calling himself back. As Beesley fought for his life, he was dimly aware of the drama playing out around him. Others were killed and wounded, but all he could do was fight his own battle with the oblivion trying mightily to consume him.

> By the sweat of your brow you will eat your food until you return to the ground, since from it you were taken; for dust you are and to dust you will return. ~Genesis 3:19

To Live

THE CORPSMAN kept working on Eddie Beesley's wounds. He used his own belt and one from another Marine to make tourniquets. Eddie asked the corpsman to give him something for the pain. *"I already did,"* the man said and moved on to help someone else. Eddie struggled to stay conscious.

Eddie Beesley

> I felt myself drifting away. Everything closed in around me. I knew I was dying.
> NO.
> I wouldn't die.
> I focused on staying alive—but with every minute that passed, I grew weaker.
> I could no longer see.
> Despite the morphine the corpsman gave me, the pain was tremendous and I was tired—so tired. It would be easy to let go—but I wouldn't.[74]

The severely wounded Marine kept drifting toward unconsciousness but continued to fight for his life. Finally, after what seemed forever, he heard the familiar sound of a helicopter approaching. He was lifted aboard by his buddies and found himself on what seemed like an unending path of medical treatment that would eventually bring him back to the States.

Eddie would be forever thankful he didn't let go on that battlefield. It would be hard to count the number of people who have been blessed by the fact that this Marine held on—and lived. Today Eddie Beesley proudly maneuvers his wheelchair among other wounded warriors from battles in the Middle East. He brings them a message of faith and courage. He inspires other veterans, friends, and the congregation of a small church he now pastors with his zest for life and determination to live fully in this life and in the next. He has made it his ministry to impart that determination to others.

> We were therefore buried with him through baptism into death in order that, just as Christ was raised from the dead through the glory of the Father, we too may live a new life. ~Romans 6:4

Catalyst

THE LIFE of a combat chaplain had its sobering moments. Lieutenant Tom Collins wryly described a lesson in humility received during his first service in the field with the 9th Marines:

> As the men gathered for services they spaced themselves and sat low in a dry rice paddy. I stood up on the dyke to preach. About halfway through the service, 10 rounds from a VC weapon whizzed by my ear. The Chairman of the Board of Deacons and six companies took care of the disturbance. Needless to say, I completed the service down in the rice paddy, on a level with the laity.[75]

The kingdom of heaven is like a mustard seed, which a man took and planted in his field. Though it is the smallest of all your seeds, yet when it grows, it is the largest of garden plants and becomes a tree, so that the birds of the air come and perch in its branches. ~Matthew 13:31, 32

The good chaplain not only learned to "stay off the skyline," he learned a lot about the men who were the focus of his ministry. They lived and worked in a harsh and dangerous environment. Many risked their lives every day and had to take others' lives all too often. Collins worked hard to understand these men and did a lot of soul-searching about how to relate to them. He observed:

> The closer we got to the front lines the more responsive were Marines to the chaplain's presence and to the worship services. Foxhole religion for the most part stands open to much criticism, but the shallow experience can sometimes act as the catalyst for a deeper religious experience. In the "grunt" I saw a lot of boys grow into men, and a lot of men grow spiritually in the chaos of war.[76]

My "foxhole religion" was as shallow as any. My prayers were fervent when the mortar rounds were falling, but were soon forgotten when it was over. Even so, I think the chaplain is right, even though I had not considered it before reading his comment. I now see my combat experience as an important catalyst for my later spiritual life. Those religious services in the field and my superficial prayers while afraid *did* lead to something deeper, even though much later. We hear the phrase often, "In God's time." We should always keep this in mind as we share the gospel with others. We never know how or when our words will be the catalyst for another's awakening.

RHIP

IN AUGUST 1965 Brigadier General John Wright took a group of field-grade officers and senior NCOs to Vietnam to select a site for the 1st Cavalry Division's base camp. After scouring Binh Dinh province, the general picked a location near An Khe in a remote valley surrounded by hills. Standing on the site with the rest of the group, General Wright saw that an airstrip would be needed with the underlying brush cut close to the ground. Realizing he had an unusually high-ranking group for such a task, he called them together to explain the task:

> Gentlemen, you will all be issued a machete or a grub hook; they both do exactly the same job. We are going to cut brush until we have a 'golf course' here. You may as well hang your rank insignia on a tree because until this area is transformed, we will all avail ourselves to this manual task. When the golf course is completed, you may then put back your rank insignia.[77]

RHIP, or "Rank Has Its Privilege," is the military expression used to explain why someone of higher rank might have certain benefits others do not. Fortunately, I have seldom heard the expression used seriously. In fact, military rank always carries more responsibility than privilege. Those of higher rank should always look first to the needs of those serving under their command. It is also important that officers show a constant and personal interest in their men. There are times when this requires a human touch and less awareness of rank. A good leader crosses this line effortlessly and often, just as a good parent does.

Our model for this kind of leadership is our Savior, Jesus Christ. Although he was the Son of God, he was never preoccupied with "rank." He not only became a man, he put the needs of other men before his own and became a servant to them. There is no higher ideal for anyone in a position of responsibility.

> Jesus said to them, "The kings of the Gentiles lord it over them; and those who exercise authority over them call themselves Benefactors. But you are not to be like that. Instead, the greatest among you should be like the youngest, and the one who rules like the one who serves."
> ~Luke 22:25, 26

Amen

DURING THE Vietnam era, affordable long distance phone calls were often available only through the MARS network of amateur radio stations. If a serviceman wanted to call home, a radio link between his overseas MARS station and one somewhere in the States had to be made. Then the stateside station would place a long distance call to the party the serviceman wanted to contact. It was usu-

MARS station at work. (U.S. Navy)

ally a tenuous connection but, when successful, provided a rare opportunity for a man to talk directly to long-separated loved ones.

David Grant helped operate the MARS station at the U.S. Army Hospital at Camp Zama, Japan, for several years during the war. His most memorable call was between a wounded soldier named Clarence and Clarence's father in Hawaii. It was not an easy connection, as repeated efforts were needed to find a Hawaiian station with a good signal.

When the link was finally established, Clarence had to explain to his father the extent of his wounds. He told him he had lost both legs at the knee. Grant would never forget the next few minutes of this phone call:

> *The conversation continued on past the normal three minutes, as it turned out Clarence had many brothers and sisters, and they all wanted to talk to him. At the end the father came back on and offered a prayer . . . He prayed for his son, but more especially he prayed for all servicemen, those stationed in Vietnam, and especially those caring for his son. I lost it. I could barely see the controls and meters on the radio, as the tears were flowing. But that's not all. After we signed off, another MARS station broke in with their call-sign and the word "Amen." Then another station broke in, with "Amen." Within 5 minutes I logged 30 MARS stations with the same message—"Amen." All these stations had heard the call, both sides, and were moved to do what they did.[78]*

The expression *amen* comes directly from the Hebrew and means "So be it" or "Truly." It is also used colloquially to express strong agreement. All these meanings were conveyed by these heartfelt responses to a father's prayer for a wounded son.

Praise be to his glorious name forever; may the whole earth be filled with his glory. Amen and Amen. ~Psalm 72:19

Mail Call

IN VIETNAM two words could make all the difference in a soldier's morale. Every man and woman waited every day to hear someone shout, "Mail call!" There was nothing more important than a letter from home. Letters from girlfriends and wives were naturally most prized, as there was absolutely nothing to compare to holding in one's dirty hands a clean envelope with familiar handwriting on the outside and the smell of perfume. When there was no mail call it was a bad day. When there was mail call and a soldier received nothing, it was even worse.

> The body is a unit, though it is made up of many parts; and though all its parts are many, they form one body. So it is with Christ. For we were all baptized by one Spirit into one body.
> ~1 Corinthians 12:12, 13

There were times when units in the field could not receive mail. Otherwise, it came with regularity. Few gave much thought to the process of its delivery. A division level post office could process more than 30,000 pounds of mail every day, as one postal officer reported:

> *Four commercial flights—two each from San Francisco and Seattle— arrive at Da Nang daily with cargos of nothing but mail. It is then transported here by C-123 and C-130 aircraft on a space available basis.*
>
> *The pallets of mail are hauled by truck from the airport to the APO, where they are broken down according to units. When unit clerks arrive to pick up their mail they bring in a load of outgoing mail, and the reverse process occurs.*[79]

Mail represents a lifeline to sanity for soldiers in every war. In the chaos of a combat zone, a letter from home reconnects them with quiet and peaceful places. Most of us have the same need. In our chaotic lives we also want a quiet place and reassurance that someone cares.

We know that our quiet place can always be found in God. Unfortunately, letters from him are not placed in our hands by a postal clerk. His letters to us are there in Scripture, waiting for us to seek them out, study them, and apply them to our lives. To help us with this task, we have the body of Christ around us in our churches. When we conscientiously study the Bible in company with fellow believers, we establish a consistent avenue for God to hold the ultimate "mail call" for each of us.

Footprints

THEY WERE saved by a footprint. Sergeant Frank Marshall was moving along a road that had just been swept for mines when he spotted one lone footprint off to the side. He called an engineer with a mine detector back to the spot, and the area was rechecked. This time the detector gave off a weak, but discernable signal. Two charges were uncovered, one of which was intricately booby-trapped. One of the engineers explained:

> Praise be to the Lord, to God our Savior, who daily bears our burdens . . . Our God is a God who saves. ~Psalm 68:19, 20

There was almost no metal used to construct the mine. That's why the mine sweeper didn't catch it on the first pass. Whoever rigged that mine knew what he was doing. The dirt was hidden in a rice paddy and all the footprints had been wiped out. Except one.[80]

The enemy soldiers who planted these mines were experts, and they were very careful. Was this footprint their one careless mistake, or did these soldiers benefit from a mysterious or even divine intervention? There is of course no answer to such a question.

I have heard another thought-provoking story about the importance of "footprints." It is about a man who had a dream in which he was walking on the beach with God. As he walked, scenes from his life flashed across the sky. In most of the scenes there were two sets of footprints in the sand—his and God's. In a few scenes, however, there was only one set of footprints. The man was troubled by this when he realized these scenes were the lowest points in his life, when he was the saddest. He asked the Lord why he had not been there for him when he needed him most. God replied, *"My precious child, I love you and would never leave you! During your times of trial and suffering when you see only one set of footprints, it was then that I carried you."*[81]

It is not unusual to look back and see God's hand in our lives. In retrospect, we can more clearly discern how he has changed us or how we could not have survived some crisis without his help. This knowledge of God in our past should give us a stronger faith in the future. We can have confidence he will always be there when we need him most.

The Painting

A WEALTHY MAN and his son loved to collect rare works of art. They had exceptional items in their collection, by artists ranging from Picasso to Raphael. They would often sit together and admire the great paintings. When the Vietnam War broke out, the son had to leave home to go to war. He was a courageous young man and died in battle while rescuing another soldier. When the father was notified, he grieved deeply for his only son. About a month later, there was a knock on the old man's door. A stranger stood there with a large package in his hands.

> There are different kinds of gifts, but the same Spirit. There are different kinds of service, but the same Lord. There are different kinds of working, but the same God works all of them in all men.
> ~1 Corinthians 12:4–6

He said, *"Sir, you don't know me, but I am the soldier for whom your son gave his life. He saved many lives that day, and he was carrying me to safety when a bullet struck him in the heart and killed him instantly. He often talked about you and your love for art."* The young man held out the package and said, *"I know this isn't much. I'm not really a great artist, but I think your son would have wanted you to have this."*[82]

The father opened the package. It was a portrait of his son, painted by the young man. He stared in awe at the way the soldier had captured the personality of his son in the painting. The father was so drawn to the eyes that his own eyes welled up with tears. He thanked the young man and offered to pay him for the picture. *"Oh, no, sir, I could never repay what your son did for me. It's a gift."*

The father hung the portrait over his mantle, the place of honor in his mansion. Every time visitors came to his home he took them first to see the portrait of his son before he showed them any of the other great works he had collected. He obviously prized this work above all the others.

Vietnamese soldiers defend Saigon.
(U. S. Army)

President Johnson decorating a soldier. (National Archives)

Take My Son

WHEN THE wealthy art collector died, there was an auction of his paintings. Many influential people gathered, excited about seeing the great paintings and having an opportunity to purchase them for their own collections. The first painting brought to the platform, however, was the portrait of the man's lost son, painted by his fellow soldier from Vietnam. The auctioneer pounded his gavel. *"We will start the bidding with this picture of the son. Who will bid for this picture?"* There was silence . . .

> For God so loved the world that he gave his one and only Son, that whoever believes in him shall not perish but have eternal life. For God did not send his Son into the world to condemn the world, but to save the world through him.
> ~John 3:16, 17

Then a voice in the back of the room said, *"We want to see the famous paintings. Skip this one."* But the auctioneer persisted. *"Will somebody bid for this painting? Who will start the bidding? $200 . . . $100?"*

Another voice said irritably, *"We didn't come to see this painting. We came to see the Van Goghs, the Rembrandts. Get on with the real bidding!"*

But still the auctioneer continued. *"The son. Who'll take the son?"*

Finally, a voice came from the very back of the room. It was the long-time gardener of the man and his son. *"I'll give $10 for the painting."* Being a poor man, it was all he could afford.

The auctioneer said, *"We have $10, who will bid $20?"*

Someone shouted, *"Give it to him for $10. Let's see the masters."*

The auctioneer pounded the gavel. *"Going once, twice, SOLD for $10!"*

A man sitting on the second row shouted, *"Now let's get on with the collection!"*

The auctioneer laid down his gavel and said, *"I'm sorry, ladies and gentlemen, the auction is over. There is a stipulation in the will that I was not allowed to reveal until this time. Only the painting of the son will be auctioned. Whoever bought that painting will inherit the entire estate, including the paintings."*[83] And so, the man who took the son got everything!

This story is representative of how God gave his son 2,000 years ago as a sacrifice for mankind. Much like the auctioneer, his question today is, *"The Son, the Son, who'll take the Son?"* And the result is the same: Whoever takes the Son gets everything.

And God to Men

EARLY IN the war a chaplain serving with Marines made some thoughtful observations on what was needed in the type of war being fought at that time:

> *In guerrilla warfare it is physically impossible to remain by the side of very many men at any given time and place. The men are widely dispersed; they hit and run; they withdraw and vanish into their hiding places. It seems to me that it is imperative that a fighting man who will operate alone or with small groups be trained and equipped not only in a military way, but also in a spiritual and moral way to withstand isolation and all the pressures that the feeling of being "cut off" brings to bear upon the mind and soul of man.*[84]

> There should be no division in the body, but that its parts should have equal concern for each other. If one part suffers, every part suffers with it; if one part is honored, every part rejoices with it. Now you are the body of Christ, and each one of you is a part of it.
> ~1 Corinthians 12:25–27

These observations are relevant to all Christians going about their busy lives, usually separated from each other. Young people face a special form of spiritual isolation in their schools and colleges. Often in the minority and faced with professors and fellow students openly antagonistic to religion, it is not unusual for them to feel "cut off" from support. As parents, we hope they will be prepared for this challenge by their early experiences at home and in church. Unfortunately, peer pressure will inevitably put a strain on these past influences.

Ultimately, it is up to the individual young person to decide what influences will dominate his or her mind and soul. An important part of this decision is the selection of friends. The wrong choices inevitably lead down the wrong paths and toward further isolation. On the other hand, a few Christian friends can be their connection to the "body of Christ" and the spiritual support that flows from it. This may or may not be a "church," but any group of fellow believers is the one group from whom young people will never have to fear being cut off or isolated.

God Can Sneak Up on You

ALBERT FRENCH served with the 7th Marines in Vietnam and afterward became a critically acclaimed writer and photojournalist. In his own eloquent style, he reflected on his thoughts while in combat and questioned the presence of God in war:

> God can sneak up on you anytime, then leave quickly. Most of the time, he comes at night when you're alone in your hole. He can just be there, you can look his way, talk, whisper to him. You can ask him why, why, why. Sometimes you won't talk to him. You don't want him close to you, messin' with your head. Things ain't never fair. Everything is upside down, everybody can get killed. Maybe God ain't here, maybe you're just talkin' to yourself, thinkin' he's here.[85]

Despite his doubts and unanswered questions, French confessed an ill-defined faith that God *was* there during his worst moment and even seemed to have a purpose for his life:

> I remember one night, perhaps I had gone too far. Maybe God didn't want me to go no further, wanted me to live, tell about it, write about what he had to watch us do. I know now he cried, it was never raindrops fallin'. No, there ain't that much rain to ever fall.
>
> I was standing in the dark, looking across the rice paddy. We were pulling back, and I was asking this guy if anyone was left back there. This guy turned and looked back too, then turned to me and muttered, "Only the dead." I turned, pulled back, came back. But I brought the time with me and turned it into words that will hopefully live forever.[86]

The doubts expressed so thoughtfully by this soldier ring true, and his story reassures us in our moments of perceived isolation God is still there. God honors our honest doubts, and rewards us with answers in his time. When we have our doubts, we should raise them in a direct and heartfelt way—and expect God to answer. He would rather deal with a passionate challenge than unspoken doubts and withdrawal.

"'If you can'?" said Jesus. "Everything is possible for him who believes." Immediately the boy's father exclaimed, "I do believe; help me overcome my unbelief!" ~Mark 9:23, 24

No Greater Love

Larry Pierce (U. S. Army)

SERGEANT Larry Pierce was a squad leader in a reconnaissance platoon ambushed near Ben Cat in September 1965. He led his men in a successful attack to neutralize an enemy machine gun position and disrupt the ambush. During the action, he saw an antipersonnel mine threatening the rest of his men. Without hesitation, he threw himself on the mine, absorbing the blast and giving his own life for the other soldiers. For his heroic actions, he was awarded the second Medal of Honor given in Vietnam. The award was made posthumously to his family by President Lyndon Johnson in the White House on February 24, 1966.

Lieutenant Colonel John Tyler was CO of the 1st Battalion, 503rd Airborne Infantry, and Pierce's battalion commander. Tyler was a Methodist from Winona, Mississippi, who once remarked to a fellow officer, *"If Christ was not the Son of God and if His death was not sufficient to atone for sin, then there is no hope for any man."*[87] This unusually spiritual officer led a memorial service for the battalion's Medal of Honor recipient, and gave a moving witness to the men of the battalion, comparing Pierce to another great hero of the past:

> Greater love has no one than this, that he lay down his life for his friends. ~John 15:13

Centuries ago there was a man who walked the dusty roads of a land far removed from us today. His life and actions produced widely diverse responses among those who knew Him. Some called Him demon-possessed; others labeled Him a winebibber; still others acclaimed Him as a prophet; and others called Him a king.

You and I know him as Jesus of Nazareth, the Son of God, the Savior. This same Jesus was slain—but not without reason. It was because of His unlimited love for men like you and me. What is even more remarkable, we are further instructed that if we are willing to place our faith in Him, we have His guarantee of eternal life.

Today, we come together to give honor to one who, like the Nazarene, gave his life that others might live. Sergeant Larry S. Pierce has put into practice for the world to see this principle:[88]

A Man's Decision

KENNETH PEEPLES did not agree with America's involvement in the Vietnam War. He was even less happy with his nation when he was drafted into the Army. Nevertheless, he followed his orders, went to Vietnam, and served with the 1st Infantry Division in the III Corps area. During his tour he was wounded in action and evacuated to Japan. While recuperating, he received a heartfelt letter of encouragement from his father:

> Let me say here and now that I'm extremely proud of you, son. You made a prudent and honorable decision. It may not matter at all to you, but you are coming home a hero to us. Not a war hero, because you had to fight and get shot, but more so because you made a man's decision and stuck it out. You should feel proud of yourself! You can hold your head high everywhere you go, and you can go anywhere you wish.[89]

Every young man of Kenneth Peeple's generation had to make a decision. For some it was easy. For some it was extremely difficult. Fortunately, most took the honorable path, as did this young man.

One of the great biblical heroes also had a difficult choice. Abram (later called Abraham) was called by God to leave his home and travel halfway around the known world to an undisclosed destination. The Bible tells us, *"Abram believed the LORD, and he credited to him as righteousness"* (Genesis 15:6). If God appeared to Abram in person and gave him a command, it is hard to understand why Abram was given such credit. Who would not obey if God spoke directly to them? I suspect that Abram was more like the soldier in this story. He was not happy when his life was disrupted. He knew the risks. Somehow, however, he discerned what God wanted him to do. Somehow he knew what was right. Even though he always had a choice, he had to make a man's decision.

> It was not through law that Abraham and his offspring received the promise that he would be heir of the world, but through the righteousness that comes by faith . . . Against all hope, Abraham in hope believed and so became the father of many nations. ~Romans 4:13, 18

A Tribute to Chaplains

ON DECEMBER 2, 1965, the Marines and Navy personnel at Da Nang celebrated the birthday of the Navy Chaplain Corps. In a ceremony honoring the service of chaplains past and present, Lieutenant Commander James Seim explained the unique ministry of these dedicated men and women:

> "The harvest is plentiful, but the workers are few. Ask the Lord of the harvest, therefore, to send out workers into his harvest field. Go! I am sending you out like lambs among wolves."
> ~Luke 10:2, 3

As desired by the churches of the land and by Navy Regulations, chaplains have taught men both secular and sacred subjects. Always they teach the larger lessons of life, the lessons of God's Word, His way for man. Chaplains have administered the sacraments. They have confronted men with the sacred acts most holy and precious to their churches, baptizing the new believers from helmets and in oceans, offering the Holy Supper, confirming, hearing confessions, blessing marriages, going with them to the final moment of life and bridging the gap with the last rites. They have brought the assurance of God's care to sailors and Marines on wooden ships, in polar ice, on violent seas, in roaring helicopters and in silent depths, in rotting jungles, on comfortable stations, in foxholes, bunkers, and bamboo chapels.

Chaplains have shown the nation the meaning of religious cooperation by working together, and have led the way, honoring one another . . . All this because we are here to serve God and the military man. It is our unique profession.[90]

All military men and women appreciate the difficult ministry of their chaplains. These dedicated people have to do their work while recognizing the military significance of rank and authority. Amazingly, they are themselves not in either the military or spiritual chain of command. They neither command the troops nor act as intermediaries between them and God. They do, however, hold a certain spiritual authority as "commissioned officers" of the church. Like all ministers, they have vital leadership duties—guiding worship services, administering the sacraments, and teaching God's Word. The troops, or laity, also have their duty—to lift up in prayer and to actively support these men and women who so bravely and unselfishly assume the mantle of spiritual authority.

Guerrilla Warfare

BY MID-1965, the Communist insurgency in South Vietnam was growing more powerful, even in the face of a massive U.S. bombing campaign. The Johnson administration announced the commitment of 125,000 ground troops to bolster the war effort with more offensive operations and to support the South Vietnamese armed forces in their continuing buildup.

By this time, Great Britain had 54,000 troops defending Malaysia from China-backed Indonesian Communists. Fearing a growing Indonesia-Vietnam-China-North Korean Communist axis in Asia, the nations of Australia, New Zealand, South Korea, and the Philippines sent forces to join the United States in South Vietnam.

Fighting the war by proxy, the Chinese continued to send massive amounts of equipment and more than 300,000 troops into North Vietnam to build and repair the country's infrastructure and to relieve North Vietnamese troops for deployment to the south. The Soviet Union also sent many of its best weapons systems and as many as 3,000 advisors to man these weapons and to train the North Vietnamese.

As U.S. military forces increased, more offensive operations were conducted from the coastal enclaves. At first these were small unit patrols and reconnaissance missions to find and disrupt Viet Cong operations. It was a frustrating type of combat for the Americans, operating in and around populated areas where the enemy, interspersed among the civilians, used mines and booby traps extensively.

Gradually, operations increased in size and scope. The term "search and destroy" was used to describe the concept of a quick thrust into a suspected area to find and dispatch an elusive enemy. On these operations infantry units were usually transported and resupplied by helicopter and supported by artillery and aircraft from nearby bases. The overall strategy adopted by General William Westmoreland, the U.S. commander, was one of attrition, based on the belief superior American firepower and maneuverability would inflict more casualties on the VC than they could replace. It was believed the Communists would eventually become convinced they could not achieve their aims in South Vietnam. On their part, the VC, supplemented more and more by North Vietnamese forces, believed they could outlast the Americans, especially in the realm of American public opinion.

After months of small unit firefights and sniper fire in the Da Nang area, the Marines got their first big intelligence break with a deserter's report of a main force VC unit located south of Chu Lai in the vicinity of the village of Van Tuong. Operation Starlite, the first major U.S. operation of the war, kicked off on August 17, 1965, as a company of the 3rd Battalion, 3rd Marines, moved over land to a blocking position north of Van Tuong. The next morning the rest of the battalion landed in an amphibious assault over beaches to the south. Simultaneously, 2nd Battalion, 4th Marines, landed by helicopter in three landing zones to the west. During the next two days of heavy fighting a VC regiment of more than fifteen hundred men was driven from its base with heavy casualties.

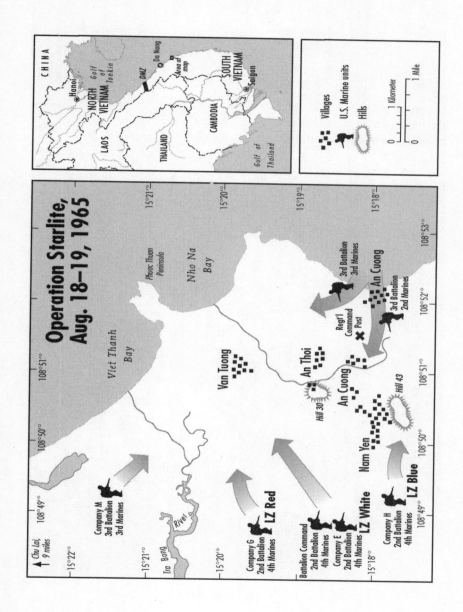

Operation Starlite, Aug. 18–19, 1965

Main map labels

Chu Lai, 9 miles

Company M
3rd Battalion
3rd Marines

Tra Bong River

Company G
2nd Battalion
4th Marines

LZ Red

Battalion Command
2nd Battalion
4th Marines

Company E
2nd Battalion
4th Marines

LZ White

Company H
2nd Battalion
4th Marines

LZ Blue

Viet Thanh Bay

Van Tuong

An Thoi

Hill 30

An Cuong

Nam Yen

Hill 43

Phuoc Thuan Peninsula

Nho Na Bay

Regt'l Command Post

3rd Battalion
3rd Marines

An Cuong

3rd Battalion
2nd Marines

108°49'° 108°50'° 108°51'°

15°22'°
15°21'°
15°20'°
15°18'°

15°21'°
15°20'°
15°19'°
15°18'°

108°51'° 108°52'° 108°53'°

Inset map (top)

CHINA

Hanoi

NORTH VIETNAM

Gulf of Tonkin

Da Nang

DMZ

Area of map

LAOS

THAILAND

CAMBODIA

SOUTH VIETNAM

Saigon

Gulf of Thailand

Legend

Villages

U.S. Marine units

Hills

0   1 Kilometer
0   1 Mile

A Marine lands at Da Nang (National Archives)

A Sign of My Frailty

CAPTAIN DICK CAMP was leading a group of his men back to base along an open road in a staggered column. He suddenly had one of those feelings something wasn't right. He stopped, hesitated briefly, and was about to shout for everyone to get off the road when an explosion ripped the earth twenty yards ahead of him. As a corpsman rushed by, he realized one of his Marines had been seriously wounded by a command-detonated mine. Private First Class Smith, one of the radio operators, lay alongside the road, barely alive. Nothing could be done for him other than call for an emergency evacuation.

> Three different times I begged the Lord to take it away. Each time he said, "My grace is all you need. My power works best in weakness." ~2 Corinthians 12:8 NLT

Back at base, word soon came that Smith had died of his wounds shortly after being picked up by the medevac helicopter. Captain Camp almost came undone at the news. Blaming himself, he retreated to his tent, overcome with grief and guilt. He couldn't remember how long he wept in solitude. Eventually, the battalion chaplain showed up at his side:

> *I don't remember what was said, but I slowly turned around and got myself pulled together. On the outside. Inside, for all the years since, I have carried the image of Smitty's death deep inside me as a sign of my frailty. I knew it then, clearly, that I never should have let the patrol proceed up that open roadway.*[91]

Good Marine officers need to be aggressive and at times fearless. To be great, however, a sense of humility born of experience is needed. Maturity in a leader requires a sense of one's own fallibility, and the ability to make decisions even knowing some will be wrong. It is no disgrace to acknowledge this kind of weakness. The apostle Paul described a *"thorn in my flesh"* that tormented him constantly. Even as he prayed for its removal, he recognized that the pain served to remind him of his weakness and protected him from being proud (2 Corinthians 12:7–9). We each have our own "thorns" that aggravate us physically or emotionally. They may also be God's gift to us to keep our feelings of self-importance in check.

For One of the Least

GUY MCPARTLAND was a battalion chaplain with the 3rd Marines operating near Da Nang. In addition to his normal duties of ministering to the men of his unit, he took an interest in the Vietnamese people he met. His infantry battalion operated far from the cities, so the people he encountered were farmers and small villagers trying to eke out a living in the midst of a violent war. Chaplain McPartland wrote home to church friends,

> *The people here are extremely poor. We've been trying to do as much as we can to improve their living conditions. For instance, introducing them to soap and toothbrushes and paste . . . The average workman draws anywhere from 50 cents to $1.00 per day . . . If any of your groups at home would like to do a real work of charity and at the same time help us win this war, they could have a little "bash" at somebody's house, take up a little collection, and send it to me via a money order. I could then convert it into piasters and put it to immediate use . . . I don't have in mind anything big . . . A $10.00 or $15.00 or $20.00 would do wonders for a child, a sick mother, or father, etc.*[92]

The chaplain later wrote that he received twenty-three dollars from church members at home and that he spent seven dollars of it on soap for three hundred fifty school kids. He was convinced these kids would either get cleaner or that their parents would have a valuable item to barter for other necessities. Either way, this small act would make a meaningful difference in a few lives.

What more can anyone expect in their work for God's kingdom? Even though there are times when the needs seem overwhelming, we should not let this deter us from doing *something* to make a difference.

> "'Lord, when did we see you hungry and feed you, or thirsty and give you something to drink?' . . . The King will reply, 'I tell you the truth, whatever you did for one of the least of these brothers of mine, you did for me.'"
> ~Matthew 25:37, 40

Maggie

MARTHA RAYE's career as a comic actress started in the 1930s and spanned more than five decades. During World War II, the Korean War, and the Vietnam War she traveled around the world entertaining and supporting the troops. Thousands of military men and women have fond memories of "Maggie," with her big smile, often bawdy jokes, and untiring energy. The men of Special Forces had a special feeling for her, as she was one of the few entertainers ever to visit the outlying Special Forces camps. She came not only to entertain, but to spend time with the troops. One soldier described her two-day visit to Kontum, near the Laotian border:

Martha Raye (Bill McDonald)

> *The war wasn't put on hold. Teams still came and went, the guard changed, life went on. But Maggie managed to lace her way into the fabric of it. She'd stop in with a team and help pack chow. She filled sandbags. She helped a team off the pad with their rucks, bringin' cool ones. She watched us go to the range, played pool, walked the berm, visited Rosie's. She was everywhere. Ate with the guys, and always had a kind word, a good story, and news of the other sites . . . She never said a monologue or stood on a stage, but she did her entertainin' job to the max. She didn't bring a piece of home, she brought herself, and gave remorselessly.*[93]

Even though Martha Raye was in her fifties during the Vietnam War, her energy and enthusiasm amazed everyone. She was always smiling: *"God, the smile went from ear to ear and back again, and it dropped twenty years off her like a shot. And she wasn't tidy with it, she spread it all over the place."*[94]

> He will yet fill your mouth with laughter and your lips with shouts of joy.
> ~Job 8:21

Martha Raye brought warmth and laughter to weary men in dreary places. Her smile will long be remembered by Vietnam veterans as a light in the darkness. Her unselfish service is an example that lives on for all of us. If we can bring the same kind of smile and genuine concern to someone in a difficult situation, it will always have a profound impact. A simple act of service at such a time shows the love of Christ in a way that will never be forgotten.

My Refuge and My Fortress

JUD SPAINHOUR was a uniquely gifted Marine officer. He was a superior athlete, highly effective troop leader, and an all-around great person. His most amazing quality was a perpetual optimism that infected everyone around him. I was fortunate to serve with him in 2nd Force Recon Company at Camp Lejeune, North Carolina, before we went our separate ways to Vietnam. Tragically, he was killed on September 15, 1966, while leading a reconnaissance patrol near the DMZ.

Even though we were good friends, I regret to say I never discussed with him the source of his positive energy and cheerful nature. Years later I read a book compiled by the Spainhour family to commemorate Jud's heroic life. In one of his letters to his father from Vietnam he explained the nature of his faith:

> He who dwells in the shelter of the Most High will rest in the shadow of the Almighty. I will say of the LORD, "He is my refuge and my fortress, my God, in whom I trust."
> ~Psalm 91:1, 2

> "Because he loves me," says the Lord, "I will rescue him; I will protect him, for he acknowledges my name. He will call upon me, and I will answer him; I will be with him in trouble, I will deliver him and honor him. With long life will I satisfy him and show him my salvation."
> ~Psalm 91:14–16

I try to constantly look after my lads and care for them and trust God to care for me. The 91st Psalm is quite appropriate—God has a place for me here and I hope that I may be strengthened by each trial and if he wills it return safely home. If not, and never fear that I will, I will have hoped to live my life as I think He would want me to, and I hope you would want me to. There's not much to worry about for I know that all things are ordained by him and I am thankful that you gave me this knowledge and are an inspiration to me when the going gets tough.[95]

When I knew him, Jud Spainhour was not an overtly religious person. I never heard him give anyone spiritual advice or counsel. He simply lived his life in a way to demonstrate the power of his own faith. In his own way he touched the lives of everyone who knew him.

A Letter to My Son

FROM CAMP Tien Sha near Da Nang, James Kline wrote a letter to his seven-year-old son to explain why he had to be away from him so long. He explained that his duty and responsibility as a father started with making the world a safer place in which his son, and perhaps someday his son's son, could grow up. He also felt the need to explain the important beliefs that had guided his life, hoping they would be important in his son's life:

> First of all, Believe in God and follow his commandments; be loyal, trust-worthy, morally clean and spiritually right. Never lie no matter what, honor and love and respect your mother and father. Respect the rights and property of others. Do not covet what belongs to others, do not steal, and do not use the word and the name of God in vain.
>
> Jesus had a cross to bear and all of us over here have our cross to bear. We may falter but must carry the load ourselves as Jesus did, but we can call on him any time the load gets too heavy or we need help . . . You have a good home, wonderful mother and many good friends, and above all else, you have God.[96]

This was a good father and a man with strong convictions. He was trying to accomplish two things in this letter. First, he expected his son, even though very young, to understand much of what he was writing and to put what he did understand into practice. Second, and perhaps more importantly, there were things he wanted to share with his son that he might never have the opportunity to explain unless written in a letter. This is not an uncommon thought for a man in a combat zone or any other dangerous place.

Now faith is being sure of what we hope for and certain of what we do not see. This is what the ancients were commended for
~Hebrews 11:1, 2

Consider what you would write to your own children if you thought there was a chance you wouldn't see them again. This would have to be the acid test of your true beliefs. Take a few quiet moments to earnestly examine your conscience—and compose your own letter.

Tedium

CHARLIE RIDGE was the objective for this recon patrol. This imposing terrain feature lying west of Da Nang was named in honor of the VC (referred to as 'Victor Charlie' in the phonetic alphabet), who still controlled most of the area. The ridgeline was a long finger with little cover or concealment running down toward the sea from an elevation of forty-five hundred feet. In addition to weapons, ammunition, and heavy rucksacks, each man in the team carried eight canteens of water, knowing that more would be hard to come by during the five-day mission.

> A man can do nothing better than to eat and drink and find satisfaction in his work. This too, I see, is from the hand of God. ~Ecclesiastes 2:24

After landing by helicopter the Marines had the uncomfortable feeling they were under constant observation by a watchful enemy. They moved only at dawn and dusk, and laid up during daylight hours to better conceal their location. Walking may have been a little easier during the cooler hours, but being still during the heat of the day was excruciating. One of the recon Marines recalled:

> We set up an OP (observation post) on a knoll in the middle of the ridge line. A very open and very dangerous position because of its high visibility. We must remain very alert and cautious. Tedium and heat are our enemy now. We have seen nothing and just sitting has us soaked in sweat. The slight breeze stirs the heat a little, but it's like stirring molasses with a straw.[97]

Combat is full of such timeless treks and exhausted waiting—the proverbial "days of tedium punctuated by moments of stark terror." In certain ways, everyday life has its similarities. If we are fortunate, most of our work and leisure are self-motivating and pleasurable. However, there are those mundane tasks that wait to be done: paying the bills, weeding the grass. Each of us has days whenwe wonder what we accomplished. At such times it is important to remember there is no task too great or too small that can't be done in a way to bring glory to God. A cheerful heart and a smile demonstrate God's presence in our lives and give a powerful witness to our faith.

VC prisoners taken during Operation Starlite. (National Archives)

4th Marines operating near Da Nang. (National Archives)

Those Ills We Have

THE PILOTS flying out of Binh Thuy airfield in the Mekong Delta called him One-Shot Charlie. He would fire just one shot at planes taking off or landing and then disappear. If the wind shifted (so flights took off and landed in another direction), he would somehow move all the way around the base to take his one shot at the other end of the runway. Patrols went after him time after time for months, but no one was able to track him down.

For all his soldierly qualities of stealth and persistence, One-Shot Charlie had one basic flaw: He was not a marksman. He never hit one of the aircraft he fired at.

> *In time the American airmen at Binh Thuy came to feel that One-Shot Charlie was the ideal sniper to have around. Some said that they should quit sending out patrols after him. After all, if he were caught, the VC might replace him with a better marksman.*[98]

In *Hamlet*, Shakespeare gave us the famous phrase about our fear of the unknown, explaining how it *"makes us rather bear the ills we have than fly to others that we know not of."* This all-too-human tendency reflects an underlying trait common to most of us. We prefer the safe and familiar to the unknown.

Sometimes we need to step out of our comfort zone. Bill Hybels said as much in the title of one of his great books: *Just Walk across the Room.* Approach that person you have passed a dozen times in the gym and introduce yourself. You may be surprised as a new door opens. Try some form of volunteer work that is different. You may gain a new perspective as you learn from your discomfort. We all need to make new friends, try new ministries, and maybe even sit somewhere else in church! Sometimes we need a few more unknowns in our lives. By boldly and prayerfully exercising our faith, we build the confidence that comes from leaning on God and overcoming our fears. With him there is no unknown we cannot risk.

> God has said, "Never will I leave you; never will I forsake you." So we say with confidence, "The Lord is my helper; I will not be afraid. What can man do to me?"
> ~Hebrews 13:5, 6

Building an Orphanage

WHEN KARL PHALEN learned that a group of Vietnamese nuns were trying to build an orphanage near the town of Rach Gia, he decided to do what he could to help. He wrote several impassioned letters to a journalist he knew in San Francisco describing the plight of the children and his belief that American bombing was contributing to the problem.

Phalen soon heard back from the journalist, who said he would help raise funds for the orphanage *if* he could publish the letters. Phalen knew this would undoubtedly jeopardize his military career. He didn't consider himself a war protester, but, thinking it would help the children, he agreed to have his letters released. Ultimately more than $15,000 flowed in from sympathetic readers in the States. For his efforts, Phalen was officially reprimanded for his public criticism of the war effort and was reassigned from advisor duty to a regular Navy unit in another part of Vietnam.[99]

> His work will be shown for what it is, because the Day will bring it to light. It will be revealed with fire, and the fire will test the quality of each man's work. If what he has built survives, he will receive his reward.
> ~1 Corinthians 3:13, 14

Like Karl Phalen, we are not always rewarded for our good deeds. On my graduation day at The Citadel, the Commandant of Cadets pulled me aside to give me one last bit of advice. He said, *"Larkin, I'm afraid you haven't had occasion to learn this up until now, but you need to realize an important truth: Virtue is not always rewarded in this life."* I have subsequently learned how true this is. There are times when you have to do the right thing regardless of the opinion of others. At those times there is only one opinion that counts, and that is the opinion of our heavenly Father. We may have to go on suffering in the present as we rest assured he understands. He knows our motives, and he is the Judge of how our actions contribute to his kingdom. His rewards will come later and last longer than any form of human recognition.

Personal Response

EVEN BEFORE the first troops entered Vietnam, senior Marine Corps commanders realized that winning the confidence of the civilian population would be the key to success in this type of conflict. Lieutenant General Victor Krulak, the senior Marine commander in the Pacific, emphasized this critical issue:

Lt. Gen. Victor Krulak (U. S. Marine Corps)

Much has been said and written about the importance of winning the hearts and minds of the people in Vietnam if we are to be successful in carrying out our mission in that war-torn country. Victory will come as the people want to help themselves. We can win everything in Vietnam but the people and suffer an abysmal defeat. We must start by knowing them as they are and building from there. It is self-defeating to be willing to do everything for the Vietnamese except understand them as persons.[100]

General Krulak ordered his chaplaincy staff to conduct a study of Vietnamese religious practices; that study eventually evolved into what was termed the "Personal Response Project." Training materials were produced for small-unit leaders, based on practical examples of likely incidents between troops and indigenous people. For some time the Chaplain Corps assumed the greatest part of this effort, even though many voiced theological reservations about participating in what they felt were "indoctrination" programs. Some were opposed to this kind of activity, while others felt it a legitimate effort to promote cultural understanding.

This controversy among the chaplains served to highlight the difficulty of their role as representatives of God trying to serve simultaneously as members of a military command. To the chaplains' credit, they

> Then he said to them, "Give to Caesar what is Caesar's, and to God what is God's."
> ~Matthew 22:21

showed a deep concern about keeping their priorities straight, as many argued for a stronger focus on serving the religious needs of the Marines in their units. Eventually, the Personal Response Project was made a command responsibility instead of a chaplaincy program. But the Marines learned early in the war they were more effective operating in areas of the country where the people were on their side.

Mines and Booby Traps

KILO COMPANY was moving carefully along a well-used trail running north from Route 9. We had discovered it earlier in the day and were ordered by battalion to check it out. The lead platoon had already found one trip wire across the trail rigged to a grenade, and I had passed the word for no one to sit down. The point man was working overtime trying to see everything while avoiding a misstep.

Capt. Spivey and Lt. Dick Hanson

The column suddenly stopped moving, and, after a few minutes, word came back along the line, *"CO up!"* My radio operator and I started making our way forward to the head of the column. I soon found Dick Hanson, the 1st Platoon commander, and the point man squatting in the trail. They motioned me forward and pointed to a trip wire across the trail. Dick then stood up and pointed into the jungle to the right. All I could see was dense foliage. As I continued to stare, I made out the tip of a sharp object and then the outline of what looked like a spear! They had found a six-foot bamboo spear rigged to a sapling, set to strike whoever tripped the wire.

Bamboo spears were a first for Kilo Company. We had encountered grenades, bouncing bettys (mines originally used by German forces in World War II), and artillery rounds rigged as mines. But somehow the primitive nature of this homemade device was at once laughable and sobering. What would we run into next?

> The LORD is my light and my salvation—whom shall I fear? The LORD is the stronghold of my life—of whom shall I be afraid? ~Psalm 27:1

Every man in the field during the Vietnam War had to deal with the fear of mines and booby traps. It was worse for some than others. Units working close to inhabited areas controlled by the VC were constantly in danger. One soldier commented, *"It's an absurd combination of certainty and uncertainty: the certainty that you're walking in mine fields, walking past the things day after day; the uncertainty of your every movement, of which way to shift your weight, of where to sit down."*[101] The hidden dangers were the worst part of the infantryman's life in Vietnam. The unremitting anxiety took its toll as each man dealt with fear in his own way.

Value of Suffering

FOLLOWING ARMY Chaplain Thomas Confroy on his dangerous rounds to the men of the 1st Division, a reporter made some insightful observations about how this godly man approached his difficult mission:

He never pressures anyone into coming to this church (a clearing in the jungle), he never asks why the buddy who came last time has not returned. He never speaks of the nearness of death—everyone knows it full well. The hardest part of Father Confroy's work comes after Mass, as he waits at the aid station for those who have received Holy Communion, struck into the jungle, and will be soon returning for Extreme Unction, the last rites of the Church. His sermons are brief and often mention the value of suffering as a means to understanding what Christ Himself endured.[102]

Dear friends, do not be surprised at the painful trial you are suffering, as though something strange were happening to you. But rejoice that you participate in the sufferings of Christ, so that you may be overjoyed when his glory is revealed.
~1 Peter 4:12, 13

I want to know Christ and the power of his resurrection and the fellowship of sharing in his sufferings. . ..
~Philippians 3:10, 11

I believe it is true every hardship gives us an opportunity to come closer to our Savior. It is unfortunate, but we all seem to need some humbling experience to turn us in his direction. When life is on an even keel, we begin to suffer the illusion we have everything under control. When the illusion is shattered, the experience is always painful. Nevertheless, this is the time our faith can grow to a new level. We simply have to remember that Christ waits for us in our pain. Through his suffering, he understands ours, and through his resurrection, he has given us hope for the glorious time ahead.

An Invisible Enemy

STAFF SERGEANT C. T. Anthony joined the 26th Marines in 1966 on Hill 55, southwest of Da Nang. With twelve years in the Corps at that time, he had plenty of leadership experience, but no actual combat. Like all Marines, he wondered how he would react under fire.

C. T. Anthony

His first mission was a night patrol to disrupt VC operations in the vicinity of the base. When an automatic weapon opened up on his column from a nearby village, he deployed his squads, directed their return fire, and advanced through the area. Although he was reassured about his ability to do his job, that night he got a taste of the kind of fighting he would continue to experience in this part of the war:

That also was my introduction to the frustrations of fighting the VC in the area of Hill 55. Lots of planted mines, booby traps, and hit-and-run tactics with seldom ever having the chance to really engage the enemy. For me it was very frustrating and like a hell of a way to fight a war. They were like an invisible enemy.[103]

Christians are acquainted with invisible enemies. We know about that small voice that tells us we shouldn't try, we aren't qualified, we don't have enough time, we can't make a difference. Whether this is Satan at work or our own rationalizations, the effect is the same. A hidden enemy seems constantly at work to deflect us from the narrow path we know we should be walking with God. When we are on that path we only hear one voice—the voice that reassures us we can do anything as long as we're walking with him.

> For wide is the gate and broad is the road that leads to destruction, and many enter through it. But small is the gate and narrow the road that leads to life, and only a few find it.
> ~Matthew 7:13, 14

Last Letter

PRIVATE FIRST Class Hiram Hickman was killed in action near Bong Son, Vietnam, in February 1966. Almost a month later someone found a notebook that had fallen beside his bunk containing a handwritten "last letter" home. In it he tried to lighten the tone by paraphrasing an apocryphal Marine poem from the Guadalcanal campaign of World War II:

> And when he gets to Heaven
> To Saint Peter he will tell:
> "One more Marine reporting, Sir—
> I've served my time in Hell!"[104]

> Do not let your hearts be troubled. Trust in God; trust also in me. In my Father's house are many rooms; if it were not so, I would have told you. I am going there to prepare a place for you. And if I go and prepare a place for you, I will come back and take you to be with me that you also may be where I am.
> ~John 14:1–3

The patriotic and spiritual young man went on to express sincere regret that his family had to read his letter, but also a lot of pride in what he was doing:

> Believe me, I didn't want to die, but I know it was my part of the job. . . . I want my country . . . to stand as a light to all people oppressed and guide them to the same freedom we know. If we can stand and fight for freedom, then I think we have done the job God set down for us. It's up to every American to fight for the freedom we hold so dear . . . God bless you all and take care. I'll be seeing you in heaven.[105]

I wonder how comforting this letter was to the soldier's family. Arriving in the midst of their grief, his patriotic optimism probably gave them somewhat cold comfort. When a son is lost, the wounds are deep and lasting. There is an optimistic note to this letter, however, in the faith evidenced by the young Marine. I hope his family was able to take him at his word and look forward to heaven with him. I pray his family was able to grieve their loss while maintaining this hope in the ultimate future. Eternity with God puts a different perspective on the life and death of every one of us. Life is preparation. Death is not a tragedy—it is the final step we take to a complete union and glorious life with our Savior, Jesus Christ.

Warning Label

THE BLAST of a Claymore mine is devastating. When set off, seven hundred steel balls are scattered in a sixty-degree pattern, wreaking havoc on everything in an area within fifty yards. In Vietnam, we put several out ahead of our lines every night, and also used them in ambushes.

Claymore mine (U. S. Marine Corps)

As shown in the accompanying photo, these mines were rectangular and convex in shape, measuring about eight inches in length by three in height with an aperture on top to permit sighting. Included in the kit were the mine itself, a detonator—called a "clacker"—blasting caps, and a length of wire. The three-and-one-half pound device was easy enough to carry and fairly simple to operate, but it was dangerous and treated with great respect. Even so, it always struck me as slightly humorous that on the outer convex surface there was an embossed warning label: *"Front toward Enemy."* In another display of super-caution, the light anti-tank assault weapon (LAAW) had a big arrow with a similar label: *"Aim toward the Enemy."*

Since these bygone days warning labels have totally taken over our modern culture, protecting us from such dire threats as hairdryers (don't use in shower), baby oil (keep out of reach of children), and matches (may catch on fire). Unfortunately, there are no warning labels to protect us from the things that can truly hurt us in this life: the presence of evil and our own lack of spiritual focus.

> Be self-controlled and alert. Your enemy the devil prowls around like a roaring lion looking for someone to devour. Resist him, standing firm in the faith. ~1 Peter 5:8, 9

I try to keep my Bible handy as my daily warning label against these threats. Our sure defense against evil is self-discipline in our prayers and Bible study. With these resources, we can draw nearer to the only Source of true protection in this world, our Savior, Jesus Christ.

I Know He Hears Me

IT WASN'T easy, but Chaplain Jim Hutchens finally reached the wounded officer. Pete Arnold had been hit by an exploding mine and was in bad shape. With multiple shrapnel wounds and blood all over his body, he was barely conscious. As medics worked on the wounded man, Hutchens kneeled beside him to see if he could comfort him in some way. He later recalled an amazing conversation:

> "Because he loves me," says the LORD, "I will rescue him; I will protect him, for he acknowledges my name. He will call upon me, and I will answer him; I will be with him in trouble, I will deliver him and honor him." ~Psalm 91:14, 15

"I'm not just talking, Chaplain. I'm praying to my God and I know He hears me. I know He loves me," he said. After a pause he added, "And I know He is going to take care of me."

"Why don't we have a word of prayer, Pete," I suggested, "and put your life completely in His hands."

He nodded his approval.[106]

Machine guns and small arms were still clattering, and artillery fire was screaming overhead. The smell of sweat and blood was mixed with the stench of combat. Through it all, however, Jim Hutchens was aware of an overshadowing fragrance from the presence of the living God hovering over him and the men around him. Every man bowed his head as the chaplain prayed:

Dear Father,
We come in the name of Jesus Christ our Lord. You said that when two or three gather together in Your name You are also there. We believe You are here. We know it. Knowing this, Lord, we put ourselves willingly into Your hands. Give us the grace and the courage for whatever is asked of us. We are not afraid of what man can do to us. We look to You for victory—to You, Lord, from whence comes our help. Right now we ask You to restore Pete Arnold to soundness of mind and body. Thanks be to God which giveth us the victory through our Lord Jesus Christ. Amen.[107]

Fortunately, Pete Arnold did survive his wounds and recovered fully. We are blessed with this insight into God's power to reassure men in the midst of the worst imaginable chaos. We are encouraged by the knowledge there is no dark place we can go where God cannot find us—there is no pit so deep he cannot lift us out of it.

Silence

IN THE jungle, silence *was* golden. Members of the 7th Royal Australian Regiment considered the old Simon and Garfunkel tune "The Sounds of Silence" to be their theme song:

> *Talking is part of everyday life. Yet in the jungle it was the thing you did the least of. Communication was done with "clicks" of the fingers, looks, nods, and hand signals that were standard for the infantry. Any spoken word was done up close and personal and very quietly. It was a time you lived in your mind, for many days at a time. The success of the silent way of the Aussies can be tested by the number of stories when the VC were sprung at close quarters in the jungle, having no idea they were in Aussie gun sights.*[108]

Silence may be golden in combat and in human affairs generally, but when we pray to God, we wish we could hear answers. In our humanness, we want to hear him speak to us in unmistakable terms. Oswald Chambers, the great Christian devotional writer, had great confidence in prayer and God's faithfulness in responding to it. However, he saw even greater significance in those times of God's silence:

> So the sisters sent word to Jesus, "Lord, the one you love is sick." . . . Yet when he heard that Lazarus was sick, he stayed where he was two more days. ~John 11:3, 6

> *Has God trusted you with His silence—a silence that has great meaning? God's silences are actually His answers . . . His silence is the sign that He is bringing you into an even more wonderful understanding of himself. Are you mourning before God because you have not had an audible response? When you cannot hear God, you will find that He has trusted you in the most intimate way possible—with absolute silence, not a silence of despair, but one of pleasure, because He saw that you could withstand an even bigger revelation.*[109]

When God is silent the faithful come closer. They pray more intensely and listen more carefully. They have confidence God will respond and that his silence is a sign of greater things to come.

Standing Up

THE DAY started at 4:00 a.m. with me yelling into a field telephone. I was trying to gather information on reconnaissance operations throughout the Northern I Corps area for the general's briefing later that morning. I was new on the job as a staff officer and still felt a little out of place as a captain standing up to brief the senior officers of the division staff.

During the previous day, one of our patrols near Khe Sanh had spotted an enemy column moving through a valley below their hilltop position. They called artillery fire on the column and then relocated to a new position, according to procedure. I talked to the patrol leader during the night and got all the details.

At the 8:00 a.m. briefing, I told the general and his staff about this incident and made a comment praising the patrol for disrupting an enemy unit and causing casualties without disclosing their own presence. At this point, the general kicked a chair across the room and shouted, *"I don't care whether any NVA were killed or not—I want to know what they're doing!"* He then went on a rant about the general ineffectiveness of his reconnaissance assets. Throughout this tirade, interspersed with my feeble attempts to respond, my immediate boss, the reconnaissance battalion commander, sat in the back of the room, never saying a word.

> I am the good shepherd; I know my sheep and my sheep know me—just as the Father knows me and I know the Father—and I lay down my life for the sheep. John 10:14, 15

For a long time I held a grudge against this officer whom I thought had failed to stand up, literally, when it counted. One day many years later I was recounting this story to my wife, who recalled my own failure to back her up on a notable occasion when she was having a problem with one of our children. There was not much I could say in reply. We both decided that the moral of this story is that there is only one perfect example of a leader truly protecting his followers, and that was Jesus Christ. The Good Shepherd came into the world to faithfully tend his flock and ultimately to give his own life for them. When it counted, he stood up for his followers, to open the way to a blessed life and an eternal future. No matter who fails us, he never will.

A Fighting Man's Prayer

IN AUGUST 1967, a prayer was published in *Allons*, the 7th Battalion, 15th Field Artillery, newsletter. This prayer by an unknown author has appeared since in many forms and places, including invocations for political assemblies, in Jewish Chanukah services, and as a Christian Christmas prayer. It has been used and adapted often and has been meaningful to many different people. However, it has never been more meaningful than on the occasion it was published for soldiers in a war zone.

> He makes wars cease to the ends of the earth; he breaks the bow and shatters the spear, he burns the shields with fire. "Be still, and know that I am God; I will be exalted among the nations, I will be exalted in the earth." The LORD Almighty is with us; the God of Jacob is our fortress. ~Psalm 46:9–11

A Fighting Man's Prayer
Let us pray that strength and courage abundant be given to all who fight for a world of reason and understanding; that the good that is in every man's heart may day by day be magnified; that men will come to see more clearly not that which divides them but that which unites them; that each battle may bring us closer to a final victory not for nation over nation but of man over his own evils and weaknesses; that the true spirit of the United States, its joys, its beauty, its hope, and, above all, its abiding faith, may live among us; that the blessing of peace be ours—the peace to build and grow, to live in harmony and sympathy with others, and to plan for the futures of our families.[110]

Of all men, the soldier is the one who prays most earnestly for peace and understanding in the world. It is a great American tradition that the soldier has no political agenda and seeks only to perform his duty to the fullest and, when called on, to fight for his nation's protection. The fighting man is the one who bears the brunt and sees the results of the evils that pit man against man and nation against nation. The "Fighting Man's Prayer" should be the prayer of every citizen, until that day when understanding and sympathy finally do rule in the hearts of men and the policies of nations.

EOD

EVERY MILITARY person is familiar with the initials *EOD*, for "Explosive Ordinance Disposal." These are the seemingly fearless people who handle the unexploded artillery shells and bombs, and somehow defuse every other explosive device known. In Vietnam, EOD was called routinely to dispose of abandoned or dud ammunition. Less routine, and much more hazardous were the enemy mines, booby traps, and other ordinance found on the battlefield. One EOD team with the Americal Division averaged one hundred thirty-five incidents per month.[111]

Loading a 40mm grenade (U. S. Govt.)

One EOD man, Captain Fred Puckett, considered the 40mm grenade round as the most dangerous ammunition he had to deal with, due to its highly unstable nature. On three occasions, he had to assist surgeons in removing these projectiles from the bodies of wounded soldiers. He said, *"It's just another explosive that has to be disposed of, as long as the thing is handled extremely gently. I treat all explosives with a great deal of respect, but I don't fear them."*[112]

Fortunately, not many of us have to handle unexploded grenades. However, we all must face our share of uncertainty. The prospect of changing careers, losing loved

> The fear of the LORD is the beginning of wisdom; all who follow his precepts have good understanding. To him belongs eternal praise.
> ~Psalm 111:10

ones, or becoming seriously ill can make anyone anxious about the future. We know that Scripture tells us, *"The eternal God is your refuge, and underneath are the everlasting arms"* (Deuteronomy 33:27). Claiming that assurance, however, is not always easy. This is probably why we admire the calm resolve of the EOD man. Respect, without fear. That's how God wants us to face our unknown dangers. Only with his help will we find this kind of confidence to live our own lives. God has authority over heaven and earth and the power to accomplish his will. In his will, we are guaranteed peace and eternal safety.

The Things They Carried

AN ANONYMOUS veteran posted an article on a military Web site detailing all the things the troops carried in Vietnam. The physical items were extensive:

> They carried P-38 can openers and heat tabs, watches and dog tags, insect repellent, gum, cigarettes, Zippo lighters, salt tablets, compress bandages, ponchos, Kool-Aid, two or three canteens of water, iodine tablets, and C-rations stuffed in socks. They carried flak jackets and steel pots, and M-16 assault rifles.[113]

Then, there were other things that weighed less but were nevertheless very real:

> They carried malaria, dysentery, ringworms and leeches. They carried the land itself as it hardened on their boots. They carried love for people in the real world and love for one another.[114]

And finally, there were other burdens, of an exalted nature, known to very few men or women:

> They carried the traditions of the United States military, and memories and images of those who served before them. They carried grief, terror, longing and their reputations. They carried the soldier's greatest fear: the embarrassment of dishonor. They carried the emotional baggage of men and women who might die at any moment. They carried the weight of the world. They carried each other.[115]

All of us shoulder burdens in life—some easy and fulfilling, some difficult. Fortunately, few have the life-or-death urgency of a soldier's. Nevertheless, Jesus has placed a unique burden on those who would follow him. First, we must deny ourselves. We do this by placing him at the center of our lives, always considering first how he would view the actions we take. Then, we must take on our burdens in his name, joyfully accepting the hardships that come our way, as a means of demonstrating his power in our lives. Christians do carry the weight of the world on their shoulders as they carry their crosses and each other.

> Then he called the crowd to him along with his disciples and said: "If anyone would come after me, he must deny himself and take up his cross and follow me. For whoever wants to save his life will lose it, but whoever loses his life for me and for the gospel will save it." ~Mark 8:34, 35

A Taste of Hell

THE ATTACK came just after midnight. Grenades fell among the recon Marines as enemy troops crawled unseen almost into their lines. Lieutenant Clebe McClary was wounded severely in the attack and evacuated by helicopter. He would linger close to death for days in what he described as "a taste of hell."[116] Suffering the loss of an eye and an arm and other painful wounds, his recovery, at first uncertain, would be long and painful. At times he would wish he was dead.

Months later, on his first leave from the hospital, McClary and his wife, Dea, attended an evangelistic crusade in Florence, South Carolina, that changed their lives. On a night in

Clebe McClary, a Marine for Christ

July 1968 they listened to several well-known sports figures give moving witness talks. Then, after a gifted evangelist explained the gospel, they both opened their hearts to Jesus Christ for the first time. Clebe explained:

> For years I had tried to live the Christian life; the difference was that now Christ was living in me. When this Marine surrendered to the Lord, it was not defeat but rather victory. In the Marine Corps I had sought only to serve my country. At last, I joined the greatest Army that has ever marched—the Army of Jesus Christ.[117]

In one of the greatest witnesses ever given to the power of God to turn bad circumstances to good, Clebe stated, "God's purpose became clear: He spared my life that I might find abundant life in Him. I did not know it at the time, but through my experiences He was to touch countless lives."[118]

After months of painful recovery, Clebe began to fulfill his new mission. He has since become a great motivational speaker, blessing countless others in every state and more than thirty countries with his unique message of faith and courage. He continues to claim the words of the apostle John as his theme for living:

As long as it is day, we must do the work of him who sent me. Night is coming, when no one can work. ~John 9:4

A New Heart

CHUCK DEAN had always wanted to be a paratrooper. He enlisted in the Army, went to jump school at Fort Benning, and volunteered for duty on Okinawa. There he joined the 173rd Airborne Brigade, one of the first units to deploy to Vietnam in 1965. His worst experience during his year in combat

> For God did not send his Son into the world to condemn the world, but to save the world through him. ~John 3:17

came on the last day. While at Tan Son Nhut Air Base waiting for his flight home, his compound was hit by VC mortars. He suffered superficial wounds, but others were not so lucky. Seven of his friends died in that attack, only hours before going home.

Ten years later, Dean's life was a shambles. Anger, depression, and drug abuse had brought him to the depths of despair. After encounters with the police and the IRS, his nervousness and depression seemed to spiral downward. In desperation, he picked up the telephone one night and called a friend named Bill, a veteran of the Korean War and former paratrooper like himself.

I called him and simply said, "Bill, I really need a friend right now."

He was quiet for a moment and then replied, "Chuck, you need the Lord."

At first I resented that he would try laying a "trip" on me about Jesus. I thought, Oh, man don't you know I'm hurting? I don't need this religious crap! But I didn't say anything because I respected Bill very much.

His statement did stun me, however. A week earlier, I might have laughed, but at that moment, with my life in shambles, something inside told me that he was speaking truth. Deep inside I somehow knew that here was the answer I'd been looking for a long time even though outwardly I had avoided for years.

"Yeah," I said softly. "I guess that's one thing I haven't tried. Maybe that's what I need to do."

Bill talked with me for a little while, and then asked if I was willing to pray with him. I agreed, because I knew that the way I was headed could only end in disaster. Then and there I prayed with him, giving my heart, soul, and life to the Lord Jesus Christ. It was a realization that I had become a friend of God. Now Jesus had shown me that he accepted me just the way I was, and he could show no greater love than when he laid His life down for His friend.[119]

7th Marine Regt. troops move along rice paddy dike. (National Archives)

C-ration cases for an altar. (U. S. Marine Corps)

Called a Friend

AFTER YEARS of running away from himself and from God, Chuck Dean came to Christ while talking to a Christian friend over the telephone. As he talked and listened, he remembered fellow soldiers in Vietnam who had given their lives for their friends, and his heart was moved by Jesus' sacrifice of his own life. Jesus had said, *"Greater love has no one than this, that he lay down his life for his friends"* (John 15:13). Somehow, in that moment, Dean finally understood himself to be one of those for whom Jesus made this great sacrifice.

> I no longer call you servants, because a servant does not know his master's business. Instead, I have called you friends, for everything that I learned from my Father I have made known to you. ~John 15:15

When he got off the telephone, there were no angels singing or rockets exploding, but he knew he had become a different person. He was filled with a peace like nothing he had ever experienced. He tried to explain it:

I was now what I had always told myself I would never be: a Christian; but I now had a new understanding of what re-birth is all about. I knew I had been remade by God and had a joy in my heart that was never there before. I knew that whatever happened now, it would be all right. This calming, secure sensibility replaced the feelings of death, fear, and agony that I had experienced and expected to experience for the rest of my life.

This was the beginning of the healing God had in store for me. I soon found out that He had erased my long dread of dying. My urge to drink and use dope vanished abruptly. The heavy symptoms of my PTSD felt like part of another life that I had once lived, but now was dead and gone.

It was as if Jesus had taken all the mental images from my subconscious mind and mounted them in a photo album. I could still see them from time to time, but they no longer impinged on my life.[120]

Chuck Dean's long road to recovery from Vietnam took on a new meaning as he came to understand that God really cared about him. He realized he did not have to pay the penalty for all the wrongs he had done—that Jesus had already paid that price long ago. With Jesus in his life and with Jesus as his Friend, his life took on a new direction—and a new hope.

A Man Like All Others

IT WAS not unusual for men serving in Vietnam as chaplains to wonder if they had accomplished their calling. Had they been good enough, or done enough? Had they been everything a man of God should be under the trying conditions of combat? One chaplain explained his answer to these imponderable questions:

> Without a doubt to some the chaplain is a rabbit's foot or a walking St. Christopher medal, to some he is a burden or a symbol of a nonpragmatic approach to life, to others a threat. To most I have found he is what he makes himself be, a man like all others, who laughs and hurts, who bleeds and grits his teeth, whose stomach rumbles for "C's" or whose throat constricts with a need for water, who prays to drown out his own terror when an 81 coughs its deadly phlegm, who endures damnable frustrations, who gets it all wired together, not because he has all the answers, but because he at least knows how to ask the right questions. I have found for myself that a chaplain can be a valued part of the team called Marines; he has a mission, he has a purpose, he has a place. It is purely, though not simply, a question of how much he is willing to give of himself, where it really is.[121]

In describing the role and attitude of a combat chaplain, this man has described the essence of Jesus' own ministry on Earth: to bring God to man, as "a man like all others." This attribute of Jesus is described in a great biblical passage from Philippians:

Hilltop service. (National Archives)

Your attitude should be the same as that of Christ Jesus: Who, being in very nature God, did not consider equality with God something to be grasped, but made himself nothing, taking the very nature of a servant, being made in human likeness. And being found in appearance as a man, he humbled himself and became obedient to death—even death on a cross! Therefore God exalted him to the highest place and gave him the name that is above every name, that at the name of Jesus every knee should bow; in heaven and on earth and under the earth, and every tongue confess that Jesus Christ is Lord, to the glory of God the Father. ~Philippians 2:5–11

Dirty Boy Scouts

RICHARD LOFFLER was an administrative clerk with the 1st Infantry Division at Bear Cat combat base, near Long Binh. His duties were somewhat routine, and he could almost have been a civilian, except for a few things that kept reminding him he was in a combat zone.

A short distance from his hut, an artillery battery would come to life at any time, most often at night. Gradually, he became all too familiar with the ritual of a fire mission. A shell would be loaded into the breech with a distinctive *clank*, followed by a *whirr* as the azimuth and elevation were set. Someone would yell, *"Fire!"* And, after an instant of silence, an explosion would rock the earth, bouncing his cot off the ground. A few minutes later the sequence would be repeated. Then, the entire battery would open up and rattle the whole base. An hour of blessed silence might pass before he would hear another clank and whirr.

> Keep your head in all situations, endure hardship, do the work of an evangelist, discharge all the duties of your ministry. ~2 Timothy 4:5

Then, there was guard duty to be performed. He frequently had to report to the command post at 2:30 p.m., where he was inspected and briefed. Then, with two other men, he was taken by some kind of vehicle out to the base perimeter where his little group would man a sandbagged bunker. Two had to stay awake, staring out the small aperture into the black night, with only the artillery fire to break the monotony.

Loffler described all this in a letter to his parents, concluding with the comment:

> Well, the routine goes on. We're just "paper soldiers," that is, the people doing administration, although somebody has got to do it. The "roughness" we endure is only the water rationing, being hot, and the somewhat dreary atmosphere of it all. Dirty Boy Scouts moved up a notch.[122]

Richard Loffler was one of thousands of soldiers in Vietnam doing their *routine* duties, supporting the line units in the field and facing their share of danger. In God's kingdom there are also many seemingly mundane duties to be done. Even the mundane, however, is important in God's eyes. Far better to be a "dirty Boy Scout" in his kingdom than a rich and powerful person in the material world.

A Free Man

SHORTLY AFTER arriving in Vietnam at the Tan Son Nhut Airport, Private First Class Carl Rogers was bused to Camp Alpha for in-processing. There he received orientation briefings on a variety of subjects dealing with the war and the country. Personal conduct was stressed in so many lectures Rogers made the wry comment that they *"deal with VD more than they do with VC."*[123] He also observed some irony in a taped speech from the commanding general:

> *So General Westmoreland tells them that the mission is two-fold, and we must fight and beat the Communist aggressor. And then he goes on to say that the second point we must make is to show the Vietnamese people what it is to be a free man. And this got a chuckle from several fellows, because there we sat with our green uniforms on and the hot sun that probably was 110 degrees. For me this had special significance, because I was sitting there in a uniform I detest, in a country that is involved in a war that I don't support, and yet I'm supposed to show these people what it is to be a free man. This is very hard to do.*[124]

Just as drafted soldiers are bound to wartime service, we are bound to the worldly concerns of this life. As Christians we know that somehow we are supposed to be "free" in Christ, yet we remain enslaved to the demands of everyday living. When our focus is on our duties, our pleasures, and our possessions, it is about as difficult for us to demonstrate freedom to others as it was for this soldier.

> You, my brothers, were called to be free. But do not use your freedom to indulge the sinful nature; rather, serve one another in love. The entire law is summed up in a single command: "Love your neighbor as yourself."
> ~Galatians 5:13, 14

The true nature of our freedom is found in the life and ministry of Jesus Christ. He came to show every one of us a clear path to God, at the same time eliminating compliance with religious law as a precondition. In this way, he replaced anxiety and guilt with forgiveness and peace. This was his gift to us—the freedom in him that goes to the depth of our souls and transcends all worldly concerns. We demonstrate this freedom to others when we understand it and use it in the way he intended.

Tough Love

LARRY WARD was one of the toughest, and yet most compassionate, Marines I ever knew. He was one of the first Marines to go into Vietnam, landing over Red Beach on March 8, 1965, to defend the newly operational air base at Da Nang. As operations officer of 3rd Battalion, 9th Marines, it was his job to deploy the battalion in defense of Hill 327, later known as Freedom Hill. He endured his share of hardship and danger leading Marines during two tours in combat.

Capt. Larry Ward

I recently met Larry at a restaurant in downtown Charleston, South Carolina, to talk about old times. During the course of our conversation, I asked him about his spiritual life while in combat. His answer surprised me. He said, *"Whenever I prayed, I always asked God for the strength and courage of my mother."*[125] At my urging, he went on to tell me about this remarkable woman.

Doris Faith Vernon married Larry's father during the Depression, and, due to his workload, raised their three children mostly on her own. She was affectionate, but extremely demanding of her kids, employing her own unique style of "tough love." She was a very spiritual person and longtime member of the Moravian Church in Winston-Salem, North Carolina. She passed away with a smile at age ninety-five after listening to her daughter read the 23rd Psalm.

I pray that God is smiling back on the soul of this strong and stoic woman from a generation gone by. She leaves behind a loving and respectful son who faithfully carried on her tradition of tough love—in service to America, the Marine Corps, and his own family.

> Listen, my son, to your father's instruction and do not forsake your mother's teaching. They will be a garland to grace your head and a chain to adorn your neck. ~Proverbs 1:8, 9

Don't Quit

THERE ARE days when we all feel like quitting—no one more than did the foot soldier in Vietnam, carrying more than a man should bear, in tropical heat, over densely covered, mountainous terrain, constantly suffering fatigue and fear. To encourage his fellow soldiers, one man circulated an uplifting poem by an unknown author, titled, "Don't Quit":

> When things go wrong as they sometimes will,
> When the road you're trudging seems all uphill,
> When the funds are low and the debts are high,
> And you want to smile but you have to sigh,
> When care is pressing you down a bit,
> Rest if you must but don't you quit.
>
> Often the goal is nearer than
> It seems to a faint and faltering man.
> Often the struggler has given up
> When he might have captured the victor's cup.
> And he learned too late when the night came down
> How close he was to the golden crown.
>
> Success is failure turned inside out—
> The silver tint of the clouds of doubt.
> And you can never tell how close you are
> It may be near when it seems afar.
> So stick to the fight when you're hardest hit
> It's when things seem worst that you must
>   not quit.[126]

> Do you not know that in a race all the runners run, but only one gets the prize? Run in such a way as to get the prize. Everyone who competes in the games goes into strict training. They do it to get a crown that will not last; but we do it to get a crown that will last forever. ~ 1 Corinthians 9:24, 25

The apostle Paul issued another and classic call to perseverance, urging us not to give up in the greatest pursuit of all: the attainment of the *"crown that will last forever."* When we accept Jesus Christ into our hearts, our salvation is assured. However, Paul compares our lives after that event to a great race in which we strive to find our true purpose for being alive—our role as members of the great body of Christ.

The Rifleman's Creed

This is my rifle. There are many like it, but this one is mine. It is my life. I must master it as I must master my life. Without me my rifle is useless. Without my rifle, I am useless. I must fire my rifle true.[127]

THESE LINES from the Marine Corps Rifleman's Creed reflect the importance of the basic and most important components of the Marine Corps combat team: the rifleman and his weapon. Every Marine, officer and enlisted, is exposed to this creed, because every Marine is trained first to be a rifleman.

Craig Tourte with M-14 rifle

Craig Tourte arrived in Vietnam in the summer of 1967 with the M-14 rifle issued him on Okinawa. After several days on the sandy beach near Cua Viet his unit was moving upriver to Dong Ha by landing craft when he came under fire for the first time. When his rifle unexpectedly jammed, his training took over:

I sat down on the deck and completely field stripped my weapon, removing the cleaning rod from the rear butt plate and locating a toothbrush I had used for cleaning. By the time I got the round removed, the sand from the receiver, barrel, chamber, and magazine, and got the weapon reassembled, our firefight was over. I was disappointed and embarrassed, but a whole lot smarter and thankful for those many hours in boot camp I had spent disassembling and assembling weapons.[128]

When Tourte left Vietnam and turned in his rifle for the last time, he said, "I know there were many like it, but that rifle was mine. It was my best friend and at times, it was my life."[129]

Christians know and regularly recite the Nicene and Apostles' creeds. I might suggest another, to more clearly focus our attention on the most basic component of our faith, the book that gives us our knowledge of God: *"This is my Bible. There are many like it, but this one is mine. It is my life. I must master it as I must master my life . . ."*

> Put on the full armor of God . . . Take up the shield of faith, with which you can extinguish all the flaming arrows of the evil one. Take the helmet of salvation and the sword of the Spirit, which is the word of God.
> ~Ephesians 6:11, 16, 17

Proverbs

EVERY VETERAN with an e-mail account is familiar with an ever-growing list of military "proverbs" that contain enough truth and humor to live on in cyberspace. A few are listed below for purposes of enlightenment and entertainment, and to direct our thoughts to the *biblical* proverbs that follow:

It is generally inadvisable to eject directly over the area you just bombed.
Whoever said the pen is mightier than the sword never encountered automatic weapons.
Tracers work both ways.
Five-second fuses last three seconds.
If your attack is going too well, you're walking into an ambush.
Any ship can be a minesweeper. Once.
If you see a bomb technician running, follow him.
Try to look unimportant; the enemy may be low on ammo.
Don't ever be first, don't ever be last, and don't volunteer for anything.
You've never been lost until you've been lost at Mach 3.
The only time you have too much fuel is when you're on fire.
Flying the airplane is more important than radioing your plight to a person on the ground incapable of understanding or doing anything about it.

In the Bible, the book of Proverbs provides advice from the wisest king of Israel on such diverse subjects as diligence, honesty, justice, knowledge, righteousness, wickedness, success, folly, and, especially—wisdom and understanding. Proverbs is a book of guidance for daily living, introduced by the following verses:

The proverbs of Solomon son of David, King of Israel: for attaining wisdom and discipline; for understanding words of insight; for acquiring a disciplined and prudent life, doing what is right and just and fair; for giving prudence to the simple, knowledge and discretion to the young—let the wise listen and add to their learning, and let the discerning get guidance—for understanding proverbs and parables, the sayings and riddles of the wise.

The fear of the LORD is the beginning of knowledge, but fools despise wisdom and discipline. ~Proverbs 1:1–7

The Red Flower

Lieutenant Sandy Kempner was killed by shrapnel from a land mine near Tien Phu on November 11, 1966. He was a platoon leader with 3rd Battalion, 7th Marines, operating in the I Corps area. A month before this tragic event, he wrote a thoughtful letter to his aunt after one of his men pointed out a small red flower growing on a hillside:

> *It is a country of thorns and cuts, of guns and marauding, of little hope and of great failure, yet in the midst of it all, a beautiful thought, gesture, and even person can arise among it waving bravely at death. Some day this hill will be burned by napalm, and the red flower will crackle up and die among the thorns. So what was the use of living and being a beauty among the beasts, if it must, in the end, die because of them?*[130]

After thinking about the lonely flower, Kempner concluded it would always live in the memory of at least one Marine. Furthermore, he realized, *"If we had never gone on that hill, it would still be a soft, red thornless flower growing among the cutting, scratching plants, and that in itself is its own reward."*[131]

It is hard to discern the religious outlook of this thoughtful young man. A flower does indeed exist for itself, without regard to our knowledge of it. A human life also has existence and significance in itself, even if unappreciated by others. However, we know there is more to the human condition than this. We were brought into this world by a God who knows us intimately: *"You created my inmost being; you knit me together in my mother's womb"* (Psalm 139:13). We were made for a reason by a God with a purpose. When we live with him in our hearts, and in accordance with his plan, our lives have a transcendent significance. We may live in a wilderness on Earth, and our work may not always be appreciated by others, but we know that who we are and what we do have eternal significance.

> What does the worker gain from his toil? I have seen the burden God has laid on men. He has made everything beautiful in its time. He has also set eternity in the hearts of men; yet they cannot fathom what God has done from beginning to end.
> ~Ecclesiastes 3:9–11

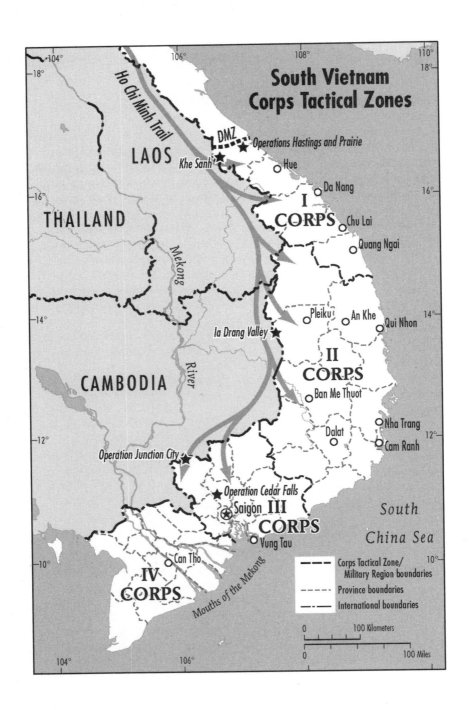

South Vietnam
Corps Tactical Zones

LAOS

THAILAND

CAMBODIA

Ho Chi Minh Trail

Mekong

River

Mekong

DMZ

Operations Hastings and Prairie

Khe Sanh

Hue

Da Nang

I CORPS

Chu Lai

Quang Ngai

Ia Drang Valley

Pleiku

An Khe

Qui Nhon

II CORPS

Ban Me Thuot

Nha Trang

Dalat

Cam Ranh

Operation Junction City

Operation Cedar Falls

Saigon

III CORPS

Vung Tau

South

China Sea

Can Tho

IV CORPS

Mouths of the Mekong

Corps Tactical Zone/
Military Region boundaries

Province boundaries

International boundaries

0   100 Kilometers

0   100 Miles

Conventional Warfare

U.S. AND South Vietnamese forces began turning the tide against the Viet Cong insurgency during 1965, causing North Vietnam to play a more direct and overt role in the war. The key to this effort was a tenuous supply route that became known as the Ho Chi Minh Trail. This trail was actually a maze of tangled routes threading westward out of North Vietnam, turning generally southward through Laos and Cambodia, and then back into South Vietnam at multiple points. Interdiction of these trails was a major objective of Allied air power, but the effort was never totally successful due to the mountainous jungle terrain. The North Vietnamese used more than 5,000 Soviet-made trucks and as many as 75,000 people staged along the network, with frequent transfers and short runs. One officer described it as follows:

> As many as twenty transfers may take place. Following a box of ammunition through the Mu Gia Pass, it moves on a truck at night. The truck moves about eight miles, then pulls into a park covered by the thick jungle canopy. He unloads. During the next day, the ammunition is loaded to another truck. He moves sixteen miles, then unloads, and so on.[132]

The first clash of American forces and the North Vietnam Army (NVA) came in late 1965 in a remote area near the Cambodian border called the Ia Drang Valley. Operating on intelligence of an NVA buildup in the area, the 1st Air Cavalry Division mounted a monthlong campaign to engage and expel the enemy force. After heavy fighting, three depleted NVA regiments pulled back across the border.

Meanwhile, reacting to the success of the III Marine Amphibious Force in controlling ever-larger regions of northern South Vietnam, the NVA massed four divisions north of the DMZ. Since U.S. policy was to not send troops north of the DMZ, these forces were allowed safe havens to attack from and withdraw to during the conflict. Later in 1966, the NVA 324B Division moved across the DMZ into Quang Tri and Thua Thien provinces. The Marines launched Operations Hastings and Prairie to successfully engage and defeat this invasion. The key maneuver element in this campaign was the infantry battalion that usually operated independently within an assigned area, frequently detaching and attaching separate rifle companies as required by the mission.

In early 1967 the NVA 325C Division began secretly occupying the hills overlooking the Marine base at Khe Sanh with the intent of repeating their 1954 victory at Dien Bien Phu. This effort was discovered by Marine patrols, however, precipitating a series of battles for the key terrain around the base. Bloody fighting ensued for more than a month, until the NVA pulled back into their bases across the border.

By 1967 American troop strength in Vietnam had risen to 400,000, enabling other large-scale operations into VC/NVA strongholds northwest of Saigon in Tay Ninh province. Operations Cedar Falls and Junction City were conducted between January and April against the area known as the Iron Triangle, containing miles of underground tunnels, weapons, food caches, and a major VC headquarters complex. More than 40,000 U.S. Army and South Vietnamese troops forced the VC to abandon the area and destroyed more than five hundred tunnels stretching over a distance of twelve miles. Large stores of weapons, ammunition, and documents were captured, as well as enough rice to feed 13,000 troops for a year.[133]

Squad Leader

LIMA COMPANY, moving along a ridgeline south of Con Thien, was attacked by a large NVA force and was taking casualties. The Marines dropped down and returned fire as the officers and NCOs tried to organize the fight. Suddenly the cry went up, *"Grenade!"* immediately followed by several explosions. Enemy troops had penetrated to within a few feet of the front line in dense undergrowth and were throwing grenades at close range.

Infantry troops assault. (National Archives)

Sergeant Marshall Jesperson, a squad leader in 3rd Platoon, decided it was up to him to deal with this threat. On his order the squad stood up and attacked into the thicket. There was a crescendo of small arms fire accompanied by shouts and the sounds of close-in fighting with bayonets and knives. The fight was swift and brutal as the Marines cleared out the threat to their lines.

The Lima Company commander later thought about the actions of his squad leader and the young Marines under him:

> *Marshall Jesperson. He realized what had to be done, and he did it. No one told him to lead the way into the thicket . . . He did what he did because it had to be done. More important, those eighteen- and nineteen-year-old Marines followed him. They could have stayed in their fighting holes. No one held a roll call. They followed Sergeant Jesperson into the thicket. That was the key.*[134]

Initiative is the hallmark of Marine officers and NCOs. The history, traditions, and training methods of the Corps are aimed at building this quality. The result is usually capable, forceful leaders. Ultimately, however, the troops who follow them bear the burden, pay the cost, and win the victory. Somehow young men and women of faith and courage have always stepped forward to shoulder the burden of defending our nation. Thankfully, it is no different today. May God bless and protect each one of them.

> Then the officers shall add, "Is any man afraid or fainthearted? Let him go home so that his brothers will not become disheartened too."
> ~Deuteronomy 20:8

Pan Am

I WENT TO Vietnam on a Pan Am charter flight. I stepped on board a Boeing 707 at Travis Air Force Base in San Francisco with one hundred fifty other Marines and was greeted by a smiling stewardess who directed me to my seat and cheerfully told me to "buckle up." The attentive crew treated us royally during the fourteen-hour flight, serving airline meals and providing a constant stream of friendly chitchat.

(panamair.org)

As we neared our destination, we got our first intimation we were not on a completely "normal" Pan Am flight. The pilot flew a tight pattern coming into the Da Nang airstrip with some sharp turns and an abrupt landing. He was obviously taking no chances in flying low over the countryside outside the base perimeter. For some reason, I was standing near the door when it was opened and found myself greeted by a blast of hot, humid tropical air and red dust. We had arrived.

My Marine Corps ancestors went to war on troop ships, steaming for weeks across the vast expanse of the Pacific, with long hours to gaze at the horizon and to gather their thoughts. I must confess I didn't mind coming home on an airplane, but I always felt that *going* that way was rather a cruel twist. To step off a civilian airliner with cool air and smiling stewardesses into the blast furnace of a combat zone was abrupt and disorienting, to say the least.

In retrospect, I take this experience to be a little foretaste of what it might be like to die unexpectedly and wake up one day in that place where none of us wants to go. No advance warning. No preparation. One minute you are going about your life, and, then, there you are, on final approach to your eternal destination. Whether you consider yourself a Christian or not, you might consider giving serious thought to the *possibility* of this scenario. Do you know for sure where you are going? Fortunately, there is a way.

> It is by the name of Jesus Christ of Nazareth, whom you crucified but whom God raised from the dead, that this man stands before you healed . . . Salvation is found in no one else, for there is no other name under heaven given to men by which we must be saved. ~Acts 4:10, 12

Deeper Is Safer

MARINE UNITS operating along the DMZ were usually on the move during daylight hours. During any prolonged stop and especially at night, defensive positions were prepared. Setting up a company perimeter became a choreographed routine. The platoon sectors were assigned, machine guns and mortars placed, and then the men would file around the perimeter and be given individual positions. No matter the events of the day or the level of fatigue, every man, including officers, would then dig in. One man in 3rd Battalion, 9th Marines, took special pride in his constructions:

> Therefore put on the full armor of God, so that when the day of evil comes, you may be able to stand your ground.
> ~Ephesians 6:13

Private First Class Charlie Lenox of Curtis, Nebraska, had already finished his excavation 100 feet to the northwest of the command post, and southwest of Churchill's M-60 position. Lenox's hole was more than four feet deep. He had a reputation for having the deepest fighting hole in the unit. "When people come back here 30 years from now," others chided him, "they'll still be able to find your pit." That didn't bother Lenox. For him, deeper meant safer.[135]

After being caught in the open during my first mortar attack, I also began to pay careful attention to the depth of my foxholes. I would make a rough rectangular outline about six feet long by two feet wide and then stick my bayonet into the ground to mark the corner nearest my head. My radio operator would measure the distance of his radio handset cord from the bayonet to the corner of his own hole. We would then start digging. If the need arose, he would toss me the handset, and I could talk to battalion while we both remained well below ground level.

The need for protection in combat is obvious. The danger is clear and always present. Unfortunately, the threats to our spiritual well-being are much more subtle and difficult to anticipate. Bad habits creep into our lives unobtrusively. My particular problem is that I drift away from God imperceptibly as I go about my daily business. I have a tendency to "go it alone," which leaves me defenseless against a nonspecific anxiety that builds in my mind as I get farther away from him. The spiritual disciplines of prayer and Bible study are my only defense. In my relationship to God, deeper is always safer.

He Took My Bullets

DURING Operation Essex, Hotel Company, 2nd Battalion, 5th Marines, was locked in a pitched battle near An Hoa and pinned down by heavy automatic weapons fire. Phil Downer's platoon tried to move to the right in an effort to outflank the enemy, but were met with a hail of bullets as soon as they moved. As Downer hit the ground to return fire, something fell on top of him. He was dismayed to discover it was his best friend, John Atkinson, mortally wounded in the crossfire.

> For it is by grace you have been saved, through faith—and this not from yourselves, it is the gift of God—not by works, so that no one can boast. For we are God's workmanship, created in Christ Jesus to do good works, which God prepared in advance for us to do.
> ~Ephesians 2:8–10

Pain and anguish washed over Downer in that moment as he realized his best friend was dead. Only a few days before, Downer had turned over the squad's machine gun to his friend, in effect making him a target for enemy snipers. He was overcome with the thought that his friend had died in his place.

For more than forty years, Downer blamed himself for the death of John Atkinson. The pain and guilt took its toll on his family. His impatience and frequent explosions of anger brought him to a low point when his wife finally announced she wanted a divorce. During this crisis, at the insistence of a friend, he attended a businessmen's meeting where the speaker unexpectedly began talking about Jesus Christ. When the speaker quoted Ephesians 2:8–10, Downer realized for the first time in his life the meaning of Jesus' death on the cross:

> He took my bullets for me voluntarily as John had involuntarily taken the enemy fire as he carried my machinegun. I recognized that I could go free of my sin and guilt by accepting what Jesus had done for me, just like I had been able to walk away from death that day with the recognition that John had died in my place.[136]

Phil Downer knew he owed his life to John Atkinson. He was finally able to acknowledge he owed even more to Jesus Christ. Thanks to Jesus, he found the forgiveness and peace that had eluded him for forty years. His life and ultimately his marriage were restored.

Huey helicopters landing troops. (U. S. Army)

Marines moving on amphibious tractors. (National Archives)

Vietnam Isn't So Bad

CHAPLAIN John McElroy was with the 26th Marines at Khe Sanh, sharing the fear and misery of life with the Marines at the besieged combat base. He lived in a bunker made from a mortar pit with walls and floor of red clay. The nearest latrine was in the open, requiring users to frequently sit in the rain. Life was not easy for anyone at Khe Sanh.

On his way to the combat base in July 1967, McElroy had stopped in Da Nang to visit a senior chaplain headquartered at the large base. He found that his superior had air conditioning, maid service, and a swimming pool. After talking for a while, the senior chaplain stood up and announced: *"Please excuse me, I have a tennis game to go to. You know Vietnam isn't so bad once you get used to it!"*[137] These words would echo in McElroy's mind during many weeks of hard duty in a dangerous place.

It would be easy and probably justified to condemn this senior chaplain's insensitivity and apparent arrogance. However, this story also causes us to take a look at ourselves. On the next cold, rainy, winter night, try to remember the homeless man you saw that day walking along the road with a bundle under his arm. Where is he sleeping? Can you conceive of telling him that life in the woods isn't so bad *"once you get used to it?"* I hope I wouldn't, but is that what I would actually be thinking? Am I like the senior chaplain in the rear area with all the comforts of home, unable to conceive of the hardships on the front line? I sadly realize I probably am.

> This is how we know what love is: Jesus Christ laid down his life for us. And we ought to lay down our lives for our brothers. ~1 John 3:16

I also realize Jesus never tried to lead from a comfortable place. He was constantly in the front lines with the people he cared about, experiencing their lives with them. He gives us a hard example to follow—a standard of loving and selfless service that requires the best within us.

Mason Jar Bombs

Birddog (U. S. Air Force)

WHILE RECOVERING from wounds, Lieutenant Tommy Franks served a short tour of duty as an aerial observer (AO), riding in the back seat of a single-engine 0-1 Cessna, known as a Birddog. The pilot would fly the little aircraft low and slow over the battlefield so the AO could spot enemy targets and call in supporting fire. One pilot, wanting to provide some of his own fire support, used a Korean War trick to turn the 0-1 into a dive-bomber:

> *Out on the strip one morning, I watched him line up six one-pint Mason jars in the shade of the wing. He then plucked six oval M-26 fragmentation grenades from his helmet bag. "You gotta make sure the bottom of the spoon's down inside the jar before you pull the pin," he said. I watched as he "loaded" the jars.*
>
> *Grenades without pins made me nervous. But, to my amazement, jamming a grenade into a Mason jar would hold the safety lever—the "spoon"—tight against the glass wall of the jar, keeping the four-second fuse from being activated until the jar smashed upon impact. The grenades worked as advertised.*[138]

Grenades without pins would make me nervous, too. I can't imagine flying for hours in a small aircraft with live grenades in glass jars sitting by my feet.

Thoughts of Mason jar bombs lead me to wonder about other kinds of lethal objects we carry around that could "go off" at any time. From my experience, I would have to put alcohol at the top of such a list. Drinking is a common social activity with an unfortunate dark side. It surreptitiously takes over the lives of some people who are always the last to

> Make every effort to live in peace with all men and to be holy; without holiness no one will see the Lord. See to it that no one misses the grace of God and that no bitter root grows up to cause trouble and defile many.
> ~Hebrews 12:14, 15

understand the lethality of what is happening. I have a friend who had problems with alcoholism in her family. She now periodically abstains from her daily glass of wine for two weeks at a time, to make sure she's not forming a dangerous habit. We can all use such an example of forbearance. The author of the book of Hebrews advised vigilance toward any practice that would impair our relationship with friends, family, or our Father in heaven.

"Incoming!"

QUICK REACTIONS become ingrained in the frayed nerves of combat troops. One day in 1967, 3rd Battalion, 3rd Marines, received hot chow at their Rockpile position near the DMZ. The men were sent to the chow line in small groups, and a line formed along the main road running through the battalion position. Due to the somewhat festive atmosphere, the officers had to constantly remind everyone to keep their interval and to not bunch up in groups. As I was standing beside the line, a jeep filled with mail bags came rolling down the road, trailing the usual plume of dust.

> Your iniquities have separated you from your God. ~Isaiah 59:2
>
> Examine yourselves to see whether you are in the faith; test yourselves. ~2 Corinthians 13:5

All at once, I heard someone say, a little too loudly, *"Hey, is that incoming?"* (referring to the mail). In the next instant, every Marine within earshot dove into the ditch beside the road, me included. There were no questions asked and no waiting to see if there was a real danger. The word "incoming" was enough to trigger a blind dash to the ground, to get there ahead of incoming enemy fire. After a few minutes, about twenty men sheepishly stood up and went on with the business at hand. The seemingly innocent question had come from a new man who was subsequently "counseled" severely by his buddies.

Warnings come in many forms and are particularly important to our spiritual well-being. We have many biblical passages, including the words of God's prophets, to remind us there are consequences to our behavior. The Bible tells us, *"The LORD warned Israel and Judah through all his prophets and seers: 'Turn from your evil ways'"* (2 Kings 17:13). Christian friends are also there to help us realize when we are going astray, if we empower them to do so. And finally, we have the warning of last resort: our own conscience. Unfortunately, it is not always reliable. Somehow, however, when we are in the wrong place in our lives, we begin to feel ourselves growing apart from God. For me, that distance is the measure of my need to examine my conscience and reevaluate my spiritual condition.

Dong Ha

A KOREAN WAR veteran once told me well-being in Korea was measured in distance from the front line. Being one hill back made a world of difference, and, of course, the farther back the better. I thought about this as I arrived at the forward Marine Corps base in South Vietnam near the little village of Dong Ha. I found a complex of windblown, tattered tents, antennae, trench lines, underground bunkers, and well-sandbagged artillery positions. Dust and dirt were everywhere, in spite of the muddy "streets." All this was within rocket range of the DMZ, so there was added purpose to everyone's movement around the compound. My stay at this garden spot was brief. Within twenty-four hours I was on a helicopter to my new unit operating north of Cam Lo. I wouldn't see Dong Ha again for months.

> "Now the dwelling of God is with men, and he will live with them. They will be his people, and God himself will be with them and be their God. He will wipe every tear from their eyes. There will be no more death or mourning or crying or pain, for the old order of things has passed away."
> ~Revelation 21:3, 4

I soon learned that Dong Ha was the "rear." My troops talked about it with a mixture of distain and longing. Their fellow Marines based there had full status as rear-area "poags" (slang for troops posted at the rear), just as if they were all the way down in Saigon. But going there, for whatever reason, was an almost heavenly respite. If a man had to go back for medical treatment or some administrative matter, he knew he would get at least one night's sleep and a hot meal. And there was a good chance he wouldn't be shot at.

It is almost unbelievable now to think how this place held such a revered status. Dong Ha may have been a spartan combat outpost, but the contrast to life in the field under combat conditions made it a "better place." Can we even imagine the contrast between our present lives and our ultimate "better place"? If we think that leaving this life is a tragedy, we must have a truly dim picture of where we're going! We need to remind ourselves of the heavenly respite we have been promised through our Savior.

Who I Am

RICHARD GOODWIN served with 1st Battalion, 9th Marines, operating near the DMZ and in places such as Camp Carroll, Con Thien, the Rockpile, and Khe Sanh. As a company corpsman, affectionately known as "Doc G" to everyone, he witnessed more than one person's share of pain and suffering. He tried to explain how this experience affected him:

> Since my people are crushed, I am crushed; I mourn, and horror grips me. Is there no balm in Gilead? Is there no physician there?
> ~Jeremiah 8:21, 22

You may wonder why I am so different
Why I have so many unusual ways
But feel not alone, for I wonder too
But in answer, this is all I can say . . .
I have witnessed pain of intolerable degree
While I held the pieces of destroyed tissue in my hands.
I was obligated to play God, and I did it
As I decided who was to live and who must die.
I have fired at the enemy with a vengeance
And I have promised to kill a friend out of mercy.
I have done these things . . .[139]

I am extremely thankful I have never been in a situation requiring me to perform triage on injured people, having to make decisions about who should receive emergency medical care and who should be considered a "hopeless" case. Many corpsmen and medics with combat units, even though not doctors themselves, have been faced with this duty in every war, including Vietnam. I can only imagine the agony of self-doubt that would come from reflecting on the decisions one made. The process could never be perfect, and mistakes are inevitable.

Mistakes are inevitable in just about every area of life, and any person should experience his or her own share of self-doubt every day. This kind of questioning is not only inevitable but, I believe, is actually a good thing. When we question ourselves, we acknowledge our human vulnerability and susceptibility to doing the wrong thing. God honors our confessions of weakness and stands ready to redeem our mistakes. In the case of corpsmen and all other emergency medical personnel, I am certain he grants special dispensation in advance. He knows they "play God" reluctantly. He understands the strain they are under and blesses the decisions they have to make. For all who perform this life-and-death duty: Thank you and God bless you.

Conspicuous Gallantry

CHARLES WATTERS was an Army chaplain with the 173rd Airborne Brigade during the Battle of Dak To on November 19, 1967. During the battle he was with an infantry unit attacking a strong enemy position. Unarmed and exposed to fire, Chaplain Watters moved about the battlefield doing his job and much more. Over and over he gave aid to the wounded, assisted in their evacuation, and encouraged everyone around him. His extraordinary deeds are recounted in his Medal of Honor citation:

Chaplain
Charles Watters
(Arlington.net)

> As the troopers battled to the first enemy entrenchment, Chaplain Watters ran through the intense enemy fire to the front of the entrenchment to aid a fallen comrade. A short time later, the paratroopers pulled back in preparation for a second assault. Chaplain Watters exposed himself to both friendly and enemy fire between the two forces in order to recover two wounded soldiers. Later, when the battalion was forced to pull into a perimeter, Chaplain Watters noticed that several wounded soldiers were lying outside the newly formed perimeter. Without hesitation and ignoring attempts to restrain him, Chaplain Watters left the perimeter three times in the face of small arms, automatic weapons, and mortar fire to carry and to assist the injured troopers to safety. Satisfied that all of the wounded were inside the perimeter, he began . . . giving spiritual and mental strength and comfort.[140]

Unfortunately, Watters was mortally wounded later that day as he continued to give aid and comfort to the wounded and to the soldiers on the line. He was awarded the nation's highest award posthumously *"for conspicuous gallantry and intrepidity in action at the risk of his life above and beyond the call of duty."* This kind of heroism was beyond the call of duty for a chaplain or any other soldier. Charles Watters's selfless action in the face of the gravest danger is one of the greatest examples of Christian service ever recorded and has been an inspiration to military chaplains ever since that day.

> Whatever happens, conduct yourselves in a manner worthy of the gospel of Christ . . . I will know that you stand firm in one spirit, contending as one man for the faith of the gospel without being frightened in any way by those who oppose you.
> ~Philippians 1:27, 28

The Long Night

LIEUTENANT Frank D'Orsi had never prayed so hard in his life. Throughout a long, rain-soaked night his small combat engineer unit was probed by NVA soldiers looking for a weak point. Twenty miles from friendly lines, D'Orsi knew there would be no reinforcements or air support if his unit was hit with a full-scale attack. All he could do was wait and pray.

> That night the LORD appeared to him and said, "I am the God of your father Abraham. Do not be afraid, for I am with you. ~Genesis 26:24

Early the day before, D'Orsi had set out from Di An with his engineers and two infantry platoons in a convoy heading north to recon roads and bridges for a 1st Infantry Division operation to follow. Late in the afternoon of the second day a radio message warned that an NVA regiment was headed toward them. As the rain came down in sheets, D'Orsi's men started making every possible improvement to their defensive positions. He sent extra two-man LPs (listening posts) out ahead of the lines. Darkness came early.

At about 1:00 a.m. one of the LPs started keying their radio handset. Unable to speak, they were frantically clicking the radio on and off to signal movement around them. Suddenly the resounding crack of multiple grenade explosions erupted in the night. D'Orsi then heard an excited voice through the static. The LP broke radio silence to report large numbers of NVA troops approaching. They requested permission to pull back into the lines. Giving one of the most difficult commands of his life, he ordered them to stay in place. He felt it was too dangerous to move.

This went on for the next three hours, as other listening posts reported movement and responded with grenades. Using the only support available, D'Orsi called in artillery fire, closer and closer to his own lines. Every man waited for the inevitable. They knew the NVA pattern was to probe the lines before massing for an all-out assault. D'Orsi waited and prayed, "God, help us through this. Please watch over us."[141]

A New Day

WHEN DAYLIGHT finally came, Frank D'Orsi looked out over an empty battlefield.

Miraculously, the expected attack never came. The NVA regiment that could have so easily overwhelmed his small force had pulled back, leaving evidence they had been there all around the perimeter. Had the artillery fire been so effective? Had they done such a good job setting up their defense? It was hard to tell. At that moment he didn't give much thought to his prayers of the night before. He went out to find his LP, fearing the worst for them.

Lt. Frank D'Orsi

There in a foxhole two hundred yards in front of the lines he found his two men, waterlogged but alive.

Frank D'Orsi grew up in a strong Catholic family in Rhode Island, where he went to parochial schools and attended church regularly. However, the importance of his religion began to wane as he progressed from high school to college and then to the Army. He measured his spiritual life by his church attendance, which gradually dwindled away to nothing.

A fearful night in Vietnam changed his course. He didn't think about God the morning after his ordeal, and didn't give him credit then for his amazing survival. Later, however, after returning home to his family, he began to count his blessings. He had made it through many dangerous times and was alive and well. He was able to look back and see God's hand in the miraculous survival of his listening post and his beleaguered unit during the most tense hours of his life. This powerful conviction brought him back to the church and restored his faith in a loving and merciful God. D'Orsi has led a productive life revolving around his work, his four children, and his faith. You still see the distant gaze, however, of a combat veteran who saw too much, but went to a deeper spiritual level in his life because of it.[142]

> And now, O Israel, what does the Lord your God ask of you but to fear the LORD your God, to walk in all his ways, to love him, to serve the LORD your God with all your heart and with all your soul?
> ~Deuteronomy 10:12

APR I L 13

Preaching

CHAPLAINS assigned to fighting units had many challenges in Vietnam. They faced the same physical danger and fear as the men they served. They often had to exhaust themselves just to visit each of their widely scattered units. A chaplain with troops in the Hoi An area explained: *"One day I began at daybreak with a service and covered six platoons with a service for each. Each of the platoon's CP(command post) was about a mile from the other, over hot sand dunes. It was a hard, hot day as my last service was completed right at dark."*[143]

Of all the challenges facing these men of God, however, the greatest lay in the spiritual arena. How to preach to men about eternal truths in a combat environment? Traditional phrases and images were inadequate for reaching men under these conditions. One chaplain, after a lot of personal soul-searching, observed:

> When I came to you, brothers, I did not come with eloquence or superior wisdom as I proclaimed to you the testimony about God. For I resolved to know nothing while I was with you except Jesus Christ and him crucified.
> ~1 Corinthians 2:1, 2

> *In the "grunt"* (infantry soldier) *I saw a lot of boys grow into men, and a lot of men grow spiritually in the chaos of war. I discovered that the chaplain must have some answers as regards war and the taking of a human life. The presence and message of the chaplain should remind them that we can never kill indiscriminately.*[144]

The chaplain was wise to recognize the special needs of these soldiers trying to make sense of their role in war. It is always important to understand who we're talking to and the situation we're in when we try to share the gospel. This can be a daunting task for those of us who are not ministers and know we don't have all the answers. Still, we should not be intimidated. To share the gospel, all we have to do is tell our own story. When we share our personal experience we do not invite an argument. We simply give an example of the power of Jesus Christ to change one life. After that, we rely on that same power to work in the lives of others. The end result is not up to us.

C-Rations

FOR A long time, I considered ineffective taste buds a distinct advantage during my military career. I ate what was presented at Marine Corps mess halls, oblivious to the angst of those around me. This was true even of the packaged fare used under field conditions of that time, known officially as Meals, Combat, Individual, or more commonly: C-rations. A rifle company in Vietnam might go for weeks eating only C-rations, and even these were frequently in short supply. They were often kicked out the door of a hovering helicopter if there had still been room on board after the ammunition and medical supplies were loaded.

C-rations came in cases of twelve meals, each with a different main course item, such as beefsteak, beans and wieners, chicken and noodles, ham and lima beans, etc. There was no individual C-ration item I couldn't stomach, and, in fact, I was usually thankful for whatever I got. There were times, however, after many days of these same twelve meals, the repetition took its toll. For a while Tabasco sauce would camouflage the taste, but this also gradually lost its effectiveness.

Unfortunately, by the time I got "fed up" with the food, my men were really depressed. It took time for me to learn not to use my own state of mind as the measure of their morale. Even today, I am still slow to acknowledge a problem. I tend to live with the situation as it is, rather than try to fix it. This trait irritates my family, but when it

> Jesus answered, "It is written: 'Man does not live on bread alone, but on every word that comes from the mouth of God.'" ~Matthew 4:4

impacts my spiritual condition, it only hurts me. When I'm not hearing God, it is because I have gradually allowed my own inner voice to take over. It's always better to fix this problem sooner rather than later. My relationship with God is the only "food" I need, and I should never let a moment go by without it.

God Bless America

IN A JUNGLE clearing a group of tired soldiers gathered in a semicircle around the chaplain. Even though they were wet and dirty, and suffered the effects of a long operation, their spirits were buoyed by the church service. Chaplain Wendell Danielson described the memorable scene and how the men were expectant about singing a special song:

(U. S. Marine Corps)

> *In a few moments we would close our services with the hymn, "God Bless America." This, for us, is difficult to sing. The words are simple enough but they compel a response. I knew the Doc wouldn't make it past the fourth line. He never finished, "From the mountains, to the prairies." Tears come to his eyes and he stops singing. Nobody, however, notices. Others would begin looking at the ground, or their hands, or at the sky. "God bless America, my home sweet home."*[145]

Irving Berlin wrote "God Bless America" during World War I. The great patriotic song was popularized in the 1930s by Kate Smith and still inspires us today.

> *God bless America,*
> *Land that I love.*
> *Stand beside her, and guide her*
> *Through the night with a light from above.*
> *From the mountains, to the prairies,*
> *To the oceans white with foam*
> *God bless America, My home sweet*
>   *home.*[146]

"Now, our God, hear the prayers and petitions of your servant. For your sake, O Lord, look with favor on your desolate sanctuary . . . We do not make requests of you because we are righteous, but because of your great mercy. O Lord, listen! O Lord, forgive!"
~Daniel 9:17–19

The distinguishing feature of "God Bless America" is the fact that it takes the form of a prayer. It is *not* a statement. It is a plea to God for the protection and guidance this nation has always needed and that only he can provide.

He Won't Let Them Down

MY ROOMMATE at The Citadel was a young man from Kansas named Sam Bird. His dynamic personality and superior leadership ability showed he was clearly destined for future top command in the U.S. Army. Our first tours in Vietnam were at about the same time, although our assignments took us to widely separated areas.

Unsurprisingly, Sam Bird was one of the best rifle company commanders ever to serve in the 1st Cavalry Division. An officer in his company tried to explain the leadership qualities of this exceptional officer:

> To describe him gives me a lump in my throat. He worries about his men like a father, yet always accomplishes the most difficult mission. His spirit is undying, his thirst for responsibility unquenchable, and his compassion for others, unlimited. He runs a good ship; flexible but not limp. His spirit is an example to these kids who have a miserable existence. They seem to know he won't let them down. I know myself. I would follow him through the gates of Hell and back.[147]

One thing about Sam that many of his men did not know was that he was a committed Christian. He read his Bible daily and drew on his faith as the primary source of a great inner strength. He did not, however, force his religious convictions on anyone under his command. As a professional soldier, he served his God, the U.S. Army, and the men under him with all his skill and energy.

Sam was seriously wounded during his tour in Vietnam, and his career in the Army was tragically cut short. While he lived and even he after passed away, he inspired his family, his Citadel classmates, and everyone who knew him with an ever-shining example of faith and courage. God bless the memory of this great human being.

> As a shepherd looks after his scattered flock when he is with them, so will I look after my sheep. I will rescue them from all the places where they were scattered on a day of clouds and darkness. ~Ezekiel 34:12

All Ready on the Firing Line

ANDY DEBONA was awarded the Navy Cross for his heroic actions while commanding a rifle company on September 10, 1967. During a search-and-destroy operation near Con Thien his unit came under attack by NVA troops estimated to be a regiment. Exposing himself to intense enemy fire, he moved among his men to direct their fire and to organize an orderly withdrawal to defensible terrain. One particular incident is described in the citation for his action:

Capt. Andy DeBona
(legionofvalor.com)

> *Shortly after dusk approximately 20 Marines became pinned down in a bomb crater 25 meters in front of the lines. Moving swiftly, Captain DeBona gathered a small reaction force and led it, under intense fire, to the bomb crater. Upon reaching the crater, he effectively organized his men into casualty bearers and a covering party. The volume of fire laid down by the covering party allowed the removal of all the casualties. Captain DeBona ordered his men to withdraw, remaining behind to cover the withdrawal.*[148]

Another Marine described the scene in that bomb crater when the rescue party arrived. Fear and confusion were rampant. Amid the chaos, DeBona yelled out in a commanding voice, *"Ready on the right. Ready on the left. All ready on the firing line!"*[149] This phrase, used by instructors on every Marine rifle range, was totally familiar to every man present. They knew they were being called to order and back from the edge of panic.

There are times when we all wish for such a clear voice of authority. We wish our heavenly Father would make his presence known and give us direct and unambiguous guidance as to what we are to do. Unfortunately (or fortunately), in his infinite wisdom he doesn't often work that way. He has decided not to directly rule in our lives and has instead given us the freedom to make our own choices. He has given us the Bible and Christian friends for most of our guidance, and wants us to use them. When he himself speaks, it is usually in a still, quiet voice, a message we have to prayerfully and diligently discern.

> My sheep listen to my voice; I know them, and they follow me. I give them eternal life, and they shall never perish; no one can snatch them out of my hand.
> ~John 10:27, 28

I Was Only Twenty

DON JACQUES was a platoon leader with 1st Battalion, 26th Marines, at Khe Sanh. As a Marine officer he knew how to take care of his men. He was first up in the morning and last to turn in at night. He knew all forty-four members of his platoon individually and tried to deal with their separate problems, considering himself something of a "mother hen" watching over her brood.

In a letter home, he commented:

Tonight I had a 19-year-old come to me for help and advice. He is married to an 18-year-old, and he was having problems. If he knew I was only 20, I wonder if he would have come. I think I helped him.[150]

I was once a twenty-one-year-old lieutenant with the same question. What kind of authority would I have with enlisted men who were not much younger than I and in some cases, much older? I quickly learned that age and appearance have practically nothing to do with the question. Some degree of authority does come with the rank insignia on the collar. However, respect is based almost completely on how well one knows his job and how well he treats the people under him. One of my great life lessons from the Marine Corps was the ageless truth, *"You can't fool the troops."*

Several years ago my church called one of the youngest-ever Episcopal priests to lead our large congregation. The Rev. Rob Sturdy answered this call with great trepidation, knowing that the vast majority of his "flock" would be much older than he. He need not have worried. His collar gave him some authority, but his knowledge and wisdom set him apart as a gifted teacher and man of God.

> When Jesus had finished saying these things, the crowds were amazed at his teaching, because he taught as one who had authority, and not as their teachers of the law. When he came down from the mountainside, large crowds followed him.
> ~Matthew 7:28, 29, 8:1

In chapters 5 through 7 of the book of Matthew, Jesus of Nazareth began his ministry as a young man by delivering what has become known as the "Sermon on the Mount." Those who listened knew that these words came from a man of few years, but were, nevertheless, words that would change the world. Regardless of his age, this was no ordinary man.

Body Bags

DURING THE second day of Operation Birmingham, the Lai Khe landing zone was busy. Lieutenant Frank D'Orsi and his engineer platoon were assigned to help out in the landing zone. Ammunition was the urgent need, and loading it was hot, exhausting work.

(National Archives)

Suddenly a helicopter landed close to D'Orsi and a group of his men, and the crew chief motioned for them. The lieutenant ran over and looked in the door. He would never forget what he saw. The plastic body bags were piled high, in grotesque shapes. Some of them were open, revealing bloody and shattered body parts. He fought back a wave of nausea. As the men behind him recoiled from the sight, he struggled to get control of himself. He gritted his teeth and resolved silently, *"Don't think about it. They are only bags."* He grabbed the nearest bag and began pulling, as he shouted angrily to his men, *"Don't think about it. Just do your job!"* It seemed like forever, but somehow they completed the gruesome task.[151]

Forty years later, Frank D'Orsi still has difficulty describing what he felt during this incident. *"On that day I had to push my emotions back into some hidden corner of my mind. Afterward, I continued doing this and even got better at it. I tried to make sure my feelings didn't enter the picture."*[152]

He brought this habit home from the war, and struggled with it for many years. At first he had difficulty opening up to his family in any way. Later, there were times when his feelings almost poured out. After many years and a lot of prayer, he thinks he is on an even keel at last. With God's help, he is even able to acknowledge the depth of his human grief in performing an inhuman task long ago in a helicopter landing zone.

> I am poured out like water, and all my bones are out of joint. My heart has turned to wax; it has melted away within me . . . But you, O LORD, be not far off; O my Strength, come quickly to help me. Deliver my life from the sword. Psalm 22:14, 19, 20

128

Chicken or Egg

A S THE USS *Whitfield County* approached the beach at Chu Lai in 1966, the Marines on board got their first sight of Vietnam and first feel for the tropical climate. One described what it was like:

It was hot. The sun itself was a burden. It sucked moisture out through the pores of my skin until I felt like a fish left to dry on the sand. Hot. My heavy pack rode in a darkness of sweat on my back as we were ordered into full combat gear for the beach assault. Web gear, pouches, packs, weapons, and ammo. Someone once observed that a Marine was nothing more than a life-support system for his rifle.[153]

This last comment brings to mind another ironic quip—"A chicken is an egg's way of making another egg." Or the age-old conundrum—"Which came first, the chicken or the egg?" This apparently unanswerable question actually alludes to one of the great unanswered questions of science—the origin of life. Evolution has explained much about how living things have changed and adapted, but not how it all started.

Scientists exploring the origins of life are confronted with an apparent paradox. DNA stores information to produce proteins and to replicate itself. Proteins are needed to interpret genetic information but are also the product of this interpretation. Biologists continue to speculate on which could have come first: DNA or functioning proteins? And how could either have come into existence without the other? To explain the origin of life, science would have to explain the origin of amino acid and protein sequencing, and the organization of proteins into cells, tissues, and organs. In other words, where did the *information* come from? So far, there is no scientific answer to this question.

Some scientists continue to hold to their *faith* in natural causes, seeking logical explanations relating to random chance or chemical necessity. Many, however, are conceding the fact that intelligent design is not only a possibility, but also the most reasonable explanation for the greatest miracle of time, space, and the universe—life.

> In the beginning was the Word, and the Word was with God, and the Word was God. He was with God in the beginning. Through him all things were made; without him nothing was made that has been made. In him was life, and that life was the light of men.
> John 1:1–4

Returning from the Dead

JOHN BENNETT was a medic with a unit of the 11th Infantry Brigade occupying a hill northwest of Tam Ky. One day a powerful thunderstorm came up, and lightning began hitting the hill. Bennett said, *"I was in the command bunker, standing near the door, when lightning struck it. That's the last thing I remember."*[154] Others in the bunker immediately went to the collapsed soldier and found he had stopped breathing. One of his friends started artificial respiration, and, soon, Bennett started to breathe again.

Once airborne in a medevac helicopter, Bennett passed out again. The helicopter crew thought he was dead and radioed the report to base. He was delivered to an aid station near the brigade command post where he soon regained full consciousness, and, in fact, found he was suffering no ill effects at all. Knowing his buddies were still on the hill without a medic, he asked to go back right away. Upon his return, mouths dropped open. There had been reports he was dead, and everyone was amazed he was there, alive. *"They had all my gear packed,"* recalled Bennett.[155]

"Watch out that no one deceives you. For many will come in my name, claiming, 'I am the Christ,' and will deceive many. You will hear of wars and rumors of wars, but see to it that you are not alarmed. Such things must happen, but the end is still to come." ~Matthew 24:4–6

I once had a similar experience during a brief return to base at Dong Ha after a long operation in the field. I met two fellow officers who expressed amazement to see me alive. They told me the "word" that I had been killed in action had gone around days before. This was one of my most vivid experiences with how rumors start and perpetuate themselves. When solid information is lacking, there always seems to be someone eager to fill in the blanks.

Since then, I have seen this all-too-human tendency at work often and have learned it never hurts to check out the facts about things I hear. Jesus warned his followers this same phenomenon will occur frequently at the time of his return.

Day by Day

During his time in Vietnam Ron Rayner carried a little pocket Bible with a steel-plated cover in his left breast pocket. It was the same Bible carried by his father during World War II. Ron kept it with him mostly as a good luck charm and for its improbable potential to miraculously stop a bullet on the way to his heart. He actually read from it only once, on an Easter Sunday, as he looked down on the Marine base at Khe Sanh from Hill 861.

(U. S. Marine Corps)

Ron had been raised attending Sunday school and church, and had dutifully memorized his Bible verses and prayers. However, from an early age he knew the difference between knowing and believing, and had never been able to believe. When he returned from Vietnam he married his childhood girlfriend and continued his token participation in church.

A door opened for Ron in 1980 when his minister asked him why he never received Communion. Ron confessed he was not a believer and felt it was wrong to fake it during the church's most important sacrament. The minister asked him to do one thing: to pray habitually every time he ate. Ron honored his request and took this small step in reaching out to God. He found himself from that moment moving in a new direction, as his prayer life grew more and more meaningful. In describing his journey, he explained: *"I believe that being a Christian is a day-by-day effort to learn more about God, His Son Jesus, and the Holy Spirit."*[156]

On his way to becoming a full member of the body of Christ, Ron found special inspiration in the words of St. Paul to the Ephesians.

> I pray that you, being rooted and established in love, may have power, together with all the saints, to grasp how wide and long and high and deep is the love of Christ, and to know this love that surpasses knowledge—that you may be filled to the measure of all the fullness of God. ~Ephesians 3:17–19

NVA soldier with rocket propelled grenade. (U. S. Army)

Troops on M-48 tank. (National Archives)

To Be Equipped

WHEN AN Army general invited a Boy Scout troop to his base for an outing, the local media were curious. A female radio broadcaster came to do a live interview with the base commander.

INTERVIEWER: *"So, General, what things are you going to teach these young boys when they visit your base?"*

GENERAL: *"We're going to teach them climbing, canoeing, archery, and shooting."*

INTERVIEWER: *"Shooting! That's a bit irresponsible, isn't it?"*

GENERAL: *"I don't see why, they'll be properly supervised on the rifle range."*

INTERVIEWER: *"Don't you admit that this is a terribly dangerous activity to be teaching children?"*

GENERAL: *"I don't see how . . . we will be teaching them proper rifle range discipline before they ever touch a firearm."*

INTERVIEWER: *"But you're equipping them to become violent killers."*

GENERAL: *"Well, being equipped for something is a far cry from doing it. They are also being equipped to defend themselves and others.*

The radio went silent; the interview had ended.[157]

This apocryphal story was circulated on the Internet for a long time as the "perfect comeback," and was a favorite of gun advocates, who include a lot of veterans. True or false, the story does have an important lesson. "To be equipped" for a task only gets us so far. We need more than capability. Faith is not faith unless it is acted upon. Although we don't earn favor with God through our good works, when we are truly his, good works come naturally.

> Show me your faith without deeds, and I will show you my faith by what I do. You believe that there is one God. Good! Even the demons believe that—and shudder. ~James 2:18, 19

Surrender

DEL WANTLAND was a rifleman with the 1st Cavalry Division patrolling through dense jungle near An Lao. He was the third man from the front of the column when his unit was suddenly ambushed. The point man and the second in line were killed instantly by the withering cross fire. Just as suddenly, Wantland was knocked unconscious by a bullet that shattered his collarbone and ripped through his spine. He regained consciousness a week later in a field hospital to find himself paralyzed from the neck down. He would be a quadriplegic for the rest of his life.

> Yet now I am happy, not because you were made sorry, but because your sorrow led you to repentance. For you became sorrowful as God intended . . . Godly sorrow brings repentance that leads to salvation.
> ~2 Corinthians 7:9, 10

Wantland did his best to return to a normal life after his medical treatment and rehabilitation. His goal was to go to college and pursue a career, but, unfortunately, an untimely divorce ruined his plans, leaving him to a lonely struggle. As he forgot about his goals, his life spiraled downward into alcoholism and abuse of other drugs. When he truly hit bottom and thought he might be losing his mind, he finally turned in a new direction—toward home. He returned to a Spirit-filled mother who helped him change his life. A fellow veteran and friend told the story:

> She listened quietly without judgment and then helped him understand that God loved him no matter what he had done. In fact, that was why Jesus, God's perfect Son, willingly suffered a cruel death by crucifixion.
> Military men are trained to never surrender. The entire concept is especially hard for veterans. But as Del listened to his mother go through the Bible passages describing how one's life gets redeemed, he knew that he had to do just that—surrender to God and trust him totally. He confessed that he had messed up his life, and surrendered, making Jesus Christ his Lord and Savior.[158]

The unwillingness to surrender is not just a military trait. Most men are driven by a primal need to stand on their own, to be "masters of their fate." We take care of our own problems. We don't ask for directions or seek help from others. Unfortunately, too many of us have to hit bottom before we look up. It takes us too long to learn that this is something we can do before a crisis gets out of hand. When we do look up, we find Jesus waiting. He is waiting for us to finally surrender ourselves to him, so he can become the Master of our fate and the Author of a new life in him.

I Finally Understood

AS THE firefight raged around him, a grenade suddenly landed inches from Michael Sofarelli. The violent explosion almost killed the young Marine. His right leg was damaged to the point it had to be amputated. Both eardrums were blown out, and shrapnel in one eye would ever impair his vision. He came close to death, but, amazingly, survived his wounds on that day in February 1967.

> The death he died, he died to sin once for all; but the life he lives, he lives to God. In the same way, count yourselves dead to sin but alive to God in Christ Jesus.
> ~Romans 6:10, 11

On a day almost thirty years later Michael Sofarelli's son, Michael Jr., was walking along the National Mall in Washington, D.C., when he took the opportunity to pay an unplanned visit to the Vietnam Veterans Memorial. It was late in the day, and the sun was fading as he approached the black granite wall. It was a tranquil scene since there was hardly anyone else present. Some distance away he noticed a man and young boy, possibly a father and son, pointing to a name on The Wall. The man touched the name, and the boy put something on the ground. Sofarelli watched them walk away, and then went over to see what had been left at the base of The Wall. He noticed a small piece of paper, and, bending down, saw written on it in red crayon, *"Happy Birthday Grandpa."* It was something he would never forget:

> *At that very moment, I realized how precious life is, and how very fast it can be taken away from us. If the grenade that wounded my father had landed inches closer to him, I would not be standing in front of this monument; instead my father's name would be on it. I walked closer to the Wall, closer than ever before. And for the very first time, I touched the Wall. I touched a name. A name I did not know. For the very first time, I cried at the Wall. I finally understood.*[159]

Michael Sofarelli Jr. had always known that his father came close to death in Vietnam. He knew what had happened, but he did not understand what it meant until this moment. So little separates the living and the dead. We tend to think of death in abstract terms and as a distant possibility. Only in rare moments do we realize how close it can be to each of us at any time and how everlasting the consequences are.

135

Something of a Miracle

AARON CARTER was a door gunner on a UH-34 helicopter based at Khe Sanh in early 1967. Late one afternoon his crew received an emergency call to extract a reconnaissance team in trouble near the Laotian border. Flying deep into enemy territory, they found the patrol on a hilltop, heavily engaged with NVA forces. The Marines on the ground had suffered two casualties and pleaded with the airmen to get them out. The pilot told them to pop a yellow smoke, and, as soon as he saw it, started the approach. They soon began taking incoming fire, and Carter responded with his machine gun, blazing away at every target he could see.

Aaron Carter(left) and fellow crewman.

Within seconds the helicopter settled into a small landing zone covered with a dense undergrowth of eight-foot-high elephant grass. Incoming fire immediately became intense. Small arms and .50 caliber machine-gun fire ripped through the ship. Carter could tell by the enemy tracers what direction to fire his machine gun, but the elephant grass severely limited his ability to see anything else.

Suddenly, Carter experienced one of the most frustrating moments in his life when his gun jammed. This had never happened before. A few seconds later the pilot decided he had to depart the zone and applied full power. As they gained a few feet of altitude, Carter looked down at the elephant grass a short distance from where they had just lifted off and saw the six-man patrol. He realized in that moment he would have killed every one of them if his machine gun had not jammed. Amazingly, once they cleared the zone, his weapon started firing again. In a classic understatement, the Marine said, *"To me, this was some kind of miracle."*[160]

> Therefore I glory in Christ Jesus in my service to God. I will not venture to speak of anything except what Christ has accomplished through me in leading the Gentiles to obey God by what I have said and done—by the power of signs and miracles, through the power of the Spirit. ~Romans 15:17–19

Semper Fi

SEMPER FIDELIS is Latin for *"always faithful."* The phrase was adopted as the motto of the United States Marine Corps in 1883 by Colonel Charles McCawley, the eighth Commandant of the Corps. It represents the bonds of brotherhood and loyalty Marines share with each other and the nation they serve. Usually shortened to *Semper Fi*, the phrase is often used in greeting others and in closing various forms of correspondence. It has its own meaning and significance to every Marine, as passionately articulated by one veteran:

> Your kingdom is an everlasting kingdom, and your dominion endures through all generations. The LORD is faithful to all his promises and loving toward all he has made. The LORD upholds all those who fall and lifts up all who are bowed down. The LORD is near to all who call on him, to all who call on him in truth.
> ~Psalm 145:13, 14, 18

It means being screamed at, and humiliated in front of others, having your rifle field stripped and stuck inside your pockets, threatened with being sent to the brig when you have done nothing wrong, and made to do push-ups in the rain and mud, until you need help just to get to your feet. After all that agony, you're called to attention, and asked by your DI if you want to quit. You respond with a resounding "NO, SIR!" and are again made to do push-ups. But on Graduation Day, that same DI finally calls you "Marine." That's Semper Fi.

Even under conditions of extreme weather, war, illness, fear, filth, and hunger, you always know that the Marines next to you will always be there for you, as you will be for them. That's Semper Fi.

When you find a quiet place after a battle or firefight, and you're still shaking, you say a prayer, or shed some tears for a lost friend, or even a few for yourself, you pick up and continue. That's Semper Fi.[161]

Marines understand that, to be *faithful*, you must be reliable and true to your word. You have to be steady, loyal, and constant. We all seek this quality in others and treasure it in our friends and loved ones. How amazing it is to realize it is one of the distinguishing attributes of our heavenly Father! Even as we waver in our loyalty to him, he is always faithful to us. He loves us unconditionally and keeps the promises he has given us in Scripture. In sickness and in health, in good times and bad, in this life and in the eternal future, he is *always faithful. Semper Fidelis.*

Paying Back

AFTER RETURNING from Vietnam, Tommy Kerr got a railroad job with Amtrak, married his sweetheart, Linda, and became an active member and associate pastor in his local church. Outside of his family, the Boy Scout troop he started became the passionate focus of his life. His boys called him "Sarge" and were an unusual mixture of kids from the church and extremely disadvantaged homes in the community. Someone joked that Troop 270 looked like the lineup of characters in a sitcom.

> If anyone serves, he should do it with the strength God provides, so that in all things God may be praised through Jesus Christ. To him be the glory and the power for ever and ever. Amen.
> ~1 Peter 4:11

Under Kerr's stern but fatherly leadership this diverse group of boys became a tight-knit unit. His policy on fighting required the winner of any fight to take on the scoutmaster. When it came time to sit around the campfire, he told them tales of the Marine Corps and war stories from Khe Sanh. He often helped the poorer kids purchase their uniforms and took special care to make sure everyone was doing their schoolwork. He provided the spark for many to make the long journey to Eagle Scout.

Tragically, Tommy Kerr died in 2007 at age fifty-nine from heart-related problems. There were many friends and family members at his funeral, and his Scouts served as pallbearers. His wife pointed out that Tommy had received a lot of help from others as a boy that *"kind of rubbed off,"* and that he had spent his life paying back that kind of help.[162]

This man's life is an inspiration to anyone wanting to serve in God's kingdom. Our heavenly Father has many ways of putting things on our hearts, and we see one in this story: the simple desire to "pay back" what others had done. Tommy Kerr listened to this message of the heart and passionately followed where it led. His life took on a purpose that blessed him and countless others.

One More Day

EVERY COMBAT veteran remembers the nights in Vietnam. Foxholes. Slit trenches. Fifty percent alert. Driving rain or high humidity. Sweat. Dirt. You were always bone tired from a day of struggle over jungle-covered hills or through waist-deep rice paddies. Darkness came suddenly and was absolute except for an occasional flare casting its eerie, moving light. Staying awake was agony, unless there was movement outside the line—then, the adrenaline would kick in. The nights were always long and often tense. One soldier had his own memories:

I can still see the faces, though they all seem to have the same eyes. When I think of us I always see a line of "dirty grunts" sitting on a paddy dike. We're caught in that first gray silver between darkness and light. That first moment when we know we've survived another night, and the business of staying alive for one more day is about to begin. There was so much hope in that brief space of time. It's what we used to pray for. "One more day, God. One more day."[163]

In Vietnam a popular refrain was "one day at a time," or even on occasion, "one step at a time." It could be an emotional catastrophe to think too much about how many more hills were ahead or how many days were left on your tour of duty.

The same habit of focusing our attention on the present moment is often needed in our daily lives. There are difficult times when our problems seem insurmountable. The whole journey ahead sometimes seems impossible. With prayer and confidence in God's guidance, we can face our hard times one day, or one step, at a time. *"One more day, God. One more day."*

"Look at the birds of the air; they do not sow or reap or store away in barns, and yet your heavenly Father feeds them. Are you not much more valuable than they? ... See how the lilies of the field grow. They do not labor or spin. Yet I tell you that not even Solomon in all his splendor was dressed like one of these. If that is how God clothes the grass of the field, which is here today and tomorrow is thrown into the fire, will he not much more clothe you, O you of little faith? ... Therefore do not worry about tomorrow, for tomorrow will worry about itself." ~Matthew 6:26, 28–30,34

Do You Want to Live Forever?

SERGEANT Dan Daly is a legend of the Marine Corps. Even though he won two Congressional Medals of Honor, he is most famous for his actions during the World War I Battle of Belleau Wood. When his men were outgunned and pinned down, he stood up and led an attack, shouting, *"Come on. . . . you [expletive] do you want to live forever?"* This famous incident was written about later:

Sgt. Dan Daly (U. S. Marine Corps)

> *They are gone now, those Marines who made a French farmer's little wheat field into one of the most enduring of Marine Corps legends. Their actions are immortal. The Corps remembers them and honors what they did, and so they live forever.*
>
> *Dan Daly's shouted challenge takes on its true meaning—if you lie in the trenches you may survive for now, but someday you will die and no one will care. If you charge the guns you may die in the next two minutes, but you will be one of the immortals. All Marines die, some in the red flash of battle, some in the white cold of the nursing home. In the vigor of youth or the infirmity of age, all will eventually die.[164]*

The point of recounting this story is not to glorify death in combat. The point is in the perspective. With eternity as the frame of reference, our lives are brief, no matter the circumstances or our age when we die. After the moment we pass away, time stretches on into the infinite future. The length of our lives, therefore, is less important than what we do while we are alive. Fighting heroically in battle is honorable and does indeed earn us a place in history. There are obviously countless other ways we can lead meaningful lives in service to our families, communities, and nation. However, God has given us only one way to truly live forever, and he gives each of us the amazing opportunity during the brief span of our lives to do one thing that matters eternally: acknowledge Jesus Christ as our Lord and Savior.

> Then Jesus said to his disciples, "If anyone would come after me, he must deny himself and take up his cross and follow me. For whoever wants to save his life will lose it, but whoever loses his life for me will find it."
> ~Matthew 16:24, 25

A Marine ready for patrol (National Archives)

Tet Offensive, January–February 1968

LAOS

DMZ

Quang Tri

Khe Sanh

Hue

Da Nang

THAILAND

Tam Ky
Chu Lai

Quang Ngai

14

Dak To

Konlum

Pleiku

19

An Khe

Qui Nhon

Hau Bon

Tuy Hoa

CAMBODIA

Mekong

River

Ban Me Thuot

21

Ninh Hoa

1

Nha Trang

Cam Ranh

SOUTH

Da Lat

An Loc

14

VIETNAM

11

Phan Rang

Tay Ninh

20

Phu Cuong

Bien Hoa

Xuan Loc

1

Phan Thiet

South China Sea

Chau Phu

Moc Hoa

Saigon

Go Cong

Phuoc Le

My Tho

Sa Dec

Ben Tre

Vung Tau

Rach Gia

Can Tho

Vinh Long

Phu Vinh

Mouths of the Mekong

Soc Trang

Ca Mau

4

Bac Lieu

Viet Cong/NVA Targets

14 Main roads

International boundaries

0   100 Kilometers

0   100 Miles

TET OFFENSIVE

IN MID-1967 the North Vietnamese high command began planning a large-scale, coordinated offensive they believed could end the war. They hoped to inflict a stinging defeat on the Allied military forces and precipitate a general uprising in South Vietnam against the American "oppressors" and what they perceived as an unpopular South Vietnamese government. After months of preparation, more than 80,000 VC and NVA forces launched the largest campaign of the war on January 30, 1968, on the first day of Tet, the Vietnamese New Year. Their targets stretched from the DMZ in the north to the Mekong Delta in the south, including thirty-six provincial capitals, major cities, and a dozen American bases.

Saigon was a major focal point of the offensive. Attacks were directed at six key objectives, including the Tan Son Nhut Air Base, American Embassy, National Radio Station, ARVN General Staff Headquarters, Independence Palace, and Long Binh Naval Headquarters. These installations were attacked by small teams of local VC units, as larger elements waited to follow up and to exploit the general uprising that was expected. To the surprise of the North Vietnamese, this uprising did not occur. The fighting was intense within the city, and thousands of civilians quickly became refugees trying to avoid the violence. Millions of Saigon residents were touched by the war directly for the first time. The presence of large numbers of journalists and photographers in the capital brought much of this action directly into American living rooms. Despite the civilian and military bloodshed, order was generally restored by about February 4 in Saigon and the other cities of South Vietnam, with a few notable exceptions.[165]

One key objective of the offensive was the city of Hue, the ancient imperial capital of Vietnam. On January 30, 6,000 regular NVA troops of the 4th, 5th, and 6th Regiments entered and took over the city. Over the next twenty-four days almost two divisions of Marine and ARVN troops were committed to retake the ancient capitol. The devastation was severe, as more than 70 percent of the homes and buildings were destroyed and high casualties sustained on both sides. The civilian population suffered a brutal political purge by the Communists, who summarily executed more than 2,000 civilian residents.[166]

Even before the start of Tet, the Marine base at Khe Sanh came under attack by two NVA divisions. The North Vietnamese had several objectives in this part of the campaign. They hoped to inflict a Dien Bien Phu type defeat on the United States while also diverting forces away from the cities during the offensive. The 6,000 Marine and other U.S. troops there suffered almost continuous mortar and rocket attack and enemy ground unit probes for three months. The siege ended in early April with Khe Sanh firmly in U.S. control.

From a military perspective, the Tet Offensive was a catastrophe for the Communists, who lost more than 40,000 dead and achieved few of their stated objectives.[167] There was no popular uprising among the people of the South, who, in fact, saw for the first time Communist brutality in its starkest form.

The perception of the Tet Offensive on the American home front was unfortunately vastly different. Because of earlier government assurances that the end of the war was in sight, the reactions of the press and certain elements of the public were extreme. All optimistic assessments by the military and government were drowned out by violent protests. In March President Johnson announced he would not run for reelection, in effect admitting the war was not close to being won.

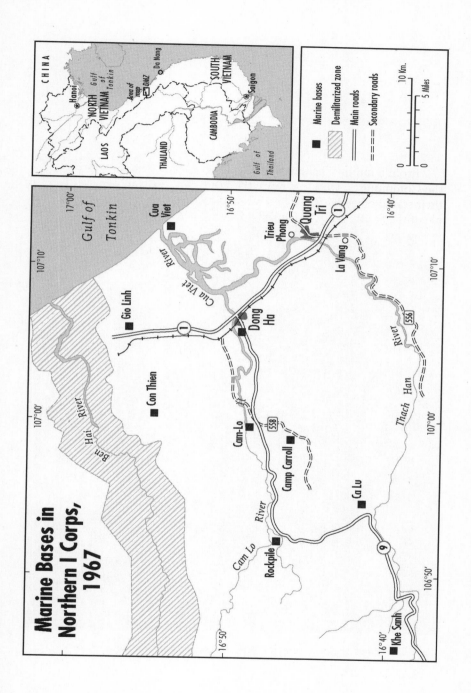

Marine Bases in Northern I Corps, 1967

Map legend:
- ■ Marine bases
- ▨ Demilitarized zone
- ── Main roads
- --- Secondary roads

10 Km.
5 Miles

Inset map labels: CHINA, Hanoi, Gulf of Tonkin, NORTH VIETNAM, LAOS, THAILAND, Area of map, DMZ, Da Nang, SOUTH VIETNAM, CAMBODIA, Saigon, Gulf of Thailand

Main map labels: Gulf of Tonkin, 107°10', 107°00', Ben Hai River, Cua Viet, Gio Linh, Con Thien, Cua Viet River, Dong Ha, 16°50', Cam-Lo, 558, Camp Carroll, Cam Lo River, Rockpile, Ca Lu, 9, 16°40', Khe Sanh, Triew Phong, Quang Tri, 1, La Vang, 556, Thach Han River, 107°10', 107°00', 16°50', 16°40'

Tanks and armored vehicles move through rough terrain (U.S. Army)

Spectators

THE MISSION of the Marines at Khe Sanh was to endure and survive. Fear and deprivation were ever present due to the constant bombardment and tenuous means of supply. Working to repair and improve their defensive positions, they often felt more like construction workers than Marines, even though this was a job site with dangers like no other.

There was not much that could be considered entertainment for the men at Khe Sanh. Even so, there were events worth watching. One of the most exciting was the delivery of supplies to the base by means of the Low Altitude Parachute Extraction System (LAPES). When a C-130 was spotted coming in, word spread quickly around the base. A fascinated Marine described the scene:

> Now that you have purified yourselves by obeying the truth so that you have sincere love for your brothers, love one another deeply, from the heart. ~1 Peter 1:22

The big plane would come in, wheels, flaps and cargo ramp down, engines whispering on low power. Close to the ground the ship would flare out, raise the nose, with the landing gear seeming to grope for the ground. The Loadmaster would pull a drogue parachute release the instant the back wheels kissed the ground, providing the impetus to start the cargo pallets moving. The pilots, still keeping the nose up, would crack the throttles up to a full-engine-power scream. The plane would simply take off again; total of maybe ten seconds ground time.[168]

The whole process was not only exciting to watch, but was also very meaningful to the men on the ground. One of them said, *"The daring and skill displayed right in front of our eyes was a distinct thrill, made complete by the sight of the aircraft lifting off and steeply clawing back into the sky, safe and sound, untouched. Those aircrews were risking their collective butts to help us stay alive. We admired them; loved them like brothers."*[169] These feelings were mutual for the men in the airplanes, equally in awe of their comrades on the ground who were cheering them on from the most dangerous spectator seats in the world.

The Enemy Is out There

ON NEW YEAR'S DAY 1968 a group of five high-ranking North Vietnamese officers were killed just outside the Khe Sanh perimeter. A map was found on the body of one detailing the Marines' defensive positions around the base and surrounding hills. With this early warning and other evidence of increased enemy movement in the area, efforts were stepped up to more closely monitor this activity. Air Force reconnaissance efforts were soon increased. Seismic and acoustic sensors were dropped at strategic locations around the base, relaying information directly into the base command center. Helicopters roamed the treetops with experimental "people-sniffers,"[170] with alarming results:

> If we claim to be without sin, we deceive ourselves and the truth is not in us. If we confess our sins, he is faithful and just and will forgive us our sins and purify us from all unrighteousness. ~1 John 1:8, 9

At the regimental briefing, a plastic overlay covering the tactical map of the area appeared like a diseased face with measles. There were hundreds of red dots. Each dot indicated a detection by low-level helicopters equipped with "people-sniffing" ammonia-detecting gear. Everyone is jolted by the realization that the enemy is indeed "out there," is present in large numbers, and is close to us.[171]

Watching television, I often get the same feeling as these men at Khe Sanh. The Enemy (Satan) is out there. Terrorists randomly kills innocent civilians in the Middle East. War breaks out among the drug cartels in Mexico. Political scandals and runaway spending plague our own government. Forces of violence, greed, and corruption surround us and often seem amazingly well organized. Whether all this evil is orchestrated by Satan himself or is instead the manifestation of human weakness is a theological question that could be debated. Our task as Christians, however, requires no debate. We must always look first within ourselves. We need to identify and confess our own faults to our Savior, constantly praying, *"Lord, have mercy on me, a sinner."* Only when we are in proper relationship with him are we equipped to stand up to the evil in others and in the world around us.

You Make Me Proud

STEVEN WIESE was a squad leader with the 26th Marines during the siege of Khe Sanh. As the daily rocket and mortar attacks grew more intense, he and his fellow Marines prepared for the expected ground assault. During this tense time word came down from headquarters that, if attacked, every effort should be made to take a prisoner. There was an urgent need to learn more about the enemy's intentions.

> Reckless words pierce like a sword, but the tongue of the wise brings healing.
> ~Proverbs 12:18

Knowing that NVA troops were all around the base, Wiese decided it shouldn't be that difficult to go out at night and snatch a prisoner. He asked for volunteers in his squad to go out with him on an unofficial patrol. Not only did everyone in his squad volunteer, but others, hearing of the plan, stepped forward as well. Unfortunately (or fortunately as it turned out), word of this venture soon filtered up to the company commander, who immediately sent for the over-eager squad leader. Wiese recalled the meeting and the biggest "chewing out" of his life:

> He told me that he had heard I was taking a suicide mission outside the wire, and in no uncertain terms that I would NOT go out. If I did, I would be busted in rank to Private, and spend the rest of my days on work details. And if I still pursued my idea, and someone was to get killed, he would make sure I was court-martialed, and put in the brig for the rest of my life. Then, as only a commanding officer can do he said, "Do you understand me, Marine?" I snapped back as if I was still in boot camp, "YES, SIR." On the way out the door the skipper said, "Corporal, you make me proud to be a Marine."[172]

With a few words, this officer turned a serious reprimand into a mild rebuke, and even a compliment. He got his point across, but left this Marine with a feeling of pride he would never forget. We should each be as adept at softening our criticism of others. If we have to criticize or correct someone, we should always look for the opportunity to inject a kind word. We should never forget that our first concern in all our relationships is to show others the love of Christ in our lives.

Irrevocable Commitment

(National Archives)

JIM ECKL was a forward observer with the 22nd Infantry Division. Although he was an artilleryman, he was assigned to an infantry unit to provide that vital link between the troops in the field and the big guns in the rear. To do his job he had to be with his unit and go wherever they went. Frequently this meant dropping into enemy territory by helicopter, not knowing what to expect on the ground:

> *Sometimes the landing zones would be large enough to allow the helicopter to set down; but other times the landing zone would be so small the helicopter could not set down, so the helicopter would just hover ten or fifteen feet off the ground, as low as it could get without clipping the trees and brush, and we would jump. Every landing zone was dangerous, but the small ones were especially dangerous because that meant the helicopter could not set down to pick us up even if we were being overrun: there was at least a chance to retreat, by helicopter, from a large landing zone, but retreat was impossible from a small one, no matter how bad things got. Jumping off the helicopter was an irrevocable commitment: There was never any going back from that moment. Sometimes I would be so scared that I could not talk. But I always jumped.*[173]

One morning in 1993 I sat at a table with a group of men with my head bowed. I had been given the opportunity to pray a prayer, asking Jesus Christ into my heart. I felt it was the moment I should do this, but my skeptical nature battled against it. I weighed my many doubts against the simple truth I had come to believe—Jesus Christ was who he said he was, the Son of God, sent into the world to restore mankind to God. To take this leap, I felt very much like the soldier in this story, jumping into an unknown landing zone. This was the ultimate irrevocable commitment. I will be forever grateful God gave me the will to make this jump and to say the prayer: *"Lord Jesus, come into my heart and take over my life."*

> Jesus said to her, "I am the resurrection and the life. He who believes in me will live, even though he dies; and whoever lives and believes in me will never die. Do you believe this?" "Yes, Lord," she told him, "I believe that you are the Christ, the Son of God, who was to come into the world." ~John 11:25–27

150

Monsoon

THE CLIMATE of Vietnam is determined by seasonal winds, called "monsoons." The northeast monsoon during the fall and winter brings months of rainfall to the central region of the country, much of it torrential. The men at Khe Sanh got to know it well:

(National Archives)

> *When monsoon rains approached we were told we would be attacked. We were attacked—by six inches of rain a day with very low temperatures due to the elevation. We could never get dry—for three months.*
>
> *Underground bunkers and trenches collapsed. One bunker collapsed killing two "short-timers" from crushed chests while many others received broken arms and ankles. Almost all the 30 or so bridges on the road connecting Khe Sanh to logistic support to the east were washed out. We were isolated. Planes no longer could provide aerial observation on enemy forces moving into the area. In addition to the rain, dense fog shrouded the airstrip making resupply by landing aircraft extremely dangerous.*[174]

The monsoon rains made life miserable and dangerous for the Marines at Khe Sanh, but, like rain everywhere, brought life to the land and people of Vietnam. For them, the torrential rains may have been an inconvenience, but they were nevertheless a normal and necessary part of their lives.

Problems seem to be a necessary part of our lives, and, at times, also seem to fall like rain. When we get inundated, it is easy to become either frantic or immobilized. We try to do too much, or we feel helpless to do anything. The only sure defense against this kind of anxiety has to come in our spiritual lives. When the problems mount up, it's time to prioritize. Jesus warned us about being overly concerned about our *worldly* problems. When we *"seek first his kingdom and his righteousness"* (Matthew 6:33), all our other concerns come into proper perspective. The rain that falls in our lives is nothing compared with an eternal future in the sunshine of our Father in heaven.

> Therefore everyone who hears these words of mine and puts them into practice is like a wise man who built his house on the rock. The rain came down, the streams rose, and the winds blew and beat against that house; yet it did not fall, because it had its foundation on the rock.
> ~Matthew 7:24, 25

It Was a Dud

RAY STUBBE was chaplain to 1st Battalion, 26th Marines, throughout the siege at Khe Sanh. In spite of the danger and hardship, he wrote to a fellow minister back home, *"I feel this is where I should be. The Spirit has been working in me here."*[175] He tried to downplay the risks he faced every day when writing to his parents, and only shared one harrowing episode after he was safely out of harm's way:

> *So many things happened at Khe Sanh—it's good I didn't write earlier— practically anything I might write would either sicken or scare you. But that's all past now. I must say the good Lord was very merciful and gracious. I didn't even receive a cut or bruise. But there for a while I was having very close calls every day. One noon, while eating brunch in my hooch, an incoming round went into my wall—through four feet of dirt, 3 feet of sandbags, and bent my steel walls held up by u-shaped engineering stakes—it was a dud!*[176]

To protect themselves in combat, troops wear helmets and body armor, erect barriers, and build the sturdiest bunkers time and resources permit. Through these measures they protect themselves from physical harm as completely as possible, realizing, however, there are forces that can conceivably overwhelm their defenses. Safety is never entirely in their own hands. The incoming artillery round may be a dud, or it may not.

> Those who carried materials did their work with one hand and held a weapon in the other, and each of the builders wore his sword at his side as he worked.
> ~Nehemiah 4:17, 18

In our spiritual battles, we also have protective measures described in amazing detail by the apostle Paul. These include the belt of truth, the breastplate of righteousness, the gospel of peace, the shield of faith, the helmet of salvation, and the sword of the Spirit. With this protection, the outcome is never in doubt. Whether we win or lose, live or die physically, our spiritual safety is assured. It is up to us, however, to keep our armor in good repair, and then to put it on.

Reaching Out

THE AMERICAL Division newsletter, Southern Cross, had an interesting headline in the June 1968 edition: "Children's Hands Hold Key to Understanding." The first lines explained:

Tiny hands are reaching halfway across the world to help create a better understanding between two nations. The hands belong to 34 Vietnamese children in Duc Pho and the children of a first grade class in St. Louis Park, Minn. Language is no barrier.[177]

(National Archives)

This effort at international diplomacy was initiated by an Army enlisted man named Howard Goldberg, who was teaching English to Vietnamese children at the Catholic orphanage near Duc Pho. To make his class more interesting, he conceived of the idea of a scrapbook exchange project. He contacted the principal of an elementary school in St. Louis Park, Minnesota, with the idea and received an enthusiastic response.

The final products of this innovative project were scrapbooks made by both the American and Vietnamese children. Each did hand drawings depicting the people, customs, and dress of their own countries. They added English explanations for the drawings, while the Vietnamese children went one step further, adding translations in Vietnamese.

It would be very naive to think we could place our diplomacy in the hands of children. The advantage children have, however, is their lack of knowledge about history. They haven't learned of past conflicts, hatreds, and prejudices. They see their counterparts simply as other children with interesting differences. A little of this attitude would go a long way in adult diplomatic affairs. We are all in actuality God's children. God wants us to live in peace and to reach out to each other just as he reaches out to us.

Then little children were brought to Jesus for him to place his hands on them and pray for them. But the disciples rebuked those who brought them. Jesus said, "Let the little children come to me, and do not hinder them, for the kingdom of heaven belongs to such as these."
~Matthew 19:13, 14

The Shower

JEROME HOWELL knew that the shower area at the Khe Sanh base was a dangerous place with little protection from incoming fire. Nevertheless, when he got the opportunity to use it, he didn't hesitate. He was filthy and his socks were so dirty they were stiff. Sure enough, just as he was getting lathered up under the warm water, an incoming rocket exploded a short distance away. He immediately ran out of the shower and made a dash for the nearest bunker. As he leaped through the small opening, another Marine inside yelled, *"What the heck!"* as this almost naked figure landed on top of him.

> Let us draw near to God with a sincere heart in full assurance of faith, having our hearts sprinkled to cleanse us from a guilty conscience and having our bodies washed with pure water.
> ~Hebrews 10:22

The two men lay beside each other counting the incoming rounds, when a huge explosion rocked the whole base. An enemy rocket had hit a pallet of antipersonnel mines stacked near the shower unit. Howell described the moment:

> *The bunker we were in collapsed on us, and the lights went out. I was stunned for a few minutes. After it was over the Marine in the hole with me says: "Man, we will have to quit meeting like this." My reply was, "Don't worry about it. I will take a spit bath from now on."*[178]

It was never easy to get clean in the forward combat bases of Vietnam. If the old proverb "cleanliness is next to godliness" were applied only to their physical condition, the soldiers and Marines would have been in a pretty ungodly state.

Fortunately, God is concerned about much more than the cleanliness of our bodies. When the psalmist prayed, he taught us where our priorities should be: *"Create in me a pure heart, O God, and renew a steadfast spirit within me"* (Psalm 51:10). He knew that nothing else about us matters except the condition of our hearts. This is what Jesus seeks to change in us through his message of reconciliation and forgiveness. When he fills our hearts, we are cleansed completely and forever in mind, body, and spirit.

Chaplain Ray Stubbe holds services near Khe Sanh. (Ray Stubbe, John A. Reid, U.S. Marine Corps)

Refugees move through U. S. lines during Tet. (National Archives)

Tet Remembered

THE STATE of Alaska announced a Tet Offensive 40th Anniversary Remembrance Month with an official proclamation:

> Then Moses said to the people, "Commemorate this day, the day you came out of Egypt, out of the land of slavery, because the LORD brought you out of it with a mighty hand. ~Exodus 13:3

WHEREAS, in early 1968 there were Alaska men and women serving in the Armed Forces of the United States, in uniform or as civilian employees within the military environment, during a time of armed conflict in Southeast Asia.

WHEREAS, these citizens of Alaska in Land, Air and Sea forces, who with countrymen, Republic of Vietnam forces, and international allies, all stood fast together and did what was right when the enemy launched a massive surprise assault early in 1968 against the populace and the legitimate government of the Republic of Vietnam.

WHEREAS, our forces properly and completely held at every point around the compass, in spite of heavy direct and indirect fire; first, stopping, defeating, and then pursuing the enemy in their many thousands.

WHEREAS, because it was so far from U.S. shores, families and friends in Alaska homesteads, people overseas, as well as citizens all across our land, heard fragmentary reporting of the great Tet battles, without context: and other than direct communication with those who were there, the American people at large have often been saturated with faulty accounts coming from the self-serving of media and academia. It is time for the bottom line truth of Tet 1968 to be told: the enemy's battle was lost, and freedom—at least for a time—was sustained.

NOW, THEREFORE, I, Sarah Palin, Governor of the State of Alaska, do hereby proclaim February 2008 as: Tet Offensive 40th Anniversary Remembrance Month in Alaska, and encourage all Alaskans to remember the courage brought forth in support and defense of freedom and render long overdue honor and respect to those who were there, drew fire, and sacrificed so much and tell them WELCOME HOME.

Dated: January 10, 2008[179]

This kind of acknowledgment of the past and sincere expression of gratitude has done much to heal the wounds of those who received so little thanks for their heroic efforts in this war. To the state of Alaska, all Vietnam veterans say, "Thank you."

If There Is a God

STANLEY HOMISKI was in a state of near shock when he wrote an emotional letter to his wife. In the letter he mourned the loss of his best friend, who was only twenty-two years old.

> *Dear Roberta,*
> *Today is probably the worst day I have ever lived in my entire, short life. Once again we were in contact with Charlie, and once again we suffered losses. The losses we had today hit home, as my best friend . . . was killed . . . I feel that if I was only a half second sooner pulling the trigger, he would still be alive.*
>
> *Strange how short a time a half of a second is—the difference between life and death. This morning we were talking about how we were only two years different in age and how we both had gotten married before coming to this place. You know, I can still feel his presence as I write this letter and hope that I am able to survive and leave this far behind me.*
>
> *If there is a place called hell this surely must be it, and we must be the Devil's disciples doing all his dirty work. I keep asking myself if there is a God, then how the h- - - do young men with so much to live for have to die. I just hope that his death is not in vain.*[180]

Fortunately, Stan Homiski did keep asking himself about God, and in 2009 was able to say, *"I have long since stopped blaming God for the deaths of my friends and now have a very strong faith in God. It wasn't until I was able to find God that I was able to rid myself of the void I felt in my heart."*[181]

The loss of any friend or loved one leaves a void within us that can never be filled completely. However, as our faith and understanding grow over time, God gives us a new perspective on time, eternity, and life itself. We still mourn our losses and don't usually understand our tragedies, but we never have to doubt the goodness of our Creator.

Trust in the LORD with all your heart and lean not on your own understanding; in all your ways acknowledge him, and he will make your paths straight. ~Proverbs 3:5, 6

157

How Many Days?

WHEN SERGEANT Jack Stoddard joined his unit in Vietnam he noticed the worn and tattered jungle uniforms of the old hands, in contrast to his own neat appearance. One of them leaned toward him and asked with a grin, *"How many days?"* Stoddard knew he meant, how many days left on his Vietnam tour. Somewhat embarrassed, he answered, *"Three-hundred-and sixty."* The trooper, enjoying his status as a "short-timer," laughed and yelled out, *"Better you than me, buddy!"*[182] All at once Stoddard felt like he was a raw recruit all over again.

My early military life also seemed to be an endless series of starting over at the bottom: military college freshman, drill team aspirant, Marine officer candidate, Ranger candidate, Vietnam BNG (brand new guy), etc. For years there seemed to be something about the military intent on making sure I never felt I had "arrived."

Reflecting on this from a spiritual perspective, I believe Jesus had the same concern for his followers. He didn't want them to get too comfortable, either. He told a parable about a man who hired workers at intervals during the day and paid them all the same wage at the end of the day. After admonishing those who complained, he made the well-known, but little understood statement:

Jesus is warning us about feeling as if we've "arrived." The workers who have labored a long time are easily tempted to feel as if they have *earned* their place in his kingdom. The new arrivals are invariably more humble and appreciative. They know they have not earned a place but, instead, have received an amazing gift. No matter how long we've been on the job as Christians, we need the attitude of the new recruit. We have not earned our place. We are thankful for the greatest gift ever given any human being—being last in his kingdom.

> "So the last will be first, and the first will be last."
> ~Matthew 20:16

It Seemed Unreal

SOLDIERS USUALLY had a number of choices for their brief five days of R&R, including such destinations as Australia, Thailand, and Hawaii. David Stafford was more fortunate than most. His wife came to Tokyo and stayed with the parents of friends in the States. David was able to catch a helicopter ride to base camp at Cu Chi, a C-123 to Bien Hoa, and, within hours, a flight to Japan. After a whirlwind reunion with his wife that ended too soon, he found himself

> What sorrow awaits you who are rich, for you have your only happiness now . . . What sorrow awaits you who laugh now, for your laughing will turn to mourning and sorrow.
> ~Luke 6:24, 25

on the way back. In the rush to catch his flight, he left his wallet and identification behind and found it interesting that this proved no hindrance to his return: *"I imagine they figured no one in their right mind would want to fake their way into the Army and a war."* He soon found himself back "in country":

> *After getting back into uniform and gathering up my gear I caught a helicopter ride back out to the ARVN infantry camp near Loc Giang. It seemed unreal as I gazed down at the rice paddies from the helicopter when not many hours before I was with my wife. Soon enough we began our descent and then landed near a smoke marker just outside the camp perimeter.*[183]

How quickly our circumstances change! Once driving through the outskirts of Miami late at night, I turned off the interstate looking for a service station. Suddenly I found myself with my family in a desolate neighborhood with deserted storefronts, trashed streets, and shady figures lurking in the shadows. It took only about half a minute to go from a situation of smug comfort to one of unexpected fear.

It is always good to keep in mind a simple truth: Our well-being *always* hangs in a delicate balance. There are no guarantees that our safety or health will last beyond the present moment. Instead of staking our happiness on our current circumstances, we have to put our faith in something that will survive any crisis. Our only real and lasting security is found in a time-tested relationship with our Father in heaven.

Khe Sanh Chaplain

LIKE MOST good chaplains, Ray Stubbe functioned on many levels. He ministered faithfully to the individual spiritual needs of his men and was also constantly concerned about their general state of morale. Concern for his beleaguered Marines grew during the prolonged siege of Khe Sanh:

> As spiritual advisors to the men, chaplains were directly exposed to the erosion of the Marines' élan. "If Jesus were alive today," one Marine asked, "what would He do if He received a draft notice?" . . . The chaplains worked hard to stay current with every factor affecting life at Khe Sanh to help them deal with the men's doubts . . . Services at one Khe Sanh mess hall had the men standing at chest-high tables, while elsewhere services were held in such places as atop beams at construction sites, in shell craters, and so on . . . Worship services, celebrations of faith, did not eliminate doubts but helped the men feel that others were with them.[184]

During the many years I maintained my firm stand as a religious skeptic, I often attended chapel services. A fellow Marine once asked me about this behavior, since it seemed contradictory to my somewhat antagonistic views toward the church and Christianity. I told him I seldom agreed with the message, but nevertheless found some comfort in being with other people seeking to learn important truths and live better lives. Like the men at Khe Sanh, I may not have had my doubts eliminated, but I did receive something important. I found a sense of community among people looking for answers to the questions we all have: What is the meaning of life? What is my purpose in living? In retrospect, God seemed to keep drawing me back to a place where I could find those answers when he was ready to reveal them to me.

> "For I know the plans I have for you," declares the LORD, "plans to prosper you and not to harm you, plans to give you hope and a future. Then you will call upon me and come and pray to me, and I will listen to you. You will seek me and find me when you seek me with all your heart." ~Jeremiah 29:11–13

The Cross

ON JANUARY 28, 1968, Chaplain Ray Stubbe held a worship service with men of the 26th Marines during the height of the siege at Khe Sanh. In the photo section on page 155 there is a famous photo of that service taken by a Marine Corps combat photographer. The picture captures a poignant moment as Stubbe prayed with his men while the fog was lifting from the surrounding hills. In the corner of the photo is a small cross.

More than forty years later Ray Stubbe was photographed again for an exhibit at the University of Wisconsin in Madison. He was asked to hold some object of special meaning from the Vietnam War. He

Ray Stubbe holding cross. (Frank Gill)

didn't have to think long about what that object would be.[185] There has never been a more meaningful reminder of the service and sacrifice he gave and saw many others give than the cross used for worship in one of the most dangerous places ever known.

Your attitude should be the same as that of Christ Jesus: Who, being in very nature God, did not consider equality with God something to be grasped, but made himself nothing, taking the very nature of a servant, being made in human likeness. And being found in appearance as a man, he humbled himself and became obedient to death—even death on a cross! ~Philippians 2:5–8

These Are My Friends

SAM MESSER was a hospital corpsman with a Navy Construction Battalion (Seabee) unit assigned to the Khe Sanh combat base. He survived seven hard months of combat, and, in spite of his own fears, gave encouragement and medical support to his

> A friend loves at all times, and a brother is born for adversity.
> ~Proverbs 17:17

friends and fellow sailors. He found his own support during the ordeal in a prayerful relationship with God. This relationship and his concern for his friends are both reflected in a poem he called "A Corpsman's Prayer":

> *Grant me, oh Lord, for the coming events;*
> *Enough knowledge to cope and some plain common sense.*
>
> *Be at our side on those nightly patrols;*
> *And be merciful judging our vulnerable souls.*
> *Make my hands steady and as sure as a rock;*
> *When the others go down with a wound or in shock . . .*
>
> *If it's Your will, make casualties light;*
> *And don't let any die in the murderous night.*
> *These are my friends I'm trying to save;*
> *They are frightened at times, but You know they are brave.*
>
> *Let me not fail when they need so much;*
> *But to help me serve with a compassionate touch.*
> *Lord, I'm no hero – my job is to heal;*
> *And I want you to know how helpless I feel . . .*
>
> *Lord, bless my friends If that's part of your plan;*
> *And go with us tonight, when we go out again.*[186]

Sam Messer provides the complete recipe for surviving any crisis. Focus on the needs of others while leaning on God for our own support.

Religious Discovery

LIEUTENANT Colonel Francis Lewis was a chaplain with the Americal Division in Vietnam. In May 1968 he addressed the troops with an amazing message that was inspiring but difficult to grasp:

> I'm sure all of us have come to the place where we despair of the blinding character of words and more words which shut out so frequently the reality of life they were originally coined to disclose. How perilous the tendency can be in religion, where theological exercises become substitutes for the religious spirit.
>
> If you and I might only have the joy of initial discovery, of genuine insight, of actual encounter with God wherein our language and our argument serve merely as vehicles of expression. Such a possibility may be had by any seeker. Such is the joy of religious discovery.
>
> To find in the order of the universe the steadfastness and dependability of God's purpose in the world. To find in that creativity of God at work in the nature of things and one's own being the affirmation of God's perfection. To find in one's moral restlessness the eternal call to turn one's own creativity into the same love for all created beings as was manifest in the initial act of creation.
>
> All this is not only to have found God in a significant sense, but to have entered upon a cosmic adventure for which there is no foreseeable end.[187]

To me this little gem of a sermon is a criticism of how we often allow form to take precedence over substance. There are times when each of us goes through the religious motions. We read, recite, and sing *"words and more words,"* without genuine insight or heartfelt experience. When this happens, we need a major wake-up call.

Incredibly, the Almighty God of the universe wants us to know him, and he has given us effective tools for this purpose. Scripture, prayer, and worship are there for our learning and spiritual growth. However, we have to remember that our efforts are only effective when we open our hearts and seek genuine discovery. We must go beyond the words. God waits for us to seek him with our whole hearts and waits to reward us with insights into his character. This is the cosmic adventure we were made for.

> He has made everything beautiful in its time. He has also set eternity in the hearts of men; yet they cannot fathom what God has done from beginning to end.
> ~Ecclesiastes 3:11

163

Proof of Life

IN HIS last letter home, Michael McAnich seemed preoccupied with time: *"It's hard to realize that I'm already in my 7th month. The time has been going by quickly for me also. Each day seems to slip away into the dusk . . ."*[188] He was expectant that his unit would soon be rotated back to the States, but, unfortunately, this did not happen until a year later. Days after writing this letter, Michael went with the 7th Marine Regiment into the Hiep Duc Valley, where he was killed by NVA mortar fire.

In loving memory of Michael, his fiancée, Joan, has created a moving Web site titled "Some Gave All," filled with pho-

"Now the dwelling of God is with men, and he will live with them. They will be his people, and God himself will be with them and be their God. He will wipe every tear from their eyes. There will be no more death or mourning or crying or pain, for the old order of things has passed away.
~Revelation 21:3, 4

tographs and letters home in tribute to him. Beneath a cross there is an epitaph and announcement of his burial in Houston on what was to be his first day of R&R, September 9, 1969. There is also an excerpt from an essay titled "Tears Are the Proof of Life," with a message to comfort any person experiencing the loss of a loved one:

"How long will the pain last?" a brokenhearted mourner asked me.

"All the rest of your life," I answered truthfully. No matter how many years pass, we remember. The loss of a loved one is like a major operation; part of us is removed, and we have a scar for the rest of our lives.

The scar is still there, and the scar tissue, too. As the years go by, we manage. But the pain is still there, not far below the surface. We see a face that looks familiar, hear a voice that has echoes, see a photograph in someone's album, and it is as though the knife were in the wound again.

But not so painfully. And mixed with joy, too. Because remembering a happy time is not all sorrow; it brings back happiness with it.

"How long will the pain last?"

All the rest of your life. But the thing to remember is that not only the pain will last, but the blessed memories as well. Tears are the proof of life. The more love, the more tears. If this be true, then how could we ever ask that the pain cease altogether? For then the memory of love would go with it. The pain of grief is the price we pay for love.[189]

Ability to Listen

JOE O'DONNELL served as chaplain on the USS *Tripoli* from September 1968 until early 1970, ministering to the ship's company and embarked Marines. He made frequent trips into Vietnam to be with the troops on operation and to conduct services in the field. Moving from unit to unit, he held as many as seven services per day. The most difficult day of his tour was spent memorializing eighteen men killed on one operation.

Based on his experience, O'Donnell later had some advice for others on the qualities most needed by a good wartime chaplain:

The first is that he or she has the ability to listen, to listen not only to words, but to, and with, both heart and soul. The ability to listen includes the ability to accept people where they are in their own understanding of life and faith, not where the chaplain would like them to be. As a chaplain, I must realize that no matter how firm I feel about my own approach to God, I cannot have the last word for anyone else.[190]

This is pretty good advice for any minister, and, in fact, any Christian trying to share the gospel. We don't learn much when we're talking, and we don't convince too many others of anything with our words. We can usually gain more influence with another person by listening. By keeping our own agenda out of the way, and by taking the time to discern someone else's concerns, we have a chance to learn what that person needs and what we can do to help. Sometimes, the biggest help is a sympathetic ear. When we are this kind of friend, we won't have any difficulty sharing the gospel when the time is right.

> My dear brothers, take note of this: Everyone should be quick to listen, slow to speak and slow to become angry, for man's anger does not bring about the righteous life that God desires.
> ~James 1:19, 20

Credibility

AFTER SERVING in Vietnam, Chaplain Joe O'Donnell described the important qualities of a good chaplain. From his experience, one of the most important was credibility:

> Now I want you to know, brothers, that what has happened to me has really served to advance the gospel. As a result, it has become clear throughout the whole palace guard and to everyone else that I am in chains for Christ.
> ~Philippians 1:12, 13

I have to live what I believe. I have to be a person of faith, and hope, and love—yes, love—in the midst of war. Over my years in service, there was ample opportunity to give moral input to human situations that were ethically difficult. Part of being credible is also that I realize I have only part of the answer, not all of it. I am a player, a teammate, a consultant, an idealist living in reality. Credibility is not a given in the military, as it may be in civilian churches or denominational institutions. One earns his or her place by being there, by listening, by keeping secrets, by speaking when it is time to speak, and not speaking when it is not. Deciding those times is not always crystal clear.[191]

In Vietnam, some chaplains earned this kind of credibility, and some did not. Those who did were the ones who shared the danger and hardship of life in the field with the men they served.

To the extent civilian pastors share the everyday concerns of the people they meet, they also have credibility with them. However, this is the area of ministry in which laypeople have the biggest advantage. Our credibility is already established with family, friends, and co-workers. We are living and experiencing what they are. When we share our frustrations and hopes, they see them as real. We expect the same will be true when we share our beliefs.

Many laypeople have an even greater credibility based on some unique experience. Someone who has suffered a great loss or fought an addiction has a special platform from which to speak. This kind of credibility cannot be achieved by a person who has not gone through the ordeal himself. Our hard times always have a meaning in God's kingdom, when we deal with them positively and use the experience gained to help others deal with the same kind of problem. Christ suffered for us, and, when we suffer for him, our pain has a greater and transcendent meaning.

Ruby

MAC DORSEY always thought his story about puppy love would make a great Disney movie. One day in late 1967 a little stray dog showed up at his base near Xuan Loc, where he was serving as an advisor to the Vietnamese 18th Division. The mangy and undernourished pup soon became the unit mascot, and everyone shared what food they had with her. Even though the diet was primarily rice, with some fish or meat, Ruby

(National Archives)

seemed to appreciate whatever she received and always returned the affection tenfold.

In January 1968, Xuan Loc became a battleground in the Tet Offensive, and Dorsey's base came under severe mortar and infantry attacks that went on for three days. When it was over, Ruby could not be found, and she was sorrowfully presumed killed in action. About a week later, however, someone found her alive and well at a nearby U.S. artillery base, where she had taken refuge with that unit's mascot, Blockhead. Blockhead not only had his own sandbagged bunker for a doghouse but was also situated right beside the mess hall. Ruby and her new friend were well fed next to a U.S. Army field kitchen.

Dorsey and his friends took Ruby back to their compound several times, but she kept returning to her new friend. The soldiers finally gave up, figuring her home was no longer with them. Dorsey wrote later:

> Over the years, as I have thought about Ruby, I have always liked to think that in the middle of the chaos, noise, danger, and confusion of battle, Ruby found true love. I can only hope it was not the material things about Blockhead's life that attracted her—the sandbags, overhead cover, and good food—but that it was really a deeper, spiritual attraction. But I'm sure that she and Blockhead lived happily ever after.[192]

The folks at Disney might indeed be interested in such a tale of a wartime canine romance. May God bless all our pets that bring so much undemanding and unselfish affection into our lives.

> Love is patient, love is kind . . . It is not self-seeking, it is not easily angered, it keeps no record of wrongs.
> ~1 Corinthians 13:4, 5

Letter from Home

NOTHING HAS ever been more important to the morale of troops overseas
than mail from home. I found this to be true
while I was in Vietnam. A letter from a girlfriend, spouse, or parent was read, saved,
and re-read many times and often carried in
the field until it virtually disintegrated. Occasionally, a not-so-thoughtful loved one
would write to unburden himself or herself
about some crisis at home and temporarily
unglue the soldier on the receiving end. For-
tunately, this was not typical, and even mail with bad news was *"better
than no mail at all."*

> In your hearts set apart
> Christ as Lord. Always be
> prepared to give an
> answer to everyone who
> asks you to give the rea-
> son for the hope that you
> have. But do this with
> gentleness and respect.
> ~1 Peter 3:15

One soldier in the 198th Infantry Brigade received a note from his
mother that was especially encouraging and a good example of meaningful support from the home front:

> *Dear Son,*
> *Sorry you are lonesome and unhappy, but it will wear off. I know how
> you feel bad, but it will soon pass off and the year will soon pass.*
> *It must have been God's plan for you to go where you are. So just
> trust in Him.*
> *Be sure to attend church and take an active part. If you just trust in
> the Lord, He will make everything better for you.*
> *Try not to worry. Make yourself active in something so you won't
> see home all the time. Remember I'm praying for you, so you pray too.
> And God will make things all right.*[193]

This mother was probably a little naive, neglecting to comment on
the fact that her son was faced with actual danger beyond his control. In
spite of that, it is hard to imagine anything more meaningful for a mother
to do for a child in a difficult situation than to express her love and share
her faith. These are the words young people need to hear, even when they
show an outward disinterest. If nothing else, these words plant a seed that
may take root when it really matters. All of us need God in our lives, and
this need is intensified during stressful times. Reminders like this from a
mother, or any other respected person, could go a long way in turning
someone in the right direction at a crucial moment.

Fighting Demons

A HARD-FOUGHT battle was waged near Phuoc An by a group of 198th Infantry Brigade soldiers and Vietnamese villagers, as reported in the division newsletter of June 1968:

> As Jesus was getting into the boat, the man who had been demon-possessed begged to go with him. Jesus did not let him, but said, "Go home to your family and tell them how much the Lord has done for you, and how he has had mercy on you.
> ~Mark 5:18, 19

PHUOC AN—*The household of Nguyen Chi sat astride the well-worn infiltration route, and every night the enemy would come through, destroying gardens, crops and the newly-planted rice. Something had to be done, and Nguyen called the help of the 198th Infantry Brigade civic action officer, Maj. Frederick W. Tonsing. The next night the trap was set.*

Then they came. Nguyen counted them—more than ten in all, and two big ones. He signaled the attack . . . from the left stormed the dogs. From the right came the villagers, armed only with spears and clubs. The battle was on. Screams, yells, grunts, and barking shattered the night around this small hamlet. The yelling and screaming villagers gained the initiative and the battle soon quieted down.

Dead on the battlefield lay five wild boars. Nguyen's crops were saved from another night of destruction.[194]

The Vietnamese villagers of this offbeat tale were fighting their demons—crop-destroying wild pigs. The story is reminiscent of Jesus' encounter with other demons, told in three different gospels. When approached by a man from Gerasa (a Gerasene) possessed with evil spirits, Jesus cast the spirits out of the man into a herd of pigs, which then stampeded into a lake and drowned. When the local people heard about this incident, they pleaded with Jesus to leave the town.

This biblical account is meaningful on several levels. Most importantly, it illustrates God's power over evil in whatever form it takes—possession, mental illness, or moral corruption. Jesus has the power and authority to drive out every evil and bring healing to our lives. The story also highlights the importance many attach to their material possessions, even at the expense of human life. This story is a powerful reminder we must not take our own possessions too seriously.

Link at a Time

A CHAPLAIN in the Americal Division told a story to encourage his troops about the importance of each man's work:

I recently read of an old blacksmith who, in the opinion of many people in the community, was foolishly careful as he worked on a great chain in his dingy shop. He ignored their adverse remarks and seemed to work with even greater care. Link was added to link, and at last the chain was finished and carried away. Later it lay coiled on the deck of a great ship, which sped back and forth across the ocean.

One night there was a tremendous storm and the ship was severely threatened. Anchor after anchor was dropped, but none of them held.

Finally the main anchor was dropped. The old chain uncoiled and soon grew taut. Would the chain hold? The vessel's weight surged upon it. The ship, the cargo, and hundreds of lives were dependent upon this one chain.

Suppose the old smith had labored carelessly upon just one link? Suppose he had yielded to the voice of his critics for just one day? He had not yielded. He had refused to compromise his convictions even once. He had put honesty, truth, and invincible strength into every part. [195]

> And we rejoice in the hope of the glory of god. Not only so, but we also rejoice in our sufferings, because we know that suffering produces perseverance; perseverance, character; and character, hope.
> ~Romans 5:3-4

The moral of this story was pretty clear to the listening soldiers. Each man was part of a team, and his work formed one link in a greater chain. For the chain to be effective, each soldier had to make sure his link was strong by doing his own task diligently. As Scripture relates: "Whatever your hand finds to do, do it with all your might" (Ecclesiastes 9:10).

This story also has a meaning for the individual person. Our character is constructed, like a chain, one link at a time. When we perform our tasks faithfully, whether great or small, we build a stronger chain. Every time we discipline ourselves to improve in our physical, mental, or spiritual lives, we add important links. The most important parts of this chain are forged in adversity. With Jesus Christ in our lives, we can face our great and small challenges confidently and overcome them cheerfully—building the chain of our Christian character, one link at a time.

Frog on the Burner

IN 1968 a chaplain wrote an article for his unit newsletter in Vietnam to show how men seem to go astray. By now, this little story has been often repeated, but I believe this chaplain may have been among the first to see the spiritual truth revealed by the story of the Frog on the Burner:

> As no one is discharged in time of war, so wickedness will not release those who practice it. ~Ecclesiastes 8:8

I am not an expert on bullfrogs. Once, however, I read the results of an experiment upon one. There is no way I can determine the truth of what was claimed, but I do believe it serves as a good illustration for all of us.

It appears that a bullfrog was put into a pan of water, which was at room temperature. A Bunsen burner was then placed beneath the pan at sufficient distance to heat the water at a rate of .017 degrees per second.

The report maintains that the frog did not move throughout the experiment and died at the end of two and one half hours. He had been boiled alive.

In the 150-minute period, the water temperature changed 153 degrees. At no time was the change abrupt enough for the frog to notice, and he was thus lulled into a state of insensitivity and died.

It is agreed that man is smarter than a frog. We can, however, fall victim to the same subtle death. The compromises and sins of today are not in such contrast with those of yesterday that we will notice them. This way there will be no pricked consciences, no need for confession and repentance.[196]

The message of this story continues to be informative about human nature. The big catastrophes of life usually start innocuously. Few people set out to become unfaithful to their spouses or addicted to alcohol. Most of the time it takes a series of small, innocent steps, enabled by the unfortunate tendency of most of us to overlook minor instances of destructive behavior. It is a well-established fact that anyone addicted to drugs or alcohol is the last person to realize that a problem exists.

Understanding that some of our seemingly harmless acts can lead to danger, we should make corrections early and often—by listening to our own conscience and to the advice of our friends and loved ones. It would be a good idea to keep testing the water—before we are lulled into ignorance of the danger overtaking us.

A Marine takes refuge in a church. (National Archives)

A Vietnamese family caught in a firefight. (National Archives)

The 91st Psalm

CHAPLAIN Ray Stubbe had never directly associated this psalm with battle until he was talking to a wounded Marine on a stretcher during the siege of Khe Sanh. The young man had been brought to the aid station and was suffering from painful wounds. In spite of his condition, he asked the chaplain to read this particular psalm. As the chaplain opened his Bible and began, the verses took on a meaning he never expected:

> He will cover you with his feathers, and under his wings you will find refuge; his faithfulness will be your shield and rampart.
> You will not fear the terror of night, nor the arrow that flies by day, nor the pestilence that stalks in the darkness, nor the plague that destroys at midday.
> A thousand may fall at your side, ten thousand at your right hand, but it will not come near you.
> ~Psalm 91:4–7

As I read him the words, they suddenly became alive with deep significance! Not being afraid of the arrow seemed to remind me of rockets and artillery. Not being afraid of the pestilence reminded me of the 40,000 surrounding us. The terror of night reminded me of the possible—even probable—assault they might launch—and did launch the end of February! A thousand falling at our side were our own casualties—a pretty good approximation! Ten thousand falling by our right hand—"right hand" always refers to power wielded—seemed to refer to the approximately 10,000 to 30,000 NVA that were killed by our B-52s and other air strikes! Of course, the numbers weren't apparent at the time I was reading the Psalm, but the other aspects of pestilence, arrows, fear, and presence were![197]

This story is a wonderful illustration of the power of Scripture to answer our individual needs. This passage has given comfort to countless men in war and to these men under siege at Khe Sanh. It is a comfort to anyone in a difficult or dangerous situation. When we read our Bibles purposefully and diligently, we always find what we need and what God wants us to hear.

Memorial Day

VETERANS OF the Battle of Khe Sanh continue to hold reunions to renew old friendships and share their experiences in one of the war's bitterest fights. They also keep the memory of fallen comrades alive. At a gathering to commemorate the start of the battle on January 31, 1968, one veteran wrote a simple but eloquent message appropriate for all Memorial Days:

Khe Sanh Veterans know there is a place in the world during the month of January, where it's foggy and cold with towering mountains looking down onto a small, isolated plateau, hallowed by many and surrounded by deep green jungle, where the many souls were of those who did not return. While in other places, it's relatively warm, the sun is out and shining from a rich blue sky onto the faces of aging men who remember that time so long ago when they were young, and are grateful now, that they no longer have to suffer through the deprivation and hardship they once experienced. Aging men and comrades who remember those who did not return, and on this most appropriate day, honor their memory.[198]

May God bless the memory of all those who did not return home from this war. Memorial Day is a time to remember and to honor them. For many of us, it is a bitter-sweet memory. Even though we remember fondly all the good times, the loss of friends and fellow Marines was tragic and heart-breaking, and these feelings dim little with time. There is also a measure of guilt that somehow we made it back, and they did not. We can only hope we have made our lives count for something and used the time we've been given in a way that honors their sacrifice. For families who lost husbands, fathers, or sons, the tragedy is even more intense. I pray that God will give all of us who remember and mourn on this day an eternal perspective on these events, along with the faith that these brave men are resting in true peace with him.

> The righteous perish, and no one ponders it in his heart; devout men are taken away, and no one understands that the righteous are taken away to be spared from evil. ~Isaiah 57:1

The Grinder

THERE IS a place at the Parris Island Marine Corps Recruit Depot that holds lasting memories for all Marines. That special place is the vast parade ground located in the center of the base, appropriately named "The Grinder." There countless recruits have spent untold hours grinding away the soles of their boots while learning the fine points of close order drill under the merciless South Carolina sun.

> Now, our God, hear the prayers and petitions of your servant . . . We do not make requests of you because we are righteous, but because of your great mercy. O Lord, listen! O Lord, forgive! O Lord, hear and act!
> ~Daniel 9:17–19

Many years after his time as a recruit, Dennis Mannion returned to Parris Island with a group of Khe Sanh veterans. At one point he wandered away from the group and walked until he found the scene of his former agony and pride. He stood on one end of the Grinder watching two platoons march over the vast space. After a while he was approached by one of the drill instructors, who asked if he needed help. Mannion asked if he could go out to the center of the Grinder. Noticing his name tag, the DI said, "*A Khe Sanh Marine, Sir? You can walk anywhere you want.*"[199] Describing the experience, Mannion said:

> *I then walked straight out until I was in the exact middle. I took in the view. The last time I had that same view with the stands in front of me and the Iwo Jima statue to the left, it was Graduation Day on 16 March 1967.*
> *I knelt right at that spot, down on two knees like in church, and said a quiet prayer for the Platoon 236 guys who never made it back, the Khe Sanh guys who never made it back, and all the Marines and Corpsmen from our era who never came home. I stood for a minute . . . brushed away a tear or two . . . rejoiced that my good wife and one of my sons were back at the PX waiting for me, then turned and walked on a 45 degree angle to reach the end of the Grinder. As I walked, I kept looking down at the concrete wondering if my spit polished boots had ever made contact in that exact same spot 3 plus decades before.*[200]

The image of a lone figure kneeling in the center of a vast parade field is haunting. Surely it is a scene God would observe kindly and a prayer he would hear sympathetically. We don't need a special place to add our voices to that prayer: *Lord, remember our comrades who didn't come home.*

We'll Take It from Here

ON SEPTEMBER 4, 2007, General Peter Pace, the Chairman of the Joint Chiefs of Staff, paid a visit to Karmah, Iraq. He was about to retire and wanted to spend some time with the unit he had started out with in the Marine Corps: 2nd Platoon, G Company, 5th Marines.

Almost forty years before, Pace had taken command of 2nd Platoon during the Tet Offensive, leading his men during the battle for Hue City. He still remembered the name and rank of every man he lost during that time. He told the Marines in Karmah:

Lt. Peter Pace (U.S. Marine Corps)

> *Guys to the left of me got shot. Guys to the right of me got blown up and nothing happened to me at all. I didn't understand that. I got out of Vietnam without a scratch on me. But I made a promise to myself back then that I would continue to serve in the Corps, in their memory, and try to do my job out of respect for them. After just over 40 years of service, when I do get out, I will still owe the Marines of 2nd Platoon, Golf Company more than I could ever repay.*[201]

General Pace met each man of the modern day 2nd Platoon and gave each a special coin. He gave the platoon leader, Lieutenant Chad Cassady, a K-bar knife, a traditional weapon carried by Marines. He also gave these men and all Marines something infinitely more valuable. He demonstrated the bonds that hold Marines together across many generations. He told them, *"Forty years from now, you'll remember these officers' names and they'll remember yours. A lot of stuff is going to happen between now and then. But you will remember this and you'll remember each other."*[202] He then told them what another young soldier had said to him a few days before: *"Sir, thank you for your service. We'll take it from here."*[203] God bless the young men and women of today who take up the burden of defending our nation. They deserve our thanks and constant prayers. They carry a heavy burden taking the place of heroes from the past such as Peter Pace.

It was he who gave some to be apostles, some to be prophets, some to be evangelists, and some to be pastors and teachers, to prepare God's people for works of service, so that the body of Christ may be built up until we all reach unity in the faith and in the knowledge of the Son of God.
~Ephesians 4:11–13

In Memory

Names cast in bronze, engraved on a wall
Faces branded upon our hearts
We cannot forget; we know them all
Soul-seared scenes that ne'er depart.[204]

IN 2008 the Khe Sanh Veterans published the names of those killed in the battles that raged on and around that small combat base in the northwestern corner of Vietnam. More than a thousand names are on the list that spans the time period from 1967 to 1972. This special publication was intended for both those who did and did not serve at Khe Sanh. For those who did serve:

This list may assist you to piece together just what happened in the chaos of battle. This list may prompt you to face your pain and, knowing the truth, be freed. This list may help you find a name of a close friend, perhaps even someone who saved your life, a name that you perhaps have since forgotten.[205]

For those who did not serve:

This list will reflect the cost of battle; it indicates the burden and the price of serving. When President Kennedy declared in his Inaugural Address of 23 January 1961: "We shall pay any price, bear any burden, meet any hardship, support any friend, oppose any foe to assure the survival and success of liberty," perhaps we really did not comprehend the magnitude of the price and the greatness of the burden when these words motivated so many to go to Vietnam.[206]

It is a sobering experience to read the names of those who did not come home from Khe Sanh. I knew many of these men and can attest to the fact that these are not just names; these were real men with real hopes for the future. They sacrificed everything for their nation and for us who survived. I pray that each has a special place in heaven with the One who sacrificed everything for them. The prophet Isaiah long ago foretold of the Savior who would eventually come to serve and save the world through his own suffering:

He was despised and rejected . . . , a man of sorrows, and familiar with suffering. . . . he was despised, and we esteemed him not . . . He was pierced for our transgressions, he was crushed for our iniquities; the punishment that brought us peace was upon him, and by his wounds are we healed. ~Isaiah 53:3, 5

177

The Children

DURING HIS time in Vietnam David Stafford served with a five-man team that deployed and operated a ground surveillance radar system. Working usually at night, his unit was able to detect foot movement as far away as eight miles. The nights were hot and long with frequent contacts and artillery missions. Early one morning, after a busy night in one of the ARVN camps, Stafford made an interesting note in his journal:

> *I can't help but notice that the children of ARVN soldiers are beginning to come out of their bunkers to play. I'm amazed how resilient these little rascals are; inventing games, running and playing with big smiles across their faces. I share some of the candy that we get in our care packages with the kids . . . I can't imagine raising kids in such an environment.*[207]

It is hard to imagine a more anomalous picture than children at play in the desolate setting of a combat base. Even so, this was not an uncommon sight in Vietnam. ARVN soldiers often kept their families close by, reflecting the length and nature of the war for them. Also, the families were probably safer at times with the army than in some supposedly safe "rear" areas. In any event, it is reassuring somehow that kids can be kids, even in a war zone. The optimistic and cheerful nature of the children seems to survive and even flourish no matter the situation.

Jesus encouraged his followers to be like this. He wants us to live in the present and to not consume ourselves with guilt over the past or with anxiety about the future. He wants us to accept plain and simple truths. Most of all, he wants us to have faith in him just like a child has faith in his parents.

> He took a little child and had him stand among them. Taking him in his arms, he said to them, "Whoever welcomes one of these little children in my name welcomes me; and whoever welcomes me does not welcome me but the one who sent me. ~Mark 9:36

Why

A S A COMBAT corpsman in Vietnam, Sam Messer saw many disturbing sights and asked God many questions about their meaning and his purpose for being there. He wrote a thought-provoking poem trying to capture these feelings:

Sam Messer at Khe Sanh

> *Oh, Lord, take me through*
> *That lustrous gate.*
> *Please take me, Lord,*
> *So that I might see*
> *Just what is going to happen*
> *To humanity!*
> *Please show me, Lord,*
> *Why I was sent here.*
> *I feel no hate,*
> *I just feel fear.*
>
> *Oh, Lord, please! What*
> *Am I doing here?*
> *(I see the young,*
> *The sick, the weak,*
> *The old,*
> *The dying, the dead.)*
> *I see in eyes*
> *The hope, the fear.*
> *Lord, please, could this be why*
> *I was sent here?*[208]

I say: My purpose will stand, and I will do all that I please. From the east I summon a bird of prey; from a far-off land, a man to fulfill my purpose . . . What I have planned, that will I do.
~Isaiah 46:10, 11

The greatest reward is found in a sense of purpose, and our ultimate purpose is found in service to God's kingdom. Sometimes this work is performed within the church, but, for most of us, it is performed in our daily environment as we work alongside other people. We serve God by serving others and demonstrating Christ's love by our actions. There could be no finer example of this than a corpsman prayerfully and heroically caring for his comrades under the harsh conditions of combat.

Marines carry wounded to landing zone (National Archives)

New Strategy

GENERAL CREIGHTON Abrams went to Vietnam in May 1967 to relieve General Westmoreland as commander of U.S. forces. Worrying that a change of command might appear weak to the public, the Johnson administration kept him on hold for a year. After the Tet Offensive, however, the president was finally ready for a new approach to the war.

On taking command, Abrams brought a new outlook on the nature of the war honed over months of observation and study. He accepted the fact that he had to fight on many levels—against guerrillas and conventional forces—and with an array of forces. From the beginning he de-emphasized large scale "search and destroy" operations and put equal emphasis on military operations, improvement of Vietnamese armed forces, and security for the indigenous population of the country.

By this time the United States had reached its peak troop deployment of 543,000, including seven divisions, 112 maneuver battalions, sixty artillery battalions, and more than four hundred helicopters.[209] Additionally, forces from South Korea, Thailand, Australia, and New Zealand were on hand, as well as ARVN forces numbering more than one million.

After Tet, President Johnson also focused his attention on the possibility of achieving peace through negotiations. The North Vietnamese agreed to meet in Paris, but showed no evidence of curtailing operations on the ground in Vietnam. After five months of stalled talks, Johnson finally agreed to a unilateral halt of all air, naval, and artillery bombardment of North Vietnam. Talks still progressed slowly and would only gain momentum under the Nixon administration with secret talks between Henry Kissinger and the North Vietnamese delegation.

During 1968, the North Vietnamese launched two more offensive campaigns, loosely termed the "mini-Tet" and the "Third" offensives. This time the Allies were not taken by surprise, launching preemptive attacks of their own. Abrams' staff had discerned the enemy's method of building up food, ammunition, and medical stocks in areas targeted for future operations. By more vigorous small-unit patrolling, there was a dramatic increase in the number of stockpiles discovered and destroyed during the second half of the year. Of twenty-seven VC and NVA battalions scheduled to attack Saigon, only nine reached the city, at horrendous cost to the attackers. During 1968 the VC infrastructure in South Vietnam was practically eliminated as a factor in the war.

Although the VC main force units were seriously degraded during 1968, the VC political infrastructure controlling more than 40 percent of South Vietnam remained largely intact.[210] This infrastructure became the focus of an Accelerated Pacification Campaign, under the direction of Ambassador William Colby, a future CIA director. The goal of the campaign was to bring security for the first time to more than thirteen hundred hamlets. Success was achieved by a vigorous campaign to increase the Vietnamese Regional and Popular Forces by an additional 80,000 men and to assign 350 five-man teams of U.S. soldiers to assist with patrolling, ambushes, and security of bridges and towns. These efforts paid off in a drastic improvement in security across the country, illustrated by 47,000 enemy troops coming over to the side of the South Vietnamese government in 1969, twice as many as the year before.

Despite improving conditions on the battlefields of Vietnam, the greater impact on the war was being felt in the United States from the escalating antiwar movement. In 1968 dissent turned violent with raids on college administration buildings and draft boards. The images of police clashing with rioters on the streets of Chicago during the Democratic National Convention went directly into every American living room and foreshadowed even more conflict ahead. The North Vietnamese persisted in their struggle in the belief this opposition on the American home front would eventually become decisive.

Machine Gunner

IN THE field every man carried a back-breaking load. The basic necessities were weapon, ammunition, grenades, entrenching tool, food, and water. Radio operators packed their radios, and just about everyone else labored with extra equipment such as batteries, air panels, and mortar rounds. The machine gunners felt that theirs was the heaviest burden.

(National Archives)

The M-60 weighed twenty-five pounds and required a lot of ammunition. One soldier explained:

He sweats, pants, shifts, stumbles, swears, and in general is miserable through the whole operation. He may carry the gun for two weeks without seeing even a footprint of Charlie's but when they do make their play he drops on the mud and all the strain seems suddenly worthwhile and he's proud of his dubious honor again for another couple of miles.[211]

Amazingly, it was not always the biggest men who carried the machine guns. My unit had several Marines of small stature who took great pride in being able to handle their guns and keep up on the march. All these gunners carried the heaviest loads, but also felt they got the biggest payoff when trouble started.

We all expect something from our work, whether our reward is pay, promotion, an occasional good word, or self-satisfaction. It is important to remember, however, that God has his own perspective on what we are doing. He judges our accomplishments on the basis of their contribution to his kingdom, and for works that pass this test, he even promises heavenly rewards we can't imagine.

Even though the work we do in this life is important to him, it is not relevant to how he judges *us*. He has given his Son to pay the ultimate price for us and to guarantee we will stand innocent before him in the end. We are saved only by our faith in Jesus Christ.

> His work will be shown for what it is, because the Day will bring it to light. It will be revealed with fire, and the fire will test the quality of each man's work. If what he has built survives, he will receive his reward. If it is burned up, he will suffer loss; he himself will be saved, but only as one escaping through the flames.
> ~1 Corinthians 3:13–15

New Guy

SOON AFTER arriving in country the new lieutenant reached his assigned unit at the Binh Phuoc firebase, south of Saigon. Reporting in to the battery executive officer (XO), he was confronted by a red-eyed, haggard man who looked older than his years. After receiving his assignment, the new officer casually asked, *"Good outfit?"* The XO looked at him skeptically and replied, *"Yeah, right."* It dawned on the lieutenant that being a new man here was different from his previous experience:

> *During the ten days I'd been in-country, being processed through the pipeline to Binh Phuoc, I'd noticed a cool formality toward replacements—not open hostility, just a certain sense of distance. There was none of the "Welcome aboard, let's grab a cup of coffee" you might expect joining a stateside unit.*[212]

During the Vietnam War, units were usually filled with individual replacements. The new men, also called BNGs (Brand New Guys) and similar abbreviations that stood for profane versions of this, were often treated coolly in combat units for a number of reasons. The veterans had lost friends and had developed incredibly close bonds with those remaining. There was a reluctance to befriend newcomers as sort of a defense mechanism against further loss. Only with time and shared trials could a new man gradually earn acceptance. When it was earned, however, he found himself part of a group who would do anything humanly possible to protect him and each other.

I tell you that in the same way there will be more rejoicing in heaven over one sinner who repents than over ninety-nine righteous persons who do not need to repent.
~Luke 15:7

Fortunately, we don't have to earn our way into God's kingdom. There is no rite of passage. We don't have to make ourselves better people or prove ourselves worthy. We have already been made acceptable by the sacrifice of God's Son, Jesus Christ. Our heavenly Father waits for us and welcomes us when we come to him. A BNG in God's kingdom is the cause of a great celebration among the angels in heaven.

Mercy

CHAPLAIN Bill Mahedy was called into the battalion commander's office. The colonel wanted to talk about a soldier in the unit who had become addicted to heroin. After a series of minor offenses and non-judicial punishments, the soldier had undergone detoxification in jail. His tour of duty in Vietnam was about up, and he was soon to return to the States. The colonel had resolved to recommend the man for an *"other than honorable"* discharge and wanted the chaplain's opinion.

> "'I desire mercy, not sacrifice.'" ~Matthew 12:7

Mahedy strongly disagreed with the colonel's decision. He could see no good reason to saddle the man with a permanent mark that would affect his future employment opportunities because of his failure as a soldier during wartime. An argument started between the two men and soon began to heat up. At one point, the colonel angrily pounded his desk and shouted, "Damn it, *Chaplain, the New Testament talks about justice!*" The chaplain stood up to the same desk and shouted back, *"Damn it, Colonel, the New Testament talks about mercy!"*[213]

The battalion commander made a mistake getting into this argument. He had the authority to make the decision about the soldier's future based on his own judgment. However, there is a higher authority about whom the chaplain knew more than did the colonel. Forgiveness and mercy were the hallmarks of Jesus' ministry and a major theme of the New Testament. Thanks to our Savior, none of us has to face the justice we deserve. In the end, the colonel bowed to this higher authority and relented in his decision. The soldier was given another chance.

101st Div. soldier manning machine gun near Tuy Hoa. (National Archives)

Helping a wounded comrade. (National Archives)

Song Fest

IT WAS another cold, wet night at the
Dong Ha combat base. Tired and dirty
men carrying out their duties slogged
through the driving rain and mud. The air
was split by the sound of howitzers sending
out harassing fire into the darkness. The cor-
respondent had just been assigned to a tent
with five other men. In his first conversation
someone pointed out the location of the
nearest bunker, in case of mortar attack.
Since it was too early to sleep and too cold
to stand around, he wrapped up in a blanket
and lay on his bunk. During a lull in the
artillery fire, he heard singing:

*Investigating, you find that the voice comes
from the tent of Father Joseph E. Ryan, a big,
graying priest from Boston who wears the silver oak leaf of a Navy commander on his collar. Ryan is the head Catholic chaplain in the
area, and several chaplains and Marines have
gathered in his tent for an Irish song fest.*

*"All soul-saving will come to a screech-
ing halt now," Father Ryan says as he pours
a libation for his guests. War being what it is,
there is no Irish whiskey at the front and the
men have to make do with bourbon.*[214]

There is a time and a place for everything.
On most days Father Ryan carried out his
priestly duties, administering religious services
for the living and last rites for the dying. He
gave advice, counsel, and encouragement to the many men who came to
him with their problems. On this night, however, for himself and others, he
tried to provide a simple respite from the misery of life in a forward combat base. By joining with others in fellowship he brought a warm, human
touch to a cold place, and, by letting his own humanity show, he only
increased the effectiveness of his ministry. It would not be difficult to come
to such a man with a spiritual question, and, if he spoke of the gospel, you
would listen. The apostle Paul took the same approach in his ministry.

> Though I am free and belong to no man, I make myself a slave to every-one, to win as many as possible. To the Jews I became like a Jew, to win the Jews. To those under the law I became like one under the law (though I myself am not under the law), so as to win those under the law. To those not having the law I became like one not having the law (though I am not free from God's law but am under Christ's law), so as to win those not having the law. To the weak I became weak, to win the weak. I have become all things to all men so that by all possible means I might save some. I do all this for the sake of the gospel, that I may share in its blessings.
> ~1 Corinthians 9:19–23

187

No Other Way

STEVEN SHEPLEY fought the "other" war in
Vietnam. After the Viet Cong were cleared from
an area by Army operations, he would take a combined civilian/military team in to help reestablish the
local government and economy. Twenty-nine years
old and fluent in Vietnamese, Shepley was part of
the Office of Civil Operations and Revolutionary
Development Support, known as "CORDS." This
organization coordinated all the military and civilian agencies working in Vietnam's forty-four
provinces in support of what was called the "pacification" effort. Shepley was in charge of the
Mekong Delta province of Ba Xuyen. He explained
his mission to a visitor:

South Vietnamese
soldier. (National
Archives)

The Army can't be everywhere. The people in the villages have got to be
induced to take over their own defense. They have to be brought under
effective administration. They've got to be given a better life and ade-
quate social services. The military can't win this war. But revolutionary
development won't work either, unless we have the military out there as
a screen.[215]

When asked about numbers, he said, *"We have RD teams in five*
other hamlets like this one. There are four hundred and fifteen (hamlets
in the province). We consider that two hundred and twenty-six are under
government control, one hundred and ten are under VC rule, and the rest
are contested."

"It's going to take an awful long time to carry out revolutionary
development in all of them, isn't it?" the visitor asked.

"Yes, but there's no other way to do it."[216]

The lessons learned during the Vietnam
War working with civilian populations have
been found very applicable today in America's
effort to counter insurgency in the Middle
East. There are, unfortunately, no shortcuts.
Military operations and a military presence
are necessary for security. But the war is won
village by village, as the people are given the
opportunity and find the means to build better lives for themselves.

The end of a matter
is better than its begin-
ning, and patience is
better than pride.
~Ecclesiastes 7:8

Sudden Loss

IT WAS a welcome relief for the soldier to be paired up on the perimeter with someone easy to talk to. He and the man everyone called "Flash" shared their memories and frustrations, talking quietly during a long night together.

Early the next morning, everyone was getting ready to saddle up, rolling ponchos and cleaning weapons, when explosions shattered the still air. Claymore mines went off as automatic weapons and small arms fire erupted on the other side of the perimeter. They were under attack. The call soon came for more ammo, and the soldier started gathering up machine gun belts and rifle magazines to take to those who needed them. He didn't get far until he ran into two men carrying someone seriously wounded. One of the men was his sergeant, who told him to help get the wounded man back to a medic. When he finally set the man down, he realized it was his new friend, Flash. He and the medic did everything they could for him, but the wounds were too severe. After a while, he had to watch as his friend died.

> "The people living in darkness have seen a great light; on those living in the land of the shadow of death a light has dawned."
> ~Matthew 4:16

As several other casualties were brought in, the attack subsided. The enemy broke contact, and all was quiet until the medevac helicopter came in. Three wounded men and Flash's body were taken out. Ammunition was dropped off. The numb soldiers were told to saddle up—they were moving out. The grieving soldier had only minutes to mourn:

I've never felt so empty, hurting and numb with shock at the same time. There was no time to say or do anything to honor our fallen comrade. It didn't seem right. We all knew what had happened, but had to prepare to go on and each deal with the loss in our own way.[217]

This story, written anonymously, reminds us why so many combat veterans have psychological problems later in life. The grieving process takes time and there is usually too little of it when it's needed most. All veterans should learn something about posttraumatic stress disorder and its symptoms. If there is even a possibility of unresolved issues of grief, anger, or guilt affecting them or their families, help is available.

I Can't Remember Your Name

CHAPLAIN Bryant Nobles had been with 3rd Battalion, 3rd Marines, for about two weeks. He walked, rode jeeps, and flagged helicopters to get around to all the rifle companies so he could hold religious services and get to know as many of the men as possible. On the night of September 17, 1969, he was with the battalion command group near the Rockpile, when around midnight, he was awakened by M-16 and AK-47 rifle fire. Realizing the Marines were under attack, he quickly jumped into his foxhole. He was soon joined by the battalion commander and a radio operator who had been forced to retreat back to his position. The battle raged for five hours, during which time twenty-five Marines were killed and forty-seven wounded.

Throughout the night, Nobles moved among the Marines giving first aid and encouragement, in his words, *"doing whatever I could while praying without ceasing. My faith in God met its supreme challenge."*[218] He was later decorated for his service to the men he had known for so short a time. His most meaningful reward, however, came the night after the battle:

> *Just before turning in for the night the Commanding Officer requested that I pray with him. After the prayer, he grasped my hand and said, "Chaplain, I can't even remember your name, but I thank God you were with us last night." This reward far exceeded the medal I later received.*[219]

Our rewards can come in many forms. Recognition from someone we respect surely ranks among the best. Sometimes there is no reward at all other than our knowledge that we have done the right thing. Whatever our rewards, or lack of them, during this life, we anticipate the time when we will stand before our Savior hoping fervently that something we have done will elicit the response that will fill our hearts for all eternity:

'Well done, good and faithful servant! You have been faithful with a few things; I will put you in charge of many things. Come and share your master's happiness!'"
~Matthew 25:21

Who's Next?

DURING THE firefight the lieutenant seemed to freeze up. Rather than make an issue of it, the CO sent him back to base camp to recover from "extreme exhaustion." This wasn't stretching the truth, since the whole unit had been in the bush constantly for three months. After a few days of sleep and regular food, the young officer seemed to return to normal. He began, however, to take extreme precautions in his habits. Unlike others in this relatively safe place, he constantly wore his helmet and flak jacket. He didn't even sleep on his cot, lying instead on the ground with his flak jacket over him and sandbags around him. One night, after a rare rocket attack on the base, a corpsman found the lieutenant dead in his hut. A piece of shrapnel had somehow found its way past the sandbags and body armor to penetrate his chest. The corpsman who discovered his body concluded:

> If someone was protected, it was the lieutenant. After that I decided that there was nothing you could do about it. Once you were there, you're there and who knows who's going to get it next?[220]

Is it ever our time to be "next"? This is a recurring question for every man in combat. I must admit, my answer at the time was about like that of this corpsman. I didn't think there was much I could do about it, and so I was resigned to my "fate," whatever that was. Since becoming a Christian, my attitude toward this question has changed totally.

I am now confident that God is in control of my life and that I will live as long as it suits his purpose. My prayers and the prayers of others have a role to play in influencing him, and he can alter the outcome of any event and the course of my life as he chooses. I also do what I can to protect myself and try to limit risks. Still, I am always aware of the fact that sooner or later, due to traumatic events or natural causes, the time will come when I will be "next." From God's eternal perspective, whether this is sooner or later makes little difference. My hope lies in the knowledge of who I belong to and where I am going.

Your word, O LORD, is eternal; it stands firm in the heavens. Psalm 119:89

"Now this is eternal life: that they may know you, the only true God, and Jesus Christ, whom you have sent." ~John 17:3

Caduceus

(U. S. Navy)

THE ROCKET attack went on as the corpsman and soldier huddled in the bunker, trying to think about other things. As dirt cascaded down from another explosion, the soldier looked over at the collar insignia on the other man and said, *"By the way, I've been meaning to ask you why doctors chose that as their symbol. It's supposed to be the scepter of Mercury. What the hell does that have to do with medicine?"* Without thinking, the corpsman gave him the answer: *"It's supposed to represent the Wings of Mercy, delivering the Staff of Life, from the Depths of Hell."* The soldier groaned as another rocket impacted nearby.[221]

The hospital corpsman's insignia, depicted on this page, is called the *caduceus,* and does in fact derive from Greek mythology. It was carried as a staff by Hermes, the messenger god (known later, in Roman mythology, as Mercury). It was adopted formally as an emblem by the Medical Department of the Army in 1902, and, after World War I, by the Navy Hospital Corps. For their symbol the American Medical Association uses a similar device called the Rod of Asclepius, also from Greek mythology, with a staff and single snake.

There is also a biblical origin to this image. After the Israelites fled Egypt and journeyed through the Sinai wilderness they began to get impatient with God and cried out, *"Why have you brought us up out of Egypt to die in the desert? There is no bread! There is no water! And we detest this miserable food!"* (Numbers 21:5), referring to the manna God was supplying them with. They realized their mistake in speaking against God when God sent poisonous snakes that bit and killed many of them. Confessing their sin to Moses, they asked him to pray to God to take the snakes away. Moses did pray, and God did mercifully respond, in an unusual way.

So Moses prayed for the people. The LORD said to Moses, "Make a snake and put it up on a pole; anyone who is bitten can look at it and live." So Moses made a bronze snake and put it up on a pole. Then when anyone was bitten by a snake and looked at the bronze snake, he lived.
~Numbers 21:7–9

What Are You Doing?

THE SOLDIER had joined the 2ⁿᵈ Battalion, 8ᵗʰ Cavalry Regiment, a few days before while the unit was on a major operation near Tam Quan. He had not been in a firefight so far and wondered if this would be the day he would have to prove himself in action. He moved cautiously as his company advanced on a small hamlet:

My squad was deployed roughly in a 'V' formation and I found myself at the apex of the 'V' facing the direction of advancement. There was gunfire to our front but I couldn't see any enemy soldiers or fortifications such as bunkers. Suddenly one of my squad members, who was located on my right rear, yelled, "C'mon, let's go!" I thought he meant "Charge," so I gripped my M16 firmly and ran towards our objective just like we learned during advanced infantry training. I remember running through the palm trees and low plants scattered about and with the sound of bullets whizzing by as the gunfire seemed to increase. The bullets passed me with a 'snap,' something like a micro sonic boom, and more rounds were hitting the palm fronds with a 'splat' and the tree trunks with a 'thunk,' and leaf debris was falling like rain about me. After 50 to 60 meters, I stopped and turned around only to see that I was all alone. I don't remember my exact thoughts but I think it was something like "Oh, God! What do I do now?" Within a few seconds the guy who had yelled "C'mon, let's go," caught up with me screaming "What the h___ are you doing? We're pulling back!" I think I felt even worse now, not only was I being shot at, but I was also in deep trouble with my squad leader. We returned to the area where we had set up a defensive position and my platoon leader was standing there with a scowl on his face.²²²

Unfortunately, most of us don't have a good squad leader to tell us we're going in the wrong direction. We usually have to figure it out on our own. This is not easy in any area of personal behavior but is especially difficult with regard to our spiritual direction. Everyday concerns take over our thoughts, and our physical needs rule our actions. We need to keep praying constantly, as we ask God, "What am I doing?" He will let us know, and he will guide us in the right direction. The definition of repentance is to change direction. Christians need to remember that this isn't something we do only once.

> Godly sorrow brings repentance that leads to salvation and leaves no regret.
> ~2 Corinthians 7:10

Hunger

THE PLACE became known as Hunger Hill. B Company, 1st Battalion, 22nd Infantry, had been in the field for thirty-four straight days, the last eight without resupply. Despite monsoon rains and fog, the helicopters usually made it in, even if a day or two late. This time, however, the fog was thick and unremitting.

After about four days, the C-rations on hand were used up. For several more days, the men found extra packets of cocoa powder, coffee, and cigarettes in their packs, and shared these as best they could. Then there was really nothing left. Hunger and depression began to take their toll. After another long, miserable night the men woke at dawn on the eighth day to a steady rain. One of the soldiers described the moment:

> As we lay in our poncho hooch trying to stay dry, no one even talking, Paul voiced what the rest of us were thinking, "We don't have one single solitary reason to even get up, or to even move for that matter; not one reason." The sense of despair hung in the air thicker than the fog. Never again would we feel such hopelessness, helplessness, and utter despair. It came to be known as Hunger Hill.
>
> I guess it also came to signify how fragile something as seemingly simple as resupply could be. Never again would we take anything for granted. We learned to always squirrel away something to eat, drink, or smoke.[223]

Many combat veterans have had their own ordeals of prolonged misery and can identify with the state of these soldiers. These kinds of experiences have a way of reordering one's priorities about a lot of things. After any serious deprivation, minor discomforts and inconveniences take on a new perspective.

There is another kind of hunger that can be an even greater blessing. Jesus taught, *"Blessed are those who hunger and thirst for righteousness, for they will be filled"* (Matthew 5:6). We are blessed by a spiritual hunger that compels us to seek the food that will truly satisfy our needs. This food can only be found in God's Word. When Jesus was hungry, Satan tempted him by suggesting he turn stones to bread. Jesus replied:

"It is written: 'Man does not live on bread alone, but on every word that comes from the mouth of God.'" ~Matthew 4:2–4

Sandbags

AN ARMY chaplain in Vietnam had some interesting observations about the humble sandbag. He reckoned it might be considered the universal piece of equipment, as it had so many and varied uses, including protection, construction, decoration, erosion prevention, and roof anchorage. He pointed out that they are also used for: *"laundry bags, grease rags, police call, and at church call to take up the offering; they are used as head covering, splint ties, for making walkways, muscle-building—you name it."*[224]

(Canadian Forces)

By way of comparison, he recommended to the soldiers an equally useful and basic tool of the spiritual realm. Also humble in nature but with universal application, he recommended the use of what he termed, *"Moments with the Maker."* These would be those little everyday opportunities to redirect our attention to God:

> *They offer protection against whatever threatens, building materials to make a more liveable life, they serve as dikes against erosion of peace, character, integrity.*
>
> *Like sandbags, "Moments with the Maker" are widely available— in a breath of prayer, a glimpse at some familiar picture or symbol, a Bible verse remembered, a snatch of truth from some moving experience.*
>
> *Imagination and need team up to discover where they can prove useful. Meanwhile, lay in a good supply, and maintain a recurring requisition.*[225]

This is a great picture a soldier or anyone else can easily relate to. We don't need to wait for worship services or dedicated quiet time to pray or to connect with God. He is as close as we want him to be in our everyday lives. A *"moment with the Maker"* before a meeting, phone call, or even a trip to the grocery store keeps us close to him and gives him the opportunity to change our perspective. When we pray, we let him bring a positive outlook and peace into our daily activities.

> Be joyful always; pray continually; give thanks in all circumstances, for this is God's will for you in Christ Jesus . . . May God himself, the God of peace, sanctify you through and through. May your whole spirit, soul and body be kept blameless at the coming of our Lord Jesus Christ.
> ~1 Thessalonians 5:16–18, 23

Voice of Authority

THERE'S AN apocryphal story told on veterans' Web sites about a misbehaving little boy on a crowded airline flight who picked the moment before takeoff to throw a wild temper tantrum. An embarrassed mother and frustrated stewardess got nowhere trying to stop the kicking and screaming, as the surrounding passengers grew more and more agitated.

> Apply your heart to instruction and your ears to words of knowledge. Do not withhold discipline from a child; if you punish him with the rod, he will not die.
> ~Proverbs 23:12, 13

Suddenly a rugged-looking man in uniform stepped forward from the rear of the plane. A Marine sergeant with a chest full of ribbons, shooting badges, and jump wings raised his hand to the mother and leaned down close to the little boy. He whispered a few words in the youngster's ear, after which the boy immediately straightened up and calmed down. The nearby passengers burst into applause.

As he sat back down, the stewardess came over to thank him, and, of course, ask what he had said. The Marine replied, *"I showed him all the medals and ribbons on my chest and told him they mean that I have special authority to throw one person off the airplane whenever I want to."*

We've all wished for that kind of voice of authority at times, if not to counsel our own kids, then someone else's. Unfortunately, control over little children, or any children for that matter, doesn't come from the perfect threat. It only comes from consistent and patient discipline. This means establishing boundaries for age-appropriate behavior and then, on most occasions, using positive reinforcement, logical persuasion, or loss of privileges. For that rare event, possibly pertaining to the child's safety, and when the parent is not acting out of anger, spanking also has a role. Timely and restrained corporal punishment gets results, and, once demonstrated, becomes ever less likely to be needed. This is the nature of that biblical guidance for child-raising given in the book of Proverbs, often paraphrased as, *"Spare the rod and spoil the child."*

Last Rites

IT WAS time for the attack. Weapons were locked and loaded. The helicopters were lined up in the landing zone, rotors turning. The 11th Infantry Division troops were about to jump off on Operation Bold, a helicopter assault on an NVA division headquarters located near the Cambodian border. Jim Eckl was ready with his forward observation team, but his nerves were on edge:

(National Archives)

Just when I thought I could not be more scared, sitting on the helicopter . . . the first helicopter of course, just ready to take off for the assault, the battalion chaplain came down the line of helicopters, wishing us luck and making the sign of the cross. I nearly fainted. I am sure the chaplain thought he would be a comfort to us but it looked to me as though he was administering the last rites ahead of time, and I figured command had already written us off as lost.[226]

A long time ago I heard a story about two boys, one Catholic and one Baptist. On different Sundays they went to each other's church to see what it was like in the other's service. At his church, the Catholic boy explained all about the procession, the priest's vestments, the Eucharist, and various statues and symbols around the sanctuary. At the Baptist service, there wasn't that much to explain, until the preacher took out his pocket watch with a small flourish and placed it conspicuously on the podium in front of him. The Catholic boy asked, *"What does that mean?"* His friend replied, *"Not a darned thing!"*

> "Yet a time is coming and has now come when the true worshipers will worship the Father in spirit and truth, for they are the kind of worshipers the Father seeks. God is spirit, and his worshipers must worship in spirit and in truth." ~John 4:23, 24

Both of these stories relate in some degree to the place of ritual in religious worship. They serve as reminders that the *form* of worship is relatively unimportant compared with what is in our hearts *while* we worship. Our Savior came into the world to give each of us a clear path to the Father. Through Jesus we can approach God directly and worship him as he deserves, with our whole being.

Perspective

PRIVATE FIRST CLASS Mike Peugh served in Vietnam with the Reconnaissance Platoon of the 1st Battalion, 22nd Infantry. While on patrol he frequently glanced up longingly at the birds soaring high above, remembering his time before the war as a licensed glider pilot. At the time, he commented wistfully:

(National Archives)

> *I often wish I had a sailplane here with me now, because these hills and valleys are just great for soaring. Why, I bet you could stay up all day in these updrafts.*[227]

I think every man serving in combat has fantasies of soaring above and away from the dirt and danger. In Vietnam, we all occasionally went somewhere by helicopter, and, for brief moments, had this amazing new perspective on the war and the country where we were fighting. For those moments, we could feel the cool air and see magnificent vistas stretching out below—lush, jungle-covered mountains, winding rivers, and neatly arrayed farmlands. It was a stark contrast to the foot soldier's daily reality of sweat, dirt, insects, and fear.

Many times our ordinary days take on some of the soldier's drudgery. Like a patrol through elephant grass, we suffer the little cuts, the tedious toil, and unending frustration. We become consumed with our problems and all the apparent obstacles to our goals and happiness. There are days when we desperately need a new perspective.

Fortunately, it isn't difficult. It only takes a moment in prayer to lift ourselves out of any quagmire. When we make this connection with our heavenly Father, he gives us a glimpse of his eternal perspective. From his point of view, our problems shrink into insignificance. Often, our perceived obstacles can finally be seen for what they are—part of his plan to shape us or to move us in a new direction. Through prayer we can feel the cool, clear air and the peace that only comes with a heavenly perspective.

> Those who hope in the Lord will renew their strength. They will soar on wings like eagles; they will run and not grow weary, they will walk and not be faint.
> ~Isaiah 40:31

Sleeping on Watch

IT WAS a most unusual wake-up call. Harold Hankins and Gary Woods, 4th Division soldiers, were leading an early morning patrol outside the wire of their combat base when they heard a groaning sound coming from a nearby thicket. They stopped the patrol and advanced cautiously to investigate. To their amazement, they found an NVA soldier, alone and fast asleep. *"We almost walked right on him,"* said Woods, *"but there he was sleeping like a baby and snoring like a train in a tunnel. After I shook him, he opened his eyes, yawned, and suddenly realized that he woke up in the wrong Army."*[228]

Since the new prisoner was immediately evacuated to the rear, the soldiers never learned why he was at the spot where he was captured. They guessed he was on a patrol also and posted on watch during the night. For some reason his unit had to pull out quickly without an accurate head count. For whatever reason, he went to sleep and was left behind.

> "Could you men not keep watch with me for one hour?" he asked Peter. "Watch and pray so that you will not fall into temptation. The spirit is willing, but the body is weak."
> ~Matthew 26:40, 41

On another long night and important occasion, Jesus kept watch and asked several of his disciples to stay awake with him. They were in the Garden of Gethsemane on the night of his betrayal, and his heart was heavy. After praying for a while, he found them sleeping and expressed his disappointment:

Jesus' admonition to his disciples is equally applicable to each of us every day. When we sleep, we lose consciousness. This is a dangerous condition when it occurs spiritually. Our Lord wants us to watch with him against the evils of the world and to be constantly prepared to resist. To do that, we have to stay awake and keep our eyes on him.

Pursue Your Dream

IN JANUARY 1968 Michael Naranjo was on patrol in the Mekong Delta with A Company, 9th Infantry. When his unit came under intense enemy fire, he found himself facedown in a muddy depression with his rifle in one hand and a grenade in the other. As he was about to pull the pin on his own grenade, an enemy grenade landed by his side. His rifle absorbed some of the impact, but the explosion badly damaged his right hand and left him totally blind.

> God is not unjust; he will not forget your work and the love you have shown him . . . We want each of you to show this same diligence to the very end, in order to make your hope sure. We do not want you to become lazy, but to imitate those who through faith and patience inherit what has been promised.
> ~Hebrews 6:10–12

Before the war, Naranjo had been an aspiring sculptor from Taos, New Mexico. As he lay in his hospital bed in Japan, he had to fight being discouraged as others told him he wouldn't sculpt again. Defiantly, he fashioned a crude figure from touch while still in his hospital bed. Since then, he has persevered with the same attitude to become a famous artist, working mainly in bronze to capture images of his Indian heritage. His pieces decorate many public buildings, and he has met with Richard Nixon, Bill Clinton, and Pope John Paul II. Trying to explain how he does what he does, he said, *"What I touch is what I see. Sculpting is putting together a puzzle with those thousands of touches. I don't know how it is done."*[229]

Michael Naranjo's story is inspiring on many levels. It shows that any person is capable of great accomplishments when they love what they are doing and persevere at it. More importantly, it puts our own obstacles in perspective. Most of us are too easily discouraged from worthwhile efforts because of self-imposed limitations. We forget that God can provide the resources we need if we are willing to make the effort. A blind sculptor inspires us to look beyond our obstacles. He tells other disabled veterans and each of us, "Don't let anyone tell you what goals you can set. Pursue your dreams."[230]

Ah, but a man's reach should exceed his grasp, or what's a heaven for?
–Robert Browning

Near Misses

THE FIREFIGHT was intense. Private First Class Larry Thorpe was standing in chest-high elephant grass, firing his weapon as fast as he could spot enemy muzzle flashes. When something hit him in the back, he thought someone had thrown a rock at him. He was momentarily annoyed but didn't pay much attention to it. A few seconds later, he squatted down to reload his rifle and noticed an enemy

(National Archives)

grenade on the ground between his feet. *"I didn't know what to do,"* he exclaimed, *"then it dawned on me what had hit me in the back. I didn't know whether to laugh or run."*[231] In the next instant, running seemed the better option, and Thorpe sprinted away from the site of his near catastrophe. He commented later, *"All I can say is I'm lucky it was a dud. Somebody must be looking after me."*[232]

We have all had our near misses—if not in combat, then on the highway or somewhere else. We can look at these events in different ways. First, there is almost always a logical explanation for how we avoided the potential catastrophe. Our quick reaction may have saved us from the accident, or the "odds" were just on our side.

The second possibility is that there really is "somebody looking after me." As a skeptic for most of my adult life, I was unable to concede the existence of a God so involved in the world. Now, however, I can offer my conviction that God has indeed protected me many times during my life. I thank him every day for this protection and try to keep my efforts in life focused on being worthy of his favor. There may be logical explanations for most events, but there are also mysteries we will

> Then Jesus said, "Did I not tell you that if you believed, you would see the glory of God?"
> ~John 11:40

never understand. Life is infinitely more rewarding when we have faith that God is in control and is capable of performing miracles that can change our lives.

Escaping Faith

L IKE EVERY soldier in a line unit, Joe Cardone counted down the days on his tour. As he approached his last week in country, word came down the chain of command: one more operation. The tension built as he faced this last hurdle to his long-awaited freedom and safety. On the night before going into the field, he wrote a moving letter home, directing most of his thoughts to God:

> *Please God, stay with me, help me never to forget that you are here with me—that there is always a chance—always hope and somehow, Dear Lord, to overcome the things that oppress us and the changes that have taken place. Never let me forget, God, and never let me go through this again.*
>
> *I want life. I want to live no matter what I must face. Where there is life, God, there is hope and a chance for things to get better. Give me the time and my life, God. Give me the chance and stay with me. That's all I ask. It's a big request. But when you realize what the meaning of this request is, it can only mean it is sacred and everyone deserves that chance. Please bring me home alive.*
>
> *Thank you, God, for everything you have done and for making my chances look good. And I know if I keep my escaping faith, I will make it.*[233]

Most of us can identify only too well with the phrase *"escaping faith."* It is an acknowledgement of those times we drift away from God, become consumed by our own concerns, and suddenly realize we have isolated ourselves from the One we need most. At those times we wonder whether we have faith or not. This uncertainty was expressed exactly by a desperate father who came to Jesus, entreating him to purge an evil spirit from his son:

> Jesus asked the boy's father, "How long has he been like this?"
>
> "From childhood," he answered. "It has often thrown him into fire or water to kill him. But if you can do anything, take pity on us and help us."
>
> "'If you can'?" said Jesus. "Everything is possible for him who believes."
>
> Immediately the boy's father exclaimed, "I do believe; help me overcome my unbelief!" ~Mark 9:21–24

Like this worried father, most of us have an imperfect faith and need to pray every day: *"Lord, help me stay close to you. Help me to continually resolve my doubts. Help me overcome my unbelief."*

The Enemy

WHEN YOU go to war there is an enemy. Mine was the North Vietnamese soldier. He was a fleeting figure on the battlefield, and I mostly knew him by the ballistic crack of his bullets and the concussion of his mortar rounds. I also knew him to be a smart, well-disciplined, and tenacious fighter never easily defeated.

(National Archives)

My perspective changed forever on the day I met him up close. The bloody and lifeless body of this NVA soldier was already rigid as I searched his pockets for documents and maps. Instead of anything with intelligence value, I found a photograph of his wife and children. My faceless enemy had a family.

I've never forgotten that photograph and the abrupt realization that my avowed enemy also had hopes and dreams of his own. I have since come to believe strongly that the veterans of my war, and any war, have much in common with their "enemy" veterans. Many have shed their blood, and all have paid a great price in service to the cause for which they were called to fight. Another veteran perceived these bonds and wrote an appeal to all warriors:

> We once prepared for battle, and served our causes as best we could.
> Yet our task is not complete until we have
>   acknowledged one another.
> Oh warrior, my brother, my sister, I offer to
>   you the following:
> I will honor your experience of service, recognizing that while your cause may not be mine, the terrors of war bind us together.[234]

Forgiveness and reconciliation start with the realization we have more uniting us than dividing us. This holds true for all who have fought or struggled with others in any arena, whether war, business, church, or family. Paul's instructions and example on this point are unequivocal.

Therefore, as God's chosen people, holy and dearly loved, clothe yourselves with compassion, kindness, humility, gentleness and patience. Bear with each other and forgive whatever grievances you may have against one another. Forgive as the Lord forgave you.
~Colossians 3:12, 13

Desperate

THE POINT man was about two hundred meters ahead of the patrol when an enemy grenade landed at his feet. The explosion sent him flying into the air and sent pain shooting through his body. Struggling to his feet, he was hit twice by rifle bullets and knocked down again. As he lay helpless on the trail, a Viet Cong soldier ran up and bayoneted him in the stomach, leaving him for dead.

> Keep me safe, O God, for in you I take refuge. I said to the LORD, "You are my Lord; apart from you I have no good thing."
> ~Psalm 16:1, 2

Roger Helle remembered nothing after this traumatic event until he woke up in a Da Nang hospital. As he drifted in and out of consciousness, struggling to live, he remembered saying aloud, *"God—if there really is a God—if you let me live, I'll do anything you want."*[235]

It took eleven months of surgery and rehabilitation, but Helle did live to walk out of the hospital and back into civilian life. Unfortunately, he was plagued with unhealed psychological wounds causing horrible nightmares, flashbacks, and excessive drinking. He became more and more desperate as he seemed on a path to losing everything. Finally, Helle remembered his conversation with God in that Da Nang hospital bed years before. He and his wife realized this was the only hope they had left:

> *One night, without fanfare or big announcements, we knelt together and cried out to God for help. We made a pact, a commitment, to live according to the Bible—our marriage, our jobs, everything we did. My life changed dramatically. Our marriage was restored. I experienced a peace and contentment I never knew before. I found the answer to my problems through Jesus Christ.*[236]

Roger Helle concluded a moving testimony with a final word directly to other veterans: *"If you are battling with any problems you think relate to Vietnam, I know Christ can help you, too."*[237]

Friendship

JOHN BLEHM was a sergeant when he joined the 1st Cavalry Division in 1969, and had been warned about the danger of making friends in a combat zone. Even so, he gradually got to know one man in particular in his squad named Lonnie Davis. During several firefights they had helped each other out and then shared a lot about themselves in conversation during quieter times. The day came when Blehm had to send his friend out on an ambush with another squad

> Two are better than one, because they have a good return for their work: If one falls down, his friend can help him up. But pity the man who falls and has no one to help him up!
> ~Ecclesiastes 4:9, 10

that was short a man. A few hours later, he learned that Davis had been killed by enemy gunfire. His thoughts about his friend and friendship in general were thought-provoking:

Here was another first, as I would later come to think of it. The loss of my first "best friend in Vietnam" was a moment that was destined to remain with me, not only throughout the war, but for all the days that followed. I thought of the warnings we had all been given, the warnings against forming any close attachments. How was this possible? I wondered. Knowing we might never see our loved ones again made it necessary, even vital, to fabricate a family of sorts in this strange and alien land. Man was not designed for a solitary life. It was senseless to expect us to suddenly adopt that manner of existence, particularly when we were forced to rely upon one another for survival. How was it possible to make such demands, and then turn away coldly from the very ones who had covered our backs? No, it wasn't possible.[238]

This is a strong reminder we are not meant to be alone in life, especially during times of great stress. Christians understand this completely. We are not designed for a solitary life. We rely on other believers for encouragement and support, just as they rely on us. These relationships are vital to our spiritual well-being and have to be nurtured carefully. There may be times when we need to be alone with God or by ourselves in the world, but most of the time we need to be firmly positioned in the midst of the body of Christ. Our brothers and sisters in Christ are there to lift us up and watch our backs.

The Dead Are with Me

HE WOULD never forget April 27. On that day in 1969 John Blehm was ordered to lead his squad on a mission to rescue wounded soldiers caught in a vicious U-shaped ambush. He repeatedly exposed himself to intense automatic weapons fire as he moved around the battlefield directing the evacuation. Painfully wounded himself, he continued the mission until all the wounded were treated and medevacked. For his actions

The righteous perish, and no one ponders it in his heart; devout men are taken away, and no one understands that the righteous are taken away to be spared from evil. ~Isaiah 57:1

on that day Sergeant Blehm received the Bronze Star for heroism in ground combat. Although cited for bravery, he considered his primary motivation at the time to be anger: *"Waves of grief, sorrow, pain, fear, and anger suddenly converged into a single emotion that had no name. Anger was fuel."*[239]

This rage over random death and the loss of comrades would haunt Blehm long after the war and would resurface in many inappropriate behaviors and failed relationships—until a day thirty years later. On that day he was driving alone, when he had an unexpected and unforgettable conversation with God. When Blehm asked the question that had plagued him for so long, a clear and unmistakable voice gave him the answer:

"That day I should have been killed three times in a matter of hours and other people were killed that day. Those guys were my buddies and they didn't deserve to die. And I don't deserve to live with the guilt I've been carrying ever since. So, where's the sense in any of it?"

"The dead are with me in a better place," the voice responded calmly.

"But you took the wrong ones!" I blatantly insisted, to Someone or no one at all. *"We've got good guys and bad guys here, and it was the good ones you took! It simply wasn't fair."*

"Wasn't it? But the good ones don't need another chance to redeem themselves."[240]

Blehm stopped his car after this exchange, shivering with cold. He wasn't sure what had happened. He had talked *at* God in many tense situations and had even made promises to him. His overriding feeling after this "conversation" was that God was somehow interested in those promises. Maybe he still had a job to do. John Blehm's long recovery from debilitating wartime anger issues had begun.

Unconditional Surrender

DESPITE HIS best efforts, John Blehm could not get his life on an even keel. He went from job to job and marriage to marriage. He was away from home a lot, which was about the only time he didn't argue with his wife. Plagued by alcoholism, he attended Alcoholics Anonymous meetings irregularly. Somehow, he knew he had unfinished business with God, but couldn't bring himself to "face the consequences":

> In a desert land he found him, in a barren and howling waste. He shielded him and cared for him; he guarded him as the apple of his eye, like an eagle that stirs up its nest and hovers over its young, that spreads its wings to catch them and carries them on its pinions. The LORD alone led him.
> ~Deuteronomy 32:10–12

> *I did what I could for myself, but I still couldn't face God. I knew I owed Him my life, but all I could think about was all of my friends who had died. Whatever I had promised God while in the throes of my fox-hole conversion seemed like a whole lot of mindless chatter now. And yet I had said things, made certain promises, and I expected to be held accountable.*
>
> *Throughout that time I went to church, but I also changed churches several times. I think I was probably looking for one that didn't place so much emphasis on certain Scriptures like: "He who lives by the sword shall die by the sword." The only problem was, those that were moving away from the Scriptures didn't seem to have much of anything to say. At least nothing I could put my finger on. I guess I wanted something to put my finger on, without having God put His finger on me.*
>
> *I was still some distance away from "unconditional surrender," but I was beginning to consider it as an option.*[241]

Having come to faith very late in my own life, I very much identify with another veteran's feelings of being pursued by God. He places within us that void only he can fill, and then, in his love for us, patiently intrudes on our conscience and patiently waits for our response. A poet described him aptly as the "Hound of Heaven," writing:

> *Is my gloom, after all,*
> *Shade of His hand, outstretched caressingly?*
> *"Ah, fondest, blindest, weakest,*
> *I am He Whom thou seekest!*[242]

Hill top chapel service north of the Rockpile (U. S. Marine Corps)

Marines boarding a CH 53 helicopter. (U. S. Marine Corps)

Better Than Counselors

AFTER YEARS of broken marriages, mood swings, medication, and counseling, John Blehm began to turn back to the one Source of help he had avoided most of his life. He found a church and a Bible and began seeking a better understanding of God. On his pastor's advice he read first through Proverbs and Psalms, and slowly began to notice a difference in himself. He began to learn that God knew him and understood what was happening in his life. As he explained:

> *I soon realized this was working and much better than the counselors and medication I had been taking. I felt like I had a direct line to God so I prayed more and more and I went to places where I could hear more people praise and pray to God. I have learned that the more time I spend with God learning His Word and ways, the better life goes for me.*[243]

As Blehm's relationship with God grew stronger, the events of his life finally began to take on a meaning he could grasp. He understood that his past suffering had been necessary to give him credibility in proclaiming a message of love and hope to others. His message continues to inspire veterans and people from all walks of life wrestling with a trauma from the past:

> *Don't give up; don't think your life is over because of what you've experienced. You can always call on God, too. If you'll go to God and ask for peace and restoration he will give it to you and you will know when it happens because you will feel like the whole world has just been lifted off your shoulders. Ask God what he has for you to do and you will be surprised at the doors that will open to help you do God's will and perhaps what you have been through and survived will be your tool to help others before something bad happens to them.*[244]

"Ah, Sovereign LORD," I said, "I do not know how to speak; I am only a child." But the LORD said to me, "Do not say, 'I am only a child.' You must go to everyone I send you to and say whatever I command you. Do not be afraid of them, for I am with you and will rescue you," declares the LORD.
~Jeremiah 1:6–8

Taking Charge

SERGEANT Tom Robison had completed more than thirty patrols deep in enemy territory and was near the end of his combat tour in Vietnam. He volunteered for one last patrol to help the new team leader learn the ropes. It would prove to be a fateful mission.

Sgt. Tom Robison

As Robison's patrol was moving to an observation post southeast of Chu Lai, the man ahead of him tripped a land mine and was killed instantly. Robison and one other man were wounded severely. In the explosion he lost his left leg completely and suffered multiple fractures to the other. He was blinded in one eye and riddled with shrapnel. As he was evacuated, covered with blood, no one expected him to live.

The ordeal that followed for this young man is almost incomprehensible. In the first ten weeks he endured twenty surgeries. Months later he started an even more painful therapy regimen to learn to walk with a prosthetic leg. Two sessions per week were prescribed, but he worked every day in spite of the pain. Eighteen months after being wounded, he walked out of the hospital on his own.

Never admitting he was handicapped, Robison left the Army, got married, finished college, and went to law school. He has since led a distinguished career in court administration and juvenile justice, helping countless young men and women overcome legal problems. He has never forgotten the ordeal that shaped his life, and has one overriding lesson to share with others facing rehabilitation from physical or mental wounds. He states emphatically, *"You have to take charge of your own recovery."*[245] The will to survive and to recover rests with the individual alone. Without that will, Robison knows he would not have even survived his wounds, much less ever walked again.

> Brothers, as an example of patience in the face of suffering, take the prophets who spoke in the name of the Lord. As you know, we consider blessed those who have persevered.
> ~James 5:10, 11

The Vision

JIMMY BARBOUR was killed on August 27, 1968, near Cu Chi, South Vietnam, while serving with the 101st Airborne Division. He was a good soldier and always one to give encouragement to those around him. His loss was a blow to his many friends in the unit.

His loss was also a blow to his family, particularly his mother. Evelyn Barbour had become pregnant with Jimmy twenty years before, after being told by doctors she would never have children. His birth was the happiest day of her life. Shortly afterward, however, she had the strangest experience of her life. While she was holding and rocking her new baby, she had a vision. A robed figure she believed to be Jesus appeared before her and said, "Love him. He will not live to be twenty-one."[246]

She never had a vision before this or after, and it was an unnerving experience she wouldn't forget. When her son left for Vietnam at age twenty, she was physically sick. On that day, Jimmy said to her, *"Mom, I have a feeling I won't be coming back. While I've got the opportunity, I want to tell you I'm right with God."*[247]

We don't know the meaning of this story. Skeptics would certainly write off this woman's vision as a hallucination. Even believers might be doubtful. We only know for sure that visions seemed to be one of God's preferred ways of communicating with certain people during biblical times. He came in this way to Abraham, Moses, and the prophets. Jesus appeared to Paul, Stephen, and Ananias. The entire book of Revelation is based on the visions of one man, the apostle John.

We can only speculate about God's purpose in revealing himself to Evelyn Barbour in this unusual way. Perhaps he meant to prepare her for a tragedy she would not have been able to handle without this warning. We do know she was able to pray after losing her son, thanking God for the years she had Jimmy.

> "'In the last days, God says, I will pour out my Spirit on all people. Your sons and daughters will prophesy, your young men will see visions, your old men will dream dreams. And everyone who calls on the name of the Lord will be saved.'"
> ~Acts 2:17, 21

The Enemy Within

WORKING IN the sparsely populated mountains of the Northern I Corps zone along the DMZ, my troops seldom encountered civilians. That was not the case in many other areas, as one soldier observed:

In the haphazardly laid out paddies below us, farmers and their families were working industriously in their fields, trying to produce a crop while seeming to ignore the war swirling around them. I had thought the country through which we moved would be vacant of people except those in groups barricaded in their villages. Instead, the Vietnamese were going about their everyday duties, singly or in groups, ignoring us as if we weren't really there, and only taking notice when we passed too close for them to ignore.[248]

The Vietnamese people, in spite of the war, tried to carry on with their lives—hoping not to alienate anyone. Unfortunately, the Viet Cong had established a presence in many areas and succeeded in recruiting locals into their ranks. They were then able to confiscate food and supplies, and intimidate others into acting as spies and lookouts. This made life extremely difficult for the American troops operating in these areas. To prevent harm to innocent civilians, the rules of engagement were strict. Before you could fire, you had to see weapons or be fired upon first. Friend and foe dressed alike and were practically indistinguishable.

We have the same problem in our spiritual lives with an enemy even more difficult to detect. Satan doesn't wear a uniform, either. He puts ordinary people or attractions in our path that lead us in the wrong direction. He speaks to us through our acquaintances with the wrong advice. He even enters our minds surreptitiously to rationalize behavior we would normally know to be wrong. He is far too cunning for us to resist on our own. We need every resource of our faith to identify and defeat this enemy. We must enfold ourselves in the body of Christ and constantly seek understanding of right and wrong through prayer and the Holy Scripture.

I am afraid that just as Eve was deceived by the serpent's cunning, your minds may somehow be led astray from your sincere and pure devotion to Christ . . . For such men are false apostles, deceitful workmen, masquerading as apostles of Christ. And no wonder, for Satan himself masquerades as an angel of light.
~2 Corinthians 11:3, 13, 14

212

Healing

CHARLES WHITFIELD was a platoon sergeant with Golf Company, 1st Battalion, 9th Marines, operating south of the DMZ near Cua Viet in early 1968. Late one afternoon, after a long, hot day moving through hostile territory, his platoon was ordered to dig in on the edge of a large rice paddy. While bent over working with his entrenching tool, a sniper's bullet grazed Whitfield's spine and struck the back of his head, knocking him to the ground. Amazed he was still alive, a corpsman dressed his wounds and called for an immediate medevac. It was the beginning of a long journey home for the wounded Marine.

> "'I saw the Lord always before me. Because he is at my right hand, I will not be shaken. Therefore my heart is glad and my tongue rejoices; my body also will live in hope.'"
> ~Acts 2:25, 26

After his recovery, Whitfield was left with seriously impaired vision. To read, he had to look obliquely at the page, using his peripheral vision. It was a slow and tedious process. In spite of this disability, and against his doctors' advice, Whitfield enrolled in college as soon as he was physically able. It wouldn't be easy for him, but he was determined to get on with his life. The turning point in his recovery came when he was temporarily assigned to help in a ward full of combat veteran amputees:

> Ambulatory patients like me helped feed and care for them. I realized how difficult it was gonna be for them, that the severity of their wounds was incredible. And then I realized how insignificant my own injury was. Sure, I had a big hole in my head, I had brain damage, eyes that were damaged, but I had my arms, both legs. I could walk, feed myself. After that, I never considered my injury being very much at all.[249]

A favorite expression of my wife's mother, Eleanor, was, *"I felt sorry for myself that I had no shoes, until I met a man that had no feet."* There is always something we can be thankful for. This positive outlook is the key to a healthy recovery from any wound, whether physical or emotional. Jesus Christ is the sure Source of this kind of optimism. Regardless of our wounds, he gives us the capacity for a joyful heart and the sure path to healing.

The Medals

THE WORD spread quickly by e-mail. Sergeant Joseph Harris' medals were being auctioned off on eBay. He had been a trooper with the 11th Armored Cavalry Regiment in Vietnam and was killed in action. When Otis Carey, a fellow 11th Cavalry veteran, heard the news and looked at the auction, he had a strange feeling: *"It was to me like the time when we returned from Nam and nobody cared. It was like someone was reaching down into this trooper's honored grave just to make a buck."*[250]

Purple Heart medal (U. S. Govt.)

Carey knew he had to do something. He first wanted to find out why these treasured memorabilia were being auctioned off. When he talked to Sergeant Harris' brother, he learned the medals had fallen into the hands of a step-father who had died and left everything to another relative who obviously had no idea of their significance.

Carey then started raising money to buy back the medals for the family. A flurry of e-mails went back and forth among other veterans and pledges were gathered. Carey and many other ex-troopers also contacted the seller, who finally discontinued the auction and agreed to turn over the medals to the family. Sergeant Joseph Harris' Bronze Star, Purple Heart, and Vietnam Service medals finally returned home where they belonged.

Since the time of the Roman legions, medals have been awarded in recognition of military service and heroism. They deserve an honored place in any family. Recognition is important to each of us in this life and in the next. Someday we will meet our Savior face-to-face, hoping we have done something to earn a word of praise from the One who deserves so much praise from us.

> "For the Son of Man is going to come in his Father's glory with his angels, and then he will reward each person according to what he has done." ~Matthew 16:27

Ann Margaret entertains troops (National Archives)

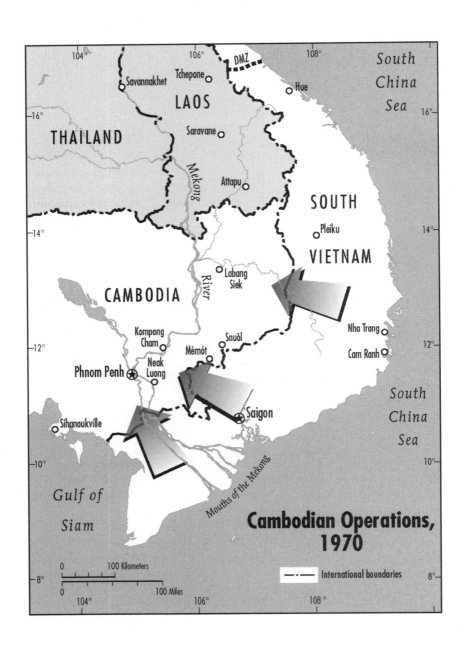

South
China
Sea

104°   106°   DMZ   108°

Savannakhet   Tchepone

LAOS   Hue

16°   16°

THAILAND   Saravane

Mekong   Attapu

14°   SOUTH   14°

Pleiku

VIETNAM

CAMBODIA   Labang
Siek

River

Kompong
Cham   Snuŏl   Nha Trang

12°   Mémót   Cam Ranh   12°

Phnom Penh   Neak
Luong   Saigon   South
China
Sea

Sihanoukville

10°   10°

Gulf of
Siam   Mouths of the Mekong

**Cambodian Operations,
1970**

0   100 Kilometers

0   100 Miles   International boundaries

8°   8°

104°   106°   108°

VIETNAMIZATION

RICHARD NIXON was elected president in 1968, pledging he had a plan to end the war in Vietnam. His basic approach was to reduce the presence of American troops, while expanding the capacity of South Vietnam to defend itself, a program eventually termed "Vietnamization." General Abrams agreed with the necessity of this approach, but came into conflict on questions of how to leave and what to leave behind. Although Nixon had ruled out a unilateral withdrawal, his new secretary of defense, Melvin Laird, went to the war zone in March 1969 to discuss U. S. troop withdrawals. The president announced soon afterward 25,000 U.S. troops would leave the country by August. By year-end 65,000 were withdrawn, and the next year 140,000.

The new administration inherited President Johnson's bombing halt over North Vietnam and the resulting buildup of enemy troops and materiel north of the DMZ, in Laos, and in Cambodia. Instead of reciprocal "restraint," the North Vietnamese launched their biggest offensive until then in early 1969 with almost one-third more separate attacks than the Tet Offensive of the year before. The attacks, however, were short-lived and costly to the Communists. The aim seemed to be a propaganda effect more than success on the battlefield. This calculation proved accurate, as the antiwar effort at home accelerated. The Nixon administration did not move to rescind the bombing halt, fearing further violence on the home front. He later characterized this as "my biggest mistake as President."[251] He said, "We should have taken on the doves right then—started bombing and mining the harbors. The war would have been over in 1970."[252]

In March 1970 the Lon Nol government took control of Cambodia and for the first time closed the port of Sihanoukville (now Kampong Saom) to the North Vietnamese, eliminating one of their most important arteries of supply into South Vietnam. Lon Nol also demanded withdrawal of North Vietnamese forces from his country, dispelling the subterfuge that none had ever been present.

In a highly controversial decision, President Nixon finally authorized a limited invasion of Cambodia in April 1970. Over 50,000 U. S. and South Vietnamese troops struck across the border at fourteen enemy base areas. This operation yielded a huge treasure of captured documents, cryptographic material, rice, weapons, and ammunition. The commanding general of the 1st Cavalry Division told his men they had captured enough weapons to equip two NVA divisions and enough rice to feed the enemy in their area of operation for a year.[253]

U.S. and South Vietnamese military efforts after the Tet Offensive in 1968 brought about dramatic improvement on all fronts of the war. As U.S. troop withdrawals went on, the South Vietnamese military establishment continued to grow in size and competence. Improvements were achieved across the board, in the Vietnamese Army, Regional Forces, and Popular Forces. Dramatic successes were achieved on the battlefield, as well as the economic and political fronts.

By late 1970 the Vietnam War was largely won from the perspective of the U.S. military establishment. The internal threat from subversion and guerilla action had been largely eliminated. The external threat of invasion had been set back for at least a year. This U.S. military perspective was based on three key assumptions: continued U.S. financial aid, logistical support, and renewed use of U.S. airpower in the event of violations to future agreements. Even though South Vietnamese forces would successfully defeat the next invasion in 1972 on the ground, these commitments would eventually be ignored.

The Forward Observer

AN ARTILLERY unit combines men, vehicles, and big guns into a force capable of delivering devastating firepower in support of troops engaged with the enemy. The firing battery, the fire direction center, and all the supporting elements of the artillery unit operate in close proximity—all except one man: the FO. The FO is the man on the ground with the infantry unit, charged with coordinating the artillery fire. As one officer charged with training this highly skilled position explained:

> *The FO is essentially the "eyes" of the artillery. The responsibilities of the FO are immense, and a great amount of skill is needed to perform the job. He cannot rely on other people for assistance. One mistake can be very costly to friendly troops. The final outcome, the success or failure of the mission, can depend on the actions and proficiency of one man on the battlefield—the forward observer.*[254]

In Vietnam I was often impressed with the critical role played by a few particular men. Sometimes an entire battalion in the field was dependent on one point man leading the column into enemy territory. An artillery battery had to rely on one FO to find the targets and direct the fire. The point men and the FOs have been called the "tip of the spear" as the men at the focal point of the action.

It is useful for the leader of any organization to pay special attention to those at the critical positions. The checkout clerks, the front-desk personnel, and the salesmen are the ones who meet the public and form the relationships vital to the success of every business. In the church, we often think of the minister in this role and overlook the critically important role of the laypeople in the church. Laypeople are the ones who get to know the visitors and who are active in the world outside the church where the gospel message needs to be taken. Every member is an ambassador of Christ, at the tip of God's great spear.

> We will in all things grow up into him who is the Head, that is, Christ. From him the whole body, joined and held together by every supporting ligament, grows and builds itself up in love, as each part does its work
> ~Ephesians 4:15, 16

One More Look

IT SEEMED like another interminable and uneventful night along the perimeter of the 11th Infantry Brigade base camp. Sergeant James Bond stood his tedious watch alone through the dark night. He had to constantly fight the urge to close his eyes. Finally, the luminous dial on his watch told him it was almost 3:00 a.m. and time to wake up his relief.

> Jesus answered, "I tell you, not seven times, but seventy-seven times."
> ~Matthew 18:22

In spite of his fatigue, he decided it might be a good idea to take one more look around. It was a good thing he did. He said, *"At first, I wasn't sure, then I saw them. There were three men trying to get through the wire. I dropped an M-79 round on them, and it looked like I got them."*[255] Soon, however, other shapes started coming out of the darkness and enemy mortar fire began falling on the camp. Fortunately, Sergeant Bond's entire unit was awake by then, firing everything available to repulse the attack.

This story is a great reminder about the value of extra effort. By going a little beyond what was expected, this man saved his unit and himself from a devastating attack.

We know extra effort pays off in many areas of life. It is the difference between a good athlete and a great one, between a worker going through the motions and a true professional, between an acquaintance and a friend. The apostle Peter once asked Jesus what kind of effort he should make to reconcile with a brother who had harmed him. Jesus' answer was astonishing and went beyond anything Peter expected. The kind of "extra effort" Jesus calls for is great and even beyond what we within ourselves can manage. Only with him in our hearts will we ever approach the level of effort *he* gives and expects *us* to give in return.

The Poor Suckers

IN A rare display of empathy, a recon Marine expressed how sorry he felt for the "grunts" in the line infantry units:

> *The poor suckers on the line moved first here and dug in, then moved there, slogging through rice paddies and bamboo and villes with hostile natives . . . After that, they got up and moved again to a place that looked exactly like the last place, but wasn't, and dug in again. All the time the sun baked their brains during the day and rains followed in the evening and made them stiff and wet and irritable and filled up their sleeping holes . . . Foot rot and crotch rot and fungi and parasites gnawed them down to moldered skin and bones. Leeches sucked what blood remained.*[256]

This graphic portrait of the grunt is pretty accurate. From the infantryman's perspective, however, the recon trooper's life seemed to have its own distasteful aspects. Patrolling deep in enemy territory with only a radio for a lifeline didn't seem like such an attractive way to live, either. Ironically, I have also heard the opposite refrain from both infantry and recon troops, complaining about how much *better* the others had it than themselves.

> "I want to give the man who was hired last the same as I gave you. Don't I have the right to do what I want with my own money? Or are you envious because I am generous? ~Matthew 20:14, 15

We all like to compare ourselves with others, sometimes with feelings of envy and sometimes superiority. Either way it is all too human to focus on these differences and the inequities of life in general. Jesus addressed this tendency in his parable about the landowner who hired workers at intervals during the day and then paid them all the same wage when the day was done. When the workers who came early complained about unfairness, he reprimanded them for failing to understand his generosity.

In this story Jesus was illustrating God's generosity in saving sinners who come to him at the "end of the day." When a person is saved later in life, this should only bring joy to the heart of a lifelong Christian. This parable also addresses envy in general and conveys the pointed message telling us we should be thankful for what we have. We are blessed that God's generosity falls like rain on an undeserving world.

221

Extraordinary Heroism

B Y MID-1971 the Khe Sanh combat base had been abandoned, and the NVA had extended the Ho Chi Minh trail network into the northwest corner of Vietnam. As enemy forces increased in the area, the decision was made to send in a patrol to gather more information. A small Special Forces unit designated Recon Team Kansas, led by a young Midwesterner named Loren Hagen, was selected for the job. Hagen and his men were inserted into an abandoned fire base by helicopter at last light on August 6. Early the next morning the soldiers found themselves surrounded and under attack by an NVA regiment. Lieutenant Hagen courageously led his men in defense of their tenuous position and, at one point, left his covered location to help wounded teammates. He was killed in the attempt. His heroic actions are vividly described in the citation for his Medal of Honor:

Medal of Honor
(U. S. Govt.)

After observing an enemy rocket make a direct hit on and destroy one of the team's bunkers, 1st Lt. Hagen moved toward the wrecked bunker in search for team members despite the fact that the enemy force now controlled the bunker area. With total disregard for his own personal safety, he crawled through the enemy fire while returning small-arms fire upon the enemy force. Undaunted by the enemy rockets and grenades impacting all around him, 1st Lt. Hagen desperately advanced upon the destroyed bunker until he was fatally wounded by enemy small arms and automatic weapons fire. With complete disregard for his personal safety, 1st Lt. Hagen's courageous gallantry, extraordinary heroism, and intrepidity above and beyond the call of duty, at the cost of his own life, were in keeping with the highest traditions of the military service and reflect great credit upon him and the U.S. Army.[257]

First Lieutenant Loren Hagen's selfless service and ultimate sacrifice live on in the hearts of the men he saved and continue to inspire leaders with the depth of one officer's commitment to his men and his duty.

> I eagerly expect and hope that I will in no way be ashamed, but will have sufficient courage so that now as always Christ will be exalted in my body, whether by life or by death. ~Philippians 1:20

Where's the New Guy?

THE SOLDIER arrived in Vietnam on Easter Sunday and began the tedious routine of in-processing. From Bien Hoa he was bused to Long Binh for assignment to a transportation unit. Finally, he arrived at his part of the war in a place called Phuoc Vinh. He soon heard stories about how often the base was hit, adding to his general state of apprehension.

> Each one should use whatever gift he has received to serve others, faithfully administering God's grace in its various forms. If anyone speaks, he should do it as one speaking the very words of God. ~1 Peter 4:10, 11

On the first night at his new base, hardly knowing anyone by name, he sat apart looking at the stars and listening to someone play a guitar. Suddenly, there was a mad scramble, and the cry went up, "*Incoming!*" Following the others, he wound up inside a bunker in pitch darkness. No one made a sound as they all listened to the impacting shells above. The soldier described what happened next:

> Out of the silence and darkness, somebody said, "Where's the new guy?"
> "I'm here," I said.
> That was that, but there was something about that little exchange in the dark that I will never forget as long as I live. That question in the dark was authentically—I don't know what the word is—generous? Caring is too big a word somehow. Generous is enough. That's a lot. That somebody even bothered to think about me. Who the hell was I? This rather quiet, slightly older new guy in clean fatigues, whose boots weren't even red yet. I was amazed.[258]

It is amazing to consider the profound effect of such a simple act. William Wordsworth addressed this phenomenon in a poem with the now-famous line, "*That best part of a good man's life, His little, nameless, unremembered acts of kindness and of love.*"[259] We often don't know the lasting effect of what we say or do, but we can be inspired by the poet and this story that anything done in kindness may not be remembered by the one who does it but will be remembered by others. Sometimes it will be *long* remembered. Think of your own anxiety in any gathering of strangers, or in an unfamiliar place. A gesture of friendship from a stranger means a lot. The effect can be profound when we reach out to someone in an unexpected way. These "*unremembered acts of kindness*" are the way we take God's love for us to the rest of the world. We know from our own experience such acts never go unappreciated.

223

The Bitterest Pang

IT WAS a deeply emotional scene. Fifty soldiers were gathered on a hilltop high in the mountains of Kon Tum province, near the Cambodian border. The view of mountain peaks, jungle valleys, and whitewater streams was spectacular. The wind and the high-altitude air were brisk. In front of the troops a lone M-16 rifle had been planted, bayonet down, in the ground. A helmet rested on the rifle—the symbol of a fallen comrade. For some reason, the words of the famous mathematician-philosopher came to the chaplain's mind as he spoke, *"Pascal once said that the solitude of death was the bitterest pang of humanity."*[260] The young soldiers, most of whom had never heard of Pascal, nodded in silence.

> On this mountain he will destroy the shroud that enfolds all peoples, the sheet that covers all nations; he will swallow up death forever. The Sovereign LORD will wipe away the tears from all faces. ~Isaiah 25:7, 8

From the philosopher's lonely perspective, the end of life would be its most severe trial. Since no one could accompany him on that journey, he anticipated enduring it alone. Fortunately, the chaplain did not stop with this thought. Instead, he began reciting the Twenty-Third Psalm. Line by line, he led the men through the greatest passage of reassurance ever written. Thanks to these verses, we know that the God who promises *"green pastures"* and *"still waters"* will also be with us even in the *"valley of the shadow of death."*

Finally, the chaplain explained to the men in their grief, *"Our heavenly Father is waiting to meet each of us . . . as He has met our fallen comrades of last week."*[261] As tears ran down the cheeks of many, the chaplain struggled to contain his own emotions. The lone rifle and helmet had been placed in symbolic remembrance of not one, but twenty-two, fellow soldiers killed in action a few days before.

Decontamination

MANY MARINES rotating back to the States from Vietnam went through Camp Hansen, Okinawa, where they underwent a process they half-jokingly called "decontamination." Some had just left their units operating along the DMZ and were still wearing the same ragged uniforms and boots they had worn for weeks. One Marine described the scene:

> I remember the tall, thin black Marine standing in front of me. He didn't even have a utility jacket; only a torn white T-shirt that was so yellow and orange you'd have never known it was once white. Another Marine had comm. wire for boot laces. My left knee was hanging out of my trousers, and I looked better than most of those standing around me. So they made us toss our old utilities and boots into a storage room in the barracks.
>
> I'll never forget the thin suffocating cloud of putrid pale red dust coming out of that little room piled high with our no longer proper uniform of the day.[262]

As they left Vietnam, these Marines had to literally "shake the dust from their feet." New uniforms, clean bodies, and haircuts helped restore new attitudes as they processed closer to home. This is a great metaphor for how lives are changed by Jesus Christ. We come to him as veterans of our own battles, with all the dirt and debris we have accumulated during our worldly lives. Through his own divine process of "decontamination," he washes the past away. He gives us fresh uniforms and new attitudes to live changed lives as members of his family.

He saved us, not because of righteous things we had done, but because of his mercy. He saved us through the washing of rebirth and renewal by the Holy Spirit, whom he poured out on us generously through Jesus Christ our Savior, so that, having been justified by his grace, we might become heirs having the hope of eternal life. ~Titus 3:5–7

Time

IN ONE of the most moving passages I have ever read, James Webb described the phenomenon of time as it related to the soldier serving his tour of duty in Vietnam:

*Time, like an ever-flowing stream, bears all its sons away.
They fly forgotten, as a dream dies at the opening day . . .*[263]

It echoed on the church walls in a piece of Hodges'
*memory, some old hymn from a saner portion of his
past. Time was everything. Time kept them there, and
time would let them leave. They were doing time, marking off the days, keeping track religiously of exactly how
long it would be before thirteen months were up and the
insanity ended. And yet the lulls and frenzies of the bush
made it a timeless world. Each day counted as one when
a man marked it off on his calendar, but a day could be
a week, an hour could be a month. An afternoon spent
under fire when a patrol was caught in an open paddy
would age them all a year, tighten their faces until the
eyeballs bulged, make them whine and leave them weak,*

(National
Archives)

*yet when the patrol came back to the company perimeter it had been a
year for them but only an afternoon for the ones who had not been on
the patrol. And when the cruel sun fell below the mountains, it still had
only been a day. All that for a stinking day.*[264]

The "old hymn" mentioned by Webb is "O God, Our Help in Ages Past." It also echoes in my memories of childhood in a small-town Presbyterian church. The hymn is based on Psalm 90, the classic assurance of God's timelessness: *"For a thousand years in your sight are like a day that has just gone by, or like a watch in the night"* (Psalm 90:4). God is not only timeless. He created time and stands outside it. He numbers our days on Earth as he holds and weighs our eternal future in his hand. We come closest to finding wisdom in this life when we learn to make our daily decisions and deal with our problems from this perspective.

> You turn men back to dust, saying, "Return to dust, O sons of men." . . . Teach us to number our days aright, that we may gain a heart of wisdom.
> ~Psalm 90:3, 12

Near-Death Experience

I T WAS one of the strangest incidents of the war. A six-man LRRP of the 101ˢᵗ Airborne Division was set up on a ridgeline overlooking the A Shau Valley, deep in enemy territory. An unusually violent thunderstorm moved in over the ridge and hit the team, gorging sheets of torrential rain and hail. As the team huddled together for protection, a violent explosion suddenly ripped them apart. They had been struck by lightning. A concussion grenade in Larry Chamber's rucksack detonated, sending him flying through the air down the hill. He and several others were knocked unconscious. All suffered from burns, cuts, and bruises, but no one was killed.

> Then God said, "Let us make man in our image, in our likeness . . ." The LORD God formed the man from the dust of the ground and breathed into his nostrils the breath of life.
> ~Genesis 1:26; 2:7

Evacuated to a hospital in Phu Bai, the team debriefed each other on what had happened. At one point, Chambers told his teammate Gary Linderer about an especially strange part of the incident:

After the explosion, it felt like I was in a dream. I felt like my body was torn apart from the blast, but suddenly a brilliant light was everywhere. I moved into the center of the light and hung there, suspended and safe. It was like something supernatural happened! I felt guarded and safe, as if everything was going to be all right. Then, when I realized what was happening, the light disappeared.[265]

When Chambers asked Linderer if he thought he (Chambers) was crazy, his friend replied, *"No, I don't think you are crazy, because I saw the same thing."*[266] They decided not to try explaining this to anyone else at the time.

Near death experiences have been studied extensively by scientists, but have not been explained. Many people resuscitated from life-threatening injuries and surgeries have reported similar experiences: detachment from their bodies, a blinding light, and a peaceful reassurance. I have always considered this phenomenon one more manifestation of the miraculous nature of human consciousness. Scientists have learned much about the natural world, but can still not account for the transcendent nature of the human mind.

I Want That Cross

ONE NIGHT four wounded Marines were brought into the Navy hospital in Da Nang. All were hurt in a land mine explosion, and one was in extremely serious condition. Still conscious, the Marine spotted a silver cross on a shirt collar and reached out from his litter to the man wearing it. *"Padre, hold my hand, will you?"* he said. The chaplain took his hand. *"Are you Catholic or Protestant?"* the boy asked.

"I'm Catholic, Son," the chaplain replied.

"I'm Baptist, but it doesn't make any difference," the wounded man said.

The Marine was then wheeled into the operating room where the surgeons had to remove a badly damaged leg. As he recovered, the chaplain came to visit him every day. The time soon came for the Marine to be flown out to a hospital in the States. During their last visit, the boy made a request: *"Father, I wish you'd give me something."*

"What do you want, Son?"

"I want the cross on your collar. It's the first thing I remember seeing after I was hit."

The chaplain unpinned the cross and put it in the Marine's hand, which he clasped tightly with both of his own.[267]

I have a little "pocket" cross I keep with me often. It serves as a small, physical reminder of my faith. There are times when I also grasp it tightly. These are the times I need the physical touch and assurance Jesus is with me. Sometimes we all need the hard evidence of his promise, *"Never will I leave you; never will I forsake you"* (Hebrews 13:5).

> "And surely I am with you always, to the very end of the age."
> ~Matthew 28:20

Sarge

ONE DAY a helicopter delivered a slingload of supplies to B Company, 8th Cavalry Regiment. As the men were unloading the gear, they found a little white puppy. One of the men took charge of the pup and named him Sarge. Everyone took to the little dog, and he soon became a regular member of B Company. He was happy to eat the C-rations no one liked, and someone even had dog biscuits shipped from home. One of the men in B Company later recounted:

(National Archives)

With the passage of time Sarge became experienced in airmobile operations and participated in many combat assaults. Unfortunately, we lost Sarge while on a mission in Bong Son. We were pulled out in a hurry and couldn't find him before we left with the choppers.[268]

Sarge is remembered fondly even today and is memorialized on the company's Web site. For a time he was the focus of affection for a group of men in a place where affection pretty much didn't exist.

As my family can attest, I have never been the world's greatest "pet person," although I try to be tolerant of the rest of humanity who are. It has always amazed me people will pass each other without a nod, but will then melt when someone comes along with a puppy.

Maybe there is a lesson here on how we can improve our relationships with other people. We could adopt a little of this puppy demeanor. We might get more attention from others if we were better at receiving it. We could respond with a bigger smile and more enthusiasm when someone shows an interest. Unfortunately, we don't have tails to wag, but we do have the ability to make the other person feel visible and appreciated. There was an occasion when a woman poured an expensive jar of perfume on Jesus' head. The disciples complained she was being wasteful, but Jesus chose to show appreciation instead:

"Why are you bothering this woman? She has done a beautiful thing to me. The poor you will always have with you, but you will not always have me."
~Matthew 26:10, 11

Keeping Watch

THERE WAS no such thing as a good night's sleep in the field. Regardless of how many miles we trekked during the day or what kind of action we were in, security had to be maintained every night. For infantry and recon units this was usually 25 percent to 50 percent alert, which meant every man was on watch for four to six hours. If someone heard a suspicious noise, the entire unit might go on alert. It was a lot to ask of men already on the edge of exhaustion. One recon Marine told about an unusual and dangerous method of staying awake on watch:

M61 fragmentation grenade (U. S. Govt.)

I would take out a hand grenade and pull the pin and hold it to my chest. As long as you didn't let go of the handle, the grenade would not go off and you could return the pin into the hole in the handle and make the grenade safe again. I would do this when I felt sleepy, and I would dare myself to fall asleep sitting there with the grenade in my right hand against my chest and the pin on my index finger of the left hand. Needless to say, I never fell asleep holding a grenade, but you know what? It's very difficult to put the pin back into a grenade at night when your hands are shaking.[269]

Although I'm glad I never saw this technique used, I was always aware of the challenge to stay alert when tired. Jesus was also concerned about his followers falling asleep on watch. He told us he is coming back, but that the day and hour of his return are known only by the Father. Equally unknown is the hour when we will go to him, if we die before he returns. Either way, we must be ready to meet our Savior at some moment we can't predict. It is simply our task to stay alert—to live our lives every day in obedience and expectancy. We don't want to sleep on this watch. The eternal future is at stake.

"Therefore keep watch, because you do not know on what day your Lord will come. But understand this: If the owner of the house had known at what time of night the thief was coming, he would have kept watch and would not have let his house be broken into. So you also must be ready, because the Son of Man will come at an hour when you do not expect him."
~Matthew 24:42–44

The Sixth Day

THE HEROES of the Vietnam War were the wives at home. Faced with the tremendous strain of separation and public controversy over the war, they faithfully carried on. With few exceptions, soldiers, Marines, and airmen knew that their families were in strong and faithful hands. Military wives were extolled in this apocryphal and fictional account of their "creation":

> The good Lord was creating a model for military wives and was into His sixth day of overtime when an angel appeared. She said, "Lord, you seem to be having a lot of trouble with this one. What's wrong with the standard model?"
>
> The Lord replied, "Have you seen the specs on this order? She has to be completely independent, possess the qualities of both a father and mother, run on black coffee, handle every emergency imaginable without a manual, be able to carry on cheerfully, even if she is pregnant and has the flu."
>
> The Lord continued, " I will give her an unusually strong heart so it can sustain the pain of separations, beat soundly when it is overworked and tired, and be large enough to say, 'I understand' when she doesn't and say 'I love you,' regardless."
>
> "Lord," said the angel, touching his arm gently. "Go to bed and get some rest. You can finish this tomorrow."
>
> "I can't stop now," said the Lord. "I am close to creating something unique. Already this model heals herself when she is sick, can put up six unexpected guests for the weekend, wave good-bye to her husband from a pier, a runway, or a depot, and understand why it's important that he leave."
>
> Finally the angel bent over and ran her finger across the cheek of the Lord's creation. "There's a leak," she announced.
>
> "What you see is not a leak," He said. "It's a tear. It's for joy, sadness, pain, disappointment, loneliness, pride, and a dedication to all the values that she and her husband hold dear."[270]

A wife of noble character who can find? She is worth far more than rubies . . . Her children arise and call her blessed; her husband also, and he praises her: "Many women do noble things, but you surpass them all."
~Proverbs 31:10, 28, 29

Military men have always been and forever will be thankful for their wives. Our nation is blessed to have women willing and able to shoulder this great responsibility.

The Grip of His Hand

ALLEN CRAVEN was newly assigned to the field hospital, but had already learned that the sound of helicopters meant casualties were on the way. Each time he was filled with a sense of dread at what he was going to see next. He had also learned that his presence meant a lot to the men coming off those helicopters. The cross on his cap seemed to be a comforting sight to many and was the focal point of one memorable incident:

I will never forget the night one Marine was brought in. His abdomen was torn, his left lung collapsed, and his legs were shattered by shrapnel. I cannot praise the team of doctors and corpsmen highly enough. They brought the boy back from death's door. The boy was going in and out of coma and thrashing about wildly. I asked the doctor if I could talk to him and he asked me to please try. I took his hand and talking into his ear told him I was the chaplain. His eyes flickered open and he saw the cross on my cap. He immediately calmed down, but my hand was in his the rest of the night. Each time I tried to remove it he would start to move around and grip my hand even tighter. I went with him to X-ray, was gowned and then accompanied him into the operating room. He was evacuated before he could recognize the things around him and he will never remember my hand in his that night, but the look in his eyes when he saw my cross, and the grip of his hand, can never be erased from my mind.[271]

This chaplain brought God to a wounded young man through the simple but powerful act of touch. With few words, he allowed the Holy Spirit to work through him, bringing comfort and healing to the young Marine. It is a lesson for any one of us seeking to help someone else. It doesn't have to be complicated. A word or a touch can be powerful in its simplicity. In a moving letter to the church in Corinth, the apostle Paul described the simple nature of his own ministry. He didn't feel the need for complicated theology in his efforts to touch the lives of others:

When I came to you, brothers, I did not come with eloquence or superior wisdom as I proclaimed to you the testimony about God. For I resolved to know nothing while I was with you except Jesus Christ and him crucified. I came to you in weakness and fear, and with much trembling. My message and my preaching were not with wise and persuasive words, but with a demonstration of the Spirit's power, so that your faith might not rest on men's wisdom, but on God's power. ~1 Corinthians 2:1–5

Religious services in the field near the DMZ. (U. S. Marine Corps)

President Nixon visits troops in 1969. (National Archives)

Teach My People

It was something that I could not really define, because I'd not heard it before. But I knew it was God. Because it was not an audible thing. But nothin' that I heard with my ears. It felt like from the depths within me, within my soul. It felt like something that just caused my entire body to tremor. All It said was that you are to teach My people.[272]

LUTHER BENTON couldn't believe that God was speaking to him, but he knew he wasn't dreaming and he hadn't been drinking. It was just another night at Hoi An as he sat on his bunker watching the flares go off in the distance. About a week later it happened again during the daytime. As he was walking along, every sound around him ceased, and the voice said simply, *"You must."*

The young hospital corpsman had one other encounter with God while serving in Vietnam. One night his compound was attacked and overrun by VC. As he was praying and shooting, a rocket-propelled grenade hit his bunker, lifting him high in the air. He lost the fillings in his teeth, but not his life. He thought to himself, *"If I lived through that, what am I s'posed to do now?"*[273]

> By faith Abraham, when called to go to a place he would later receive as his inheritance, obeyed and went, even though he did not know where he was going.
> ~Hebrews 11:8

Back in the States he began to answer that question. He went to a church near his base in Norfolk and talked to the minister. He started working with the young people of the church and organized a Bible study program. A few years later he left the Navy and enrolled in the National Theological Seminary and College in Baltimore. After graduation, he became a licensed minister in the Baptist Church and returned to the same church in Norfolk to lead a teaching ministry.

Our call from God may not be as clear and direct as that of this man. It may take much more prayer and discernment on our part. Our answers may not even come directly, but may take the form of doors closing and opening in our lives. There are many ways to discover the purpose God has for each of us. True fulfillment comes when we find what that purpose is and live it out in our lives.

CAP

JACK CUNNINGHAM received orders straight out of boot camp. He was going to Vietnam for assignment to the Marine Corps Combined Action Program (CAP). These small units were sent to Vietnamese villages where they worked with local militia units. The basic concept was simple: The Marines brought their weapons and tactical expertise, while the local troops contributed their knowledge of the terrain and enemy, as well as the motivation to defend their hometowns.

(National Archives)

Cunningham went to Phu Da, a hamlet twenty miles southwest of Da Nang in the An Hoa Valley, about three miles from the nearest Marine combat base. At times it was a lonely spot for the few Americans. He observed, *"Eleven Marines and one Navy corpsman living in a village . . . can get a little hairy at times."*[274] The Vietnamese were not the most reliable troops, as might be expected with part-time militia. They sometimes disappeared when serious trouble started. Overall, however, the relationship proved very beneficial. As trust with the local villagers and troops was built up over time, security against VC attacks improved. The locals were able to live somewhat normal lives in the midst of a combat zone and, in return, were confident enough in their own protection to give the CAP Marines tips on VC movement, storage areas, and locations of mines and booby traps.

This work required men with special talents. Professional skill had to be combined with compassion and a motivation to help others. The men fulfilling this lonely and somewhat obscure duty were the unsung heroes of Vietnam. Thanks to their selfless and courageous efforts, vast areas of South Vietnam were removed from VC control and given the chance to live in relative peace and security.

> We who are strong ought to bear with the failings of the weak and not to please ourselves. Each of us should please his neighbor for his good, to build him up. For even Christ did not please himself.
> ~Romans 15:1–3

The Dream

WHEN Jack Cunningham started yelling in his sleep, one of his buddies woke him up. He had a terrible nightmare of two Marines being killed while on patrol. Awake, he found himself bathed in sweat and trembling violently. *"Nothing like that feeling ever happened to me before. I never felt a death was going to happen. I couldn't get it out of my mind. It took complete control over me."*[275]

> Since no man knows the future, who can tell him what is to come? No man has power over the wind to contain it; so no one has power over the day of his death.
> ~Ecclesiastes 8:7, 8

The next day two patrols were going out, one in the morning and one in the afternoon. Cunningham was scheduled for the morning, but he was still almost overcome with feelings of dread and asked his friend Robert to switch with him. Strangely, he had no premonition about the afternoon patrol. He didn't explain to his friend or anyone else about the dream. He prayed silently when the patrol left the perimeter.

About an hour later, explosions were heard in the distance, and the radio came alive with frantic shouts from the scene. Two men had stepped on mines. One was dead, the other seriously wounded. The wounded man was Cunningham's friend Robert. As he listened to the chaos, Cunningham became frantic: *"Over and over again, I begged God to let Robert live. I even begged God to take my life instead."*[276] Unfortunately, word soon came back that his friend had died from shock and loss of blood before reaching the hospital in Da Nang. Cunningham was overcome with feelings of remorse and guilt. *"I felt so alone. I was a coward and someone got hurt because of it. (Robert) died when I should have. I felt that even God let me down."*[277]

There is no rational explanation for this strange story of premonition and guilt. We know in biblical times God did give certain people insight into future events, and he may still do so. I have never had such a warning and don't know how I would react if I did. Before taking action, however, I believe I would prayerfully seek spiritual counsel from clergy and friends. I would also take comfort from God's promise that he is in control of the future, and my future is secure in him.

A Known Way

CHAPLAIN Jack Randles wrote an article in the Americal Division newsletter to give his fellow soldiers in Vietnam a practical insight into God's love. He told a story about a father who wanted to send his young son on an errand to an unfamiliar village. The son was hesitant because he couldn't see the destination from where they lived. His father told him to follow the road to a landmark and a point where the road turned, and, once there, he would be able to see the village where he was going. The chaplain explained:

> *The love of God quite often withholds the view of the entire distance of the bending road of life. He reveals it step by step and from corner to corner. Thus, it is necessary for us to trust Him, because He alone knows what is beyond the next turn.*[278]

In the dark days before World War II, King George VI of England gave a radio address to give reassurance to his countrymen. At that time there was great uncertainty about the future as war clouds were building over Europe. The king showed a strong faith that God would lead his nation through the uncertain times ahead. Quoting an old poem, he told the citizens of Great Britain:

> *Go out into the darkness, and put your hand into the Hand of God. That shall be to you better than light, and safer than a known way.*[279]

The chaplain and the king give us a simple and clear message. There is no certainty for any of us about the future. In our lives we do not know what lies on the road ahead or where the road is going. We need to go step by step with God, praying for his guidance at every turn. God never lays out the entire future for us, but we can trust that every step we take under his control is truly "safer than a known way."

I guide you in the way of wisdom and lead you along straight paths. When you walk, your steps will not be hampered; when you run, you will not stumble.
~Proverbs 4:11, 12

"For I know the plans I have for you," declares the LORD, "plans to prosper you and not to harm you, plans to give you hope and a future."
~Jeremiah 29:11

237

Understanding

AMERICAN soldiers have always been known for their generosity, especially toward children. In Vietnam, however, the troops had to learn that gift giving required some understanding of local customs, as explained in a unit newsletter article:

(National Archives)

Children and soldiers are the same all over the world; the children love to receive gifts and the soldiers love to give them. But there is a right way and a wrong way for a GI to show his affection and liking to the Vietnamese children.

The proper way was exemplified earlier this month by various units of the division when they presented youngsters with gifts during Tet Trung Thu, the Vietnamese national holiday. They learned it is a time for gaiety and dancing. But equally important, they understood that only elders, parents, or extremely close friends may present gifts directly to the children. It would be considered a loss of face to the family for an outsider to do so.

Therefore, according to custom, each of the units presented the gifts to district, village, or hamlet elders on Oct. 5, the day before Tet Trung Thu. The elders in turn distributed the toys and candy to the children at the celebration.[280]

Generosity is one thing. Understanding is another. Giving presents may make us feel good, but understanding another culture or another person takes time and effort. This is especially true and important within our own families. Men in particular have a way of focusing on the physical needs of their wives and children, while neglecting their deeper needs for affection and visibility. Meeting these needs requires time, conversation, patient listening, and prayer. The Bible says, *"Understanding is a fountain of life to those who have it"* (Proverbs 16:22). Husbands and fathers can become a fountain of life to their families when they lovingly give the time and effort needed to understand the hearts of their wives and children.

> The purposes of a man's heart are deep waters, but a man of understanding draws them out.
> ~Proverbs 20:5

The Airwaves Opened

AN UNFAMILIAR call sign on the battalion radio net aroused Dennis Ostrowski's curiosity. As a radio operator with the 4th Division he was familiar with all the units passing traffic on his net, and this was not one of them. To find out more, he initiated a call to the unknown station. The response was difficult to discern at first through the static, until the word was spelled out phonetically: Kilo-Oscar-Romeo-Echo-Alpha—Korea. He was talking to other GIs 3,000 miles away! Describing the conversation, he said:

> After talking with the unit we found out they were a military police detachment, located 40 miles north of Seoul near the Demilitarized Zone. We could hear them very clearly in our conversation.[281]

Other men in Ostrowski's unit soon heard about the radio contact, and those with friends or brothers in Korea crowded in to try to get messages through. The troops in Korea were amazed to be hearing directly from frontline troops in Vietnam. This contact was repeated once more a few nights later, but was then gone, not to be reestablished. Whatever atmospheric condition had opened up this airwave, it closed just as quickly.

There are times in our lives when the "spiritual airwaves" seem to open for us and we find ourselves in more intimate contact with God. We are blessed by these moments when the music is uplifting, the sermon thought-provoking, or our prayers especially meaningful. A breakthrough with God, sometimes called a "mountaintop experience," can happen in church, while walking on the beach, or even on an actual mountain, when God dazzles our senses and awakens our hearts.

> He who forms the mountains, creates the wind, and reveals his thoughts to man, he who turns dawn to darkness, and treads the high places of the earth—the LORD God Almighty is his name.
> ~Amos 4:13

If these spiritual airwaves close, however, it is not time to despair. God is still with us. He doesn't expect us to stay on the mountaintop all the time. We have work to do. We have to remember that faith is not a feeling; it is a decision. It is up to us to continue faithfully in our work for his kingdom, trusting he will give us the level of intimacy we need with him. When he is ready the airwaves will open.

Memorial

THE MEN of the 1st Battalion, 22nd Infantry, gathered around the newly erected monument. The white stone obelisk stood in stark contrast to the camouflaged bunkers, green tents, and dirt streets of the barren combat base. The soldiers were assembled at the battalion headquarters in Camp Enari in October 1969 to commemorate comrades who had fallen during the house-to-house fighting in Kontum during the Tet Offensive and the bloody victory at Chu Moor Mountain, and to dedicate a memorial:

> They saw the memorial and remembered. They remembered the men who had come before and who had died here—the men who have given their lives for the cause of freedom in South Vietnam.
>
> Those men will be remembered by all who see the memorial. They'll be remembered with a simple thought, one that echoes the spirit of the plaque—"LORD, MAY THESE BRAVE MEN REST IN PEACE."[282]

I pray the same prayer for every man and woman in uniform who has paid the ultimate price for our nation and the cause of freedom. I pray that God has somehow provided for these heroes who died too soon; who may not have had time to find all the answers. Jesus said, *"Come to me, all you who are weary and burdened, and I will give you rest"* (Matthew 11:28). If any of these young men and women had not heard these words or had not understood them, I pray that God somehow gave them another chance. He gives us so many chances while we are living—we should have cause to hope that he gives one more to a soldier. In the words inscribed on the Camp Enari memorial, *"Lord, may these brave men rest in peace."*

> "Take my yoke upon you and learn from me, for I am gentle and humble in heart, and you will find rest for your souls. For my yoke is easy and my burden is light."
> ~Matthew 11:29, 30

Detached Violence

THE BIGGEST artillery piece used by U.S. forces in the Vietnam War was the 175-mm gun. Mounted on a tracked vehicle, it weighed a total of twenty-six tons and fired a one-hundred-forty-seven-pound projectile twenty miles. It was often the only fire support that could reach troops deep in enemy territory.

(U. S. Army)

The gun emplacement, whether simple or elaborate, was called the pit. It was where the gun crews spent most of their waking hours. Routine duties were interrupted when the alert sounded: *"Fire mission!"* At the call, the eight-man crew would swing into action, positioning the gun, manhandling the powder and projectiles, and firing the weapon. The physical labor was exhausting, the noise ear-splitting, and the shock effect of the gun violent.

Another unusual aspect of the artilleryman's job was the fact it was done miles away from the target, where the shells fired were impacting. One officer said, *"They never see what they are firing at and they normally don't learn of any material results unless a sweep is made of the area afterward."* He termed the whole operation a *"detached violence."*[283]

I have often considered this phrase a fitting description of many things that happen in daily life. When we say bad things about someone who isn't present, we don't see the immediate impact. When we are rude to another driver, we don't have to deal with or even think about his reaction. We are especially prone to this kind of detachment when dealing with children. We forget they are not able to react to our outbursts and tend to internalize abuse. Often the results of our ill-conceived criticisms or corrections are only seen much later. To avoid inflicting "a detached violence" on others we should more seriously consider the impact of our words and deeds and the ability of others to respond. Jesus gave us the ideal prescription:

> "Do to others as you would have them do to you. "If you love those who love you, what credit is that to you? Even 'sinners' love those who love them . . . Be merciful, just as your Father is merciful."
> ~Luke 6:31, 32, 36

Cooperation

AS PART of the effort to bolster the South Vietnamese Army, certain units were paired with U.S. counterparts in 1969 to share artillery and air support. At an informal meeting, the commanding officers of the 3rd Battalion, 503rd Infantry, and the 53rd ARVN Regiment were discussing recon-

> "For everyone who asks receives; he who seeks finds; and to him who knocks, the door will be opened." ~Matthew 7:8

naissance operations. A number of Vietnamese soldiers had recently attended the U.S. Recondo School at Nha Trang, and the Vietnamese colonel was concerned about immediately introducing these men to long-range patrols in enemy territory.

The U.S. commander offered a solution:

> *If you'd like, you can break in your new men with my experienced recon and ambush teams. I'll match you man for man. Your people can teach mine about trail reading and other things they've learned at Recondo School. My Hawk teams had to learn their business largely on the job. I think they could benefit from working together with school-trained personnel.*[284]

This conversation led to a program of combined U.S./ARVN patrols that proved beneficial to both forces. The American officer commented, *"I'm trying to encourage [my counterpart] to ask me for assistance beyond what he's supposed to get according to established agreements. I do this simply by asking him for favors myself."*[285] This officer was successful in building mutual reliance by showing he could receive help as well as give it.

Jesus said it is more blessed to give than to receive. I think this idea is firmly planted in the ethical outlook of most Christians. At the same time, however, I know many Christians who, on the personal level, find it difficult to *receive* help from others. Many of us, especially men, are very reluctant to ask for anything or to even share our problems. When carried too far, this trait, unfortunately, stunts the growth of our friendships. The surest path to a deeper relationship with someone lies in giving that person a chance to help us, and in receiving that help graciously. The same idea holds true in our relationship with God. He doesn't *need* anything from us. He simply wants us to receive his grace.

Duty First

DURING THE withdrawal of U.S. forces from Vietnam, units that had fought for years finally were able to stand down and prepare to go home. General Creighton Abrams usually paid a visit to these units to thank them personally and to say goodbye. In 1970, as the 1st Infantry Division prepared to redeploy to Ft. Riley, Kansas, he made these remarks to the men of the division:

Gen. Creighton Abrams (U. S. Army)

In a changing world, changing times and changing attitudes . . . the 1st Infantry Division, more than any other division in our Army, represents a constancy of those virtues of mankind—humility, courage, devotion, and sacrifice. The world is changed a lot, but this division continues to serve, as it had in the beginning. I choose to feel that this is part of the cement, and the rock, and the steel that holds our great country together.[286]

America's greatness is based to a large extent on the freedom that allows the entrepreneurial spirit and individual initiative of great men and women to flourish. The drive and genius of many visionary leaders have created our industries, built our cities, discovered cures for diseases, and explored outer space. General Abrams reminds us, however, of another aspect of America's greatness: those exceptional men and women, the soldiers, policemen, firemen, medical workers, teachers, and so many others whose lives are based on service to others. The great Christian virtues—humility, courage, devotion, and sacrifice—are indeed the cement that holds our great country together.

As servants of God we commend ourselves in every way: in great endurance; in troubles, hardships and distresses; in beatings, imprisonments and riots; in hard work, sleepless nights and hunger; in purity, understanding, patience and kindness; in the Holy Spirit and in sincere love; in truthful speech and in the power of God; with weapons of righteousness in the right hand and in the left; through glory and dishonor, bad report and good report; genuine, yet regarded as impostors; known, yet regarded as unknown; dying, and yet we live on; beaten, and yet not killed; sorrowful, yet always rejoicing; poor, yet making many rich; having nothing, and yet possessing everything.

~2 Corinthians 6:4–10

243

I Want to Go Home

DAN DOYLE's worst day in Vietnam was March 1, 1968. While trying to link up with another unit, his rifle platoon took fire from a concealed enemy bunker. One man was wounded by the opening shots, and then two others who tried to help him. As the platoon leader, Doyle knew it was up to him to lead the effort to save these soldiers. He asked for volunteers, and two of his best men came forward. As they tried to advance under covering fire, both of these men were killed. One died in his arms crying, *"Don't let me die. I want to go home."* Later, Doyle recounted, *"There was nothing I could do to save his life. The only thing I could have given him, I gave him. He didn't die alone."*

> "For whoever wants to save his life will lose it, but whoever loses his life for me and for the gospel will save it. What good is it for a man to gain the whole world, yet forfeit his soul?"
> ~Mark 8:35, 36

After the war, Doyle returned home to Virginia, earned a PhD in psychology, and ran a veterans' center in Richmond. He dedicated himself to helping others heal from their wounds. His experience led him to an unusual observation about the effects of war:

> *I make a distinction between hearts and souls. Wounded hearts heal, wounded souls change. This is how I explain the changes in me: I've had broken hearts before, girlfriends, that sort of stuff. I got over it and I was the same. I am not the same person I was before Vietnam.*[287]

This thought-provoking statement seems to be telling us that souls cannot be healed. It's a point theologians might argue. The soul has been defined as the center of human consciousness and the thing that makes human beings unique. The Bible tells us mankind is made in God's image, and I believe we see this manifest in the existence of this consciousness. Whether a soul changes in this life is less important than its eternal fate. We clearly have the opportunity to affect that by the choices and decisions we make while we are living. Through our Savior, Jesus Christ, we can be assured of our place in God's eternal kingdom. In the end, we want to be able to say to him, *"I'm ready. I want to go home."*

Red Roses

ON MOTHER'S DAY 1968, the doorbell rang early in the Tousey household. Georgia Tousey went to the front door, where she found a flower delivery man waiting. He handed her a beautiful arrangement of red roses. When she read *"From your son"* on the card, she almost fainted. Two months before, she had buried her only son, Gary. He had been killed in Vietnam. She had no way of knowing he had left money for Mother's Day flowers with a friend before leaving to go to war. He had never done anything like that before.

Gary Tousey did not have to go to Vietnam. At the time he received his draft notice, he was married with two children and could have gotten a deferment. However, there was a tradition of military service in his family, and he considered it his duty to answer his country's call. He felt he was protecting his country and the family he loved. He was assigned to the 9th Infantry Division, operating in the Mekong Delta, where his unit fought an intense battle with VC forces in February 1968. He was one of nineteen Americans killed.

> "Do not let your hearts be troubled. Trust in God; trust also in me. In my Father's house are many rooms; if it were not so, I would have told you. I am going there to prepare a place for you. And if I go and prepare a place for you, I will come back and take you to be with me that you also may be where I am."
> ~John 14:1–3

Years later, Georgia Tousey, writing in her journal, tried to say goodbye to her son:

> We wear our gold stars for you and are proud of your medals; our son. We are keeping fresh the good memories and more often now, as we speak of you, it is with joy.
> The red roses you ordered for Mother's Day, 1968, for me, were just beautiful. It was as if in all finality, you were thanking me and telling me of the love we shared together.
> We who loved you and buried you thank you eternally.[288]

Gary Tousey's mother will remember him and love him forever. I would like to consider the amazing delivery of these roses as a sign from God that her son also continues to love her, and that this kind of love does not die.

Marines patrolling near Rockpile. (U. S. Marine Corps)

Troops board UH-1(Huey) helicopters (Dept. of Defense)

Ticket to the World

THE ATTACK on Fire Support Base Buttons started at 1:15 a.m. As tracers crisscrossed through the night, a rocket-propelled grenade suddenly rocked Lieutenant Ty Dodge's vehicle, sending shrapnel flying through the interior and wounding the entire crew. Dodge himself was hurt the worst, suffering multiple shrapnel wounds all over his body and severe trauma to his right leg. Somehow, during the confusion of the battle, several men got him off the front line and back to the rear. His last memory of that night was four men carrying him to a helicopter. Out of the corner of his eye he noticed one was a chaplain. Ever since that night he considered these men his *"tickets to the world,"* even though he never knew who they were.

> In his great mercy he has given us new birth into a living hope through the resurrection of Jesus Christ from the dead, and into an inheritance that can never perish, spoil or fade— kept in heaven for you, who through faith are shielded by God's power until the coming of the salvation that is ready to be revealed in the last time. ~1 Peter 1:3–5

In 1992 Ty Dodge and his wife, Florence, attended their first 11th Cavalry reunion in San Antonio, Texas. She was looking over a row of tables in the banquet room when she found a handwritten note that said simply, *"My name is Chaplain Gene Allen, 1st Cav, FSB Buttons. I did a lot with the 11th when they were attacked outside the berm at Buttons. Call me if you remember."*[289] With his heart in his throat, Dodge made the phone call. After twenty-three years, he had found one of the men who saved his life.

Dodge soon realized the reunion site was, by chance, in the place where the chaplain had retired. The chaplain happened to be doing a seminar in the same Holiday Inn on the same day when he noticed the 11th Cavalry poster in the lobby. These *random* circumstances gave Dodge a chance to thank someone who had saved his life.

Fortunately for us, there is no uncertainty about the identity of and means of contacting our "ticket to the *next* world." We know our Savior by name, and we know he has already done all that is necessary to ensure our safe passage to be with him in eternity.

Rear Guard

STEVE WILLIAMS would never forget Hill 474. His unit first climbed it uneventfully in early January 1970. He was on rear guard as they moved up the hill when something caught his eye in the bushes. After stopping and looking intently, however, he couldn't see anything. After one of his buddies dropped back with him and could find nothing, they moved cautiously on up the hill.

Steve Williams

Several days later, Williams's unit encountered fire from NVA troops on another part of Hill 474. In a series of hard-fought battles, the soldiers fought their way back to the top of the hill, where they finally discovered an elaborate underground base camp for an NVA battalion.

Two weeks after his first walk up Hill 474, Williams' unit was leaving the area when an NVA soldier was captured. He stood nearby while the prisoner was being interrogated, and noticed that the enemy soldier kept pointing at him. The translator later told him that the man had been beside the trail two weeks before and had seen Williams pass by on rear guard. He was about to open fire when he heard others coming up the trail, so he pulled back. Williams realized this was the movement that had caught his eye that day when they first climbed the hill. He described his reaction:

Chills ran up my back as I realized how close to death I had come. What footsteps could he have heard, as I was clearly the last person up the hill? I knew that my family and friends back home were praying for my safety. Looking back, I believe the Glory of the Lord was protecting me that day on Hill 474 in answer to the prayers being lifted up for me back home.[290]

Williams later found his own verse of Scripture in the words of the prophet Isaiah, describing the ultimate "rear guard" that protects each of us:

Then your light will break forth like the dawn, and your healing will quickly appear; then your righteousness will go before you, and the glory of the LORD will be your rear guard. ~Isaiah 58:8

Angel in Disguise

IN MAY 1970 Steve Williams went into Cambodia with the 101st Airborne Division. The operation was successful but intense. Enemy contacts were frequent, and Williams' unit captured large quantities of food and ammunition bound for Vietnam. At the conclusion of the operation, his unit moved to a small landing zone for evacuation back to base. There the platoon leader organized the men into five-man teams for the helo lift and assigned Williams to the first group. He described what happened then:

"Saved to serve"

> *When the choppers came in, our teams of five were ready: three men on one side of the field and two of us on the other side. When the #1 chopper was about to land, we ran toward it quickly so it would be on the ground only seconds before taking off again. I was to be the last man on. I watched the three on the far side get in, and then the guy with me got on. I turned and tried to back in, but something hit my backpack and stopped me. I looked around and was startled to see a man already in "my" spot. He was sitting there with his head down. Suddenly, the chopper pilot turned around and shouted to me, "We're full!" I said, "But I'm supposed to be on this chopper." Again he said, "We're full!" and then he quickly took off.*[291]

Williams ran back to tell his lieutenant what had happened. The lieutenant didn't understand it, but assigned the soldier to another team for the next lift. This time everything went according to plan, and he was soon airborne. Within a few minutes, however, the pilot turned to tell the men behind him, *"#1 chopper just got shot down!"* Williams thought to himself, *"#1 was to have been my chopper!"* He also thought of the man sitting in *his* place, *"Who was that man and where did he come from?"*[292]

Williams has never answered that question completely. However, as his jacket shows in the accompanying photograph, he is certain he was "saved to serve." As a member of Pointman Ministries he has been part of a Christian organization of veterans helping other veterans find their way back from war to a normal life.

> "For I know the plans I have for you," declares the LORD, "plans to prosper you and not to harm you, plans to give you hope and a future.
> ~Jeremiah 29:11

Lost Illusions

A FEW MONTHS after the Tet Offensive, 3ʳᵈ Battalion, 3ʳᵈ Marines, was sweeping an area below the DMZ when it uncovered an NVA regimental command post. In a daylong battle, the battalion assaulted and took the position while sustaining heavy casualties. Private First Class T. J. Kelly was with a forward air-control party and in the middle of the action. At one point, a bullet meant for his chest struck and shattered his rifle instead. It was just one more episode in his "growing up" process:

I was still pretty new at the time, and in my head, this was the kind of thing that I really wanted to be . . . a hardened combat veteran Marine. That lasted about five months. About five months of that before all of a sudden my eyes opened up and I realized that hey, this isn't a movie, this is for real. I came to be thinking that an awful lot of guys were naive like me and went over to get themselves involved in a war not really for very honorable or patriotic reasons but because they maybe saw too many John Wayne movies and wanted to see themselves as heroes, this sort of thing. I sort of smartened up after a while, especially when I saw so many young men die. You didn't change what you did . . . you fought even harder after that silliness wore off because you wanted to live.[293]

It doesn't take long for green troops to become *"hardened combat veteran[s]"* when they become aware of the life-or-death consequences of their actions. This is the kind of realization all too often lacking in our spiritual lives. Some of us who have received Jesus Christ into our hearts have grown used to our lives in the Spirit and have lost sight of the pain or urgency that brought us to him in the first place. We forget the darkness others are living in without him, and the futility of a future with only our own thoughts to guide us. We don't know what hell is like in the afterlife, but we know what hell on earth is like when we live only for ourselves. The world needs our Savior. It is a life-or-death matter. Our actions in bringing others to him are crucial.

> But now that you have been set free from sin and have become slaves to God, the benefit you reap leads to holiness, and the result is eternal life. For the wages of sin is death, but the gift of God is eternal life in Christ Jesus our Lord.
> ~Romans 6:22, 23

Burial at Sea

CASUALTY Notification Officers had to personally bring bad news to families when their sons were wounded or killed in the war. Lieutenant Colonel George Goodson served two years in this difficult duty and paid a heavy emotional price. His last mission was to a family on the eastern shore of Maryland whose son had been killed in action. The father was a retired Navy man and called Goodson late one night with an unusual request. He wanted his son buried at sea. *"Can you make that happen?"* he asked. Goodson replied, *"Yes I can, Chief. I can and I will."* His wife had been listening to the telephone conversation, and said, *"Can you do that?"* and Goodson answered, *"I have no idea. But I'm going to break my* [expletive] *trying."*[294]

(U. S. Navy)

Within minutes Goodson was on the telephone to the Commanding General, Fleet Marine Force, Atlantic, and early the next morning stood before a Navy admiral. He was given a destroyer and four days to prepare the crew and make all the arrangements. On the appointed day, the ship, sailors, band, and honor guard were ready. They sailed out of the Norfolk Naval Base to the 12-fathom depth, where a service took place that no one present would ever forget:

> *The sun was hot. The ocean flat. The casket was brought aft and placed on a catafalque. The Chaplain spoke. The volleys were fired. The flag was removed, folded, and I gave it to the father. The band played "Eternal Father, Strong to Save." The casket was raised slightly at the head and slid into the sea.*[295]

For two years Goodson dealt with the most tragic part of any war, the families grieving for lost loved ones. By his extraordinary efforts, he demonstrated to all of them their sons were not forgotten. His story is also a stark reminder to those of us who were with those sons in battle: We, most of all, must never forget.

> "I tell you the truth, unless a kernel of wheat falls to the ground and dies, it remains only a single seed. But if it dies, it produces many seeds." ~John 12:24

ARVN troops advancing through rough terrain (National Archives)

1972 EASTER OFFENSIVE

I N THE early stages of Vietnamization, U.S. forces represented one-quarter of the total Allied manpower available in Vietnam, and the most effective part of the total. Replacing this lost capability was a formidable challenge. Fortunately, continued gains in the pacification program freed more and more ARVN units from static defense to field operations. Also, the successful Cambodian incursion in 1970 further degraded North Vietnam's ability to mount major unit offensives that year—giving more time for redeployment and improvement of the ARVN.

With the loss of their Cambodian ports and the increased difficulty confiscating supplies in country, the North Vietnamese became almost totally dependent on their supply lines through the Ho Chi Minh Trail network. Due to the effectiveness of U.S. sensor technology and more targeted aerial interdiction, enemy use of the network became ever more costly. Accordingly, the North Vietnamese high command focused its planning for 1971 on the northern sectors of Vietnam, where its supply lines were shortest. Early in the year a major buildup was detected in Laos, centered on the city of Tchepone.

On February 8, 1971, the South Vietnamese launched Operation Lam Son 719, a major offensive thrust, westward along Route 9 into Laos, spearheaded by an armored brigade. On either flank infantry units advanced on key terrain by helicopter. U.S. forces, due to the Cooper-Church Amendment to the 1970 Defense Appropriations Act, were legally prohibited from entering Laos. Nevertheless, full U.S. air and artillery support from across the border were provided. After a month of heavy fighting, the Vietnamese reached Tchepone. At that point, on the advice of subordinate commanders, General Lam decided to accept his gains and terminate the operation. Both sides declared victory in this bitterly fought campaign. General Abrams was frustrated that a battle that could have been decisive in the war was not fought. Even so, North Vietnamese offensive efforts in 1971 were largely thwarted.

Seventy thousand U.S. troops were scheduled for withdrawal in the spring of 1972, representing the largest single reduction of the war, practically eliminating a U.S. combat presence. Concurrently, the North Vietnamese decided to invade South Vietnam directly across the DMZ in a bid to finally end the war. Thrusts were also planned for the Central High-lands and Binh Long province. As the enemy buildup became more and more obvious, all General Abrams could do was muster every available air and naval asset to assist the South Vietnamese in their life-or-death struggle.

On March 30, 1972, two NVA divisions struck across the DMZ against heavy resistance. By mid-May a hard-fought campaign took them to the My Chanh River, the southern boundary of Quang Tri province, where they threatened Hue, but were unable to advance farther. Then, in a series of counterattacks, the South Vietnamese began to roll back the advance, first in Quang Tri, then in the other provinces. All territory was not regained, but the invasion was defeated.

To support the South Vietnamese during the Easter Offensive, Operation Linebacker kicked off in early April. U.S. air forces conducted an intense interdiction campaign on the battlefields, supply lines, and military targets throughout North Vietnam. Even with the air campaign, however, the key to the successful defense of South Vietnam was a valiant effort on the ground. The South Vietnamese officers and soldiers, themselves, had to stand and fight, which they demonstrated the ability and desire to do.

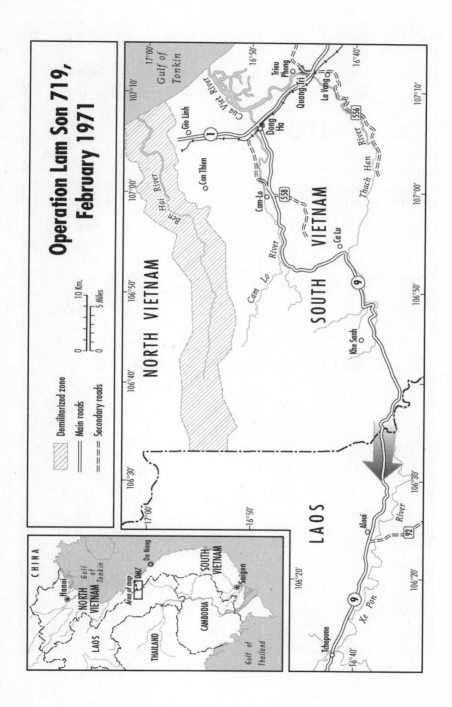

Operation Lam Son 719, February 1971

Legend:
- Demilitarized zone
- Main roads
- ===== Secondary roads

Scale: 10 Km. / 5 Miles

Main map labels:
NORTH VIETNAM
SOUTH VIETNAM
LAOS
Gulf of Tonkin
Cua Viet River
Ben Hai River
Cam Lo River
Thach Han River
Xe Pon River
Gio Linh
Con Thien
Dong Ha
Cam Lo
Trieu Phong
Quang Tri
La Vang
Ca Lu
Khe Sanh
Aloui
Tchepone
1
558
556
9
92

Inset map labels:
CHINA
NORTH VIETNAM
LAOS
THAILAND
CAMBODIA
SOUTH VIETNAM
Gulf of Tonkin
Gulf of Thailand
Hanoi
Da Nang
Saigon
Area of map
DMZ

255

North Vietnamese Easter Offensive, 1972

LAOS

THAILAND

CAMBODIA

Phnom Penh

Gulf of Siam

DMZ

Đồng Hới

Đông Hà
Quảng Trị
Cam Lộ
Huế

Da Nang

Chu Lai

Quang Ngai

Đăk Tô

Kon Tum

Pleiku   19   An Khe   Phù Cát

Qui Nhon

SOUTH VIETNAM

Nha Trang

Cam Ranh

Lộc Ninh
Quan Lợi
An Lộc

Phan Rang

Tây Ninh

Saigon

Vung Tau

Can Tho

South China Sea

Mekong

River

Mouths of the Mekong

International boundaries

0   100 Kilometers

0   100 Miles

The Bridge

BY MARCH 1972 most Americans had left Vietnam. Among the few remaining were a small core of advisors to the South Vietnamese army, including Captain John Ripley. He was assigned to a battalion of Vietnamese marines operating near the DMZ. Ripley volunteered for this duty even though he had already served a full year in combat as a rifle company commander with the 3rd Marines.

> I eagerly expect and hope that I will in no way be ashamed, but will have sufficient courage so that now as always Christ will be exalted in my body, whether by life or by death.
> ~Philippians 1:20

On March 30 the North Vietnamese army launched its 1972 Easter Offensive, sending two divisions, spear-headed by tanks, south across the DMZ. The invasion force moved along Route 1 directly toward Ripley's unit, located twelve miles south at the town of Dong Ha, on the south bank of the Cua Viet River. As refugees and dispirited South Vietnamese soldiers streamed through the town, a column of two hundred tanks and armored personnel carriers approached the bridge from the north. Ripley could see that the only way to stop the invasion was to blow up the Dong Ha bridge. Over a period of hours he manhandled more than five hundred pounds of TNT and C-4 explosives along the steel I-beams under the bridge, all the time under fire. He had to drop below the I-beams frequently, holding on only with his hands and completely exposing himself to the enemy guns.

For destroying the Dong Ha bridge and delaying the Easter invasion, John Ripley was awarded the Navy Cross. In commenting on this action, Vice Admiral James Stockdale said,

It's easy to give your all when victory appears to be around the corner. The real hero is the man whose sacrifices for his brothers-in-arms come from a sense of sheer duty, even though he knows his efforts are probably doomed to failure.[296]

There are times we get discouraged because faith seems to be losing out to the forces of secularism in our modern culture. Despite this trend, we know where our duty lies. Regardless of the odds, our lives are dedicated in service to the One who served us; in sacrifice to the One who sacrificed for us.

No Difference

Capt. John Ripley (U. S. Marine Corps)

DURING HIS time as an advisor, Captain John Ripley thought he would never understand the South Vietnamese man he called "Three-Finger Jack." This intense and withdrawn soldier was the bodyguard of the commander of the battalion Ripley was attached to. The man's eyes were a distinguishing physical feature—hard and expressionless. Another feature was the missing index finger of his left hand, which he had cut off himself to demonstrate loyalty to his leader. Ripley always felt he was being evaluated and judged by this battle-hardened warrior from a different time and culture.

As the North Vietnamese Easter Offensive pushed southward in 1972, Ripley became separated from his unit when he stopped to help his mortally wounded radio operator. Struggling with the man's body and trying to reach friendly lines, he came under fire by advancing NVA troops. Suddenly, Three-Finger Jack appeared with a group of Vietnamese Marines to cover the American and help him to safety. It was a moment he wouldn't forget:

> "Gia cam on *(Thanks, Buddy),*" Ripley called. And, for the first time, he saw the bodyguard's face open up in an unrestrained smile. Reason had told him he would never understand this man, his language, his history, the loyalty he had shown to Binh (his commander) and now, just as intensely to him. But for one moment that changed. The world seemed to come to a stop; all its energy and light turned toward Jack, illuminating the lines in his face, and Ripley saw him as if not an inch of space stood between them. The stillness and clarity washed all reason away. There was no past and no future, no subject and no object, no difference between him and Three-Finger Jack.[297]

Many differences are resolved in combat. The same is true when we struggle with others toward any worthwhile goal. Differences between Christians, especially, fall away as we climb along our various paths toward Jesus, all the while growing closer to each other.

> There is one body and one Spirit—just as you were called to one hope when you were called— one Lord, one faith, one baptism; one God and Father of all, who is over all and through all and in all. ~Ephesians 4:4–6

The Soldier

IN 1970 a poignant description of the infantry soldier bearing the brunt of the Vietnam War appeared in the 4th Infantry Division newsletter:

(National Archives)

> *He has no last name. At best, he's Bill—but more often he's simply "Brooklyn" or "Short Round" or "Cool Breeze."*
>
> *He's of varied background: He's the freckle-faced Irish redhead from the streets of Chicago, he's the lanky black with the keen sense of humor from Los Angeles, he's the Puerto Rican who can speak two languages fluently from New York.*
>
> *His helmet is his diary: It announces each of his firebases—Marty—Hardtimes—it advertises his loved ones, Joan and Marie—and it clicks off his months in country; May is about to be crossed off—and it reaffirms his faith, "God is my point man."*
>
> *A battered rope rosary often dangles from his neck—and at times a peace symbol is prominently displayed, or a symbol fashioned from shrapnel removed from his leg.*
>
> *In his pocket there's always a P-38, a church key, and a small pocket Bible. And on his back is a rucksack that weighs twice as much as him but which he carries gladly, because in that sack is all the ammo that will keep him alive.*
>
> *His hospitality shows no bounds; always room for one more in the bunker. He never hesitates to break open another box of C's for a friend. He'll share even his last cold beer with a visitor.*
>
> *He is the indispensable man. More senior men draw up the strategy and issue the orders and supervise the operations—but it is he who gets the job done. It is he who drives the trucks, loads the choppers, mans the tanks. It's he who drops into hot LZs, marches down hostile trails, and rappels from choppers. And, ultimately it is he who shoots and gets shot, who kills and gets killed.*
>
> *Without him there would be no army, and for that matter, there would be no America.*[298]

> Endure hardship with us like a good soldier of Christ Jesus.
> ~2 Timothy 2:3

Four-and-a-Half Hours

RICHARD FORD twice received the Bronze Star as a rifleman with the 25th Infantry Division. He considered them both "accidents." Once he thought he saw a small animal scurry into the underbrush near where his patrol was taking a break. Investigating, he flushed out three VC soldiers apparently intent on ambushing his unit. Another time on listening post just before dawn, he thought he saw a water buffalo moving in front of him. Unsure of what it was, he opened up with his machine gun, disrupting an NVA attack on his lines. He never considered himself a hero, even though he saw more than his share of combat.

> Then my soul will rejoice in the LORD and delight in his salvation. My whole being will exclaim, "Who is like you, O LORD? You rescue the poor from those too strong for them." ~Psalm 35:9, 10

Ford came from a religious family and found great comfort from his faith during the war. He carried his sister's Bible and a little bottle of oil his pastor had blessed. During basic training he had seen a lot of guys who professed to be atheists—but he didn't see that many in the front lines. Everyone seemed to have a cross, and everyone was quick to ask God's protection in a firefight.

The young soldier was generally not happy about the war or his role in it. When he got home, he found little respect for what he had accomplished. He considered himself blessed, however, to have found a deeper faith because of his experience. When he got home, his first stop was his church:

> It was Saturday evening when we landed. Nineteen sixty-eight. I caught a cab from Dulles and went straight to my church. The Way of the Cross Church. It's a Pentecostal holiness church. I really wasn't active in the church before I went overseas. But a lot of people from the church wrote me, saying things like, "I'm praying for you." And they said they were glad to see me. But I went to the altar and stayed there from seven o'clock to about eleven-thirty. I just wanted to be by myself and pray. At the altar . . . I was glad to be home. I was thankful that I made it.[299]

Vietnamese soldiers with U. S. advisors. (U. S. Army)

Litter bearers evacuate wounded. (National Archives)

The Mirror

IT WAS one of those unforgettable moments. The soldier had been on operation for fifty-four exhausting days. Now back at base, he was able to shower, eat, and have a beer. Then there was time to just soak up the euphoric feeling that comes from a mixture of being physically spent but safe. As he entered his hut, he sensed someone over his shoulder and turned to look. That's when it hit him:

> I realized I was looking in a mirror and hadn't recognized my own reflection. Was that me? I had to smile to make sure. I was looking at a stranger. I'd changed. I'd never seen myself before. I'd become one of those guys that I'd seen when I first arrived in country. Now I had that look in my eyes.[300]

The "look" is the stare of a combat veteran. There is a hardness to it from the strain of constantly trying to see everything and of then seeing too much. There is a constant wariness, tinged with sadness. Seeing this look in a mirror, the soldier realized he was a different person.

All of us change over time and usually fail to notice as we go along. We gain weight. We age. We have imperceptible changes in attitude. As some of us get older we have to guard against a creeping cynicism toward current events, politics, and even the culture in general. We have seen it all before—we are not impressed.

These subtle changes in attitude are generally benign, unless they begin to affect our spiritual energy. We can't expect to stay at a high emotional state all the time, but we should be aware when our enthusiasm wanes too much. If the gospel message seems less powerful and immediate in our lives, it is not the gospel that has changed. It is time to take stock within ourselves. We need a spiritual mirror to see ourselves and to assess where we stand with God. Our friends and spouses can provide this to a degree. However, the best and constant source of the feedback we need is God himself. When we pray often and earnestly he gives us what we can only find in him: a mirror to the soul.

> Now we see but a poor reflection as in a mirror; then we shall see face to face. Now I know in part; then I shall know fully, even as I am fully known.
> ~1 Corinthians 13:12

Tracers

Red-orange fireballs erupted wherever mortars impacted, and enemy green tracers crossed paths with friendly red tracers. Seeing the colorful pyrotechnics, it was easy to forget how deadly the attacks could be. The American red tracers poured out in defense, and the enemy tracers converged inward like a million fireflies at war.[301]

His tracer rounds ricocheted in lazy, bright-red arcs, a breath before the first pinging sounds of steel on steel returned to the south bank. Streams of tracer fire converged on the target, bouncing off in a crazy-quilt pattern and joining four times as many invisible rounds in a giant buzzing hornet's nest of sound. Then the machine guns on the north bank opened fire in short stuttering bursts and the enemy's tracers, bright green, came vaulting over the river.[302]

(Dept. of Defense)

EVERY FIFTH round in a belt of machine gun ammunition is normally a tracer. These are special bullets with a hollow base filled with a bright burning pyrotechnic material such as phosphorous or magnesium. When fired, they create a red or green streak that enables the gunner to follow the trajectory of his rounds and adjust his aim accordingly.

Unfortunately, there is an old military adage that points out, *"Tracers work both ways."* The bright red streaks that help gunners adjust fire also mark their position for the enemy. Hence, the converging red and green fireworks described above.

The apostle Paul described a similar principle governing our behavior by using an agricultural metaphor: *"A man reaps what he sows"* (Galatians 6:7). He points out the obvious: When you plant corn, you can expect to harvest corn. When you send out indifference or irritation toward others, you can expect the same in return. Conversely, a smile or friendly gesture will usually lead to something good. The people in our lives and God himself will sooner or later follow the tracers we send out—back to their source.

> The one who sows to please his sinful nature, from that nature will reap destruction; the one who sows to please the Spirit, from the Spirit will reap eternal life. Let us not become weary in doing good, for at the proper time we will reap a harvest if we do not give up. ~Galatians 6:8, 9

An Eternal House

BOBBY COX had just taken his boots off when the first mortar shell exploded. He grabbed his gear and started running for the command center as fast as he could. Amid the din of incoming fire and confusion he didn't realize he had a shrapnel wound until someone pointed to the piece of metal in his arm. He pulled it out, and blood went everywhere. On reaching the command center, he dressed his wound and prepared for the worst.

Bobby Cox

Cox would never forget the night of February 18, 1972. He was assigned to an advisory team at a small Vietnamese Regional Force compound called Hiep Hoa. His job was to man a ground surveillance radar system, and, when he got to it that night, it told him more than a hundred VC were coming through the wire. Cox and the small team of Americans were in the basement of an old French building, with a perimeter defense around them manned by farmers and merchants serving as part-time soldiers. All he could do at that point was to wait—and pray. It was a little after 2:00 a.m., and his waiting and praying would go on for hours.

As the time passed, Cox's thoughts went back thirteen years to when he had become a Christian in an American Baptist Church in Bamberg, Germany. The preacher was an Army first sergeant named Howard Wiseman, who frequently quoted his favorite verse of Scripture:

Cox had received Jesus Christ into his heart and accepted that heavenly promise on that day in 1959. During a long night he kept praying and reassuring himself Jesus would look out for him, either in his earthly tent or in a heavenly one. Fifty years later, this soft-spoken man would say quietly and sincerely, *"We were saved that night by the grace of God."*[304]

> Now we know that if the earthly tent we live in is destroyed, we have a building from God, an eternal house in heaven, not built by human hands.
> ~2 Corinthians 5:13

One by Truck

THE FOG was thick and rain was falling around Camp Holloway in the Central Highlands. The radio crackled to life with an urgent call for a medevac. Captain Charles Fairchild was the pilot on duty that night, but, looking outside, he could hardly see his helicopter. He radioed back that he didn't think he could make it. A doctor at the outpost, eight miles away, answered, *"The man won't live until morning if you don't get him to a hospital."*[305] Fairchild turned to the rest of his crew and asked if they wanted to give it a try. They all nodded, and climbed into the Huey.

Fairchild tried every way possible to get to the sick man. He flew slowly twenty feet in the air along the road, but soon lost sight of it. After returning to base, he tried flying on a compass heading just above the trees with a searchlight, but became disoriented. In frustration, he returned to base, only to hear another report that the man was sinking fast.

> We also rejoice in our sufferings, because we know that suffering produces perseverance; perseverance, character; and character, hope. And hope does not disappoint us.
> ~Romans 5:3–5

It was not in the nature of the airmen to leave a man in the field who needed help. Fairchild radioed to have the man brought out on the road in an armored personnel carrier. He said, *"I'll drive out and get him in a truck."*[306] The rest of the crew overrode his order to stay behind. They picked up rifles and boarded the truck with the captain. At great risk they made the hazardous journey, picked up the soldier, and delivered him to a hospital. The patient was suffering from internal bleeding, but was saved by this heroic effort.

When Fairchild completed his tour of duty, he had medivacked 1,604 wounded and sick soldiers to hospitals—1,603 by helicopter and one by truck. The single-minded devotion of this airman to aid a fellow soldier in need reassured countless other men in the field that no medical emergency would go unanswered. It inspires us today to see what can be accomplished by someone dedicated to a mission, willing to persevere—and to improvise.

Nurses

HER FATHER was an infantry-man and her mother an Army nurse during World War II. Kathy Emanuelsen followed this military tradition by becoming an Army nurse during the Vietnam War. She served in the 12th Evacuation Hospital at Cu Chi, the combat base of the 25th Infantry Division. Her medical unit was housed in Quonset huts on the base, with a helipad nearby. There were wards for soldiers, Vietnamese civilians, and prisoners. The staff consisted of about fifteen doctors, twenty-five nurses, and various other medics and support personnel. She spent most of her tour working twelve-hour shifts in the emergency room treating gunshot and shrapnel wounds, as well as other injuries. There were times when incoming mortars exploded near the hospital, and the staff had to crawl around on the floor to tend to the wounded.

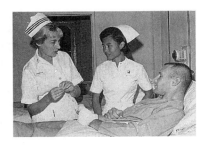

(National Archives)

Emanuelsen learned to cope with the stress of her job by focusing on the living and by remembering the men she and the rest of her medical team had saved. She later said, *"That wall in Washington would be double in size if it wasn't for the medics, dustoff choppers, and everybody who gave so much of themselves. These were human beings in a very inhuman place, trying to do the best they could. I had my successes and failures. But I did my very best."*[307]

Kathy Emanuelsen and her fellow nurses did save countless lives in Vietnam, and they hold a revered status among all veterans for their service. They also blazed a path in the U.S. military for women of the future. After Vietnam, women would be integrated more directly into all the services than ever before.

> You are all sons of God through faith in Christ Jesus, for all of you who were baptized into Christ have clothed yourselves with Christ. There is neither Jew nor Greek, slave nor free, male nor female, for you are all one in Christ Jesus.
> ~Galatians 3:26–28

Heart and Soul

HARRY HORTON and B. G. Burkett were roommates at Ft. Hood, Texas. Horton had dropped out of the University of Texas to join the Army and attend Officer Candidate School. Several times he told his friend that somehow he knew he was going to be killed in Vietnam. One night, Burkett asked him why he had volunteered for the Army if he thought he was going to die. Horton told him simply, *"Because America needs me."*[308] And he meant it.

> His work will be shown for what it is, because the Day will bring it to light. It will be revealed with fire, and the fire will test the quality of each man's work. If what he has built survives, he will receive his reward.
> ~1 Corinthians 3:13, 14

A month after his friend left for Vietnam, Burkett sent him a Christmas card that came back marked "Deceased." It took some time to learn what happened. He found the details in the Silver Star citation awarded posthumously to his friend. Horton had become a rifle platoon leader with the 25th Infantry Division and during a battle had been pinned down with his platoon by an enemy machine gun. Not wanting to send any of his men on such a dangerous mission, he charged the enemy position himself and was mortally wounded. Burkett later wrote these words about his friend:

> *Horton never hesitated. He did his duty to America without flinching. Harry wasn't an intellectual, nor was he particularly athletic or even very handsome. He was simply the heart, soul, and backbone of America. In times of crisis, it isn't the politicians or generals who save us. It's the Harry Hortons. Had he lived, Harry would have a wife, two kids, and a house in the suburbs. He would teach his children honesty, integrity, patriotism—and probably how to put frogs in the teacher's desk and play hooky. He'd make sure they all went together to church on Sunday. America didn't even notice the passing of Harry Horton, but she is substantially poorer in his absence.*[309]

This eloquent tribute to a man who didn't come home stands as a tribute to all others who suffered the same fate. I often think of the friends lost and the lives they should have lived. They never knew the children and grandchildren who would have been theirs to influence and love. The ultimate effect of their loss is truly incalculable. I pray that God has rewarded these heroes in ways we cannot begin to imagine.

Without a Scratch

MY WIFE and I were married at the Fort Myer Chapel in Arlington, Virginia, on Dec. 5, 1970. One of our groomsmen and sword bearers was a lieutenant and friend named Peter Pace. Little did we know then this energetic and highly competent young officer would someday be the Chairman of the Joint Chiefs of Staff and highest-ranking Marine in history. We have followed his career with great interest and admiration.

> When I felt secure, I said, "I will never be shaken." O LORD, when you favored me, you made my mountain stand firm; but when you hid your face, I was dismayed. To you, O LORD, I called; to the LORD I cried for mercy. ~Psalm 30:6–8

When General Pace retired from service in 2007, he made an unusual gesture in seeking out in Iraq the platoon he had served with in Vietnam. While talking to these Marines about his time in combat, he made a comment that caught my attention: *"Guys to the left of me got shot. Guys to the right of me got blown up and nothing happened to me at all. I didn't understand that. I got out of Vietnam without even a scratch on me."*[310]

These comments caused me to think about my own experience in Vietnam, where I also came through months of combat without a scratch. While thinking about this, I have had the startling realization that this charmed condition continues in my life. Lani and I have seen many good people suffer and succumb to depression, alcohol, failed marriages, and other maladies. Meanwhile, except for deceased parents, our family seems to go on, relatively untouched by disease or disaster. We look at each other and ask, "Why are *we* so blessed?" We can't answer this question, and we know this charmed state cannot continue forever. There are times ahead when we will be tested. Those of us who so far are relatively unscathed can only thank God for the blessings we have, and pray we are using them wisely. We need to grow closer to God and to each other today, knowing that these relationships are what will see us through the hard times of tomorrow.

Thanks, Doc

A FEW MINUTES past 7:00 a.m. the flight line telephone rang three times, the signal for an emergency medevac. The crew took off running for their helicopter—the pilots, door gunners, and two corpsmen. Gary Panko was one of the corpsmen. It was his job to fly with the helicopter to administer first aid and take care of any wounded Marines during the flight to the hospital. In the air they learned a patrol was in trouble, with two Marines hit by small arms fire and in need of evacuation.

Over the landing zone Panko looked down to see a firefight in progress. The patrol was receiving intense mortar and small arms fire. As the pilot started his approach, two jet fighters streaked by, slamming bombs and rockets into the VC positions. Before the smoke cleared they touched down in the landing zone, which was still under fire. The wounded Marines were rushed to the helicopter, and they all lifted off immediately.

Panko described what happened after they were airborne and safely out of the line of fire:

> After that I finally caught my breath and checked one patient over. He asked me for a cigarette so I lit one and gave it to him. The poor kid looked scared, but didn't cry or scream once. He was really a brave boy. All the time back to the hospital I kept holding his hand for comfort, and wiping some blood off his face.
>
> When we got there and I started unloading him, he looked up and smiled and said, "Thanks, Doc." Then he shook my hand. I felt like crying.[311]

There are few rewards greater than this—a simple "thank you" from someone who understands exactly what trials you have been through— even someone who has been through them with you. We each look forward to that amazing day when we will meet our Savior face-to-face—the One who truly understands everything about us and has been there with us. We know we can't earn our way to that meeting, but we can aspire to do something worthy of the greatest reward attainable in God's kingdom—the reward that will make all other rewards pale in comparison. We can only hope we hear our Lord and Savior, Jesus Christ, say:

"'Well done, good and faithful servant!'"
~Matthew 25:21

News

TOM FITZHARRIS spent his time in Vietnam working in a staff position at the Long Binh logistics base. Every day, he went from his room to the mess hall to his office, where he pored over reports, statistics, and photographs. As this routine went on for months, he began to feel disassociated from the war. He occasionally heard helicopters and artillery fire, his only reminders combat was taking place somewhere.

Fitzharris knew that when he went home, people would ask him about the war. He realized, however, he knew no more about what was happening in Vietnam than the average person in the States who watched television or read the newspaper. In fact, he might know less, considering he heard it all much later than anyone did back home. He commented:

> Consequently, you are no longer foreigners and aliens, but fellow citizens with God's people and members of God's household, built on the foundation of the apostles and prophets, with Christ Jesus himself as the chief cornerstone. In him the whole building is joined together and rises to become a holy temple in the Lord.
> ~Ephesians 2:19–21

> *It's weird how we get the news. It goes from correspondents here back to the States and then back to us. All the news reports I read have 'AP' tacked on them.*[312]

Most of us in Vietnam shared these sentiments. We occasionally saw an old issue of *Stars and Stripes* to learn what was happening around us. Anyone who has lived through a hurricane can identify with this phenomenon. You might know you have no electric power and see the wind blowing, but you don't know much else until someone tells you on your emergency radio. When you're in the news, it's difficult to get news.

We have a similar problem in our spiritual lives. We often have difficulty seeing ourselves and understanding where we are in relation to God unless someone else helps us with some perspective. This is true in most areas of personal behavior, but especially when issues of addiction are involved. For some reason, the person affected is the last person to understand there is a problem. This is why we can never afford to isolate ourselves as Christians. We need the body of Christ around us to help us see ourselves. Every member of the body is vital to the whole and to each other.

The Sinner's Prayer

BOBBY WELCH was a reconnaissance platoon leader with 1st Cavalry Division in Vietnam, where he was severely wounded and decorated for bravery in action. While recovering from his wounds, he rededicated his life to Christ and eventually became a Baptist minister. Years later, he was named president of the Southern Baptist Convention. Ironically, the great evangelist did not have a religious childhood.

Welch grew up in a small mill town in Alabama in a family of non-believers. His first interest in church was stimulated by a girlfriend. Just to be with her, he began going to the local Baptist church and gradually got to know the pastor, the Reverend Bob Mowrey. After many weeks, Welch went to Mowrey to talk about where his life was going. The minister knowingly and patiently talked the sixteen-year-old through three critical New Testament passages explaining Jesus Christ:

Sensing the young man was ready to make a commitment, the preacher suggested they pray together. Welch described the most important moment of his life:

> We knelt on our knees, and he led me to pray what's affectionately called: "the Sinner's Prayer": "Dear Jesus, I believe that You died on the cross for my sins and that You arose from the grave. I now ask You to forgive me of my sins, come into my heart, and save my soul."[313]

For all have sinned and fall short of the glory of God. ~Romans 3:23

For the wages of sin is death, but the gift of God is eternal life in Christ Jesus our Lord. ~Romans 6:23

Here I am! I stand at the door and knock. If anyone hears my voice and opens the door, I will come in and eat with him, and he with me. ~Revelation 3:20

For anyone who has not had such an experience in his or her spiritual life, Bobby Welch made a direct and urgent appeal: "If you are not certain you would go to heaven when you die, let me urge you to sincerely pray that simple 'sinner's prayer' as your own heartfelt commitment to Jesus."[314]

God Help Me

BOBBY WELCH will never forget the day he suffered a gunshot wound to the chest from close range. Bleeding profusely and unable to move or talk, he lay on his side, his face inches away from a pool of his own blood. As his fellow soldiers tried to stem the bleeding, he felt his life slipping away.

Bobby Welch in Vietnam

At that moment two shadowy figures appeared before him, and he had the strong sense that God and Jesus Christ had come for him. In that moment he was overcome with regret over the years he had let himself drift away from the commitment he made as a sixteen-year-old. At that point, he had given up hope to live and could only plead for mercy. With what seemed like his last breath, he repeated the prayer, *"God, help me! God, help me!"*[315]

The wounded soldier was loaded that night into a helicopter for evacuation to a field hospital where his life hung in the balance for days. During a brief moment of consciousness he promised God to be better, whether he was to live or die. He prayed, *"Lord, I intend to live for You from this day on."*[316] He later explained his thoughts at that crucial moment:

> *I was not playing "Let's Make a Deal" with the Lord. There were no strings attached to my prayer. No, this was a sincere and earnest commitment to Jesus Christ by a soldier of this country to become a soldier of His cross, until promoted to everlasting service for all eternity.*
>
> *The Lord Jesus Christ who had the love and power to reach down to an ungodly, dying soldier on a lonely jungle trail, halfway around the world from home; a soldier given up for dead and face down in a puddle of his own blood—that same Lord Jesus who worked a miracle to save a soldier's life, change him, and use him—is the same Lord Jesus who can do that for anyone! Don't you feel the thrill of that truth? "Wow, what a Savior, Lord, God!"*[317]

We pray this so that the name of our Lord Jesus may be glorified in you, and you in him, according to the grace of our God and the Lord Jesus Christ.
~2 Thessalonians 1:12

All My Luck

IT WAS the last day in the field for Captain Vernon Campbell. He was in command of an infantry company operating west of Quang Ngai. As he moved along a jungle trail with his unit, he stepped on the cardboard top of a C-ration box. Suddenly there was a small explosion that threw Campbell off his feet.

> *It sounded like three blasting caps going off at once. We all froze, and when I looked around I saw a small cloud of smoke, then there was more smoke and a sputtering sound off to one side of the trail. After a while, the sputtering stopped and the shell didn't explode.*[318]

The smoke and sputtering came from a 4.2-inch mortar shell. Campbell had stepped on the igniter of a booby trap that would have killed him instantly along with every man around him if it had gone off. It was a dud.

Campbell's last day in the field wasn't over yet. Even though he and his men were checking carefully for other booby traps, he stepped into a well-camouflaged punji pit. Fortunately, the stakes in this trap were old and broke off when the captain's foot went down on them. He suffered a few minor cuts, but none of the stakes penetrated his foot. He commented later on all of his "good fortune," saying, *"Some people may think I used up all my luck that day, but as far as I'm concerned, I've got plenty left."*[319]

> "Are not two sparrows sold for a penny? Yet not one of them will fall to the ground apart from the will of your Father. And even the very hairs of your head are all numbered. So don't be afraid; you are worth more than many sparrows."
> ~Matthew 10:29–31

While in combat, I was less sanguine about my reservoir of luck. I felt there was a finite amount of it and that I was using up some of it every time I came under fire. Since becoming a Christian, however, these confused thoughts about life and luck have disappeared. They have been replaced by confidence in God's plan and by the understanding he is in control of my life. I know that God knows me and has a plan for me that ultimately includes being with him. Until then I live with confidence and purpose, trusting in his *eternal* protection.

They Wanted to Know the Truth

DAVID GRANT was an Army medic serving in Japan when he received a Red Cross message notifying him a friend of his family had been wounded in Vietnam and was at the 106th General Hospital in Kishine Barracks, Japan. Within a few days, Grant made the trip by train and found the wounded soldier in the burn unit of the hospital. It did not look promising.

The wounded man was Warrant Officer Clarke Pederson, nicknamed "Corky." He had been shot down while flying a helicopter on a reconnaissance mission and had been thrown through the cockpit canopy. He was in very critical condition. Grant stayed with him for several days, but the wounded man remained comatose. When the inevitable occurred, Grant reported: *"Corky did go home. He passed into the Kingdom of God on that following Sunday."*[320]

Months later, when he returned to the States, Grant was able to visit Corky's parents. It was a poignant scene:

> *He was the only son. I talked for great length with his mother and sister, however his father stayed out of the conversation. I was one of the last to see him alive and they wanted to know what I saw. No, I didn't lie to them, because they wanted the truth.*
>
> *One other thing I told them, which also was the truth, was the dedication of the doctors, nurses, and medics who cared for him.*[321]

This young medic can teach us a lot about compassion. He cared enough about a fallen soldier and that soldier's family to pay a visit that was very important to the family in their time of grief. His words to them were honest, as he described the facts of their loved one's death. He didn't stop there, however. He gave them a positive image to remember, a picture of the care surrounding their son during his ordeal. As Christians, we have an even greater comfort to share with others in times of grief. We can tell of the care surrounding each of us—as promised by our Father in heaven.

> I will lead the blind by ways they have not known, along unfamiliar paths I will guide them; I will turn the darkness into light before them and make the rough places smooth. These are the things I will do; I will not forsake them.
> ~Isaiah 42:16

Doing unto Others

SOMETIMES our efforts to follow the Golden Rule go awry. A story published in the Americal Division newsletter in May 1968 makes the point:

> "Let your light shine before men, that they may see your good deeds and praise your Father in heaven.
> ~Matthew 5:16

> *Chu Lai—Army Staff Sgt. Cleve Watson, of Sikeston, Mo., discovered recently that "brotherly love" can sometimes backfire.*
>
> *"What are you doing here?" he roared at his younger brother, Floyd, a Marine, when the two met in Da Nang.*
>
> *"I volunteered to keep you from being sent," was the answer.*
>
> *Each had volunteered last summer to keep the other from having to serve again in Vietnam—but each kept the secret from his brother.*
>
> *The secrets were kept so well, in fact, that neither knew the other was in the war zone until a sister-in-law casually mentioned it in a letter to Cleve.*
>
> *"It's pretty funny now, but I was furious at Floyd for a while. He was kind of mad at me, too," laughed Cleve, a signalman with the 198th Infantry Brigade.*
>
> *Each had served a previous tour in Vietnam only a year ago.*[322]

This story recalls an incident in my family from an earlier era. My brother served in the Korean War, and, on his return, was assigned to Wright Patterson Air Force Base in Dayton, Ohio. My parents had not seen him for a long time, and decided to make a surprise visit over a long weekend. On that same weekend, my brother managed to get a training flight to South Carolina to surprise my parents. Somewhere between the two destinations, they passed each other.

Although the surprise backfired in both these stories due to a lack of communication, the impulse that motivated everyone's actions was good. Jesus told his followers, *"Do to others as you would have them do to you"* (Luke 6:31). A similar edict in the Old Testament tells us, *"Love your neighbor as yourself"* (Leviticus 19:18). Some expression of this ethical principle, commonly known as the Golden Rule, is found in every religion. It serves as a universal guide to ethical behavior in just about every aspect of life. We should always be considerate of how someone else feels, including their possible reaction to an unexpected "surprise.".

Passover

PASSOVER WAS a special event for the Jewish Marines in and around Da Nang. It was a rare opportunity for small groups from scattered units to come together for a special celebration of their spiritual heritage. The ceremonial Seder meal was served in the 3rd Division mess hall, where the staff went all out to make the event as authentic as possible. A sumptuous four-course meal was served to the ninety participants, including the traditional gefilte fish and matzo ball chicken soup.

> Then Moses said to the people, "Commemorate this day, the day you came out of Egypt, out of the land of slavery, because the LORD brought you out of it with a mighty hand."
> ~Exodus 13:3

Many kosher items came from Jewish organizations in the States. There were also Passover greeting cards sent from a Catholic war veterans group in Newark, New Jersey. The cards came with a note, explaining that they were written by school children:

> Please distribute the Passover cards to our Jewish brothers or to the Jewish Chaplains. The children sent these messages with love; the notes they wrote are from the heart. We send Passover greetings to our Jewish brothers on their holy day just as God sent his son to earth; to show us how to live as brothers. The significance of both holy days show that all people should live in peace and freedom.[323]

All these efforts were successful in enabling these men to feel part of a larger religious community beyond their immediate surroundings. Even though they were in a strange land, 8,000 miles from home and family, they could still be part of that community. Paradoxically, these soldiers had a significant spiritual advantage over their brothers and sisters living in peace at home. In the midst of a war themselves, they could more completely identify with the struggles of their forbearers, the earliest Israelites, undergoing hardships long before in another hostile place.

Baby Kathleen

KATHLEEN CORDS-EPPS is a mother of three daughters, now living quietly in a small town in northern California. Her journey to this place in life is an amazing story.[324]

In 1969 a group of 1st Division soldiers were moving through a Vietnamese hamlet destroyed a short time before by the VC. In the midst of the devastation, the soldiers heard a baby crying and, after a search, found a tiny three-week-old infant girl still clinging to her dead mother. They took the baby to the 3rd Field Hospital, where a nurse named Donna Rowe took over. She named the baby Kathleen and had the Catholic chaplain baptize her so she would be taken in by a nearby Catholic orphanage.

Sometime later, a naval officer named Marvin Cords heard about Baby Kathleen during a church service in Saigon. This was the beginning of a long quest by Cords to adopt Kathleen and bring her home to America. It took a year of paperwork and the signature of the president of South Vietnam to finalize the adoption. At last, this young girl completed the journey from a devastated Vietnamese village to a life filled with opportunity as part of an American family.

> Yet to all who received him, to those who believed in his name, he gave the right to become children of God—children born not of natural descent, nor of human decision or a husband's will, but born of God.
> ~John 1:12, 13

This story is not only an example of how adoption can be an amazing lifesaving event. It also gives a small insight into the nature of God's love for us. Although we are God's *creation,* we are not automatically his *children.* Through his Son, however, he gives us the opportunity to be adopted into his family as his own: *"So you are no longer a slave, but a son; and since you are a son, God has made you also an heir"* (Galatians 4:7). Like the baby Kathleen, we are able to go from a life of separation and isolation to one of inclusion in the greatest family of all. We are also able to claim our inheritance: a joyful hope in an eternal future of love and acceptance.

The Nurse

S HE WAS younger than the others—a second lieutenant working twelve-hour shifts giving special attention to the soldiers who couldn't do much for themselves. The sight of any American woman was like a tonic to the men serving in Vietnam, but was especially uplifting to the wounded undergoing treatment in field hospitals. This young nurse was friendlier than most, with a kind word for everyone despite her heavy workload. Everyone called her "Pinky" in recognition of her red hair and freckles.

> "Now that I, your Lord and Teacher, have washed your feet, you also should wash one another's feet. I have set you an example that you should do as I have done for you." ~John 13:14, 15

One evening at quitting time, she approached a wounded soldier with a bottle of lotion in her hand. The young man watched in amazement as she opened the bottle and, as he described, *"Proceeded to give me the best (and at that point the only) back rub I had ever experienced in my life."*[325] The soldier realized this gesture was beyond the call of duty for the nurse, and, even though he didn't know her full name, was forever grateful for this kindness. Speaking for all American servicemen during the war, he later said:

> *I believe she typifies the type of American woman that participated in Vietnam in any one of a variety of roles as nurses, donut dollies, civilians—volunteers all. Not one of them was drafted. They didn't just have a couple of missions go bad. Many witnessed the worst of times—certainly they saw, on a regular basis, the results—the negative sides of our experience in Vietnam. Yet, they stood tall—did their duty and then some—despite their pain, their suffering. God bless them all.*[326]

To this special nurse, he offered special thanks:

> *"Pinky, wherever you are—and all the 'Pinkies' who are out there—you deserve our gratitude, our love, our affection, and everything we could ever hope to have to offer you for your friendship, understanding, and, most of all, your love and the way you touched our lives. I personally owe you for the first real insight into the human spirit. Thank you."*[327]

I Can't Find It

WHEN HAROLD BRYANT went to visit the Vietnam War Memorial, the first name he looked up was that of James Plummer. As he stood staring at the name engraved in the black marble mingled with his own reflection, he started crying. This man had been his best friend from the first day in Vietnam, serving with him in the 1st Cavalry Division. One day he had seen Plummer working near the ammunition dump when it was hit by incoming mortar fire. Bryan was horrified to see the explosion obliterate his friend. Of all that happened to him during the war, this was the one thing he could not reconcile. His faith had also been obliterated by that blast:

> If any of you lacks wisdom, he should ask God, who gives generously to all without finding fault, and it will be given to him. But when he asks, he must believe and not doubt, because he who doubts is like a wave of the sea, blown and tossed by the wind.
> ~James 1:5, 6

> *I guess deep down in my head now I can't really believe in God like I did because I can't really see why God would let something like this happen. Specially like to my friend Plummer. Why He would take such a good individual away from here.*
>
> *I guess I got kind of really unreligious because of my Vietnam experience. Oh, I went to church once in my uniform to please my mother. But I haven't been back since except for a funeral. I've talked to chaplains, talked to preachers about Vietnam. And no one could give me a satisfactory explanation of what happened overseas. But each year since I've been back, I have read the Bible from cover to cover. I keep looking for an explanation. I can't find it. I can't find it.[328]*

This cry for help was written in 1984, and I pray that this sincere young man has somehow been able since to find a sense of peace about this event. There is no way to "explain" such a tragedy, and I wouldn't presume to try. I am sure, however, God honors every sincere plea made to him, even if it is in the form of a challenge. God hears us in our time of grief and doubt, and gives us the answers we need when we are ready to receive them. Only in him will we ever find peace of mind as we try to answer the unanswerable questions of life.

Guardian Angel

CRAIG ROBERTS escaped Vietnam with both legs intact. It was a close call. At first the doctors told him he would lose one of his legs below the knee because of an infected punji stake wound that showed signs of gangrene. Since childhood, Craig had always felt the presence of a guardian angel who protected him from death. He knew his angel would be with him on the operating table, but he wasn't so sure he was covered for the loss of limbs. He later thanked God the doctors were wrong and that his leg was saved.

In 1997 Roberts found himself in another operating room in Tulsa, Oklahoma. Chemotherapy for colon cancer had destroyed his immune system, resulting in internal infections and massive loss of blood. In an ambulance on the way to the hospital, he had heard an EMT say, *"This guy's not going to make it."*

> The angel of the LORD encamps around those who fear him, and he delivers them.
> ~Psalm 34:7

He was met at the hospital by his cancer surgeon. *"We're running some tests,"* he said. *"Do you have a living will?"*

Roberts asked, *"What's that?"*

"In case you have to go on life support. We've already told your wife. You're not going to make it. We're going to lose you. You're losing all your blood. We have five doctors working on you."

Roberts rallied, *"Right up front, Doc, let's get this straight. You have six doctors."*

"Six?"

"God's here. He's in charge. You listen to Him and do what He tells you to do."

The doctor had no answer for this statement and could only reply, *"We're going to need all the help we can get."*[329]

Craig Roberts entered an operating room for the second time in his life with confidence in the outcome. He had placed himself partly in the hands of capable doctors and fully in the hands of God. With the help of *all* his doctors, he did survive.

Marines land on operation near Phu Bai. (U. S. Marine Corps)

South Vietnamese Popular Forces. (National Archives)

The Dark Room

AS CRAIG ROBERTS was about to enter the operating room, he was at peace. The doctors and nurses were busy all around him as he had his last conscious thought: *I'm outa here.*

In what seemed like the next instant he found himself sitting in a large, dark room. He had an amazing sense of physical well-being, as if he were young again and in perfect health.

He was aware of someone behind him, touching his shoulder reassuringly. His guardian angel said to him, *"Remember? I told you when we were in the Legion that it wasn't your time. A decision is now being made on whether to take you on from here or to let you go back."*[330]

> He has also set eternity in the hearts of men; yet they cannot fathom what God has done from beginning to end.
> ~Ecclesiastes 3:11

Roberts was aware there were two paths before him, and he felt at perfect peace regardless of the outcome. Soon, he realized the decision was made. He was going back. His mind was filled with a flood of thoughts that seemed to be wisdom meant for others back in the world. Time seemed to have no meaning in the room, but it felt like only minutes had gone by. He opened his eyes to find family, friends, and doctors staring anxiously at him. Eighteen hours had passed.

"I don't know where you've been," the doctor said, *"but we lost you. You flatlined. You were dead. We gave up and started to unplug you— but then, after three minutes, we got a heartbeat again."*[331]

Near-death experiences have been studied by scientists for more than thirty years, and countless other stories such as this one have been documented. This body of evidence is one of our best proofs that human consciousness transcends the physical functioning of the brain. To scientists, this remains a great unsolved mystery. To the religious, it is another proof of the existence of the soul and the divine nature of mankind.

Act of God

A SOLDIER HAD a friend die from drowning while on R&R. He had seen a lot of death in combat, but this event affected him in a different way:

> *You know what scared me in Nam? We had a guy die from an act of God. He was swimming on vacation and he drowned. I had forgotten that you still had to contend with God, too. I didn't have it figured in the plot. That scared the (expletive) out of me.*[332]

It's a thought-provoking comment. Here is a man who sees God's hand in only *certain* forms of death. The unstated assumption is that deaths in combat are human acts of violence outside of God's purview. It raises the question: When is God involved? Does he determine our time of death, or not? Does it make a difference whether we are in a war or a traffic accident?

I haven't checked my answer to this question with theologians, but I don't think God decides when we are going to die. He undoubtedly *knows* when this will happen, but, nevertheless lets us make our own choices. We can take certain risks, or not. We can be harmed by the choices of others. Meanwhile, the natural world unfolds according to the dynamics God set in motion. He doesn't direct the path of hurricanes, germs, or bullets.

> The LORD is a refuge for the oppressed, a stronghold in times of trouble. Those who know your name will trust in you, for you, LORD, have never forsaken those who seek you. ~Psalm 9:9, 10

I don't mean to imply there is any limit on what God *can* do. He listens to our prayers. He intervenes in the natural world and performs miracles when they are in accordance with his purpose. Even though he doesn't protect us from all harm in this life, he watches us every moment of it and waits for us to put our trust in him.

I Have a Friend

A STORY OF unknown origin is posted on a veterans' Web site as a cautionary tale about our attitudes toward other people. Titled "A Soldier's Story," it tells of a young man who returned from the war in Vietnam and called his parents from San Francisco. He explained he wanted to bring a friend home with him who had lost an arm and a leg from a land mine. Since his friend had nowhere else to go, he wanted him to live with his family. Over the telephone, his father responded: "Son, you don't know what you're asking. Someone with such a handicap would be a terrible burden on us. We have our own lives to live, and we can't let something like this interfere with our lives."[333]

> This is how we know what love is: Jesus Christ laid down his life for us. And we ought to lay down our lives for our brothers. ~1 John 3:16

After the telephone call, the parents didn't hear from their son again. A few days later, however, they heard from the San Francisco police. Their son had died falling from a building. The police thought it was suicide. The shocked parents immediately flew to San Francisco and were taken to the morgue to identify their son's body. They recognized their son, but, to their horror, found that he had only one arm and one leg.

I think most of us would resist the full impact of this story by thinking to ourselves the son should have explained himself better. The parents would not have turned their own son away if they had known. The son, however, was trying to gauge the attitude of his parents, and he got an honest, but unfortunate, response. Do we think our attitudes toward others who are "different" in some way would be better? This is a matter of conscience for each to decide. We know there is One who accepts us and every other human being as his own, regardless of how different we are. He wants us to have the same attitude toward others.

They Got the Message

(U. S. Army)

THE COLONEL was incensed when he got the report. Vietnamese militia troops, sent to guard a nearby village, were, in fact, stealing from the villagers. Lieutenant Colonel John Warr, commanding the 5th Battalion of the Royal Australian Regiment, had spent a lot of energy developing good relations with these villagers and wasn't going to stand for this kind of abuse.

Colonel Warr loaded some of his men into an armored personnel carrier and drove directly into the Vietnamese unit headquarters. He lined all forty of the militia troops up at the point of a .50 caliber machine gun. As one of his men trained the gun on the line of troops, he spoke through an interpreter,

> We have been asked to come into this country to help the Vietnamese Army and government to drive the VC out and get the country back on its feet. We propose to do just that. We drove the VC out. We have been getting along well with the people here and we don't propose to have all this work undone by you. Keep out of the village.[334]

When the situation improved, the colonel remarked, *"It is quite clear that they got the message."*[335]

Sometimes we feel like taking drastic action ourselves when someone who should listen doesn't. It can be especially frustrating with our kids. Lining them up in front of a machine gun is out, but, still, when they just don't get the message, parents get frustrated. When the "line in the sand" is crossed, we start looking for a bigger "weapon." As one who has been there, I offer this advice to young parents: Don't back down, but don't keep escalating. Patience and persistence will pay off. Depending on the child, it may take a long time to see positive results, but loving consistency will pay off eventually. God blesses parents trying to do what is right, and he responds to prayers for wisdom and patience.

> The end of a matter is better than its beginning, and patience is better than pride. Do not be quickly provoked in your spirit, for anger resides in the lap of fools.
> ~Ecclesiastes 7:8, 9

Digging Ditches

THE SOLDIER and the company commander had quite a debate. Private First Class Bob Stokes was nearing the end of his tour of duty in Vietnam and his enlistment in the Army. He had been a good soldier, and the captain thought he should seriously consider reenlisting. However, nothing seemed to move the private. The officer explained all the benefits of an Army career and pointed out that Stokes would probably make sergeant one day, but the soldier continued to voice his resolve to "get out" as soon as possible. The officer reminded Stokes he had little education and that the Army would help him learn a trade, but again to no avail. Finally, getting a little heated, the captain threw out how hard it was going to be for Stokes to get a job on the "outside." He exclaimed, *"Go out and maybe you'll wind up digging ditches!"*

> God made you alive with Christ. He forgave us all our sins, having canceled the written code, with its regulations, that was against us and that stood opposed to us; he took it away, nailing it to the cross.
> ~Colossians 2:13, 14

"Maybe so," said the soldier, *"but at least I won't have to sleep in them at night."*[336]

In thinking about the soldier's clever rejoinder, it occurred to me many of us do manage to sleep in our ditches. We make mistakes, we get into trouble, and we just keep digging. Our ditch gets longer and deeper, and we stay in it. After a setback, we dwell on our own faults, and drift into depression. The old expression, *"As you make your bed, so you must lie in it,"* often works deep in our thoughts. Consciously or unconsciously, we keep on living with the results of our mistakes.

I don't want to make light of personal responsibility in any way—sometimes our actions are misguided and should have consequences. However, we don't have to let our mistakes continue affecting our attitudes and our lives indefinitely. Jesus promises us a clean slate and a fresh start when we repent of our wrongs and ask for forgiveness. There are ditches we can't get out of on our own, but there is none he can't *lift* us out of through his grace.

No Stained Glass Windows

LIEUTENANT Ronald DeBock was assigned as one of the first chaplains in the field hospital run by Company C, 3rd Medical Battalion, known throughout I Corps as "Charlie Med." He made it his duty to meet jeep and helicopter ambulances day and night to be one of the first to offer comfort to the casualties as they arrived. He often stayed with the seriously wounded in the operating room and followed up with frequent visits to the wards, bringing reading material, praying, and just talking with the men. He helped some of them make commitments to Christ.

> To you, O LORD, I lift up my soul; in you I trust, O my God . . . Show me your ways, O LORD, teach me your paths; guide me in your truth and teach me, for you are God my Savior, and my hope is in you all day long.
> ~Psalm 25:1, 2, 4, 5

On Sundays he held services in the hospital chapel, a fly tent pitched beside a nearby rice paddy. The chaplain had good memories of his primitive but spiritual "church":

It had no stained glass windows or even a single picture, but our blessed Lord was ever present, and the men knew it. They sang and worshipped as they had back home. They gradually adjusted to the sights and sounds of the area, and continued to pray or sing despite the noises of jets, helicopters, or artillery fire. Attendance at worship services was generally in small groups. In the hospital area and in nearby troop sites large assemblies of personnel were neither practicable nor desirable. Nevertheless, they came to worship God. The Marines seemed to take their religion as seriously as their duties.[337]

There is a small chapel at Camp St. Christopher on Seabrook Island, South Carolina, with only one noteworthy amenity. It has a large window over the altar with a view of the Edisto River and Atlantic Ocean. As the palm fronds sway and seagulls coast by on the breeze it is not difficult to go to a deeper level spiritually. God doesn't require much to enter our thoughts. He waits patiently for us to give him our attention. We can worship him in cathedrals or in tents. It has more to do with our own sense of urgency and our own understanding of how much we need him in our lives.

The Best Show

ONE DAY the chaplain ran out of wine for Communion. He knew an officer who had some scotch whisky, and prevailed on him to part with it for "a good better than his good." When the first Marine in line took a sip, he looked up in surprise, and took a second drink. The chaplain laughed, thinking this was the most unique Communion he had ever offered.

Religious services in the field were usually unique, although never elaborate. Chaplain Bob Bedingfield explained:

> I learned early on that the best service was a service that went no more than twenty minutes. Because, first of all, you didn't want to group people and, secondly, our attention spans ran awfully short. So the words were always words that were very simple and plain and the words were always words that ended with communion. I carried a chalice and by the end of my ten months with 3/3 [Third Battalion, Third Marines], I had been on my third chalice . . . the third one was pretty bent and bruised by the time we finished . . . I suppose we always had awfully splendid attendance because in the field I was always the best show in town.[338]

Under combat conditions, religious services were clearly a respite from the constant pressure and physical hardships of life in the field. Many of us did attend when possible, and, for a few moments, were able to reorient our thinking to a different place and a different concern. As a skeptic, I never gave much thought to the actual presence of God in these services.

As a believer, I now realize any worship service is truly the best show in town. Our daily lives are filled with pressures that often seem like combat. It is our greatest blessing to have the opportunity to come into God's presence to reorient ourselves and to strengthen our relationship with him. We can of course do this at times on our own, but we need to realize there are limits to our own thoughts. We need other input on a regular basis to lift us out of ourselves, and there is no better place to get it than a worship service with fellow Christians. We belong to the body of Christ. We need them, just as they need us.

> Come, let us bow down in worship, let us kneel before the LORD our Maker; for he is our God and we are the people of his pasture, the flock under his care.
> ~Psalm 95:6, 7

Eighteen Hours

Ed BLANCO's "freedom bird" landed at Travis Air Force Base on November 3, 1968. He changed uniforms and caught a bus to San Francisco for his final flight home. With his duffel bag over his shoulder he stopped in an airport bar for a beer to calm his nerves. He hadn't been away from the war long enough to really relax.

> "This is the covenant I will make with the house of Israel after that time," declares the LORD. "I will put my law in their minds and write it on their hearts. I will be their God, and they will be my people."
> ~Jeremiah 31:33

The bartender seemed to eye him cautiously as he stepped up to the bar. He was wearing dress greens, jump boots, airborne patch, and combat ribbons. He could feel the shell fragments still embedded in his jaw and neck. He ordered a beer. The bartender said, *"I'm sorry, soldier, but I need to see some ID. You have to be twenty-one to drink in California."*[339] Blanco thought the man was joking. Unfortunately, he was serious. He explained he could lose his job by serving minors. As Blanco quietly fumed over this absurdity, he thought to himself:

This meant one thing. I was back in the Real World. The war was back there with its own terrible rules. Goodbye to all that. For me, the war was over. I was now expected to live by another set of rules. In the Real World they had rules about who could and couldn't drink beer. The problem was that I didn't have a switch in my head that I could flip to make an immediate adjustment. I wasn't ready to accommodate these new rules. It was too sudden. Eighteen hours wasn't enough.[340]

Life in a combat unit isn't pretty, but it is simple. Authority is clear and the rules are few and self-evident. You don't need a lawyer. You take care of your weapon, your personal hygiene, and your buddies. The "regulations" of peacetime duty seem to fade away.

The Christian life isn't combat, but it shares an important similarity: It is also simple. When Jesus Christ enters your heart there is no longer any question of authority. With him within, the struggle with rules and regulations diminishes, because you know in your heart what is right. You can spend a lifetime learning theology, but the essential truths are simple: Love the Lord and love your neighbor.

Tank firing during road sweep (National Archives)

THE WAR ENDS

A FTER THE defeat of the North Vietnamese Easter Invasion in 1972, another period of outward calm settled over Vietnam. General Vo Nguyen Giap was replaced as commander of the NVA, as North Vietnam embarked on yet another rebuilding program. It would be several years before the Communists would be able to undertake another major offensive.

During this lull in the fighting, activity increased at the ongoing peace negotiations in Paris. By the fall of 1972, the United States had already made several key concessions. Unilateral troop withdrawals had begun, and Henry Kissinger had secretly agreed to allow NVA forces to remain in the South after a truce. When North Vietnam offered to drop its insistence on the removal of the Thieu government, it appeared an agreement was finally within reach. An accord was drafted providing for a cease-fire with forces in place, withdrawal of all U.S. forces, release of POWs, cessation of infiltration from the North, supervised elections, and a ban on introduction of new war materiel.

When President Thieu learned NVA forces would be allowed to remain in South Vietnam, he publicly denounced the agreement on October 24, 1972. Negotiations quickly fell apart in Paris as the North Vietnamese delegation walked out. President Nixon personally gave Thieu specific guarantees of U.S. support if the agreement were violated and also threatened to go ahead without him. He also approved a new bombing campaign to get the North Vietnamese back to the table. Finally, on January 27, 1973, over the objections of South Vietnam, an "Agreement on Ending the War and Restoring Peace in Vietnam" was signed in Paris. After one of the longest negotiations in history, lasting four years and nine months, the war was ostensibly over.

In February, Operation Homecoming commenced, bringing U.S. prisoners of war home from Hanoi. By April, 591 Americans were repatriated. As these men came back, it was finally revealed just how brutal their treatment had been. In the notorious Hoa Lo prison, known as the "Hanoi Hilton," the North Vietnamese had beaten their captives with fists, clubs, rifle butts, and rubber whips, and had inflicted other brutal tortures to elicit information and confessions. Starvation diets and poor to nonexistent medical care were standard as prisoners were isolated, unable to communicate with each other or the outside world. Nevertheless, the prisoners resisted in every way humanly possible, enduring torture, giving nonsensical confessions, and communicating secretly with each other.

Meanwhile, in South Vietnam, the thirteen NVA divisions left in place by the peace accord began deliberately violating the terms of the peace. The logistics flow to these units sharply increased as the new NVA buildup proceeded. The Soviet Union and China stepped up their support. During 1974 and 1975 the quantity of war materiel moving south through the pipeline was more than one-and-a-half times greater than the previous thirteen years of the war. Compared with 1972, six times as many weapons and ammunition stocks, three times as much rice, and twenty-seven times as much fuel were delivered.[341]

No U.S. effort was forthcoming to deal with these infractions. Instead, the U.S. Congress cut off funding for any further U.S. military action in or over North Vietnam, South Vietnam, Cambodia, or Laos. Congressional actions also cut promised financial and logistical aid to South Vietnam to almost nothing during 1974 and 1975.

In January 1975 North Vietnam sent their forces into Phuoc Long province, northeast of Saigon, and soon captured the capital city of Phuoc Binh. The U.S. State Department issued a "strong protest." When there was no U.S. response from the air, the North Vietnamese leadership knew the time had arrived for the final invasion. The beginning of the end came in early March, when twenty divisions commenced a drive to the south. Despite valiant stands by South Vietnamese troops in many quarters, the enemy advance inexorably ground forward to Saigon. On April 30, 1975, the last helicopter pulled off the roof of the U.S. Embassy, and the government of South Vietnam unconditionally surrendered.

Guilt

SOLDIERS AND Marines are taught how to kill. Basic and advanced infantry training includes hand-to-hand combat with knives and bayonets, rifle and pistol shooting, and familiarization with crew-served weapons such as machine guns and mortars. Every aspect of training is designed to build the aggressiveness needed to close with and destroy an enemy.

"You have heard that it was said to the people long ago, 'Do not murder, and anyone who murders will be subject to judgment.' But I tell you that anyone who is angry with his brother will be subject to judgment."
~Matthew 5:21, 22

All this training is usually effective in giving soldiers the skills needed to do their job and to survive in combat. Yet, no preparation has been found for actually taking another life. After his first firefight at close range, one young soldier in Vietnam had to unburden himself in a letter to his parents:

> Mom I don't know if I should tell you this or not, but I have to tell somebody and I can't tell Linda because she would worry too much, and I think you might be able to take it better than her. I think I might have killed a person but I am not sure, we were fired at and I seen men running with rifles so I opened fire on them and one of them fell to the ground. I just pray to God for forgiveness. I just hope you can forgive me.[342]

The Bible states it simply: *"Thou shalt not kill"* (Exodus 20:13 KJV). Theologians have tied themselves in knots delineating exceptions to this rule. Most would agree that a person defending his family, and soldiers fighting in so-called "just" wars, are not condemned by God for these actions. Still, God's guidance is emphatic. If we ever depart from it, even for reasons that are justified, there should be many conflicting feelings, including some measure of guilt. It is a great credit to this soldier and his family that he felt the need for forgiveness.

Further, we should also realize Jesus expanded the traditional definition of killing to include even anger toward others. Love cannot coexist in our hearts with feelings of anger or hatred. When we realize how often these feelings consume us, we understand how desperately we need forgiveness every day.

MEDCAP

Lt. Cal Cunningham

AFTER COMPLETING Navy Flight Surgeon School, Cal Cunningham was assigned to a Marine F-4 squadron at Chu Lai. In addition to his regular duties, he had the opportunity several times each month to go with medical civic action patrols (MEDCAPS) into nearby Vietnamese villages. Each patrol had several doctors, corpsmen, and a squad of Marines for protection. It was a strictly voluntary assignment that Cunningham accepted whenever asked. On every occasion the MEDCAPS were thronged by men, women, and children with every imaginable medical problem.

One day an infantry Marine came up to Cunningham at the base camp and said, *"Doc, last night we killed a few of your 'patients' in a fire-fight. We recognized the bandages and found some of the pills you gave them."*[343] The young doctor was stunned to realize he must have treated Viet Cong soldiers on one of his mercy missions.

I recently had a conversation with a member of my local city council, explaining all the good things my church was doing for the homeless in the community. His comment was, *"Well, you are just adding to the problem. You're attracting more homeless people to our town."*

Cal Cunningham and I were both victims of unintended consequences. We knew we were doing good things, but there were other ramifications the possibility of which hadn't occurred to us. Nevertheless, Cal didn't stop treating whoever came to him on his MED-CAP missions, and our church hasn't stopped feeding the poor. Faced with such ethical dilemmas, we sometimes have to look at our WWJD? bracelets, and prayerfully ask, "What *would* Jesus do?" The answer is usually not hard to find.

> *"For I was hungry and you gave me something to eat, I was thirsty and you gave me something to drink, I was a stranger and you invited me in."*
> ~Matthew 25:35

Prayer of Thanksgiving

A WOUNDED MAN immediately fears the worst. His first conscious moments are spent inventorying body parts and assessing how life-threatening his wounds are. Sometimes complete reassurance is a long time coming. A chaplain discovered he had to be careful how he approached these men:

> *There is one complication of which the chaplain needs to be aware. Because the wounded Marine is sometimes fearful for his life, the offering of prayer on his behalf carries for him the connotation of death. It then becomes necessary to assure the patient that you are sharing with him a prayer of thanksgiving for his having been spared and for full restoration to health. In every case when he understands that prayer is not being offered because he is dying, prayer is requested and welcomed.*[344]

Chaplains, unfortunately, have to face many negative connotations of their presence. In combat, a wounded man may presume the worst when a chaplain starts praying for him, and sadly, there are times when these fears are justified. On the home front, the worst moment in any military wife's life is to see an officer, accompanied by a chaplain, approaching the front door. Religious men and women have to face these dire situations as part of their professional lives.

> Sing to the LORD a new song, for he has done marvelous things; his right hand and his holy arm have worked salvation for him. ~Psalm 98:1

The rest of us also have to face our share of dire situations, helping friends and loved ones cope with tragedy in some form. As "nonprofessionals," we naturally have many doubts about what to say or do. Unfortunately, there is no formula for these situations, and each calls for its own prayerful discernment. I believe that the combat chaplain's advice does give us a useful insight. No matter what has happened, all people have something in their present and past lives for which they can be thankful. We can at least spend some time talking about those things, and we can say a prayer of thanksgiving to God for the many blessings he has given us.

There Goes the Light

IN A world without electricity, nighttime brings darkness suddenly and completely. It was an unnerving experience for infantry troops operating away from their bases in Vietnam. A soldier described the sensation:

> *But then the sun goes down and I could feel my stomach sinking. There goes the light. There goes one of your senses, the most important one. Life stops. There's no electricity. There's no technology . . . You think about people back in the world walking around downtown, going out for a beer. You'd be staring into the dark so hard, you'd have to reach up and touch your eyes to make sure they were still open.*[345]

I've never experienced anything more unnerving than darkness in a combat zone. Sounds are magnified when you can't see. Your imagination works overtime. You make mistakes. You get lost. Every time you move around, you put your life in the hands of others around you who are just as nervous as you are.

There is another form of darkness that is even more intimidating. When we live in spiritual darkness, we lack what is truly our most important sense: our sense of moral direction. It may be possible at times to figure out right from wrong intellectually. However, it is always difficult and often impossible to act on this knowledge. By completely changing our hearts, Jesus Christ brings a light that gives us an internal moral compass to guide our thoughts and actions. There may be times we fall short of Christ's ideal, but we know when it happens. He is always there within our hearts to give us forgiveness and support as we keep trying to be better for him. He is the light that never dims.

> I am writing you a new command; its truth is seen in him and you, because the darkness is passing and the true light is already shining. Anyone who claims to be in the light but hates his brother is still in the darkness. Whoever loves his brother lives in the light, and there is nothing in him to make him stumble. ~1 John 2:8–10

The Overlay

Sgt. George Graves

AS THE sun rose on another sweltering day in the Central Highlands, the patrol left the safety of Camp Enari for a two-day mission outside the wire. Sergeant George Graves was a member of the twelve-man group, led by a new staff sergeant he did not know. They labored across the rugged terrain all day, until dusk, when they stopped and went into a perimeter for the night.

Standard procedure at the time was for the patrol leader to call for an artillery flare to be fired just after dark. He would then shoot a compass azimuth to the flare and report this to base, to accurately fix the patrol's position. Over the radio, the usual artillery alerts were heard: *"Shot, out,"* meaning the round had been fired. A few seconds later, *"Splash."* Everyone looked skyward expectantly to see the flash. Instead, there was only darkness.

After this process was repeated several times without success, Graves asked the patrol leader for a look at his map. The sergeant put a plastic overlay on top of the map with the patrol route marked in grease pencil. Graves looked for a few seconds and then announced to the staff sergeant, *"You've got the overlay upside down!"*[346] No wonder they couldn't see the flares! They were as far off course as they could get.

Have you ever been completely turned around? It's not that difficult when you travel in unfamiliar places and/or in the dark. It helps to check yourself as you go along, but it is absolutely essential you orient yourself accurately at the beginning. If you make a fundamental error at that point, you will be forever lost. I find being preoccupied with myself is my way of turning the "overlay" upside down. Self-concern orients me in the wrong direction, and self-control leads consistently off course. My overlay is on straight when God is the focus of my journey and in control of it.

> Show me your ways, O LORD, teach me your paths; guide me in your truth and teach me, for you are God my Savior, and my hope is in you all day long. Remember, O LORD, your great mercy and love. ~Psalm 25:4–6

Prayed for Every Day

MIA bracelet
(American History Museum)

DURING THE Vietnam War Carol Bates was a college student looking for some way to give positive support to the troops overseas without getting embroiled in the student controversies over the war itself. She and several friends came up with the idea of wearing bracelets to stimulate concern for prisoners of war and those missing in action. Starting on a shoestring, her little group began making small quantities of these bracelets and eventually found themselves processing 12,000 requests per day. These bracelets were originally made of donated brass and copper and were engraved with the name, rank, and date of loss of the serviceman.[347]

In 2008 a young woman wrote a poignant letter to the family of a man remembered by one of these bracelets:

> Recently I was going through a hope chest and came across my mother's POW/MIA bracelet for Capt. Bernard Plassmeyer, 9-11-1970. I received this bracelet after the death of my mother. It brought back a lot of memories and prayers I remember hearing . . . I was 10 or 11 years old at the time and she kept it on for many years. I remember her every night while we said our prayers . . . for all service men and women. She would rub her bracelet and include Capt. Plassmeyer's name. I remember thinking at the time how important this was and how his family must be so scared.
>
> I was told that these bracelets are not to be returned until the soldier is brought home. But I thought if it was me, I would love to have this for my family history. To know that it has been kept safe by someone that cared about our son, father, or husband and thought of so much. And prayed for every day.[348]

This simple program has continued to touch the lives of thousands of servicemen and service-women and their families. These bracelets have kept memories alive and served as the focal point of countless prayers. We all pray that every missing person will eventually be accounted for and that every bracelet will someday be retired.

> Then Jesus told his disciples a parable to show them that they should always pray and not give up. ~Luke 18:1

Faith of a POW

ON HIS eighty-seven combat mission, F-105 pilot Roger Ingvalson was strafing a convoy of Russian-made trucks near Dong Hoi in southern North Vietnam when his aircraft was suddenly rocked by an explosion. His cockpit filled with smoke, and he was forced to eject. On the ground, he was soon captured, beginning an ordeal that would last five years.

When asked after his release how he survived, Ingvalson said simply, *"There is one word, and that is faith."*[349] His faith remained strong during captivity, as he often felt God's reassuring presence, even at the worst times.

Capt. Roger Ingvalson

On one occasion, his cell door was opened, and a Bible was tossed into his cell without explanation. Four days later he was brought into an interrogation room and abruptly informed his wife had died. Normally, he wouldn't believe his captors, but he knew this news was true because she had been in bad health. Overcome with grief, he returned to his cell. His only relief came as he immersed himself in his newfound Bible. That night he dreamed of his wife, not in the crippled state he had left her, but whole and healthy. He was certain the presence of that Bible was God's way of giving him hope and comfort, and that his dream was God's reassurance his wife was restored to perfect health in heaven.

One rock-solid principle we see repeated in Scripture is that God will never forsake his faithful followers. No matter what remote place we find ourselves in, either physically or mentally, he will not let go of us. Even in the darkest prison cell in the most remote corner of the world he will seek us out to give hope and reassurance.

> The LORD himself goes before you and will be with you; he will never leave you nor forsake you. Do not be afraid; do not be discouraged.
> ~Deuteronomy 31:8

Walking with God

WORSHIP SERVICES required a lot of imagination in a P.O.W. camp. The American prisoners were isolated from each other, and any noise or communication was severely punished. Even so, they persisted. One described his own way of bringing everyone together:

> "For where two or three come together in my name, there am I with them." ~Matthew 18:20

> *At a certain time every Sunday, I started whistling "The Lord's Prayer." All the guys with whom I and my buddies could get in touch agreed to have a regular church call at that same period.*
>
> *Once I stood next to my window, peering down through the little cracks where I could see a little bit of sunlight. It was time for church call, and I whistled "The Lord's Prayer." At that time I thought I whistled it alone. Suddenly an armed guard came running around the corner, headed for my cell.*
>
> *I obviously was caught, but I moved to the other side of my room and stopped whistling. But the whistling continued. Other men, whom I had not heard because all of us were in perfect unison, kept the tune going. The guard was confused. He could not be certain who was breaking the rule of silence and who was not—and so he could not stop the whistling. It went on, Sunday after Sunday, many of us whistling together to share with one another, "The Lord's Prayer."*
>
> *The help I received from those common—though distant—worship experiences was a big part of survival for me. Not only did they serve as a break in the boredom, but worshipping God kept constantly before me that he still was around. God was there for me, and he helped me make the best of a bad existence . . . Hand in hand with one another and with God, we walked through that valley.*[350]

We are not meant to follow Christ by ourselves. We are all parts of the body of Christ and each of us has a unique contribution to make to it. The church is not a collection of buildings, but is instead the Christians who fill them. The church needs us, just as we need the church. As we provide our talents in service to God's kingdom, we need the intellectual and emotional support that can only come from fellow Christians. We should pray for the same sense of urgency as did a group of prisoners of war as they risked their lives for this kind of fellowship.

Amazing Grace

DURING SOLITARY confinement, prisoners often passed the time thinking through their past lives. During the long days and nights in a place called The Zoo, Ralph Gaither went over it all. As he did so, he paid special attention to the path of his spiritual progress. He was raised in the Methodist Church, attended regularly, and participated in youth fellowship. He was encouraged by his mother to try other denominations and often went to different churches. His choice was frequently centered on the girl he was dating at the time.

At the insistence of one particular girl, Ralph went to a Christian retreat with a group of other teenagers, where he participated in group activities and a lot of singing. He was seventeen years old. At one point the group sang the moving hymn "Amazing Grace," and Ralph remembered, *I thought my heart would come out.*[351] At the conclusion of the song, the leader put down his guitar and opened a Bible. He read from Ephesians:

At that moment, Ralph's heart was filled with God's grace. Amazing grace. He remembered what went through his mind: *"I had always thought being a Christian meant earning your way. The difficulty of the Christian life had dominated my thinking about salvation. That night I found Christ as my Savior."*[352]

> For it is by grace you have been saved, through faith—and this not from yourselves, it is the gift of God—not by works, so that no one can boast.
> ~Ephesians 2:8, 9

Every Christian at some point in his or her spiritual journey experiences the breathtaking simplicity of the gospel message. We don't have to work our way to God. We simply have to receive a gift. By his grace and through his Son, God opens the door for us to be with him in this life and for all eternity.

South Vietnamese troops in the field. (National Archives)

Refugees crowd on board the USS Montague. (National Archives)

Finding God in Prison

RALPH GAITHER thought he had faith. However, after months of captivity, it wasn't working. He prayed for physical relief from his suffering, but only felt the cold, the hunger, and the pain more intensely. He tried to thank God for what he had, but found himself hating everything—his cell, the darkness, the guards, the pitiful food—with growing intensity. God did not seem to be listening.

> "Then you will call upon me and come and pray to me, and I will listen to you. You will seek me and find me when you seek me with all your heart."
> ~Jeremiah 29:12, 13

In desperation, Gaither began making promises to God of all the good things he would do in return for some relief from his pain. It dawned on him, however, God did not need his good deeds. He finally remembered God's promise of grace. Amazing grace. The words of his favorite hymn came to him: *"When we've been there ten thousand years . . ."* He went to his knees in prayer, and except for eating and sleeping, stayed there for three days.

During these days, the young man thought of Job's suffering and how he never lost his faith: *"My heart cried. I gave God everything I had, every bit of faith in my heart and soul."*[353] He sought only God's assurance in the present moment, and finally came to a point where he realized it was there:

> And then he came, and it wasn't in a ball of fire. It wasn't a voice or an angel. It was nothing like that. My life changed, and I felt the change in my mind. I knew it without any question of a doubt. I knew the Lord was with me and that he would watch over me from that point on. I had a confidence in my heart that told me God would give me the strength and patience I needed.[354]

I have never heard a greater story of faith through adversity. It teaches us to never give up—that God is always there. It reminds us that, if, in a crisis, we are able to come closer to him, then that crisis will eventually be one of our greatest blessings. When times are hardest, we must persevere more than ever in our faith.

Communion

FOR PRISONERS, communicating with each other was an urgent need, leading to dangerous and ingenious schemes. In his book, *With God in a P.O.W. Camp*, Ralph Gaither stated that all of the methods used could not be revealed in print, because they were still considered vital tools for captured soldiers. However, their usual means were to speak quietly when possible or to tap out coded messages. Those involved in any kind of activity such as these risked severe reprisals if discovered.

Ralph developed a close friendship with a fellow prisoner named Bill Shankel in the cell next to his, even though he was not able to see him directly. They set up a routine of "talking" twice a day. Bill had learned the Lutheran Communion service from another prisoner, which he shared with Ralph. Together they established another routine: Every Sunday they held a Communion service.

> Then he took the cup, gave thanks and offered it to them, saying, "Drink from it, all of you. This is my blood of the covenant, which is poured out for many for the forgiveness of sins. I tell you, I will not drink of this fruit of the vine from now on until that day when I drink it anew with you in my Father's kingdom. ~Matthew 26:27–29

> *We saved a little water and rice for the occasion, and at the proper time one of us initiated the service. A light tapping on the bars signaled the start. When both of us had time to get in position with our elements, a second tapping started us in unison speaking the words for the bread. Then a third tapping and we took the wine, again speaking the words in unison.*[355]

We know that Jesus himself initiated the sacrament of the Last Supper. He shared a meal with his disciples before his crucifixion and told them to continue the practice. It has been continued and is a vital observance of the church and an important way in which Christians renew their faith on a regular basis. We should approach it with the same reverence as two prisoners of war, risking their lives to be in communion with their Savior.

Making Bibles

PRISONERS HAD no Bibles. They had to make them in their minds. Anyone who could remember a verse would share it with others by code. These were passed along until everyone had heard each one. Some tried to commit them all to memory, and some tried to hold onto them in written form. One prisoner explained the techniques:

> *We wrote them down when we could. We wrote on the floors of our cells with rocks. We wrote on that sandpaper-like stuff that passed for toilet paper. Our ink in those early days was made from brick dust or soup, in later days from coffee or whitewash. Sometimes we used our lead toothpaste tubes, which made a pretty good black mark.*[356]

These homemade "Bibles" were crude, but effective. Few verses were accurate word for word and many were out of order, but the basic meanings were there. In addition, songs and poems were shared and memorized, and were an important part of the prisoners' common knowledge. Sometimes remembering an entire song was a slow and agonizing process. It took one man four years to piece together one particular hymn. He concluded God has a way of letting us remember things we need when we most need them.

Few, if any of us, will ever face a situation in which we will be denied access to our Bibles or hymnbooks. This story should serve primarily to heighten our thankfulness that these resources are so readily available. A spiritual life without the Bible would be difficult if not impossible for most of us. God has provided his Word in this amazingly complex volume to give us food for daily living throughout our lifetimes. Each one of us can make better use of this gift, and each of us can do more to share it with those who do not have it.

> You have known the holy Scriptures, which are able to make you wise for salvation through faith in Christ Jesus. All Scripture is God-breathed and is useful for teaching, rebuking, correcting and training in righteousness, so that the man of God may be thoroughly equipped for every good work.
> ~2 Timothy 3:15–17

The Flag

MIKE CHRISTIAN knew the risks, but was doggedly determined to complete his project. After finding a handkerchief in the gutter, he had a vision of it as a flag. The other POWs gave him bits of soap to clean it, ground-up pieces of red and blue roof tiles to color it, and small amounts of a watery rice glue to paint on the colored pieces. Finally, he labored under his mosquito net at night, secretly sewing on the stars with bits of thread from his blanket and a handmade bamboo needle.

One morning, when no guards were nearby, he called out to everyone and lifted his "flag" high over his head, waving it as in a breeze. The other prisoners stood proudly at attention, many with tears in their eyes, and saluted. They finally had their most cherished symbol of home: an American flag.

> For the message of the cross is foolishness to those who are perishing, but to us who are being saved it is the power of God. For it is written: "I will destroy the wisdom of the wise; the intelligence of the intelligent I will frustrate."
> ~1 Corinthians 1:18, 19

Unfortunately, Mike's flag was soon discovered by a guard. The retribution was swift and severe. He was taken from his cell and beaten all night. He recovered slowly for two weeks—and then began to work on another flag. One of his friends later commented, "*The Stars and Stripes, our national symbol, was worth the price to him. Now whenever I see the flag, I think of Mike and the morning he first waved that tattered emblem of a nation.*"[357]

Our symbols grow in importance when they represent cherished things we have lost or could lose. The flag to a group of POWs is a clear example. This story should also be an inspiration to Christians regarding our own symbols. The emblem of our Savior's suffering and death is becoming more and more important as we strive to carry his message to an indifferent culture. It's nice to see a cross in church, but is even more uplifting to see one on a necklace, a lapel, or a car—identifying a fellow soldier in the army of Christ.

Christmas Tree

THE APPROACH of Christmas only deepened the gloom of a cold, barren prison cell. Temperatures in the forties weren't quite cold enough to freeze the captives. However, the cold sapped their strength and quickly burned the few calories they were able to ingest. Ralph Gaither stayed cold, and he stayed hungry. It had been two months since his F-4 had been shot down during a bombing run on the Red River Bridge, north of Hanoi. He had suffered beatings, torture, solitary confinement, and constant handcuffs.

> The gift of God is eternal life in Christ Jesus our Lord. ~Romans 6:23

Christmas brought tantalizing thoughts of where he most wanted to be: home. In his mind he pictured his family's traditional Christmas tree and imagined everyone around it opening presents. He thought of parties in friends' homes, each with a Christmas tree at the center of the celebration. He longed for a tree of his own to celebrate the season, but knew how completely impossible this was: "*We were not allowed to bring a stick even the size of a match into the room. Nothing was allowed into our cells, and the frequent searches made sure the barrenness.*"[358] Still, the young airman dreamed of a tree and what it represented. He prayed.

> *Then one afternoon after washing my dishes, I turned to take the one step back into my cell. I looked down, and on the threshold of my door was a tiny leaf blown by the wind. I picked it up with my toes and carried it inside. The door slammed behind me. I carefully took the leaf from between my toes and looked at it for a long time. I held it to my nose. The perfume of freedom raced up my nostrils and infused my mind with its power. I fondled the leaf. It was real. I held it in my hand. God had not forgotten me. I set the leaf on the little ledge by the window. Its greenness stood out in stark contrast to the dull, gray bars. Tears rolled down my cheeks. God had given me a Christmas tree.*[359]

At Christmas and on every other day of the year I pray to be as thankful for the abundant blessings in my life as this young man was for a simple leaf. I have so much to be thankful for, and I know that all good things come from God.

Values

BARRY BRIDGER was a highly decorated F-4 pilot with two hundred combat flying hours and seventy missions. On January 23, 1967, he was shot down over North Vietnam and spent six years as a prisoner of war in the notorious "Hanoi Hilton." To survive this ordeal he had to come to terms with what was really important in life:

POWs (U. S. Naval Academy)

I think that you could appropriately say that there wasn't much of a difference in the attitudes of most of us young men who walked into the prison camps in North Vietnam. We all probably thought that success in life was how fast you could run the 100 yard dash, how quickly you could be promoted . . . but when you were actually cast into the encroaching environment of a POW prison camp you began to focus very rapidly on ideas that were more meaningful, which is your faith, family, and friends, and doing something worth remembering.[360]

Bridger concluded from his experience that, during a crisis, *values* are the most important things in life: *"rugged individualism, caring and respect for others, good character, being confident."*[361] These values are common to most Americans and can be traced back through preceding generations to our Founding Fathers. With faith in God first and foremost, these are the values that enabled our prisoners of war to survive the impossible conditions of their captivity. These are the same values that will enable this generation and future generations of Americans to live meaningful lives and survive whatever hard times are in store.

Therefore, since we have been justified through faith, we have peace with God through our Lord Jesus Christ, through whom we have gained access by faith into this grace in which we now stand. And we rejoice in the hope of the glory of God. Not only so, but we also rejoice in our sufferings, because we know that suffering produces perseverance; perseverance, character; and character, hope. And hope does not disappoint us, because God has poured out his love into our hearts by the Holy Spirit, whom he has given us. ~Romans 5:1–5

Circuit Breaker

PAIN IS the body's natural defense. When something hurts, we usually quit doing it. However, when the pain is not under our control and reaches a certain level of duration or intensity, there is a circuit breaker in our brains that short-circuits the pain, at least for a while. This circuit breaker was tripped often for prisoners of war under interrogation and torture in North Vietnamese prisons. When that point of extreme pain was reached, the prisoners either passed out or went into a zone where the pain no longer mattered. The interrogators came to understand this phenomenon and found ways to work around it. By putting their victims in uncomfortable positions for days and even weeks, they inflicted pain that became more and more excruciating, but never tripped the breaker.

> Then he called the crowd to him along with his disciples and said: "If anyone would come after me, he must deny himself and take up his cross and follow me."
> ~Mark 8:34

Hopefully, we will never have to experience this kind of torture. We will all, however, face varying degrees of frustration and misery over the misfortunes of life. The vast number of people suffering from depression attests to this fact. Fortunately, God has provided a circuit breaker to make any pain or frustration bearable. His circuit breaker is found in the assurance that he knows our burdens and will never be give us more to bear than we can endure. A soldier from another war found affirmation about this aspect of God's nature in a reflection titled "Your Cross":

> The everlasting God has in his wisdom foreseen from eternity the cross that he now presents you as a gift from his inmost heart. The cross he now sends you he has considered with his all-knowing eyes, understood with his divine mind, tested with his wise justice, warmed with his loving arms, and weighed with his loving hands to see that it be not one inch too large and not one ounce too heavy for you. He has . . . taken one last glance at you and your courage, and then sent it to you from heaven . . . alms of the all-merciful love of God.[362]

The Lord Is My Shepherd

THE PRISONERS were filled with foreboding as they were herded into trucks and blindfolded. This was the first time they had moved during daylight hours. Something big was up, and they could only suspect the worst. When they were forcefully removed from the trucks and their blindfolds were taken off, they realized they were in downtown Hanoi.

> Even though I walk through the valley of the shadow of death, I will fear no evil, for you are with me; your rod and your staff, they comfort me. You prepare a table before me in the presence of my enemies.
> ~Psalm 23:4, 5

Ralph Gaither could see he was near the end of a line of about sixty prisoners, surrounded by a surging mob. Political cadres yelled to the crowd with loudspeakers, whipping them into a frenzy. The guards ordered the prisoners to move along the street and to bow their heads. One of the prisoners spoke out: *"Stand tall, you're an American."*[363] Gaither and the others held their heads high—and paid the price. The crowd roared. They were struck over and over with fists and rocks. Children kicked their legs. People broke in front of them and spat in their faces. The women took off their shoes and beat them with the wooden heels.

Progress was slow and halting. Men went down and were helped up by others. The violence of the crowd was unremitting. Gaither stumbled and a friend caught him. His friend went down. They finally locked hands to support each other. Someone repeated, *"Stand tall, you're an American."* They kept going. Nearing exhaustion, Gaither started reciting the Twenty-Third Psalm. Others around him picked it up: *"The Lord is my shepherd; I shall not want . . ."* Gaither said later, *"Hand in hand with one another and with God, we walked through that valley . . . I did not try to test God; in fact, I tried very hard to survive. But I had no fear for the next day. God was with me, whether I was to live or die."*[364] In a very real "valley of the shadow of death," these men were able to lean on God for strength and reassurance. In spite of their hopeless situation, they remained strong in their faith. God did not desert them.

Thanks to God

TO THE prisoners of war in the so-called "Hanoi Hilton," bombs falling on the North Vietnamese capital meant one thing: America was trying to win the war. When Linebacker II ended and the bombing stopped in December 1972, a pall of uncertainty settled over the ever-expectant American captives.

Hanoi Hilton (U. S. Air Force)

Robert Certain languished in the Hanoi prison as the days and weeks of captivity ticked by. He could only guess at the meaning of the bombing halt and continue to speculate if the war would ever end. Although his living conditions were deplorable, the young airman continued to thank God for what he had:

> *Sanitary conditions did not improve. There was no medical care. Baths were only allowed once a week. Toilet buckets were in the anteroom and were emptied daily, except on Sundays. Rats visited nightly, crawling over us in search of dropped food. Meals consisted of bread made with rat-dung-and-insect-contaminated flour, and the usual cabbage soup containing similar contamination and undercooked pork fat and skin. The morning beverage continued to be the sweet reconstituted powdered milk that came from Poland. We had to eat to maintain our strength; but the meals were becoming boring, repugnant, and hard to swallow. Nevertheless, I always offered thanks to God for the food and for life.[365]*

I know what it is to be in need, and I know what it is to have plenty. I have learned the secret of being content in any and every situation, whether well fed or hungry, whether living in plenty or in want. I can do everything through him who gives me strength.
~Philippians 4:12, 13

Only God can give meaning to our suffering. When we rely on him, times of adversity can bring us to a deeper relationship with him. Hard times also present opportunities for us to give a powerful witness to others. Thankfulness in the face of adversity is a strong testimony to God's saving grace. The apostle Paul suffered greatly during his ministry, often as a prisoner. He modeled the attitude we need to adopt during our own trials, whether great or small.

311

I Thank Thee

AS 1972 came to an end, peace rumors began to fly and life began to change in the North Vietnamese prison camps. The food, treatment, and living conditions improved noticeably. More worship services were allowed, and, on one Sunday, Ralph Gaither was asked to speak on the subject of "blessings." Reflecting on his seven years of captivity, he remembered a lot of suffering. He nevertheless felt he had a lot to be thankful for as well. In fact, when he started actually counting his blessings, he knew there were too many to cover in only one service. When he woke up that Sunday morning, a poem came to his mind and seemed the best way to address his feelings. Trying to speak for himself and his fellow prisoners, he wrote:

> I thank thee, Lord, for blessings, big and small;
> For spring's warm glow, and the bird's welcome call;
> For summer's lease, with clouds that dance in rain;
> For autumn's hue, and winter's snow white shawl.

> I thank thee for each sunset in the sky;
> For sleepy nights, the bed in which I lie;
> A life of truth, and peace, a woman's love;
> Her hand in mine, until the day I die.

> I thank thee, Lord, for all these things above;
> But most of all I thank thee for thy love.[366]

When we consider the physical circumstances of the man who wrote this poem, we should be inspired to count our own blessings. Thankfulness is always the most appropriate attitude to adopt toward our Father in heaven. King David endured his own trials and still left us the classic expression of thanks and praise to God:

> I will praise you, O LORD, with all your heart; I will tell of all your wonders. I will be glad and rejoice in you; I will sing praise to your name, O Most High . . . The LORD is a refuge for the oppressed, a stronghold in times of trouble. Those who know your name will trust in you, for you, LORD, have never forsaken those who seek you. ~Psalm 9:1, 2, 9, 10

Jane Fonda

CHUCK DEAN was talking to a group of Vietnam veterans on the subject of anger management when one of the vets expressed his hatred for Jane Fonda (in recounting this story, Dean referred to her as *"a Hollywood actress known for her vocal and active opposition to the Vietnam war"*). When he asked for a show of hands of those who agreed with this sentiment, every hand shot in the air, and in some cases, both hands.

> Bear with each other and forgive whatever grievances you may have against one another. Forgive as the Lord forgave you.
> ~Colossians 3:13

Dean used the occasion to talk about one of the most important subjects veterans need to address: forgiveness. He cautiously explained he had decided some time earlier to let go of his anger toward this person. His anger had formed a "relationship" with her that he didn't need and in effect put him in bondage to his own feelings. The only way he could let go of these feelings was to forgive this person. He also said, *"Forgiving someone takes a lot more courage than charging an enemy bunker, or walking exposed across an open rice paddy."*[367]

Many in the group decided that day to forgive Jane Fonda and to let her walk out of their lives for good. The group prayed together for forgiving hearts. Afterward Dean was witness to one of the most amazing events he had ever seen:

> *I don't see many miracles in my life, but that day I did when one particular Marine veteran forgave this celebrity. This man had been wounded by a .50-caliber round, and was paralyzed from the waist down and in a wheelchair for more than two decades. By a simple act of faith, he forgave this infamous woman, and within a couple of hours was out of his chair for the first time in twenty-three years. He stood and walked away from his wheelchair that day, never to return to it. For some reason only known to God, that bitterness and unforgiveness was keeping him bound to a life without walking.*[368]

Our own unforgiveness may not be crippling in a physical sense, but it undeniably impairs us emotionally. By forgiving someone of something we are holding inside, we free ourselves from bondage. In a small way, we also follow the example of the One who brought forgiveness to us and the whole world, our Lord Jesus Christ.

To Volunteer

LIEUTENANT Pat Brantley served proudly as a nurse in Vietnam. She was most enthusiastic about her volunteer work with a civic action team in a Vietnamese village near her base:

Pamela and Lani with Rwandan children

Yesterday was one of the most rewarding days I've ever spent since I've been here. I went on a junk (a Vietnamese boat) to a small fishing village south of here on the coast . . . It's strictly voluntary on off-duty time, and they go up every Sunday. It's set up by the Navy. Five nurses, two doctors, and the dentist with our hospital went yesterday. We take medicines and supplies along, and set up a clinic right outdoors for anybody who needs to come—and believe me, they come! I've never washed so many babies and children in my life! They had so many sores a lot from just a lack of using soap and water. Then we applied Furacin ointment. A lot of people had infected places and we gave out antibiotic pills.[369]

Recently my wife, Lani, and her friend Pamela went on a medical mission to Rwanda. One of their most startling discoveries was the prevalence of infections from what had initially been small cuts and sores. Left untreated for long periods of time, some of these wounds had become life-threatening. Never was the adage, *"An ounce of prevention is worth a pound of cure,"* more appropriate to a situation. The medical team cleaned and dressed countless cuts to prevent infection and spent many hours debriding old wounds to get advanced infections under control.

Back at home, Lani and Pamela have undertaken a mission to build a medical clinic in Rwanda to continue and to expand these treatments. The clinic has to be built and a staff trained. These will not be easy tasks. The two women are motivated to do God's work and inspired by the fact that, in that environment, a little goes such a long way. No one can solve all the ills of the world, but God bless those who do what they can.

> "'When did we see you sick or in prison and go to visit you?'
>
> "The King will reply, 'I tell you the truth, whatever you did for one of the least of these brothers of mine, you did for me.'" ~Matthew 25:39, 40

A Revolution Based on Reality

P. J. O'Rourke, the best-selling author and writer for *Rolling Stone* magazine, had some interesting observations on the things he believed as a hippie during the '60s:

> Restore us again, O God our Savior, and put away your displeasure toward us. ~Psalm 85:4
>
> Surely his salvation is near those who fear him, that his glory may dwell in our land. ~Psalm 85:9

You name it and I believed it. I believed love was all you need. I believed drugs could make everyone a better person. I believed Mao was cute. I believed the NLF were the good guys in Vietnam. I believed wearing my hair long would end poverty and injustice. With the exception of anything my mom and dad said, I believed everything.[370]

One of the most pervasive beliefs in O'Rourke's circle was an ill-defined Marxism, based on collective ownership and shared wealth. As he considered how the value of anything would be established in such a system, he observed that the wildest hippie and most dedicated member of the Politburo shared the same daydream: *"that a thing might somehow be worth other than what people will give for it."*[371] He finally came to realize that anything based on such a false premise was bound to fail. He also came to a new appreciation for his own nation:

Maybe we should start by remembering that we already live in a highly idealistic, totally revolutionary society. And that our revolution is based on reality, not buncombe. Furthermore, it works. We have to remember it was the American Revolution, not the Bolshevik, that set the world on fire. Maybe we should start acting like we believe in that American Revolution again. The President and his advisors will not have to sit up late working on a speech to fire the public in this cause. There's a perfectly suitable text already in print:[372]

"We hold these truths to be self-evident . . ."[373]

P. J. O'Rourke's political life changed when he realized the Declaration of Independence had more wild ideas than anything he had dreamed of as a hippie. A government established under God designed specifically to serve the governed remains the greatest revolutionary idea in history.

Vietnam Peace Agreement signed Jan. 27, 1973. (National Archives)

Newly released POWs board aircraft for home. (National Archives)

God in the Battle

WHILE TALKING to a group of university students recently, former Khe Sanh Chaplain Ray Stubbe was asked about the spirituality of the men he served with in combat. He answered that at least two dozen former "grunts" had later become ministers. He also pointed out one of the great spiritual lessons he had learned from these men:

In their conversations with me, they said they were aware of the presence of God precisely in the midst of the terrors and horrors of war there. God is with us precisely in the dark times of life, in horror and terror and war. God is on the cross, identifying with us when we face death. We have peace, in the original sense of "Shalom," which is not the absence of conflict, but the presence and blessing of God precisely IN the battle.[374]

The chaplain is reminding us of one of the great attributes of God. We know he doesn't prevent war, and that he doesn't shelter us from life-or-death situations. Neither, however, does he in times of extreme stress abandon those faithful to him. He knows where we are, and he hears our cries. Most Christians I know look back at the crises in their lives as the moments God was closest. When we have this kind of faith, there is no crisis that can't eventually have a silver lining. We need to use our moments of vulnerability as opportunities to lean more completely on God and to grow closer to him. To those who did reach out in faith, he was there in Vietnam, even in the midst of the battle.

You have laid your hand upon me. Such knowledge is too wonderful for me, too lofty for me to attain. Where can I go from your Spirit? Where can I flee from your presence? If I go up to the heavens, you are there; if I make my bed in the depths, you are there. If I rise on the wings of the dawn, if I settle on the far side of the sea, even there your hand will guide me, your right hand will hold me fast . . . Even the darkness will not be dark to you; the night will shine like the day, for darkness is as light to you.
~Psalm 139:5–10, 12

Refugees

TAN SON NHAT Air Base was in chaos. Buildings and aircraft were burning. Overhead, a C-119 gunship was hit by ground fire and went down in flames. U. T. Nguyen and his new wife, Dao, huddled under the wing of a C-130 cargo plane, praying fervently that the rockets would miss them for a few more minutes. Finally, the Nguyens and a group of three hundred other Vietnamese airmen and their families scrambled aboard the aircraft as it taxied out to the runway for a hazardous takeoff for an unknown destination. At that moment on April 29, 1975, U. T. Nguyen left his life as a Vietnamese citizen and career air force officer to become a refugee.

Lt. U. T. Nguyen

The odyssey of this man and his wife took them from the burning runway of Tan Son Nhat to a refugee center in Fort Smith, Arkansas. There they found themselves with thousands of others facing an uncertain future. After days of anxious waiting, U. T. heard his name on a loudspeaker, calling him to the Red Cross office. There, someone handed him a telephone. He placed it to his ear and heard a familiar voice from the past saying, *"U. T., you're coming to Nashville to live with us."*[375] Lieutenant Colonel Talf Davis, U. T.'s former flight instructor at Keesler Air Force Base, had remembered his student and learned of his plight. Davis took the young couple into his home to give them a chance for a new life.

It is difficult to imagine losing everything. It is true, nevertheless, that ultimately each of us will be a refugee at some moment in the future. As we depart this life we will lose everything of this world and find ourselves in desperate need of a final and eternal lifeline. Will this be your moment of greatest uncertainty, or will you be confident of your place in God's family?

> Let us then approach the throne of grace with confidence, so that we may receive mercy and find grace to help us in our time of need.
> ~Hebrews 4:16

The Best Policy

STARTING A new life in America wasn't easy for U. T. Nguyen. With the help of a former flight instructor, he and his wife, Dao, went to Nashville, where he got a janitor's job at Vanderbilt University Hospital. He was thankful for his miraculous survival, but the menial work required in his job was a long way down from being a pilot and former air force officer.

U.T.and Dao Nguyen

One day U. T. was approached by a reporter for a local newspaper doing an article about the Vietnamese community in Nashville. He and several other former military officers were interviewed at the same time. Each was asked the question, *"Do you like your job?"* One by one, the others said they did, giving what seemed the "politically correct" answer. When the question came to U. T., he said, *"No. I don't like being a janitor."* He told the reporter he was doing what he had to do to survive but knew he was capable of much more. The reporter was drawn to this man and his straight answers.

Soon afterward, a newspaper article appeared featuring U. T. and his story. The manager of a computer center saw the article and offered the Vietnamese janitor a chance at a new job. U. T. did not waste the opportunity. He learned quickly and advanced rapidly. In 1979 he moved his family to Houston to pursue a challenging and successful career in management with Mars Inc., the candy manufacturer.

> LORD, who may dwell in your sanctuary? Who may live on your holy hill? He whose walk is blameless and who does what is righteous, who speaks the truth from his heart. ~Psalm 15:1, 2

U. T. considers his honest answer to the reporter's question to be the event that changed his life. Being truthful with others is always important. However, he says it is even more important to *"be honest with yourself."*[376] Those of us who tend to be "long-suffering" can benefit from this advice. Only when we acknowledge our own feelings will we be able to relate to others in a meaningful way. Self-delusion leads nowhere. Honesty *is* the best policy.

Legacy

A FEW DAYS before the fall of Saigon, Lieutenant Pham Van Hoa put his family on a military aircraft bound for Guam and safety. As an air force officer, he felt it his duty to remain and fight, even though on April 30, 1975, it was evident the final collapse was in progress. He watched in shame as other South Vietnamese soldiers took off their uniforms and threw away their weapons to avoid capture by the North Vietnamese. Unable to bring himself to do the same, he was soon arrested and imprisoned.

Hoa's family was taken to California, where they began a new and difficult life. His wife spoke no English and had never been out of Vietnam. She had to raise and support a son and three daughters by herself. Hoa was subjected to hard labor in a series of prison/reeducation camps where he was treated brutally. At one point, he came close to death. After twelve years of this treatment, Hoa was finally allowed to emigrate to the United States to rejoin his family. In 1999 he proudly became an American citizen and was sworn in by a judge who was himself a veteran of the Vietnam War.

> Blessed is the man whom God corrects; so do not despise the discipline of the Almighty. For he wounds, but he also binds up; he injures, but his hands also heal.
> ~Job 5:17, 18

Pham Van Hoa had every reason to be a bitter and disillusioned man. However, bitterness was not his legacy. His son memorialized him with these words:

> My father had somehow managed to move on about the Vietnam War before I could. His refusal to blame anyone for the betrayal of South Vietnam, his lack of bitterness for his imprisonment, his avoidance of hatred were his greatest legacies, affecting me more than his military service.[377]

Before his death, he told his children, *"I'm not afraid to die. I've lived a full life, I have no regrets."*[378] Throughout his life, Hoa was the victim of events beyond his control. The one thing he *could* control was his attitude toward those events. This spirit of optimism was his greatest gift to his family.

Arlington Ladies

VIETNAM VETERANS and Navy officers Bob Godman and Slim Russell were buried at Arlington National Cemetery in Arlington, Virginia, on October 30, 2009, with full military honors. Present at the funeral was a special woman representing a little-known group who call themselves the "Arlington Ladies." This woman came to give personal support to the families and to deliver the official condolences of the Chief of Naval Operations.

(arlingtoncemetary.org)

The Arlington Ladies date back to 1948, when Gladys Vandenberg, the wife of the Air Force chief of staff, observed many bleak and friendless funerals being conducted at Arlington with only a chaplain and an honor guard in attendance. Feeling that no one should be buried alone, she resolved to be there as often as possible herself, while enlisting the support of other military wives. Since then, the group has become a self-perpetuating organization of volunteers who send someone to every Arlington funeral. The mission is simple: to honor the fallen and help the families.

It is always a challenge for these women to hold in their emotions as they deal with the pain and loss suffered by these grieving families. One explained, *"They would want to be treated as someone who gave their life for their country. They served their flag. It covers their casket. In life, the soldier honored the flag and in death, the flag honors him."*[379] Another said, *"I always let them know that I am here for them today and in the future. I tell them I hope one day their memories will overshadow their heartache. Every person buried at Arlington National Cemetery is a hero. An Arlington Lady lets that hero know he's not alone."*[380]

> He who dwells in the shelter of the Most High will rest in the shadow of the Almighty. I will say of the LORD, "He is my refuge and my fortress, my God, in whom I trust."
> ~Psalm 91:1, 2

Old Soldier

ON THE eve of the invasion of Iraq in 2003, General Tommy Franks sat in the command center of his headquarters in Saudi Arabia, surrounded by all the accoutrements of modern war: digital maps, satellite communications equipment, and professional staff. Waiting for the final word to launch Operation Iraqi Freedom, his thoughts turned to another war a long time before:

Gen. Tommy Franks (U. S. Army)

I had learned my first lessons about war's harsh reality as an artillery forward observer in the rice paddies and mangrove swamps of Vietnam's Mekong Delta thirty-five years earlier. Tonight, as our soldiers and Marines bulldozed through the thick sand berm on the Iraqi border and rolled north into the dark fields of landmines, they would be ready to shed their blood, following the orders I would transmit to their commanders.[381]

I once asked my father for help in preparing a high school commencement address. He suggested a simple theme: The young person's contribution to the world should be enthusiasm; the older person's should be knowledge. General Franks has demonstrated this theme as it applies to a military career. A general officer wields great power and is expected to possess a vast array of skills and knowledge. The battle must be won, however, by young soldiers fighting bravely at the point of attack. The general has true wisdom when he combines his knowledge of the big picture with remembrance of what it's like to be on the front line.

The young people in our lives deserve this kind of wisdom from those of us who might be considered "old soldiers." They need to know we understand what they are facing. We pray that God grants us this wisdom over time as we walk with him and seek his counsel in meeting the challenges that form the basis of a more mature knowledge about life.

> God said to Solomon, "Since this is your heart's desire and you have not asked for wealth, riches or honor, nor for the death of your enemies, and since you have not asked for a long life but for wisdom and knowledge to govern my people over whom I have made you king, therefore wisdom and knowledge will be given you. And I will also give you wealth, riches and honor."
>
> ~2 Chronicles 1:11, 12

The Pedicab Driver

IT WAS one of those Da Nang downpours. The sound on the tin roofs was deafening as the floodgates seemed to open. The city was engulfed in darkness as everyone scattered for shelter, leaving the streets deserted. Janice Hermerding found herself alone in a small shop, suddenly fearful to be so far from the safety of her gated compound. The young medical technician was working at a Da Nang laboratory as part of an American medical mission. She had been in the sprawling, chaotic city for only a few days, and was now sick that she had ventured so far off by herself. She was alone in a place where no one spoke English or seemed sympathetic to her plight. Visions of being lost, mugged, or kidnapped by the VC ran through her head. Silently and fervently, she started praying. *"God? God, are you listening, Sir?"*[382] She didn't even know what she was praying for—a divine guide, perhaps.

> I sought the LORD, and he answered me; he delivered me from all my fears . . . The angel of the LORD encamps around those who fear him, and he delivers them.
> ~Psalm 34:4, 7

Then, as she stared out the shop door, a pedicab pulled up and stopped a few feet away. The driver looked at her. He was dressed in water-soaked black pajamas, again raising the specter of being taken away to a VC hideout. She kept praying. To get into that cab would require the greatest leap of faith in her life. As she continued to pray, she found herself reaching a resolve to put herself in God's hands, to relax and let him handle this situation. She got into the pedicab as a wave of relief swept over her that everything was going to be all right.

A short time later the little vehicle stopped in front of Janice's compound. The driver helped her out, but refused payment. He bowed three times with his hands clasped together as in prayer. Before he turned to go, a smile crossed his sad, weathered face. It was a face and a look she would never forget. Ever since, on rainy days, she remembers her mysterious rescuer. She also gives thanks to God for not deserting her in a frightening moment—and for deepening her faith that he would always provide help in time of need.

The Last Soldier Killed

Col. William Nolde (U. S. Army)

IT WAS a bleak winter day at Arlington National Cemetery as the Army buried the last man killed in Vietnam. After the final Mass in the red brick Fort Myer Chapel, the flag-draped casket was taken on a caisson drawn by horses to the hilltop burial site. A riderless horse accompanied the procession. A squad of riflemen fired a three-volley salute, followed by the haunting strains of "Taps" sounded by a lone bugler. Finally, the casket flag was folded and reverently presented to the grieving widow.

Colonel William Nolde, 43, had been killed by artillery fire eleven hours before the final cease-fire in Vietnam on January 27, 1973. He was the senior American advisor in Binh Long province and one of the last remaining Americans in country at that time. Other Americans died later in Vietnam and other Vietnam veterans died in the United States, but Nolde was the last official combat death before the truce.[383]

Colonel Nolde was a career Army officer and a good man. To be the last to die in a war would be a dubious honor at best, a distinction no one would wish for. In a sense, however, his death is no more or no less than those of a long line who went before and served honorably in an honorable cause. Like thousands before him, he persevered in his duty and saw it through to the end. We honor each of them for their service and resolve to never forget their sacrifice.

> You too, be patient and stand firm, because the Lord's coming is near . . . As you know, we consider blessed those who have persevered. You have heard of Job's perseverance and have seen what the Lord finally brought about.
> ~James 5:8, 11

Fog moves into the Ashau Valley (National Archives)

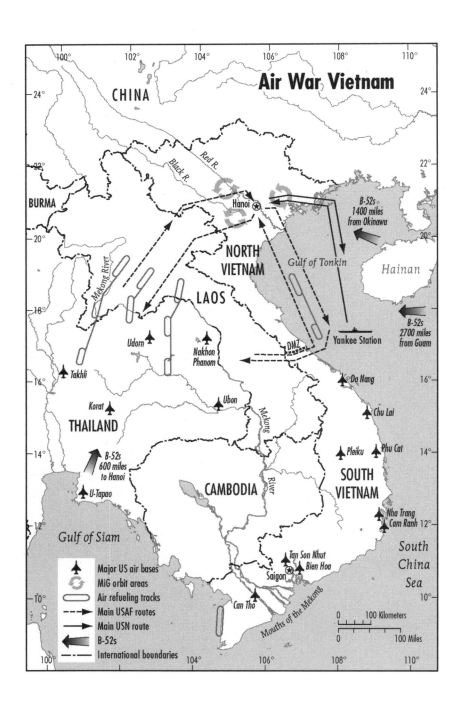

Air War Vietnam

CHINA

Black R.
Red R.

BURMA

Mekong River

Hanoi

NORTH
VIETNAM

Gulf of Tonkin

B-52s
1400 miles
from Okinawa

Hainan

LAOS

Udorn

Nakhon
Phanom

DMZ

Yankee Station

B-52s
2700 miles
from Guam

Takhli

Ubon

Da Nang

Korat

Chu Lai

THAILAND

Pleiku

Phu Cat

CAMBODIA

Mekong
River

SOUTH
VIETNAM

B-52s
600 miles
to Hanoi

U-Tapao

Nha Trang
Cam Ranh

Gulf of Siam

Tan Son Nhut
Bien Hoa

Saigon

South
China
Sea

Can Tho

Mouths of the Mekong

✈	Major US air bases
♺	MiG orbit areas
▭	Air refueling tracks
--- →	Main USAF routes
→	Main USN route
⬅	B-52s
–·–·–	International boundaries

0   100 Kilometers

0   100 Miles

AIR WAR

AIRPOWER WAS vital to the Allied effort in the Vietnam War. About 75 percent of missions flown during the war were over South Vietnam in interdiction strikes and direct support of ground troops.[384] The F-4 Phantom, flown by Air Force and Marine pilots, was a familiar sight to Marines and soldiers, strafing and bombing ahead of the lines or along convoy routes. Amazingly, the F-4 could carry twice the bomb load of a World War II B-17 bomber.[385] Many of these missions were flown at night or in inclement weather under radar guidance. B-52 bombers flying from Guam, Okinawa, and Thailand were also used in support of the ground war. They conducted "Arc Light" strikes, saturating large areas of known enemy activity with 500-pound and 750-pound bombs.

Missions over North Vietnam were fewer in number but much more dangerous and costly. The country was divided into six zones from south to north, called route packages. Number 6 included Hanoi, defended by a heavier and more accurate concentration of firepower than any target in any previous war.[386] In all, more than 1,100 airmen were killed and more than 400 captured in this theater during the course of the war. More than half the sorties flown were Navy aircraft, including A-4 Skyhawks, A-6 Intruders, A-7 Corsairs, and F-8 Crusaders, operating off aircraft carriers on Yankee Station (officially "Point Yankee") in the Gulf of Tonkin. Air Force F-105 Thunderchiefs, or "Thuds," flying from Thailand, flew the bulk of Air Force missions over the North.

In early 1972 Operation Linebacker was conducted over the southern areas of North Vietnam and the DMZ in one of the most intense bombing campaigns of the war. U.S. airpower was used in this operation to help the South Vietnamese army defeat the NVA Easter Offensive. In December of that year, Linebacker II was unleashed over Hanoi and Haiphong to break deadlocked peace negotiations in Paris and to bring the war to an end. B-52s were employed against these targets for the first time, as well as an array of fighter-bomber aircraft. After the nine-day campaign, peace talks resumed and were concluded within the next month.

The workhorse of the Vietnam War was the helicopter. During this conflict, these aircraft were used extensively for the first time to move troop units in tactical operations. They were also used in their well-established supply and medical evacuation roles. Unfortunately, during the course of the war, the VC and NVA became more and more proficient at engaging the slow-moving craft and destroyed more than 2,000 U. S. combat helicopters.[387]

The Army pioneered the concept of "air mobility," integrating helicopters with infantry units and conducting large-scale operations with as many as one hundred aircraft. The Bell UH series, commonly referred to as "Hueys," were the most widely used helicopters in the war, with more than 7,000 committed to service.[388] Most carried troops, while some were configured as gunships, with machine guns and rocket pods. After the Korean vintage H-34 was phased out, the Marines relied primarily on the CH-46 Sea Knight.

No Vietnam combat veteran will ever forget the *WHAP-WHAP* sound made by the rotor blades of these helicopters. They can still identify them a mile away. Sometimes the sound brings a sense of dread as a precursor to impending action. More often, however, it brings a sense of excitement and relief—the sound that always carried the message, "Help is on the way."

Spooky

RON BURKS flew an AC-47 gunship. These aircraft operated all over Vietnam giving close support to beleaguered infantry units. With three side-mounted miniguns and 24,000 rounds of 7.62-mm ammunition, a "Spooky" (named for its radio call sign) could stay on station for hours. At night, they would drop flares to light up the battlefield and then deliver steady streams of

Spooky (U. S. Air Force)

accurate fire laced with tracers. These bursts of fire emitted the eerie groaning sound that made "Spooky" such an appropriate name. To carry out their mission in Vietnam the pilots had to fly these obsolete aircraft at slow speeds and close to the ground. It was dangerous duty.

When Ron went to Vietnam he left behind a worried wife, Denell, and two sons, one twenty months old and one five days old. Denell took her little family back to her hometown of Milwaukie, Oregon, a suburb of Portland. Like many service wives of this war, Denell found support and unexpected inspiration from others in her same situation:

> *During that time, I was a member of the Officers' Waiting Wives Club. It was an organization which included all of the branches of the military. It was a relatively small group of young women who met monthly to go to dinner, socialize, and lift our spirits. I will always be grateful for the collective emotional strength of that group. I will always remember one gorgeous, exhausted, and very brave gal who was the wife of a Navy pilot who had been an MIA (missing in action) for several years. I figured, if she could be upbeat, so could I.*[389]

This young Navy wife demonstrates how we often find our ministry in the midst of our troubles. When we help someone else and show our faith during our own hard times, it is a powerful witness. Our faith not only sustains us but also blesses others in ways we may not even be aware of at the time.

> I was shown mercy so that in me, the worst of sinners, Christ Jesus might display his unlimited patience as an example for those who would believe on him and receive eternal life.
> ~1 Timothy 1:16

Trust

HELICOPTER pilots in Vietnam were my personal heroes. It is one thing to be on the ground locked in combat. It is quite another thing to be orbiting safely above looking down on the fight. Many helicopter pilots looked down on chaotic scenes

> "Whoever can be trusted with very little can also be trusted with much." ~Luke 16:10

of crisscrossing tracers, explosions, and smoke. When called in for help it was always up to the pilot to decide whether or not to risk himself, his crew, and his aircraft. I never knew one to refuse the call. Another Marine at Khe Sanh had similar sentiments:

> *Heroism was routine. The helicopter zones were always "hot." The enemy's weapon of choice to attack them was the 120mm mortar, which was always deadly . . . Seven helicopters were shot down, yet we never called for a medevac that didn't come.*[390]

The trust between air and ground units in Vietnam went both ways. The pilots knew the infantrymen would risk their own lives to get the wounded to the helos. The pilots also knew they would be called only when lives were at stake. Those of us on the ground could trust the airmen to be there when it counted. This trust was a major factor in the attitude of every soldier, sailor, airman, and Marine who saw combat in Vietnam. We knew we were never completely alone. The best medical system in the world was within reach of every man, thanks to the possibility of air evacuation.

Trust is important in every area of our lives and determines how we relate to family, friends, and everyone else we know. It is especially critical in our relationship to God. When we rely completely on his promise that he will always be there to support and forgive us, we have a freedom to live our lives that can be found nowhere else. If we want to be worthy of this kind of trust—we must strive to be more trustworthy ourselves. We want to be the kind of men and women God can count on.

We Help

I LIKE TO take every opportunity to thank helicopter pilots for their heroic service. They were the true heroes of every "grunt" in Vietnam. The foremost reason for this veneration is the fact that these pilots and their aircraft revolutionized medical care in this war. Often, wounded men arrived at field hospitals and received lifesaving treatment within minutes instead of hours or days. The men who performed this dangerous duty took it very seriously. Their attitude was epitomized by the words painted on the side of one medevac aircraft: *God saves, but we help.*[391]

This same thought was expressed by John F. Kennedy in his first inaugural address, delivered in 1961:

> *With a good conscience our only sure reward, with history the final judge of our deeds, let us go forth to lead the land we love, asking His blessing and His help, but knowing that here on earth God's work must truly be our own.*[392]

> The eye cannot say to the hand, "I don't need you!" And the head cannot say to the feet, "I don't need you!" On the contrary, those parts of the body that seem to be weaker are indispensable, and the parts that we think are less honorable we treat with special honor . . . God has combined the members of the body and has given greater honor to the parts that lacked it, so that there should be no division in the body, but that its parts should have equal concern for each other.
> ~1 Corinthians 12:21–25

The apostle Paul eloquently described how Christians are to do their work in the world as part of the "body of Christ." We are individuals in the larger body, each with responsibilities given according to our respective talents. Some are to be apostles, some prophets, some teachers, some healers, some administrators, etc. Whatever our contribution, we are each unique and indispensable. Every body needs all its parts to accomplish God's work here on Earth. God is the one who saves, and our purpose in life, working within the body of Christ, is to make the contribution for which our talents are most suited in support of this great mission.

I Want to Be a Pilot

THE HUEY gunship crews were a special breed. Unlike their fixed-wing counterparts that came in at supersonic speed from high altitude, the gunships did their work at ground level. The Hueys were armed with fixed machine guns and rocket pods on each side, and this firepower was delivered at slow speed as they flew or hovered over the front line in support of the troop transport helicopters or men on the ground. The men of the 13th Aviation Battalion, based at Can Tho, took special pride in their ability to do this difficult work, and could only laugh at the innocence of a fifth-grader's letter, published in the squadron newsletter:

Huey gunship (Richard Seaman)

I want to be a pilot when I grow up, because it's a fun job and easy to do. That's why there are so many pilots today. Pilots should be brave so they won't be scared if it's foggy and they can't see or if a wing or a motor falls off they should stay calm so they'll know what to do. Pilots have to have good eyes so they can see through clouds and they can't be afraid of lightning or thunder because they are closer to them than we are. I hope I don't get airsick because if I get airsick I couldn't be a pilot and would have to go to work.[393]

Leave it to a child to put serious "grownup" business into a different perspective. No matter how unrealistic, we appreciate the simple honesty and innocent wonder of a child's viewpoint. Also, it never hurts to have our pride pricked a little. Sometimes our children help us see ourselves as we really are. What our children see in us is closer to God's perspective than most. They judge our qualities as parents rather than as pilots.

This is what the Lord says: "Let not the wise man boast of his wisdom or the strong man boast of his strength or the rich man boast of his riches, but let him who boasts boast about this: that he understands and knows me." ~Jeremiah 9:23, 24

We Thought It Was a Trap

BURIED IN the summary of 1st Air Cavalry Division operations for the day, one item popped out at the staff officer: *"At 1030, Vicinity BR 695789, in the middle of a village, a woman took off her clothing, laid down and made an attempt to get an aircraft to land.*[394]

The pilot who made the report was summoned for an explanation:

We were flying in our OH-13 helicopter over a village and we saw a woman in black pajamas standing next to a bombed-out building in sort of a patio surrounded by hedgerows. There was no one else in the immediate area. The woman was a real beauty. She started to dance. Then she took off her pajama top and beckoned us to land. We thought it was a trap—Charlie could have been waiting in a nearby building . . . we orbited over her at twenty-five feet of altitude, watching. Next thing we knew, she took off her pajama bottoms and lay down on the ground, naked. She kept waving her arms for us to land.[395]

Asked how long this went on, the pilot responded, *"Thirty minutes, Sir."* When asked why he left, he said, *"We were running out of fuel, Sir."*[396]

Fortunately, these airmen realized that, a beautiful woman beckoning from below was a temptation too good to be true. It would be nice if all our temptations were so obvious. Unfortunately, this is usually not the case. Our temptations are more often the kind where we can say to ourselves, *"One time won't hurt, or I can fix this later."* We gratify an impulse or take a shortcut that seems innocent in itself, and only much later do we see the damage. It is even difficult to discern the point where we actually go astray.

The apostle Paul precisely described our predicament in his letter to the Romans. He explained we are continually thwarted in our efforts to do what we know is right by our humanness: *"I do not understand what I do. For what I want to do I do not do, but what I hate I do"* (Romans 7:15). He also gave us the only cure for this human condition:

> Who will rescue me from this body of death? Thanks be to God— through Jesus Christ our Lord! ~Romans 7:24, 25

A Sign on the Face

A SOLDIER DESCRIBED the tension-filled moment he and his comrades had to leave the relative safety of a covered position and dash into an open landing zone to get to a helicopter:

> They came in low and hot, close to the trees and dropped their tail in a flare, rocked forward and we raced for the open doorways. This was always the worst for us, we couldn't hear anything and our backs were turned to the tree line. The best you could hope for was a sign on the face of the man in the doorway, leaning out waiting to help with a tug or to lay down some lead. Sometime you could glance quickly at his face and pick up a clue as to what was about to happen.[397]

I was fascinated with this soldier's predicament—unable to see what was happening behind, he looked in the face of someone else who could. One of my favorite poems addresses this phenomenon of how we see many important things indirectly:

> For while the tired waves vainly breaking
> Seem here no painful inch to gain,
> Far back, through creeks and inlets making,
> Comes silent, flooding in, the main.
>
> And not by eastern windows only,
> When daylight comes, comes in the light,
> In front the sun climbs slow, how slowly,
> But westward, look! The land is bright.[398]

This principle is often at work when we try to discern God's working in our lives. It is always difficult to grasp his purpose or his perspective in the present moment. I often see what he has been doing only in retrospect, as I look back and see where I've been and how I've changed, and indirectly grasp what he has done. Every achievement and every tragedy in my life has worked to deepen my faith in God, and, over time, draw me closer to him. This faith gives me confidence he is directing my path and watching over me even during those times I have difficulty feeling his presence.

> "For I know the plans I have for you," declares the LORD, "plans to prosper you and not to harm you, plans to give you hope and a future."
> ~Jeremiah 29:11

1st Division troops attack from helicopters. (1st Division Museum)

CH 47 Chinook resupplies hilltop position.
(U. S. Army)

Cornerstone of My Character

JOHN GALKIEWICZ was a twenty-year-old helicopter pilot when he had to face one of the toughest choices of his life. In March 1968 his assault helicopter company had its worst day of the war in support of a Special Forces operation in the A Shau Valley. Eight Hueys were shot down in and around a key landing zone trying to take infantry troops out of the valley for return to base. That evening Galkiewicz faced the fact that the next day, he and only one other helicopter would have to extract more than one hundred men left on the ground in close contact with the enemy.

He didn't like his chances. After writing a "goodbye letter," sleep eluded him as he went over the mission in his mind. He wondered if twenty years in prison would be worth it if he refused to go. He then thought about one of his good friends who was still out there in that landing zone, waiting:

> *We had come into the unit together and he was now stranded down there and needed help. If I were in his shoes I sure would want someone trying their very best to come get me out. I made the decision to fight and unknowingly set in place one of the cornerstones of my character.*[399]

Galkiewicz went into action early the next morning. Amazingly, the extraction was accomplished without further loss of aircraft—and the airman was forever thankful he made the difficult but right call.

No matter where we are in life, we occasionally face decisions that have the potential of forming a "cornerstone" of our character. Taking an easier path, giving up too soon, or giving in to other temptations is often appealing, but unfortunately sets the tone for other choices to come. Every one of our decisions should be considered prayerfully before God, and, with his help, all its possible ramifications. When Jesus is in our hearts, we know we will never go too far wrong—we know the ultimate cornerstone of our character is in place.

> Yet to all who received him, to those who believed in his name, he gave the right to become children of God—children born not of natural descent, nor of human decision or a husband's will, but born of God.
> ~John 1:12, 13

Prayer of Thanks

THEY KNEW they would only have one chance to make it. The landing zone was small and the trees ahead were more than a hundred feet tall. The helicopter was dangerously overloaded with its crew and the recon patrol who had just piled in.

> Give thanks to the LORD, for he is good; his love endures forever.
> ~Psalm 118:1

Enemy fire ripped through the helicopter as every man fired back with everything he had.

Mike Vaughn was the door gunner and by now had almost burned up his M-60 machine gun. As they approached the tree line, he prayed for airspeed. He knew the pilot would have to wait until the last second to pull up and then hope they were moving fast enough not to stall and drop out of the sky. He yelled for the recon soldiers to jettison their gear. Vaughn described the next frantic moments:

> *The chopper starts a rapid climb; the g-force pushes me down against my seat. I watch the low rpm light on the dash of the helicopter . . . the red warning light is flashing like crazy. The helicopter made a quick climb to just about treetop level, then just seems to float there for a second. The AC [pilot] instantly drops the nose of the chopper, it's his only hope to get back some of his airspeed. The chopper begins slipping through the tops of the tree; the branches are hitting my M-60. The tree limbs are like giant fingers, reaching up from the jungle floor, trying to rip us from the sky. For awhile the bottom of the chopper is actually flying through the tops of these huge trees. By the grace of God and the phenomenal ability and courage of our pilots, we begin to gain some valuable airspeed and altitude.*[400]

Somehow Vaughn and the others made it out of that landing zone and returned safely to base. On the ground they discovered severe damage to the main rotor blade from the trees. The leading edges were so battered they were starting to come apart from the rest of the blade. They were within minutes of complete rotor failure. Vaughn described his reaction:

> *I began to relax a little . . . for the first time I tell myself . . . we made it. I sat quietly thinking, How in the hell did we ever get out of there? The shock and the terror started to really take hold . . . death seemed a certainty on this day. I took a brief moment to say a short silent prayer of thanks to God for His merciful protection.*[401]

Training Takes Over

THE CHINOOK helicopter settled gently into the landing zone at Fire Support Base Keene. Gary Roush, the aircraft commander, was assisting the pilot during the landing when a severe shock through the aircraft told him a serious blade strike had occurred. Emergency lights lit up the control panel. Roush went through the shutdown procedure, not noticing that the other crew members had abandoned the helicopter.

Suddenly, he saw a fire rapidly spreading toward the cockpit and realized he was trapped. His mind raced:

> As I experienced several times in Vietnam, during periods of pure terror, training takes over and everything fortunately happens in slow motion. I remembered being told in flight school about the emergency escape door each pilot had which was operated by a black and yellow striped handle located just above my head on the left. I grabbed for the handle and jerked down. To my horror and surprise the handle broke off in my hand and the door did not pop out like my training said it would . . . The voice in my head started again. "If the emergency handle fails then the door can be kicked out." . . . Well I kicked and kicked but nothing happened. There was not much room to kick. "Well, I will take one last look at my fate"—Surprise! The fire had backed off just enough for me to get through the companionway and over the right door gun.[402]

In the end this pilot was saved by the random course of the fire itself. Even so, it is amazing to see the disciplined thought process of a well-trained aviator. His training enabled him to mentally work through every action that could save him in this emergency.

> For these commands are a lamp, this teaching is a light, and the corrections of discipline are the way to life. ~Proverbs 6:23

Fortunately, our spiritual check list in a crisis is a short one. It begins and ends with prayer. We hope we will be ready when the time comes by virtue of our own "training" during quieter times. When we build our relationship with God through regular worship and frequent prayer, we become stronger in our faith and better able to deal with true emergencies. The calm strength that comes through prayer is the only sure defense against confusion and panic in a crisis situation.

Insertion

THE TENSION built as the helicopter's turns grew tighter. I was barely able to keep the small landing zone in sight as we were thrown about by the violent movement. Suddenly, we began to flare out and sink below the nearby tree line as the brush below blew in waves from the rotor wash. Above the noise, the crew chief yelled, *"Go! Go! Go!"* with three feet left between us and the ground. Several of us fell as we hit the ground hard, weighed down by our weapons and fifty-pound packs. The helicopter lifted off.

Suddenly, we were immersed in an eerie, palpable silence. We were on our own.

Third Reconnaissance Battalion sent many patrols into the mountains west of Hue. Practically every patrol started like many operations in the Vietnam War, with a helicopter insertion. That moment of touchdown was shared by thousands of soldiers and Marines who had to face this sudden vulnerability. We made it off the LZ that day unopposed, but many others did not. Another soldier described the same experience: *"Then the choppers flew off. Whether the LZ was hot or cold, the departure of the helicopters was a profound moment. The grunts felt an awful sense of abandonment and vulnerability. The sense of power and security the choppers could provide was gone."*[403]

> Yours, O LORD, is the greatness and the power and the glory and the majesty and the splendor, for everything in heaven and earth is yours ... In your hands are strength and power to exalt and give strength to all.
> ~1 Chronicles 29:11, 12

There are inevitably moments in life when we are suddenly vulnerable. We have all experienced near misses on the highway that leave us gasping. I have seen a day in the sunshine on a boat quickly turn into a life-or-death struggle with the elements. As we ponder how powerless we are in these situations, we are blessed to acknowledge the One whose power is never limited. God has ultimate control over all things and is always there for us as we face our emergencies. We can take action to protect ourselves and our loved ones with a clear mind and calm resolve based on our faith in his presence and our ultimate place at his side.

Prayers Work

IT SEEMED like a hopeless situation. They were dangerously low on fuel and, below them, an unending layer of fog blanketed the ground. To make matters worse, they were flying over the infamous Ho Bo Woods in Binh Duong Province, a VC stronghold laced with tunnels and fighting positions of the 4th VC Region Headquarters. Bill McDonald was flying crew chief on a Huey trying to resupply a friendly unit below the fog. However, they couldn't find their destination or any other place to safely set down. They were rapidly running out of options.

> I have set the LORD always before me. Because he is at my right hand, I will not be shaken. Therefore my heart is glad and my tongue rejoices; my body also will rest secure.
> Psalm 16:8, 9

When the fuel warning light flashed on and the audio alarm started beeping, the pilot asked McDonald, *"How long can we last after that thing goes off?"* He replied, *"Beats me. I've never tried to find out!"*[404] At that point, McDonald recalled, *"I began silently talking to God, asking for his divine help to find us someplace to land before we crashed into the forest below."*[405]

As they were descending to an unknown fate, an opening in the fog below gave them a glimpse of a grassy meadow and possible landing zone. As the pilot steered for the spot, the engine quit a few seconds before touchdown, resulting in a hard landing but no damage. Looking around, the crew saw movement on all sides. Fearing they were in the middle of a VC unit, they jumped out of the helo with what weapons they had and prepared to defend themselves. Ready to go down fighting, they soon recognized American uniforms and friendly soldiers. Amazingly, they were safe. On their deliverance, McDonald commented:

> It was a very lucky or blessed day, depending on how you viewed the events. Just good luck you might say, maybe? But then, perhaps other forces were at work. Maybe the power of a small silent prayer opened a big hole in the fog . . . I do not need anyone to tell me that prayers do work—I believe.[406]

Seventeen Bullet Holes

I N 1967 Bill McDonald was flying as door gunner in a Huey helicopter with ARVN soldiers on board. The fire was intense as they touched down in the landing zone near Cu Chi.

Bill McDonald

Suddenly and inexplicably, one of the Vietnamese soldiers turned, aimed his automatic weapon directly at McDonald's chest, and pulled the trigger. "I had slightly turned my head in time to see nothing more than a stream of light entering my body. I could feel the impact of something hitting me hard in the chest, directly in the heart, or what should have been my heart if I had not had a ceramic protective plate on my chest . . . I thought I was dead."[407]

Examining himself in the confusion, he saw smoke seeping from a deep cavity in his chest protector, but there was no blood or sharp pain. Later, after the battle, he and others examined the helicopter and were struck by disbelief. The transmission housing partition directly behind McDonald's position showed no damage. However, the partition directly on the other side of the aircraft showed exit holes where seventeen bullets had passed through.

> An Army safety board investigated and was as puzzled as all of us who had lived through the experience. It was impossible that it could have happened as we saw it. But the holes were there. We saw what we saw. There were those 18 rounds fired directly at me—one entered my chest protector and the other 17 exited the far side of the aircraft without ever hitting me. It was as if they went through me.[408]

Bill McDonald was never able to offer anything more to explain this amazing incident, except to affirm his faith that *"There must have been some kind of 'spiritual armor' that protected me from harm's way on that fateful morning along the Saigon River."*[409]

Stand firm then, with the belt of truth buckled around your waist, with the breastplate of righteousness in place, and with your feet fitted with the readiness that comes from the gospel of peace.
~Ephesians 6:14, 15

Train Like You Fight

AN "OLD CORPS" aviator explained the training techniques devised in an earlier war to more closely resemble actual combat flying against ground targets. Training targets were selected in remote areas around Moffett Field, California, such as power plants, lakes, and small bridges. As the training progressed the objectives grew more difficult, until:

> All Scripture is God-breathed and is useful for teaching, rebuking, correcting and training in righteousness, so that the man of God may be thoroughly equipped for every good work. ~2 Timothy 3:16, 17

The target for the final flight in the target location phase was one of those old Foster and Kleiser signboards located . . . out in the boondocks. The regime required the pilot to report to the squadron skipper after the flight and tell him the words that were printed on the signboard. There was no way that you could read the big orange letters on that sign without dropping wheels and flaps, dragging the terrain at very low level and a slow speed while trying to read the sign. Several pilots took more than one hop to graduate. The words were "Orange Crush," and were one of the best-kept secrets of Naval Aviation. No one was going to reveal the answer to a teammate. It took some training and a bit of courage to learn those words.[410]

It has always been a military axiom that you *"train like you fight."* Put another way, *"Sweat in peacetime saves blood in wartime."* All professions require some amount of continuing education, but the military services are unique in their emphasis on constant and repetitive training, done as realistically as possible.

In the spiritual realm, we need to similarly "train" ourselves for God's work. The "full armor of God" includes one offensive weapon: *"The sword of the spirit, which is the word of God"* (Ephesians 6:17). We need an intimate knowledge of his Word through Bible study to train for the work of his kingdom. In bringing others to Christ, our own witness may often be more important than our knowledge of Scripture. Even so, there will be occasions when challenges and questions come our way requiring biblical knowledge. Our training for these moments should be continual and thorough. We should always be in a Bible study.

Switching Seats

IT SEEMED like a good idea at the time. Since there were two student pilots on a long training flight in an AD-5 Skyraider, and only the pilot in the left seat got to log the flying hours (due to the location of the controls), the students decided to switch seats at 20,000 feet to provide equal hours to each. Not only was the cockpit cramped, both men were on oxygen and would have to unplug during this totally unauthorized exchange.

AD-5 Skyraiders (U. S. Navy)

After one of them gave the signal to start, they commenced furiously unbuckling harnesses and disconnecting hoses. One man leaned back and stepped across the center console. One leaned forward and attempted to do the same thing. It was a tighter squeeze than they thought, however, and both were soon hung up. Considering the awkward and ridiculous position they were in, one of them started chuckling to himself. The other also began, and soon both were laughing hysterically. One of the men later explained:

> Then it came to me in a rush. We were hypoxic! By now we had been deprived of oxygen for over a minute. Unexplainable giggling was one of the first symptoms. Dizziness was the next phase, followed by hallucinations, convulsions, unconsciousness and finally death. This was not funny . . .[411]

With a last, desperate lunge, both men threw themselves across the console, replugged their oxygen hoses, and got control of the aircraft. In retrospect, these young pilots concluded that this maneuver was not so smart. Oxygen deprivation is an insidious danger difficult to diagnose.

We deal with spiritual dangers equally insidious. From day to day it is easy to drift away from a close relationship with our Savior and, as with oxygen deprivation, not be aware of it. I find the best gauge of my spiritual condition to be my sense of peace. When peace is lacking, I am usually in a place I don't want to be. Anxiety is the measure of my distance from Jesus.

> "Peace I leave with you; my peace I give you. I do not give to you as the world gives. Do not let your hearts be troubled and do not be afraid."
> ~John 14:27

The Right Thing

THE WITHDRAWAL from Kham Duc had gone on all day. Fifteen hundred American and Vietnamese troops had been evacuated by air at a cost of eight aircraft and two hundred fifty-nine lives. At about 5:00 p.m., as the operation was ending, word came by radio that a three-man air control team was still on the ground by the airstrip, in danger of being overrun by advancing NVA units.

> Everyone who competes in the games goes into strict training. They do it to get a crown that will not last; but we do it to get a crown that will last forever.
> ~1 Corinthians 9:25

The last transport aircraft on the scene was a C-123 piloted by Lieutenant Colonel Joe Jackson. Looking down at the devastation below, he could see damaged aircraft blocking much of the runway, as well as enemy automatic weapons, mortars, and recoilless rifle fire raking the area. The runway was engulfed in smoke, and nearby ammunition dumps were exploding. Fully aware of the danger and the high probability he would fail in the mission, Jackson took his aircraft down. The next fifty seconds of heroism are summarized in the Medal of Honor citation for this amazing feat:

> *Displaying superb airmanship and extraordinary heroism, he landed his aircraft near the point where the combat control team was hiding. While on the ground, his aircraft was the target of intense hostile fire. A rocket landed in front of the nose of the aircraft but failed to explode. Once the combat control team was aboard, Lt. Col. Jackson succeeded in getting airborne despite the hostile fire directed across the runway in front of his aircraft.*[412]

Shedding some light on the kind of character that produces this kind of heroism, Joe Jackson later wrote:

> *When I was a young boy about the age of twelve, I became a Christian. One of the things my mother and my minister taught me was to always do the right thing. I've tried to live up to this requirement, not always being successful—but I've always tried. The right thing may not be what you as an individual would like, but if it is the right thing, then do it. Major decisions become a lot easier when the right thing is used as a benchmark.*[413]

Honeymoon Helo

GREEN AND yellow smoke grenades heralded the arrival of the Honeymoon Helo at the Chu Lai airstrip. *"Just Married"* was conspicuously painted across the nose, and the crew wore neckties instead of body armor. The "mission" for the day was to transport a pair of newlyweds to their honeymoon cottage near the South China Sea. The pilot of the helo had crashed twice while extracting wounded soldiers and had been rescued each time by the groom. He said, *"He has pulled me out twice after I was shot down. It was real great flying him from his wedding."*[414]

On July 13, 1968, Warrant Officer Don Sewell and Captain Patricia Mann were married at the Chu Lai base chapel in a rare military wedding held during the Vietnam War. He was a helicopter pilot with an air ambulance company, and she was a nurse with a field surgical hospital. Sewell commented, *"Three days after I met her I knew we were going to be married."*[415]

> "Haven't you read," he replied, "that at the beginning the Creator 'made them male and female,' and said, 'For this reason a man will leave his father and mother and be united to his wife, and the two will become one flesh'? So they are no longer two, but one. Therefore what God has joined together, let man not separate."
> ~Matthew 19:4–6

The administrative process for servicepeople getting married in a combat zone was not easy. The "request for marriage" took seven weeks to make its way up the chain of command, and the couple then had to go to Saigon for a civil ceremony. Sewell was almost at the end of his tour and so extended his time in country to coincide with hers. They at least got time off together for R&R and a brief honeymoon in Hong Kong.

Although the warrant officer was outranked by his wife, she said, *"He will be the boss"* of the family. *"I wear the bars, but he wears the pants,"* she said.[416]

God at the Controls

IT WAS the day John Galkiewicz came closest to dying. He was flying copilot in a Huey helicopter on a reconnaissance team insertion west of Kontum. There were two troop ships on the mission, escorted by several gunships armed with rockets. The team went into the small landing zone uneventfully just before dark. But as the helicopters began their departure, the radio came to life with shouts from the team on the ground. They had landed in the middle of a company-sized NVA unit and were under heavy fire. In danger of being overrun, they urgently asked for an "emergency extraction."

> I know, O LORD, that a man's life is not his own; it is not for man to direct his steps. Correct me, LORD, but only with justice—not in your anger, lest you reduce me to nothing.
> ~Jeremiah 10:23, 24

The first troop ship made it back into and out of the landing zone through heavy ground fire, picking up part of the team. The gunships started firing rockets into the tree lines around the landing zone at about the same time Galkiewicz went in. The rest of the team scrambled aboard, and the pilot put on maximum power to clear the zone as fast as possible. As they were picking up speed, a call came from the first aircraft warning them of a .50 cal. machine gun in the tree line directly ahead. The pilot yanked back on the controls in one of tightest turns ever executed by a helicopter. Galkiewicz saw the ground through the Plexiglas over his head. Helicopters aren't made to fly upside down, but, somehow, they recovered from this maneuver and made it out.

As Galkiewicz was catching his breath, a call came on the radio from one of the gunships: *"When you made that turn you turned into the path of a set of rockets that had already been fired and while you were upside down one of the rockets went straight through your open cargo compartment and blew up when it hit the ground!"*[417]

Galkiewicz later said, *"Though at the time I wasn't much in line with the Lord, I sure am glad he was on the controls for that one."*[418]

The Lives I Took

Capt. John Tuthill.

THE ROTO-ROOTER man arrived less than an hour after the call. John Tuthill had just moved his family to Dallas and already had a plumbing emergency. Within a few minutes, he learned the plumber was a former Marine, as was John. Tuthill had been an F-4 pilot, the plumber a Force Recon ground pounder, and they had both served in Vietnam, at about the same time. As they talked, a bond gradually formed between them unique to military men with so much in common.

It had been more than ten years since Tuthill had been in combat, and he had seldom talked about his experiences with anyone. For some reason, however, he shared with this Roto-Rooter man one of his most memorable days. It was a mission to help a unit in trouble:

> *Eight Marines were being pursued by an entire company of NVA troops and in imminent danger. Helicopters had gone in twice in attempts to extract these men, and twice they had been repelled by intense enemy fire. The enemy had closed within 50 meters of the Marines, and without immediate action, their survival was in doubt.*
>
> *. . . It was easy to see where to drop after I rolled in and got the target in sight. The top of the mountain lit up like sparklers on the 4th of July as the NVA filled the sky in front of me with intense small arms automatic weapons fire. I zeroed in on the muzzle flashes and released my nape [napalm] to land right in the middle of the area where the muzzle flashes emanated. I passed over the target at 500 feet altitude, pulled off hard left at four to six Gs, and turned my head back towards the target to see if we got a hit. Right on, right on.*[419]

Back at base, Tuthill learned that rescue helicopters came in right after his bombing run and pulled out the beleaguered Marines without any enemy fire. He later commented: *"Not a day has passed since I came home in June 1970 that I haven't thought about those who served, those who survived, those who died, and those whose lives I took on a day like that."*[420]

O LORD, do not rebuke me in your anger or discipline me in your wrath . . . My guilt has overwhelmed me like a burden too heavy to bear. ~Psalm 38:1, 4

347

Boulders in the Road

A S JOHN TUTHILL told his story of saving a recon patrol in Vietnam, the Roto-Rooter man listened intently:

> As I finished, the former Marine I was talking to became obviously emotional about my story. He asked the location of the action, he asked about the plane I flew; he asked if it had a blue sword across the fuselage. All questions I answered, now with an emotion equal to his. Yes, we had a blue sword across the fuselage; we were the Crusader Squadron. Yes, the time of year for the action was the same as his. Yes, we were together again, eleven years, 12,000 miles, and it was us—alive, living, with families—we could hardly talk![421]

John Tuthill finally learned for sure that all eight Marines got out that day and made it home. They had been so close to the falling bombs that napalm actually splashed onto the arm of one of them. The two men were almost overcome with emotion at this amazing reunion.

Soon, the plumber had to go, leaving Tuthill with his thoughts: "*What had happened was over, and the impact God had intended was there.*"[422] He felt the event had helped him understand he was okay in God's eyes.. He explained:

> We all pick up burdens as we travel the road of life, and the Vietnam Veteran has more than his share. These burdens look like boulders on life's road behind us. We can't remove those boulders from our past, all we can do is recognize them for what they are, accept them, and be watchful that we keep life's road ahead of us clear. God doesn't want us to forget the past. He wants us to understand it, to accept its unchangeability, to learn from it, to remember our friends, to look at those boulders as signposts to help keep us and others from creating more boulders because of a focus on that which we cannot change.[423]

As John Tuthill took another step in his unique spiritual journey, he realized intuitively that God would not hold his past against him. He couldn't forget the dark side of his war, but somehow knew he had to stay focused on the future.

> If you, O LORD, kept a record of sins, O LORD, who could stand? But with you there is forgiveness; therefore you are feared. I wait for the LORD, my soul waits, and in his word I put my hope. ~Psalm 130:3–5

Drawn to Christ

IN RETROSPECT, John Tuthill came to see the encounter with the Roto-Rooter man as a tap on the shoulder from God, one he managed to largely ignore for a long time. The walls he had built in his mind to protect himself from thinking of his wartime experiences remained intact. He tried to explain:

> No one can see these walls or detect their existence. On the outside you see what to you is a perfectly normal person, however, if you live with someone in this state eventually you feel a distance developing and you don't understand why. Particularly with wives and children this is true because the amount of love getting through is insufficient for healthy relationships.[424]

For years after this incident, Tuthill continued on a winding spiritual journey. At first, as a self-described "good perfunctory Christian," he went through the religious motions. He persisted, however, and kept participating in church activities and Bible studies. Over time, his protective wall started coming down. It wasn't easy, as he said, *"The Vietnam experience was always there because, you see, when you've killed another human being, no matter how, it is with you every day for the rest of your life."*[425] It wasn't easy, but he kept going. In time he was rewarded for his perseverance:

> After a couple of years of this formal Bible study, more and more of the walls came down, and I could feel the presence of Christ in my life. Weakly at first, but stronger every year thereafter. I still have miles to go, but the process is well underway and I'll not let it stop—for once you can "feel" Christ in your soul you will never not feel it again.[426]

In describing his spiritual journey, Tuthill took no credit for success, quoting John's Gospel:

In praise and thanksgiving, he said, *"It took some real drawing for me to get to where I am today. God never stopped loving me and drawing me to Him."*[427]

> "No one can come to me unless the Father who sent me draws him."
> ~John 6:44

Twenty-Five Thousand Feet

PANCHO PASQUALICCHIO figured he had the best job in the Air Force. Commanding a squadron of twenty-two F-4 Phantoms, he deployed to Vietnam early in 1966. Operating independently out of Da Nang, he got his missions from MACV headquarters in Saigon with virtually no oversight. With twenty-four years experience as a fighter pilot, he didn't miss having someone looking over his shoulder.

One morning Pancho received an order from Saigon directing him to escort a flight of F-105s into North Vietnam on a bombing mission. The 105s were assigned an altitude of 20,000 feet, and his fighters 22,000 feet. He didn't like these orders because he knew if enemy MIGs attacked he would need more altitude and airspeed to close quickly with the attackers. He immediately got on the landline to Saigon and told the operations officer he wanted to fly at 25,000 feet. He was told, *"Definitely not. Carry out your orders."* He then asked the ops officer for his boss, General Simler, and was told, *"He's out to lunch."* Pancho responded, *"When the General gets back from lunch, tell him Pancho is flying at 25,000 feet!"*

That afternoon, Pancho's escort aircraft engaged and dispersed a group of attacking MIGs before they could reach the bombers. Later, an apparently irate general called the squadron leader, growling, *"Pancho, don't you ever violate one of my orders again! Unless you're right."*[428]

During a brilliant career as a fighter pilot in three wars, Pancho Pasqualicchio flew 350 combat missions. Along the way he got into his share of trouble for violating the letter of rules and regulations, because he found in wartime these rules and regulations were often obstacles to getting the job done. This highly decorated officer risked his life for others on countless occasions and never failed in a mission. His duty was written clearly on his heart.

> I will put my laws in their minds and write them on their hearts. I will be their God, and they will be my people.
> ~Hebrews 8:10

The Power of the Cross

PANCHO PASQUALICCHIO served two tours of duty in Vietnam and had many interesting experiences as an F-4 squadron commander and advisor to the Vietnamese air force. His most phenomenal story of faith and courage, however, came from a different war.

In April 1951, his friend, Captain Bob Ward, was shot down over enemy lines in Korea. As Ward ejected from his P-80 jet fighter, both his legs were broken when they struck the canopy. Quickly captured and held in an enemy trench, he suffered severe pain and diarrhea for days without medical attention. Thinking he wouldn't last much longer, he fashioned two sticks together with some string, making the form of a cross. He then did some serious praying. One of his captors noticed the cross and quietly asked, *"Christian?"*

> For Christ did not send me to baptize, but to preach the gospel—not with words of human wisdom, lest the cross of Christ be emptied of its power. For the message of the cross is foolishness to those who are perishing, but to us who are being saved it is the power of God.
> ~1 Corinthians 1:17, 18

Ward nodded. *"Yes."*[429]

Amazingly, this same soldier was assigned to take Ward by truck to a rear area prison camp. During the nighttime trip the North Korean unexpectedly pulled off the road. He picked up the injured airman and carried him to the top of a nearby hill, chosen for being in the path of American bombers making night raids. As aircraft passed overhead, the guard flashed a makeshift light toward them. This went on for two long nights until a helicopter mission was launched to investigate.

Early the next morning, a helicopter crewman spotted a Korean waving frantically from a hilltop with another man beside him on the ground. Within minutes, Ward was snatched from the hill with his new friend and "savior." Both were flown to safety and a new life.

Bob Ward and Pancho Pasqualicchio have ever since considered this miraculous story of survival and redemption an amazing demonstration of the "power of the cross."

I Never Knew You

MICHAEL MURPHY would never forget a day on the flight deck of the USS Coral Sea. Afterwards he wrote a moving letter to a fellow sailor named Norman Ridley who died tragically that day:

I never knew you in life.

We may have passed each other at some time on the ship or in port and never knew it. We met on the flight deck the day you died.

. . . the plane was launched just as you were pulling the fuel hose across the deck. My back was to you and I saw part of your ear protectors and goggles blow down the deck, I knew that something terrible had happened. You were lying on the deck about 20 feet from me. The wing had hit you in the head as the plane launched. I looked down at you as I walked by. I did not stop, I had planes to de-arm, I just walked by.

When I finished my job I went below deck to the ordnance shop and thought about your death. Where was God this day, why did this happen, what purpose did your death accomplish? . . . I went down to dinner and on with my life, but I never prayed again.

You have never been far from me, sometimes I wonder about what your hopes and dreams were, what you wanted to do in life . . . In 1979 I cried for you for the first time, I cried again when I went to the Wall in 1987, I was back on the flight deck I could hear the Jets and the Helos, I could smell it, feel it and I could see it. You will be in my memory till the day I die.

I only knew you in death.[430]

We don't know the end of this story. We can only hope this man found some sense of peace and returned at some point to God. There is no greater test of anyone's faith than the premature and apparently random death of another human being. It is natural to question God at such a time. It may take time for us to see any meaning in a tragic event. We know, however, that when we question God sincerely, in his time he will give us the perspective and peace only he can give, to enable us to live with the aftermath of any tragedy.

> Then the end will come, when he hands over the kingdom to God the Father after he has destroyed all dominion, authority and power. For he must reign until he has put all his enemies under his feet. The last enemy to be destroyed is death
> ~1 Corinthians 15:24–26

To Keep Going

WITH A typhoon off the coast, high winds and heavy rain were hammering Kadena Air Force Base on the island of Okinawa. In spite of the storm, Tom Webb and his crew made their way to their assigned B-52 bomber. By the time he completed the preflight check outside the aircraft and climbed into the cockpit, he was thoroughly soaked. Takeoff was at 4:00 a.m. for the eight-hour bombing run from Okinawa to Vietnam. Soldiers on the ground needed air support, and it was their job to provide it.

Lt. Tom Webb

The rain kept falling in sheets as the 488,000-pound aircraft, fully loaded with bombs and fuel, began to lumber forward on its long takeoff roll. As they slowly gathered speed, Webb peered ahead but could not even see the white lines painted on the runway. Finally, the hurtling B-52 lifted off the ground. In that instant, as he was retracting the landing gear, the blinding blue-white flash of an explosion erupted from the left wing. Warning lights for the number 1 outboard engine immediately lit up. They were hardly off the ground, and all he could do at that moment was shut down the engine and keep flying.

Webb would learn later that the alternator had exploded in that engine, blowing off the cowling and causing extensive damage. From the cockpit, he could only guess at what had happened as he assessed the aircraft's condition. He checked instruments, made adjustments, and found he could still fly the aircraft. They would continue the mission. Hours later, their bombs would be on target, helping some beleaguered unit on the ground in Vietnam.

Tom Webb's quiet and unpretentious courage inspired others at that time just as it inspires his friends (including me) now. I know him to be a dedicated Christian gentleman who works behind the scenes for his church and community. As he demonstrated on a stormy night over the South China Sea, he would never turn back from an important mission nor let someone down who was depending on him.

> We continually remember before our God and Father your work produced by faith, your labor prompted by love, and your endurance inspired by hope in our Lord Jesus Christ.
> ~1 Thessalonians 1:3

Bombing Hanoi

THE WING commander mounted the podium and faced the packed briefing room. He announced, *"Gentlemen, your target for tonight is Hanoi."* Operation Linebacker II was beginning. The B-52 bombers of 43rd Strategic Wing were now committed to the most dangerous mission of the war. Captain Robert Certain, a navigator for one of the bombers, felt a flood of complex emotions. There was a powerful elation at being part of such a massive

B-52 drops bombs (USAF Museum)

operation that could possibly end the war. There was also anger at having to fly a mission on the last day of his tour of combat duty. Stronger than either of those emotions, however, was an almost overwhelming fear of the dangers that lay ahead. In this intense moment the airman's thoughts turned to God:

> *Once again, my prayers reflected these emotions as I alternately railed at God and sought his protection. I was fearful of the probable danger of a B-52 strike over the capital of North Vietnam, with more defenses than any city in the world other than Moscow. We would face anti-aircraft artillery, Russian-built MiG fighters, and surface-to-air missiles (Soviet SA-2s), both going in and coming out.*
>
> *I turned to the Lord in prayer for skill, wisdom, insight, and calm as I prepared myself for Monday's flight into the jaws of hell.*[431]

Robert Certain was a spiritual young man who would eventually go into the Episcopal priesthood. Even at this point in his life, as a combat airman, he held an ongoing dialogue with God that is an inspiring example of the purpose and power of prayer. We build a relationship with God through conversation. God wants us to share our thoughts and emotions openly, honestly, and regularly. He wants us to have what we so desperately need: a closer and deeper relationship with him.

> Let us then approach the throne of grace with confidence, so that we may receive mercy and find grace to help us in our time of need.
> ~Hebrews 4:16

Better Men

S T. JOHN'S EPISCOPAL Church in Agana, Guam, had a unique feature. There was a glass wall behind the altar with a magnificent view of the Pacific Ocean. The vista also included a view of the final approach to Anderson Air Force Base and the B-52 bombers returning from their missions over Vietnam. While attending church services, B-52 crewman Captain Bob Certain had the opportunity to ponder a recurring dilemma. Although the motto of Strategic Air Command was, *"Peace is Our Profession,"* he was obviously engaged in waging a brutal war. He wondered why the Air Force chaplains never seemed to address this conflict for the benefit of the bomber crews. As he considered the possibility that answering such questions

> You who ride on white donkeys, sitting on your saddle blankets, and you who walk along the road, consider the voice of the singers at the watering places. They recite the righteous acts of the Lord, the righteous acts of his warriors in Israel.
> ~Judges 5:10, 11

might be his own calling, he relied at that time on a quotation, familiar to most military men and women, from the 19th-century philosopher John Stuart Mill:[432]

> *War is an ugly thing, but not the ugliest of things: the decayed and degraded state of moral and patriotic feeling which thinks nothing worth a war, is worse . . . A man who has nothing which he is willing to fight for, nothing which he cares more about than he does about his personal safety, is a miserable creature who has no chance of being free, unless made and kept so by the exertions of better men than himself.*[433]

I reveal my own military bias by strongly supporting the assertion there are things in this world worth fighting for and my belief that God blesses those who take up arms when it is necessary. This is not to make light of the difficult process of determining when military action is just or to suggest we are always right in that determination. However, I believe that these bomber crewmen and all other veterans of this war carried out their dangerous missions with God's blessing and understanding.

F-4 Phantoms in formation. (U. S. Air Force)

A-6 Intruders. (National Archives)

Bug's Prayer

JOHN ROACH, nicknamed "Bug," flew F-8 Crusaders during the Vietnam War, making three combat cruises with three different carrier air groups. He became famous for his expertise as a landing signal officer (LSO) and for his ability to handle any emergency. He brought in aircraft with battle damage, engine trouble, and missing landing gear. On one occasion he brought down six aircraft despite a total electrical failure on his ship. With a flight deck illuminated only by tractor headlights, he talked the pilots down with a hand-held radio. The Navy League later sponsored an award to recognize superior LSO performance and named it in his honor.

LSO at work (U. S. Navy)

Bug Roach was not only a highly skilled and professional naval aviator, he was a down-to-earth, humble guy who liked everyone and was liked by everyone in return. He was also known on occasion to pray for his fellow aviators.[434] One of his prayers reflected his own intense patriotism and personal faith:

Lord, we were conceived in freedom, and dear God, if you are willing, in freedom we will spend the rest of our days. May we always be thankful for the blessings you have bestowed upon us. May we be humble to the less fortunate and assist those in need. May we never forget the continuing cost of freedom. May we always remember that if we are to remain the land of the free, we must continue always to be the home of the brave. May our wishbone never be found where our backbone should be. May we possess always, the integrity, the courage and the strength to keep ourselves unshackled, to remain always a citadel of freedom and a beacon of hope to the world. We are the nation . . . this is our wish . . . this is our hope and this is our prayer . . . Amen.[435]

Bug's prayer might by summarized in the familiar slogan *"Freedom Isn't Free."* Our nation has been blessed with men and women of great courage and faith, like Bug Roach, who have made great sacrifices for it. Our nation will continue to be free as long as it is worthy of this kind of sacrifice.

> Be devoted to one another in brotherly love. Honor one another above yourselves. Never be lacking in zeal, but keep your spiritual fervor, serving the Lord. Be joyful in hope, patient in affliction, faithful in prayer.
> ~Romans 12:10–12

Others before Myself

ONE OF the most dangerous missions of the war was flown by the Navy pilots of Observation Squadron 67. Operating out of an airfield in Nakhon Phanom, Thailand, they flew twin-engine OP-2Es (converted P-2V Neptune subchasers) in low-level flights over enemy territory, dropping electronic sensors along the ground. These large, slow-moving aircraft were easy targets for NVA gunners, and suffered heavy losses.

On February 27, 1968, Commander Paul Milius and his crew were flying over the Ho Chi Minh trail in Laos when their ship was hit by ground fire. The blast killed one crewman and started a fire inside the aircraft. When it became obvious the airplane couldn't be saved, Milius ordered the crew to bail out. The cockpit rapidly filled with smoke as he struggled to hold the aircraft straight and level so that each crewman could make a safe exit. Seven crewmen made it out and were later picked up by rescue helicopters. Milius was seen parachuting from the burning aircraft, but was never found. Officially declared MIA, he was posthumously awarded the Navy Cross in 1978 for *"extraordinary heroism and inspiring devotion to duty."*[436]

> "My command is this: Love each other as I have loved you. Greater love has no one than this, that he lay down his life for his friends."
> ~John 15:12, 13

In 1995 the guided missile destroyer USS *Milius* (DDG 69) was commissioned at Pascagoula, Mississippi, the first ship named for a Vietnam MIA. The warship's motto, *"Alii Prae Me,"* or *"Others before Myself,"* was chosen to reflect the personal ethics of Paul Milius throughout his career, and his supremely selfless actions to save others from a burning aircraft.[437]

Quick Response

THE SURFACE-TO-AIR missile exploded directly in front of the B-52, scattering red-hot shrapnel through the aircraft, knocking out engines and cutting hydraulic lines. In the dark, Captain Robert Certain, the navigator, checked the gauges with his flashlight and found they were in a rapid descent. He shouted an escape heading to the pilot over the intercom, noticed a fire behind him, near the bomb bay, and ordered the bombs jettisoned. Over the intercom he heard, *"EW's leaving,"* followed by the explosion of an ejection seat.

North Vietnamese surface-to-air missile (U. S. Air Force)

Everything seemed to unfold in slow motion. *"From that point forward, I was truly on auto-pilot, reacting in the way I had been trained. Thank God it worked!"*[438] He pulled down his visor, cinched up the oxygen mask, turned on the oxygen flow, kicked back into the leg restraints, grabbed the ejection handle between his knees—and pulled. His next sensation was tumbling through darkness at 31,000 feet in minus-fifty-five-degree air. As he began stabilizing his fall and checking his equipment, he realized again that his training was working:

> My mind was racing through checklists and training manuals and all those boring safety lectures I had sat through for the last four years. I was amazed and calmed that I seemed to be remembering so much.[439]

Thankfully, few of us have to face emergencies of this magnitude. Even so, we know disasters can strike, and the wise make plans to deal with them. We hope we will do the right thing when it counts. Preparation is even more important for the spiritual crises in our lives. When Jesus was tempted by Satan, he relied on Scripture to counter Satan's arguments. The Bible is our "training manual," with guidance for our own emergencies. We need to prepare ourselves, just as our Savior prepared himself, by studying it and storing it within our hearts.

> The tempter came to him and said, "If you are the Son of God, tell these stones to become bread." Jesus answered, "It is written: 'Man does not live on bread alone, but on every word that comes from the mouth of God.'" ~Matthew 4:3, 4

The Third Man

MOON VANCE was a legend among Navy aviators. As a landing signal officer (LSO) he skillfully guided countless pilots to safe carrier landings from an exposed platform beside the flight deck. His only escape in an emergency was a safety net beneath his platform that would funnel him to the deck below.

> Who among you fears the LORD and obeys the word of his servant? Let him who walks in the dark, who has no light, trust in the name of the LORD and rely on his God. ~Isaiah 50:10

One dark night, an A3J Vigilante called in with engine trouble requiring an immediate landing. At the last second before landing, Vance saw that a successful landing was hopeless, screamed, *"Eject, eject, eject!"* and dove for the safety net.

Two rocket-propelled ejection seats left the aircraft a bare instant before its fiery crash on the flight deck of the carrier. Using searchlights, the plane-guard helicopter pilot quickly found the airmen in the water and hoisted them into the helicopter. He then radioed a startling message to the carrier: *"Tower, this is Angel Two Four. How many crewmen are there in a Vigie?"* He was told there were two. *"That's what I thought, Tower. But I just picked up three people!"*[440]

The third man was Moon Vance. He had missed the safety net! He had suffered the equivalent of a seven-story fall and landed in the dark, turbulent water behind the carrier. Somehow he was miraculously spotted by the rescue helicopter. If he hadn't been seen in that instant, it would have been hours before he would have been missed, and he would have been many miles separated from the ship at night.

There are times when we all struggle in dark waters and wonder how we will ever get free of the grief, guilt, or depression that threatens to engulf us. Amazingly, God always continues to search for us, even in these dark places. Miraculously, he passes us a lifeline we have but to reach out for and grasp. When we take hold of that line our rescue is certain.

Full Power

FROM THE air, landing an aircraft on something that looks about the size of a paper clip seems totally impossible. It is in fact probably one of the most dangerous and difficult feats devised by man. There are few things as violent as a high-performance aircraft hitting an aircraft carrier flight deck. In addition to the speed and weight of the aircraft, the engines are at *full power* at the moment of impact. One observer explained:

> By faith Abraham, when called to go to a place he would later receive as his inheritance, obeyed and went, even though he did not know where he was going.
> ~Hebrews 11:8

You might expect them to pull off the power. The reason they don't is because if they get a "bolter" (the tail hook skittering over all the arresting wires without catching one), they need full power to get airborne again. Particularly with the F-4. To get on the power late—even a second late—in an F-4 is extremely dangerous. In the event of a go-around this big heavy plane will not rotate quickly once the nosewheel slams down. The night before I came aboard, Constellation lost a pilot and radar man in an F-4 on a night go-around attempt. All he did was hesitate with his power on a long landing—and when he finally got to it, it was too late. They went into the water with full burners. Neither survived.[441]

Applying full power at the moment of landing is a very counterintuitive act and a great demonstration of faith. The pilot has to take this action with complete trust the equipment will bring his surging aircraft to a halt.

Many of our instructions from Jesus seem equally counterintuitive. For example, his injunction to *"love your enemies"* (Matthew 5:44; Luke 6:27, 35) turned the world upside down. He focused our attention on the blessings due the poor in spirit, the humble, the mourners, the merciful, and the persecuted. Many of his words do not make sense to the "objective" reader. Only when he has taken possession of our hearts do these words make perfect sense. The more we learn, the more certain our faith becomes that his words are perfect; that we can apply them with full power to our lives—and know he will catch us when we stumble.

F-105s refueling (National Archives)

RECONCILIATION

RECONCILIATION between those who fought the Vietnam War and those who resisted the war effort has come slowly. Most veterans feel they fought honorably for freedom in that war, including the freedom of their fellow citizens to demonstrate and oppose their own government. In most cases, veterans concede the motives of the antiwar protesters were honorable, but have been forever bewildered by the antagonism directed at them as the ones who had to do the fighting. Many came to the conclusion the protesters had somehow achieved the aim suggested by the writer Tom Wolfe, transforming *"the shame of the fearful into the guilt of the courageous."*[442] Even though disaffection has dissipated slowly between these groups, there have been significant events to reconcile both groups to their nation.

As a first step toward healing the wounds of the war, President Gerald Ford established a clemency program for draft evaders in 1974 conditioned on two years' civilian service. In 1977, Jimmy Carter fulfilled a campaign pledge to grant an unconditional pardon to all those who evaded the draft either by not registering or by going abroad. This did not include deserters, those with less-than-honorable discharges, or civilian protesters who initiated acts of violence. Of an estimated 100,000 draft dodgers who fled to Canada during the war, about half returned home to take advantage of their government's pardon.[443]

In March 1979, Jan Scruggs, then a low-ranking Labor Department employee, conceived of the idea of a memorial to recognize Vietnam veterans for their service and to honor those who did not come home from the war. He began talking to veterans' groups, congressmen, and the press. He attracted a core of supporters dedicated to building a monument beside the Lincoln Memorial, funded entirely by private donations. Before groundbreaking in 1982, the group raised more than $9,000,000 in small donations from 650,000 contributors.[444]

From start to finish, the project to build a memorial to those who died in the Vietnam War generated controversy. The antiwar protesters vehemently opposed anything that might glorify the war. Within the veteran community itself there were disagreements on the purpose and design of the memorial. Finally, a panel of well-known artists and designers was appointed to select a design from more than fourteen hundred proposals.

Amazingly, the panel members were unanimous in choosing the work of a twenty-one-year-old Yale undergraduate named Maya Ying Lin. Describing her concept, a *New York Times* editorial commented:

> *The V-shaped, black granite lines merging gently with the sloping earth make the winning design seem a lasting and appropriate image of dignity and sadness. It conveys the only point about the war on which people may agree: that those who died should be remembered.*[445]

The opening ceremony and celebration was held in November 1982, with more than 100,000 veterans coming together for the event. It was only then the full effect of the memorial was revealed. The black granite wall seemed to go on forever. The polished panels displayed more than 58,000 names in chronological order of death, as well as the reflection of the viewer—drawing each observer deep into the panels. As Maya Lin had conceived it, The Wall created a thin boundary that narrowly separated the living and the dead.

The Wall soon became more than a memorial to deceased servicemen. One journalist said, *"Veneration occasionally imparts something more to a hallowed site: a spiritual dimension that transforms it into something like a sacred shrine, where pilgrims come and devotions are paid."*[446] The Vietnam Veterans Memorial has truly become a national shrine. Hundreds of thousands of visitors leave behind an amazing collection of letters, poems, flowers, military medals, and other personal items, trying to bridge the chasm to lost loved ones. Dedicating the memorial, Air Force Chaplain Owen Hendry prayed,

Your presence is felt in this place as a mighty wind, O God, echoing again the words once spoken by your prophet Isaiah, 'I have called you by name, you are mine.' Keep them close to you, O God, in your eternal peace.[447]

The Names

LATE ONE night in March 1979, Jan Scruggs couldn't sleep after watching a movie called *The Deer Hunter*. The graphic scenes of cruelty and violence kept taking him back to Vietnam. He sat in his kitchen with a bottle of whiskey, reliving his worst memory of the war: an exploding ammunition truck that decimated a group of twelve of his friends. As he came running to the scene of

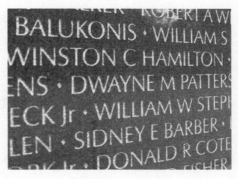

(Dept. of Vet. Affairs)

devastation, bodies were everywhere, and he was helpless to do anything except scream for help.

As the scene flashed through his mind, he remembered the faces of his friends. He realized no one else even knew the names of these young men. He thought, *"The names. No one remembers their names."*[448] The next morning he announced to his wife, *"I'm going to build a memorial to all the guys who served in Vietnam. It'll have the name of everyone killed."*[449] Jan Scrugg's vision would eventually result in the construction of the Vietnam Veterans Memorial. The distinctive feature of its design would be the complete listing of every person killed in the war: 58,000 names, in chronological order of death.

Names are important. No one wants to be thought of as a number; no one wants his name abused; no one wants his name forgotten. This human trait comes directly from our Creator. God knows each of us by name and also wants us to know him by name. He has also given us the one name by which we can be reconciled to him.

> "You shall not misuse the name of the LORD your God." ~Exodus 20:7

> "He calls his own sheep by name and leads them out." ~John 10:3

> "There is no other name [Jesus] under heaven given to men by which we must be saved." ~Acts 4:12

Its Words Were the Names

BEFORE THEY could build the Vietnam Veterans Memorial, Jan Scruggs and his fellow veterans had to fight long and torturous battles to raise funds and obtain government approvals. Every official and bureaucrat found it easier to either say no or to find a reason for delay. The biggest crises, however, came over the design itself.

Shortly after Maya Lin's plan was made public, there was an outcry from many prominent veterans that the proposed memorial was not heroic or uplifting. James Webb held a press conference. *"Why is it black?"* he asked. *"Why is it underground?"*[450] Another disgruntled veteran coined the phrase, *"black gash of shame,"* which numerous newspapers, including the *New York Times,* prominently printed. Ross Perot came to Washington with a proposal to fund a Gallup Poll to see if veterans approved of the design.[451]

Late one night Scruggs walked the Mall and stood before the Lincoln Memorial. Looking up at the statute of the great president, he thought to himself:

> *The Civil War had been America's bloodiest conflict, and yet this memorial carried no sense of violence. It was nonpolitical. Nothing favored the North or the South. Like Maya Lin's design, it provided a sense of history, it was simple, and it relied on words. People could read Lincoln's Gettysburg Address and Second Inaugural Address, think about the words, stand quietly, and let the feelings flow.*
>
> *Maya Lin's design would do the same thing. Its words were the names. Even those who wanted glory had only to pick a name at random. Who could deny the glory in a young man willing to risk—and give—his life for his country?*[452]

That night Scruggs resolved that the Memorial had to be built so the American people could gather before it to hear the eloquent words spoken by 58,000 names. It would be up to the individual onlooker to interpret the meaning of those words.

And the words of the LORD are flawless, like silver refined in a furnace of clay, purified seven times. ~Psalm 12:6

"For by your words you will be acquitted, and by your words you will be condemned.
~Matthew 12:37

Parents and Children

ON HIS first visit to The Vietnam Veterans Memorial Wall, David Rosenthal was amazed by the people he saw there. He knew beforehand the Wall had been designed to memorialize fallen comrades and had been built for the benefit of veterans such as himself. Looking around, he did see his contemporaries, some dressed in Vietnam-era uniforms, some in civilian clothes. However, as he stood there he began to see more and more people who did not fall into the age bracket to be veterans of that war. He said it was like *"getting hit over the head with a sledge hammer"* when he realized who these people were:

> The wicked return to the grave, all the nations that forget God. But the needy will not always be forgotten, nor the hope of the afflicted ever perish. Arise, O LORD, let not man triumph; let the nations be judged in your presence.
> ~Psalm 9:17–19

> *Not only had I made the trip with, and found myself in the company of my "brothers" when I arrived, but now I found myself completely enveloped by the men and women who were the parents and children of the colleagues whom we had come to memorialize.*
>
> *Where had I been all those years? I was then, and remain today, humbled beyond words by the presence of these—our Gold Star mothers, fathers, and children. The depth of my feelings defies my ability to put into words how I am affected. For these, of diverse ancestry, culture, or religious family, for their sacrifices and sacrifice made by their loved ones, I can only say, "God Bless America."*[453]

This thoughtful veteran's observations serve to remind us the Vietnam War touched not only those who fought there. There were also countless loved ones who were affected deeply, either by living with those who came back or by remembering those who did not. Our veterans served America proudly in an unpopular war. Their wives, children, parents, and siblings carried the same burdens, and continue to do so, serving their nation at home. Our veterans of the past, and their extended families, form the hard core of patriotic Americans who stand behind our Armed Forces today and serve as the backbone of a strong America. May God continue to bless every one of them.

Two Walls

JAMES GRIFFITHS served as a machine gunner and scout driver with F Troop, 2nd Squadron, 11th Armored Cavalry Regiment, in 1968 and '69. When he first visited The Vietnam Veterans Memorial Wall in 1984 he found it a place of healing, fellowship, and homage. Yet, he still felt that closure to a war he never really understood was lacking.

> It is for freedom that Christ has set us free. Stand firm, then, and do not let yourselves be burdened again by a yoke of slavery.
> ~Galatians 5:1

Closure finally came in 1989 with events surrounding another wall. In November of that year the destruction of the wall between East and West Berlin became the ultimate symbol of the end of the Cold War. Griffiths observed:

> *The Berlin Wall fell with a thunderous seismic crash that hopefully rattled the very foundation of the Vietnam Veterans Wall in Washington, D.C. The Cold War was ending.*
>
> *The Berlin Wall and the Vietnam Veterans Wall in Washington are inexorably linked. It is my belief that the destruction of the Berlin Wall was contributed to by the men whose names appear on the Vietnam Wall. The Vietnam War was a smaller part of the overall struggle called the Cold War and the American side prevailed in the Cold War. There is no greater symbol of the forces of democracy being victorious in that epic struggle than the destruction of the Berlin Wall.*
>
> *The all-elusive closure sought by me concerning the meaning of the war has been moved forward. The ultimate sacrifice of the 58,000-plus names on the Vietnam Wall was a monumental contribution to those hundreds of millions of people that were to breathe free with the fall of Communism. Knowledge of this has brought a higher degree of closure to me concerning the meaning of the Vietnam War.*[454]

All Vietnam veterans made a significant contribution to democracy and freedom in the world. Though unpopular, the Vietnam War needed to be fought, and was an important part of that larger victory. The protests at home were disheartening to many, but no protests were ever held in the Soviet Union until its final and ultimate collapse. The veterans of Vietnam fought to preserve this right and the many other freedoms that have made our nation great and worthy of victory in this epic struggle.

They Force Us to Think

MA VAN KHANG was born in Hanoi in 1936 and lived in North Vietnam through more than thirty years of war. Many of those years were spent under constant threat of air attack and included long hours with his family in underground shelters. His entire family was affected deeply when his brother was killed in 1972 near Quang Tri. Since the end of the war he has been a teacher, writer, and journalist. One of his most moving experiences was seeing the Vietnam Veterans Memorial, which he described in his own eloquent way:

> Your glory, O Israel, lies slain on your heights. How the mighty have fallen! . . . How the mighty have fallen in battle! . . . The weapons of war have perished!
> ~2 Samuel 1:19, 25, 27

The Vietnam Wall is like a book with many pictures and pages, which to truly appreciate requires an inner perspective.

Those are pages cast in stone, beautiful and sad, with hundreds of lines standing mute, one after another inscribing the names of those American soldiers who died. They force us to read slowly; they force us to think.

My father said "If you know how to learn, even mountains and rivers are books." The Vietnam wall is a book. War is a great book that we all need to read. And so I have read the Vietnam wall slowly, carefully, line by line. I tried to read it with a great deal of thought, with calmness to achieve a measure of peace. It was Dostoevsky who said, "Great ideas are spawned in sufferings." After a great loss comes experience and growth. To meditate on the war, on the loss of loved ones, is to meditate on how to live rightly in peace and friendship among ourselves.[455]

These thoughts from a Vietnamese writer would have been gratifying to Maya Ying Lin, the twenty-one-year-old Yale undergraduate who designed the Vietnam memorial. She specifically insisted on listing those killed in the war chronologically, rather than alphabetically. She felt that only in this way would The Wall stand as an epic story, with the fallen scattered, as on a battlefield. Her view prevailed, adding to The Wall's unique power to "force us to think" about war and those who pay the price of it.

Bagpiper at Vietnam Memorial, Washington, DC

Marine wives greeting POWs at Camp Pendleton. (National Archives)

Contrasting Emotions

WHEN CHAD DAUGHERTY was two months old, his father was killed in Vietnam. His mother, in anguish, threw out all the photos and other reminders of the man she would not see again. She also remarried while Chad was very young, and so his father was rarely mentioned in the household. Nevertheless, he was frequently haunted by fantasies of his father returning.

> Honor your father and your mother, so that you may live long in the land the LORD your God is giving you. ~Exodus 20:12

At age seventeen, Daugherty went to the Vietnam Memorial to find his father. After going through the search process, he finally stood before Panel 57, looking at the name he sought. His fingers brushed over the letters. He later wrote a composition, describing himself in the third person and his feelings at that moment:

> From his heart rose a feeling he just could not explain. It only seemed to occur at that place while gazing at the name and dark reflections in the wall. The feeling seemed to torture the heart. Contrasting emotions of love and hate; happiness and sorrow; pride and shame were all felt at once. Why did he put himself to this torture? he wondered. There was no reason to come. No one made him come. Yet he came willingly.[456]

The Wall became the place where Chad Daugherty resolved the conflicting emotions of his childhood. There, he talked to his father. He shared all his accomplishments and dreams for the future. He told him how much he loved him. He left a letter saying, *"Dear father, you shall always be remembered. Your loving son."*[457]

There are probably very few men who do not have conflicting emotions about their fathers. They are fortunate if their fathers are still living, giving them an opportunity to resolve these feelings directly. Many of us unfortunately don't have that option. We need a wall of our own to go to where we can acknowledge the man who was probably the best father he was capable of being, and was the one our heavenly Father meant us to have. Whatever his faults, he helped make us what we are. Whether talking to the man or to a wall, the best place to start is, "I love you, Dad."

Help to Heal

THE MOVING WALL, a replica of the Vietnam Veterans Memorial in Washington, D.C., has traveled the United States since 1984. Jim Schueckler served as a volunteer when the Wall came to Batavia, New York. During his time on duty, he met mothers, fathers, sisters, brothers, aunts, uncles, cousins, and friends of fallen heroes, as well as fellow veterans. There were also visitors with no relation to the fallen who were simply curious or wanted to pay respect. He heard comments such as:

> If one falls down, his friend can help him up. But pity the man who falls and has no one to help him up!
> ~Ecclesiastes 4:10

"I came to see my son's name."
"He's my brother."
"I took him hunting."
"He was the little boy who lived across the street."
"We were going steady in high school."
"I was his Boy Scout leader."
"He went to our church."
"We were classmates for twelve years."
"He went out on patrol in my place that day." [458]

Schueckler's duty was to help people find and make rubbings of the names they searched for. Even more significant, he gave hurting people a chance to talk:

> *While searching the directory or leading a visitor to the name they sought, I would quietly ask, "Was he a friend or a relative?" Over the six days, I began conversations that way with several hundred people. Only a handful gave me a short answer; almost everyone wanted to talk. Each had their own story to tell. For some, the words poured out as if the floodgates of a dam that had been closed for thirty years had just burst open. For others, the words came out slowly and deliberately between long pauses. Sometimes, they choked on the words and they cried. I also cried as I listened, asked more questions, and silently prayed that my words would help to heal, not to hurt.* [459]

We all worry about what to say to a friend who has lost a loved one. This story is a reminder it doesn't have to be complicated. During such times, everyone needs a friend who will listen and share memories of the person they are mourning.

A Living Memorial

GEOFFREY STEINER's life after Vietnam was difficult. He spent time in a VA psychiatric ward, fought a drinking problem, got divorced, and even tried to commit suicide. He finally ended up at the end of a dirt road on a one-hundred-acre parcel of land in a remote part of Minnesota. His own healing began when he started planting trees. He seemed to reach a truce in his long, personal war as he dug into the soil and put down the roots of new life.[460]

Steiner gradually began to visualize a larger purpose to his efforts. He would plant a tree for each of the 58,000 lives lost during the Vietnam War. His task would not be easy. By 1989 he had planted 30,000 trees and run into financial difficulty. On the day the bank was to foreclose on his property, a number of veterans' groups and a local beer distributor came to the rescue, paying off his debt. *"I think the good Lord sent them,"* said Steiner, as he continued with his lonely work.[461]

The Living Memorial Forest is now officially recognized by the state of Minnesota. The site is on a hilltop with older birch trees looming over the thousands of new seedlings and young trees planted in recent years. Veterans frequently visit the site to find a quiet moment of reflection in the peaceful setting. Geoffrey Steiner chose purposely not to build a memorial of stone or sculpture, saying, *"What we're trying to do is heal people. This is a living memorial."*[462] At the center of the site are a flagpole flying an American flag and a stone marker with a moving biblical passage:

Rescue those who are unjustly sentenced to die; save them as they stagger to their death. Don't excuse yourself by saying, "Look, we didn't know." For God understands all hearts, and he sees you. ~Proverbs 24:11, 12 (NLT)

PTSD

COMBAT VETERANS, policemen, and firefighters have a lot in common. Men and women in uniform have been required to face danger and deal with violence. They have repeatedly confronted horrific images while working in professional cultures that value personal stoicism. Shunning help from others, they deal with a lot of disturbed feelings that get shoved below the surface.

Ron Rayner

Sometimes, often much later, problems begin to surface in the personal and family lives of these dedicated people. Irritability, quick temper, outbursts of anger, road rage, depression, and thoughts of suicide are some of the symptoms of a condition known as post-traumatic stress disorder, or PTSD. Ron Rayner is a Marine veteran of the Vietnam War and career firefighter. He described a dilemma common to this condition:

> *The real problem with PTSD is not that people are mentally wounded from a traumatic life-threatening event . . . The real problem is that most of the victims are in denial and will not seek help for this life-threatening disability. These courageous individuals who risk their lives for others cannot accept that they may also need help from a mental health professional.*
>
> *I know that I personally was in denial. I always thought I was a tough guy and didn't need help. Being tough is definitely part of the job that these occupations demand. But what I have learned and what these brave people have to realize is that mental wounds can ruin your life and kill you just like a physical wound.*[463]

We have to acknowledge a problem before it can be solved—but the person suffering from PTSD is usually the last to see it. Unfortunately, understanding often comes only from a catastrophic event. We would all benefit from talking out our problems with Christian friends or professional counselors, before they explode harmfully on others. Prayerfully examine your conscience and look objectively at your own behavior. Do you need help? If so, do your family a favor. Don't be the last person to acknowledge it.

Dear friends, do not be surprised at the painful trial you are suffering, as though something strange were happening to you. But rejoice that you participate in the sufferings of Christ, so that you may be overjoyed when his glory is revealed.
~1 Peter 4:12, 13

Anger, Depression, Guilt

THE DOWNWARD spiral often starts with anger. I've seen men break down with rage after battling elephant grass, leeches, and debilitating heat for too many hours. Losing friends and fellow Marines in a firefight was bad enough, but random death to mines and booby traps nurtured a frustrated anger that festered even deeper. The crowning blow came for many with a hostile reception on the home front from people who didn't seem to know or care about what was really happening in a place that wasn't even real to them.

> "Come now, let us reason together," says the LORD. "Though your sins are like scarlet, they shall be as white as snow; though they are red as crimson, they shall be like wool."
> ~Isaiah 1:18

The problem for many Vietnam veterans has been the tendency to absorb all this anger and turn it inward, as one writer described:

> *"A person may become angry with someone or with a situation over which they have no control. They feel powerless, and anger begins to build inside. Most depression is a result of what counselors call 'frozen anger,' or anger turned inward."*[464]
>
> *This inward-directed and unresolved anger leads often to depression and guilt, the natural hazards threatening all combat veterans: "That's why many veterans never talk about their combat experiences. Burying their memories and guilt, they try to put the war behind them. Guilt and war go together."*[465]

The Vietnam Veterans Bible addresses the issues of anger, depression, and guilt that plague many veterans. Professional counselors and veterans' groups are recommended, but there is also insight on the ultimate solution—forgiveness:

> *Of course true and complete forgiveness can only come from God. Ultimately, all sin is against him. And the great news is that he stands ready to forgive and forget, if you'll let him. This means that all the horrible things you are carrying around have to be released—and only God can carry that burden for you. But you have to be willing to give it up. Thousands of veterans just like you have found the freedom that God gives. You can have it too.*[466]

Amnesty

IN 1971 the debate over amnesty for draft dodgers was heating up. Many Americans supported the idea, although President Nixon and many others strongly opposed it. In Montreal, Mike Wallace of *60 Minutes* spoke with Ken Duff, a nineteen-year-old deserter from the Marine Corps who longed to return home even though he showed little remorse for what he had done. Talking about those who did go to war, Duff said, *"These people did what they thought was right and what was their duty. But my ideal of what America should be and what America should do as a country is different from theirs."*[467]

Following this encounter, Wallace traveled to Connecticut to interview Duff's parents. He found a mother generally supportive of her son, but with conflicted feelings about his actions. When asked about the other mothers who had lost their sons in the war, she broke down. Wallace recalls,

> The Lord is not slow in keeping his promise, as some understand slowness. He is patient with you, not wanting anyone to perish, but everyone to come to repentance.
> ~2 Peter 3:9

> *I immediately called a halt to the interview. Nor did I do that only for her benefit, for in truth my own feelings were edging out of control. I've always tried to maintain emotional distance from the people I interview. But that was one time when the normal defense mechanisms failed me, and I think I know why. After all, I, too, was a parent . . . So my heart went out to the Duffs as they struggled to cope with the moral dilemma of their son's desertion and the bitter resentment it aroused in other parents who had lost their sons in Vietnam.*[468]

Mike Wallace and this mother both wept over a dilemma without an earthly solution. We may love our children, but, in fairness, we know breaking the law calls for punishment. God himself has a similar dilemma. He loves us as his children and also does not want to see us punished. However, he is a just God and has to deal with our unrighteousness. He solved this dilemma once and for all by sending his Son into the world to reconcile mankind to himself. It is up to us to freely and earnestly repent of our wrongdoings and turn to him for forgiveness. Through Jesus Christ, our amnesty is assured.

Looking for a Helicopter

DONALD SMITH was discharged from the Army immediately after returning from Vietnam. His abrupt separation from a way of life he had known for three years was disorienting. He was glad to leave the war behind and to get home at last, but the friends he had grown so close to were gone, leaving no one to talk to who understood what he was feeling. For some reason, he had recurring visions of helicopters:

(U. S. Marine Corps)

> *In my mind I could still hear the sound of choppers overhead. I'd day-dream so much. Waiting to see if a helicopter would come and take me away. I used to dream about that a lot—I was going to be airlifted out of there. Any helicopter that goes by with the right pitch on those blades . . . I just look up at it. I just think, "At any moment that thing's going to land. I'm going to see some blue smoke or green smoke or something else, yellow smoke. That thing is going to land and pick me up, take me away. Who knows where."*[469]

To appreciate this soldier's fixation, imagine being airlifted out of a steaming jungle. You are sweat-soaked, filthy, and afraid. Suddenly, you are safely above the fray, looking down on a scenic panorama, in cool, brisk air. It's like going to heaven. Who wouldn't have recurring visions of such an experience?

Heaven is indeed a glorious prospect, especially for those living in a present state of hardship or misery. Unfortunately, our own visions of heaven may not be so vivid if our lives are filled with a certain amount of physical comfort. Jesus had this human tendency in mind when he said, *"Blessed are the poor in spirit"* (Matthew 5:3). From an eternal perspective, our time on earth is brief. If our pains and trials serve to keep our focus on eternity, then we are truly blessed. If we are "cursed" by a comfortable life, we need an even more exalted vision of heaven and the glorious life that awaits us there with our Father.

> "Blessed are you when people insult you, persecute you and falsely say all kinds of evil against you because of me. Rejoice and be glad, because great is your reward in heaven."
> ~Matthew 5:11, 12

I Sent Him Home

WILLIAM CRAPSER did not readjust to civilian life easily. Resentful and angry, he turned to drugs for relief from the mental agony he suffered, living for years just on the edge of sanity. His story of healing is an unusual journey of redemption:

> *The first decision I made which led to my recovery was to recognize him as me. That, yes, I was the nineteen-year-old Marine who had killed and, at times, killed without remorse. I realized I could not fight him anymore or deny him.*
>
> *So I began meditating on him . . . until I could see him very clearly in my mind. He looked sad and he was very tired. I too felt sad for what he had gone through and I realized how badly I wanted him out of the war.*
>
> *I decided to bring him home. I began by picturing the nineteen-year-old "me" stopping, then dropping his rucksack, his suspender straps and web-belt, his gas mask and K-bar knife. Then I watched him throw his rifle on top of the pile. Then I watched him take off his camouflage utilities . . . dress in jeans and a sports shirt and a light jacket. . . . When he was done, I told him he was going home, that he didn't have to fight anymore, that he was being discharged. He burst into laughter and tears and ran toward me, his arms wide as if to embrace me. And inside me we embraced. Then I put him on a plane and sent him to someone I knew would love and care for him. I sent him home to me.*[470]

It never hurts to stop and think about who we are and what we have become. It is easy to drift spiritually and, without realizing it, come to a place far removed from God. Self-absorption, anxiety, and creeping pessimism are sure signs of this condition. Take a detached look at yourself and assess why "this person" is so troubled. Maybe you need to be "discharged" from some worry by refocusing and reconnecting with God and asking him to share your burden.

> "Come to me, all you who are weary and burdened, and I will give you rest . . . For my yoke is easy and my burden is light."
> ~Matthew 11:28, 30

Planting a Seed

IT WAS an unusual and history-making event. In July 2007, a government delegation from Vietnam came to an evangelical church in North Texas for a three-day visit. The delegation was led by Nguyen Van Kien, director-general of the People's Aid Coordinating Committee. The purpose of the visit was, as stated by Mr. Kien, "to convey the gratitude of our people."[471]

> "The kingdom of heaven is like a mustard seed, which a man took and planted in his field. Though it is the smallest of all your seeds, yet when it grows, it is the largest of garden plants and becomes a tree, so that the birds of the air come and perch in its branches."
> ~Matthew 13:31, 32

For more than a decade, members of the North Wood Church in Keller, Texas, have been going to rural areas of Vietnam to install water filtration systems and to work in schools, orphanages, and medical clinics. The ministry was started by Bob Prough, a church member and former helicopter pilot from the Vietnam War. With his encouragement, the church sent a fact-finding mission and found that little was being done in that country by U.S. churches, and that the needs were great.

The pastor of the North Wood Church, Bob Roberts, has eagerly supported this ministry and has made dozens of trips to Vietnam himself. He acknowledges he is nervous about the country. You can wind up in jail for trying to start churches or for overtly evangelizing. Even so, he feels, "If Jesus were walking on this world today, he would be serving the Vietnamese. He wouldn't say, 'Change your government and I'll serve you.'"[472]

It is always easy to focus on the obstacles. The Communist government of Vietnam puts up harsh roadblocks to spreading the gospel. In the same way, we all know individuals who have equally tough personal defenses against intrusions of the Spirit. Our efforts to share our faith may often seem futile. When faced with seemingly insurmountable obstacles, all that we may reasonably expect to accomplish is to plant a seed. Someday the government of Vietnam will change. Someday our skeptical friend may face a crisis and have a change of heart. In his own time, God will use the seeds we have planted to produce something new and amazing.

The Vietnam Project

JAMES RECKNER was a career Navy officer who served two tours of duty in Vietnam as an advisor to Vietnamese riverine forces. After his retirement he joined the faculty of the history department at Texas Tech University, where he taught courses in U.S. Navy history. In 1989 he was teaching a course on the Vietnam War when he realized the university had very little material relating to that conflict. With a small group of local veterans and a handful of donated documents, he started the Vietnam Project.

Today the Texas Tech University Vietnam Center and Archive contains more than 20,000,000 pages of documents, a 12,000-volume library, hundreds of oral histories, and thousands of carefully catalogued boxes of material relating to the Vietnam War.

> What causes fights and quarrels among you? Don't they come from your desires that battle within you? ~James 4:1

Guest lecturers are brought to the university representing different viewpoints on the war, and hundreds of scholarships have been sponsored for Vietnamese and Cambodian youths in their home countries.

Unfortunately, the Center is not without controversy. When a former South Vietnamese ambassador to the United States came to speak a few years ago, members of the faculty protested his presence on campus. There seems to be suspicion within academia that the Center is trying to portray the war in Vietnam as too "noble" an effort. The undercurrents of conflict seem to continue between the antiwar movement of that era and those who fought the war. This attitude has saddened and angered Dr. Reckner. When Nguyen Vinh Uoc, a senior North Vietnamese military officer, visited the Center, Dr. Reckner told him, "You and I have more in common than I have with some American people who favored your side during the war—devotion to duty, respect for the chain of command, and dedication to service."[473]

Most veterans are proud of what they accomplished in the Vietnam War and will always have much in common with other veterans from both sides who served their nations. They pray that feelings of opposition to the war will ultimately be supplanted with respect for those who fought it.

Trying to Remember

PHAM TIEN DUAT was a soldier in the North Vietnamese army who, after the war, became a well-known writer and journalist. In recent years he has been surprised to discover a large number of women war veterans who have become nuns. These women were either widowed, wounded severely, or who were simply too old after the war to get married and start families.

NVA woman soldier. (vhpa.org)

Like other veterans, these women want to put the war behind them. However, they are haunted by memories of their lost loved ones and their own lost youth. Duat has become very philosophical about the need for them and his nation to close these doors to the past:

> In order to close a door, it's worthwhile to understand what it is that we close. Sadly, after over twenty years have passed since the war ended, many can still only vaguely see the contour of that door as if looking through a veil of mist.
>
> Perhaps in order to really forget something, we first have to know fully what it is that we want to forget. And it is a difficult thing: There is a limit to how much we can remember. When I asked the name and age of a nun in Thai Binh province, she went rummaging through her old papers to find a piece of paper with my own handwriting on it. Only then did I recognize her as a beautiful soldier I knew during the war.[474]

This thoughtful and eloquent writer seems to be looking at the issue of reconciliation through the lens of modern psychoanalytical thought, which suggests we need to delve deeply into the past, bring our traumatic experiences to light, and then deal with them in the open. This approach forms the basis for much of present-day psychology and has obviously helped many people. I believe, however, that Jesus Christ gave us a better way to put our anger and guilt behind us. He brought forgiveness to those who seek it, and, in return, expects those who are forgiven to forgive themselves and each other. There are times when it takes more than our own analytical ability to reconcile with ourselves, with others, or with God.

> Bear with each other and forgive whatever grievances you may have against one another. Forgive as the Lord forgave you. And over all these virtues put on love, which binds them all together in perfect unity.
> ~Colossians 3:13, 14

We Hurt Ourselves

AS JULIE WEAVER listened to the news and the antiwar rhetoric about the Vietnam War, she went along with it and gradually "turned against the war." When her brother came home from duty in the war, she didn't hesitate to tell him what she thought of it. For years they didn't speak.

> For if you forgive men when they sin against you, your heavenly Father will also forgive you. ~Matthew 6:14

Many years later her attitude began to change when she saw a photograph depicting the anguished face of a veteran at the Vietnam Memorial. She began to realize she had never considered the price paid by the men who fought. To atone, she wrote a moving open letter to all veterans, excerpted below:

Dear Hero:

Have you been to Vietnam? If so, I have something I want to say to you—Thank you for going! Thank you from the bottom of my heart. Please forgive me for my insensitivity. I don't know how I could have been so blind, but I was. When I woke up, you were wounded and the damage was done, and I don't know how to fix it. I will never stop regretting my actions, and I will never let it happen again.

Inside of you there is a pain that will never completely go away . . . and you know what? It's inside of us, too; because when we let you down, we hurt ourselves too. We all know it . . . and we suffer guilt and we don't know what to do . . . so we cheer for our troops and write letters to "any soldier" and we hang out the yellow ribbons and fly the flag and we love America. We love you too, even if it doesn't feel like it to you.

Please say you will forgive us and please take your rightful place as heroes of our country.[475]

This letter has been posted on many veterans' Web sites and has generated many positive responses. My own response is one of appreciation. Thank you, Julie, for taking such a risk, and, for what it's worth, I add my forgiveness to that of many others. In actuality, we fought for your right to form and express your own opinion and for the right of others to express theirs.

Still with Us

THIRTY YEARS after the Vietnam War, one thoughtful person felt the need to give a heartfelt apology and word of thanks to those who received so little recognition at the time of their service. This message was posted recently on an 11th Armored Cavalry Regiment Web site:

> *It has been over 30 years now, your tour in Vietnam has ended, but, it is still with you!*
>
> *. . . Maybe it was because you were so young and impressionable back then. You were open to all the excitement of being a young man, facing your future, and you were thrown there, to "Hell" on earth. It wasn't fair, but the reality of war dampened your spirit, and it is still with you!*
>
> *Listen! You need to hear this. Your fighting, as well as your survival, was for us, your brothers and sisters back home. We could say "thank you" until we're blue in the face, but the words to truly thank you for what you did for us simply don't exist. We can welcome you home with "open arms" now. We know it's much too late to let you know that you truly were our heroes, but we want you to know, not only that, but also that our total lack of appreciation back then,* **is still with us!**[476]

Often the thoughtless things we do or fail to do hurt others. What we sometimes overlook is the harm done to ourselves. Jesus himself gave us a simple command: *"Love each other as I have loved you"* (John 15:12). He considered his followers as his friends, not uninformed underlings. His commands therefore did not rely on blind obedience, but were meant to be stored in our hearts, to guide all our actions. When we drift away from his simple ethical code, we drift away from him. Our thoughtless acts are very much more harmful to ourselves than to anyone else.

"Greater love has no one than this, that he lay down his life for his friends. You are my friends if you do what I command. I no longer call you servants, because a servant does not know his master's business. Instead, I have called you friends, for everything that I learned from my Father I have made known to you."
~John 15:13–15

The Only Salvation

JOHN TUTHILL attempted to describe the mental process that separated him from others as he tried to live with himself after his wartime experience as a combat pilot:

When anyone . . . is threatened daily with the potential end of their life and they have to kill other human beings or be killed . . . [they] become callous to every emotion you can imagine. These things are done involuntarily and to some extent in the subconscious part of our brain. The interesting thing is that not only does nothing get into your soul through these walls, nothing gets out either. Even love is hindered in both directions.[477]

> "I am the way and the truth and the life. No one comes to the Father except through me. If you really knew me, you would know my Father as well. From now on, you do know him and have seen him."
> ~John 14:6, 7

To illustrate the extent of his detached indifference, he related an incident when his wife, Penny, was grief-stricken over the death of her mother. After watching her cry for several days, he said coldly, *"Penny, get over it, everybody dies."*[478] It would take years for him to appreciate the cruelty of this statement and to realize how impenetrable the wall around his own emotions had become.

Since becoming a Christian, Tuthill has shared his spiritual journey freely with other veterans. He tries to convince them of the one proven way to break through the barriers separating them from their loved ones and their own emotions:

The only salvation for anyone in that environment, as I have learned from personal experience, is to study the Bible and develop a personal relationship with Christ. There is no other answer no matter what you hear from the psycho-babble of the news or doctors who have no combat experience. I know it to be true because it took 29 years from coming home in 1970 to get it and have it begin in earnest in me in 1999. Don't let a family member or friend go that long without encouraging them to seek their answer in the only place found, the Bible and Christ. . . . It's the only thing that works![479]

Vietnam veterans gather at the Memorial. (U. S. Marine Corps)

Marine body bearers fold the flag. (U. S. Marine Corps)

Failure

IN A newsletter for Vietnam War veterans, the Disabled American Veterans national chaplain, Rev. Oscar Wilkie, wrote a moving article to help veterans restore some needed perspective to their lives. Pointing out how our "win-lose" culture seems to prize winners and to aggrandize athletic and financial superstars, he acknowledged the pressure ordinary people are often under to "succeed." We all feel this pressure to win, but must inevitably face a certain amount of failure in our lives. Reverend Wilkie observed, *"Losing is depressing for most of us, but life does not afford us the luxury of choosing whether or not we are going to play. We know what it is to fail, and what we need is a way to redeem those failures."*[480] To accomplish this, he offered an insight into God's perspective on our struggles:

> Simon Peter answered, "You are the Christ, the Son of the living God." Jesus replied, "Blessed are you, Simon son of Jonah, for this was not revealed to you by man, but by my Father in heaven. And I tell you that you are Peter, and on this rock I will build my church.
> ~Matthew 16:16–18

> *The ultimate tragedy in life is not failure. The ultimate tragedy is to be unwilling to take risks when significant purposes present themselves! I think if someone is keeping score and "grading" us on life, during the times we don't quite make it He gives us an "incomplete" rather than a "failure." This means even when we fail on occasion, we are not "failures," just "incomplete" in the process of "becoming." "Incomplete" means there is still room to grow.*[481]

There are many biblical examples of spectacular failure, later redeemed by God. The apostle Peter's denial of Jesus at the critical moment of Jesus' trial before the Crucifixion stands out: *"Then Peter remembered the word Jesus had spoken: 'Before the rooster crows, you will disown me three times.' And he went outside and wept bitterly"* (Matthew 26:75). Even though Peter was utterly humiliated by his failure, Jesus still redeemed him to become a great leader in the church. Through this famous failure, Peter's boldness was tempered with humility, enabling the Savior to use him in a mighty way.

America Is Good Enough

IN HIS book, *My Losing Season*, Pat Conroy described his limited involvement in the antiwar movement during the Vietnam War. Going against his own military roots and college background, he organized the only antiwar demonstration ever held in Beaufort, South Carolina. Later in life he thoughtfully reassessed his attitudes of that time and concluded,

> Clothe yourselves with humility toward one another, because, "God opposes the proud but gives grace to the humble." Humble yourselves, therefore, under God's mighty hand, that he may lift you up in due time.
> ~1 Peter 5:5, 6

In the twenty-five years that have passed since South Vietnam fell, I have immersed myself in the study of totalitarianism in the unspeakable twentieth century . . . I read the newspaper reports during Pol Pot's shameless assault against his own people in Cambodia, and the rise of Saddam Hussein and Gadhafi of Libya. I have watched the fall of Communism in Russia . . . Many times I have quizzed journalists who reported on wars in Bosnia, the Sudan, the Congo, Rwanda, Angola, Indonesia, Guatemala, El Salvador, Chile, Northern Ireland, Algeria—I have come to revere words like "democracy" and "freedom," the right to vote, the incomprehensibly beautiful origins of my country, and the grandeur of the extraordinary vision of the founding fathers. Do I see America's flaws? Of course I do. But I can now honor her basic, incorruptible virtues . . . I have come to a conclusion about my country that I knew then in my bones, but lacked the courage to act on: America is a good enough country to die for even when she is wrong.[482]

I greatly admire Conroy's honesty and humility in admitting something he came to see as a mistake in his past. He gives each of us a great example to follow. The path to forgiveness and reconciliation starts with an admission of our failures and wrongdoing. Jesus came to save those with flaws, not those who consider themselves perfect. Our first act before him every day should be to pray simply, *"God, have mercy on me, a sinner"* (Luke 18:13). When we adopt this attitude, we open our hearts to him and to the power he alone has to heal and reorient our lives.

That Flag

AL KRABOTH attended The Citadel and played basketball with Pat Conroy. While writing his best-selling book, *My Losing Season,* Conroy interviewed Kraboth and his wife at their home in New Jersey. When the discussion turned to Vietnam, Kraboth told an amazing story.

Kraboth was the navigator of an A-6 Intruder when it was hit by gunfire while bombing somewhere in South Vietnam. He lost consciousness and didn't even remember ejecting. When he woke up on the ground, he found that he had broken bones in his neck, back, and scapula. He was captured by the Viet Cong and forced to walk at gun-point through the jungle. In spite of his injuries, he was marched barefoot over the worst imaginable terrain for three months, through rain and mud, mostly at night, to the final destination, Hanoi. He told of harrowing episodes when people along the way tried to kill him and of how close he came to dying due to sickness and starvation.

> Now if we are children, then we are heirs—heirs of God and co-heirs with Christ, if indeed we share in his sufferings in order that we may also share in his glory.
> ~Romans 8:17

The most memorable and moving event of his ordeal came on the day of his repatriation. As the big C-141 landed at the Hanoi airport, he said he watched without emotion—until he saw the flag painted on the plane's tail:

> The flag. It had the biggest American flag on it I ever saw. To this day, I cry when I think of it. Seeing the flag. I started crying. I couldn't see the plane, I just saw that flag. All the guys started cheering. But that flag . . . that flag.[483]

We probably don't understand this kind of emotion for a flag or any other symbol unless we have suffered for it. The symbol of our faith, the cross, represents Jesus' suffering for us, and takes on a deeper meaning when we suffer in some way for him. It's unlikely we will ever face an ordeal like that endured by this POW, or especially the ordeal endured by our Savior, but any risk we take, or sacrifice we make, to share our faith will bring us closer to the place we need to be—the foot of the cross.

Reunion

BILL MCDONALD returned to Vietnam in 2002. He traveled north from Saigon with several companions and a guide looking for old battlefields. He found that his old compound at Phu Loi had become a People's Army base. Everything else seemed to have returned to nature. The grassy fields and farms that now occupied the former military facilities were somehow comforting to McDonald and his friends.

Bill McDonald

As the small group was traveling along Highway 13, formerly known as "Thunder Road," McDonald realized they were entering the "Iron Triangle," one of the major VC strongholds for many years of the war. They stopped along the road to take photos of a Vietnamese tank that had been left as a monument to the war. There they met an old man, a former VC officer and doctor. He invited the group into his home to meet his family and to have refreshments. They all spent a pleasant afternoon together.

McDonald reflected on this meeting with a former foe:

> *The irony of it amused me, but also made me feel good that real recovery from any war is possible. Here were all of us old warriors sitting around a former VC's dinner table talking about our grandchildren. What a difference 35 years made! This showed me that forgiveness and understanding were as much a part of nature as were the devastated forests and jungles of Vietnam that are growing back.*[484]

If former enemies can come together in friendship years later, maybe combat veterans hold the key to future peace. Of all people, veterans know that their former foes are human beings like themselves, trying to survive their own difficult times. Of all people, veterans are most capable of applying this insight to our present conflicts and our present enemies.

> He will judge between the nations and will settle disputes for many peoples. They will beat their swords into plowshares and their spears into pruning hooks. Nation will not take up sword against nation, nor will they train for war anymore. ~Isaiah 2:4

A Gracious God

SHARON WAS six years old in 1972 when her father, Captain Stephen Rusch, was shot down over Laos. His body was never found, and Sharon grew up with an ever-present void in her heart and in her family's life. *"I've missed my Dad,"* she said. *"I miss him every day of my life. I think about him all the time."*[485] Her father's memory played an all-important role in her career choice. Sharon Bannister became an officer in the U.S. Air Force and rose to the rank of full colonel.

Col. Sharon Bannister receives flag. (arlington-cemetary.net)

After years of excavation and analysis, a joint U.S./Laotian search team identified the remains of Stephen Rusch in 2007. Sharon traveled to Honolulu to view the remains in a military laboratory and to accompany the casket home. *"This is harder for me than I thought it was going to be,"* she said. *"But it's great for our family. It brings us some closure."*[486]

Her father was buried with full military honors in Arlington National Cemetery. Sharon commemorated her earthly father and extolled the amazing nature of her Father in heaven—revealing the power of a faith that sustained her family throughout her life:

> God gave my Dad the gift of true freedom. Because he is a gracious, loving God he wanted my Dad, and indeed each of us to know we are accepted, secure, and significant. Let me repeat that in case you missed it: Because he is a gracious, loving God he wanted my Dad, and indeed each of us to know we are accepted, secure, and significant. In this we are free to live life fully and experience eternity.[487]

For he chose us in him before the creation of the world to be holy and blameless in his sight. In love he predestined us to be adopted as his sons through Jesus Christ, in accordance with his pleasure and will—to the praise of his glorious grace, which he has freely given us in the One he loves.
~Ephesians 1:4–6

Thanksgiving

IN 1621 the survivors of the "New World" colony of Plymouth (spelled "Plimoth" by its first governor) gathered together to celebrate their meager harvest and to thank God for what they had. Soldiers have always had a lot in common with these early settlers, fighting to survive in strange, faraway lands. An Army chaplain in Vietnam explained to his men:

> Sing to the LORD a new song, for he has done marvelous things; his right hand and his holy arm have worked salvation for him. The LORD has made his salvation known and revealed his righteousness to the nations. ~Psalm 98:1, 2

God was not incidental to this hearty group (the Pilgrims). He was not an appendage to life. He was their life. Nothing seemed more appropriate than to render their heartfelt thanks and gratitude to Almighty God.

We who are to spend this Thanksgiving Day 1968 in Vietnam will be deprived of family gatherings and family traditions. One could sit down and wallow in the puddle of self-pity because of this. Or, one could thank God that he has the privilege of marching with that noble band of the ages who have repeatedly demonstrated there are some things more important than comfort.

I am confident that the band of courageous Pilgrims who came to Plymouth 348 years ago did not come merely for personal gain. They sought a land and a governmental institution that would give freedom to their children and their children's children. The soldier should not find it difficult to understand this motive.[488]

Those of us living comfortable lives would do well to remember the Pilgrims and our soldiers. They were and continue to be thankful in spite of hardships and danger—possibly more so than we are in our bounty.

Thanksgiving is a time to turn to God and to acknowledge all he has done for us. He has provided for our physical needs in abundance. More importantly, he has also provided a way for us to be restored to him in this life and throughout eternity. His greatest gift to us, our greatest cause for giving thanks, is his Son, our Savior, Jesus Christ.

A General's Thanksgiving

IN NOVEMBER 1968, Major General Charles Gettys, the Commander of the Americal Division, sent a heartfelt Thanksgiving message to all the men and women under his command:

> *Cicero, the Roman orator, said more than 2,000 years ago, "A thankful heart is not only a great virtue, but the mother of all other virtues."*
>
> *Our nation has always acknowledged its dependence on God. One facet of this acknowledgment takes the form of an officially designated National Day of Thanksgiving each November.*
>
> *On one side of the ledger, this Thanksgiving Day may appear as a day of privation for you. You will be absent from family reunions and neighborhood gatherings. However, on the other side of the ledger, your unselfish spirit and service here guarantees a continuance of our nation "under God."*
>
> *While eating our traditional turkey dinners, we must give thanks for all of the wonderful things our nation stands for and has enabled us to enjoy. Look to the future with confidence and hope, with full knowledge that our heritage will prevail against those who would deny it.*
>
> *When I compile my personal list of things for which I am thankful this year, the officers and men of the Americal Division will head the list. May God bless us all on this Thanksgiving Day.*[489]

Shout for joy to the LORD, all the earth.
Worship the LORD with gladness; come before him with joyful songs.
Know that the LORD is God.
It is he who made us, and we are his; we are his people, the sheep of his pasture.
Enter his gates with thanksgiving and his courts with praise; give thanks to him and praise his name.
For the LORD is good and his love endures forever; his faithfulness continues through all generations. ~Psalm 100

No leader of an army, a nation, or a family can do more for those under their care than to encourage them in their faith, and to point them toward the most fundamental act of faith—acknowledging God by expressing the profound gratitude he deserves for the wonder of his creation and our lives within it. This is the thankfulness that is truly the "mother of all other virtues."

Ash and Trash

NOT ALL missions were combat. Pilots called the routine, service-oriented flights "ash and trash" runs, apparently named by someone who had the childhood job of taking the fireplace ash and household trash out to the street every day. One pilot had to periodically deliver the *Stars & Stripes* to outlying bases, reminding him of his first job delivering newspapers. The only difference was he was using a million-dollar aircraft instead of a ten-dollar wagon to carry the papers.

Eric Bray flew with the 162nd Aviation Assault Company out of Can Tho in the Mekong Delta and recalled his favorite "ash and trash" mission: delivering holiday meals to the troops:

> Each one should use whatever gift he has received to serve others, faithfully administering God's grace in its various forms . . . If anyone serves, he should do it with the strength God provides, so that in all things God may be praised through Jesus Christ. To him be the glory and the power for ever and ever. Amen.
> ~1 Peter 4:10, 11

The Thanksgiving Day meals that I delivered were prepared by the mess people back at the main base in Ca Mau and put into what looked like these giant lunch boxes. Each "lunch box" looked like it could feed a whole squad of soldiers. The entire mission was well organized because there was one of these containers for every one of those little outposts where the U.S. soldiers were stationed and acting as the advisors to the ARVN forces . . .

We would land near the little base and the U.S. forces would rush out to meet the aircraft as happy as a lark because the higher ups had remembered them with a good traditional American holiday meal. I know this mission raised their morale and made them feel great just for a little while with a little taste of home.[490]

These flights were so memorable because they gave these airmen the opportunity to do something for someone else. As Bray explained, *"These missions helped make the tour of duty a little more bearable for a lot of GIs whom we will never know their names and will just remember the smiles on their faces."*[491] This is the attitude the apostle Peter encouraged all Christians to incorporate into their lives.

He Who Humbles Himself

JESUS WAS once talking to a group of people who felt superior to others based on their "righteousness." To illustrate their condition, he told a story:

> *"Two men went up to the temple to pray, one a Pharisee and the other a tax collector. The Pharisee stood up and prayed about himself: 'God, I thank you that I am not like other men—robbers, evildoers, adulterers— or even like this tax collector. I fast twice a week and give a tenth of all I get.'*
>
> *But the tax collector stood at a distance. He would not even look up to heaven, but beat his breast and said, 'God, have mercy on me, a sinner.'*
>
> *I tell you that this man, rather than the other, went home justified before God. For everyone who exalts himself will be humbled, and he who humbles himself will be exalted." ~Luke 18:10–14*

Bill Mahedy was an Army chaplain during the Vietnam War and has devoted himself since to helping veterans. In his book *Out of the Night* he cites this parable as a cautionary tale. Anyone who would assume a morally superior position to those who had to fight in Vietnam risks hypocrisy in its worst form.

The soldier himself, on the other hand, experienced the evils of war firsthand and, in fact, may have been drawn into that evil himself. If he served on the front lines, he had to kill others and often endured the rage that comes from seeing friends killed. He became acquainted with the dark side of his own soul. As Mahedy explains:

> *I believe the implicit acknowledgment of sin—which is what the war stories are all about—is much closer to the kind of humility mentioned by Jesus in the parable than most of what passes for virtue in America. Perhaps Vietnam vets—angry at God, confused by evil of an immense magnitude, walking in unaccustomed darkness—are actually very close to the kind of spiritual emptiness that God fills with His gracious presence. As the parable reminds us, there is no room for God in those who are puffed up with self-righteousness.*[492]

When a soldier, or any one of us, can sincerely pray, *"God, have mercy on me, a sinner,"* we are in the place where God wants every human being to be, the place where we give up our self-importance and rely on him in complete humility, the place where he promises to meet us in our need.

Where Was God?

DURING MY time in combat I was not a believer. Like many others I saw what appeared to be totally random death and destruction, and questioned how there could be a God who would sanction this kind of tragic violence. If there was a God, where was he? The Vietnam Veterans Bible tries to answer the question, *"Did God go AWOL?"*

> *God created human beings with a "will," the ability to follow him and live his way or to go off on our own. Since Adam and Eve, we have consistently turned away from God. Unfortunately, history is littered with the results of humanity's self-centered disobedience and independence. God doesn't start wars, people do—fueled by self-interest, blind hatred, and retaliation.*
>
> *God is not to blame for Vietnam. Sinful individuals and nations are. And God was not absent. He was there and in control. Instead of being AWOL, he kept men and women alive, and brought them safely through for a purpose.*
>
> *In the midst of any kind of torment or struggle, it may be difficult to see God. But he is there, working in your circumstances. And what God wants most of all is to have a personal relationship with you.*[493]

"The God who made the world and everything in it is the Lord of heaven and earth and does not live in temples built by hands. And he is not served by human hands, as if he needed anything, because he himself gives all men life and breath and everything else . . . God did this so that men would seek him and perhaps reach out for him and find him, though he is not far from each one of us. 'For in him we live and move and have our being.'"
~Acts 17:24, 25, 27, 28

It may be difficult to accept the idea that God kept certain men and women alive, if this implies he condemned others to death. But I don't think this is the case. Wars and natural disasters have taken millions of lives, and I believe it's true that God does not cause these events or desire these deaths. When these tragedies occur, however, it is clearly within God's power to intervene to alter the course of events and to answer prayers when it is in his purpose to do so. In every case, he promises to be with us and our loved ones during hard times to give us courage to go forward and peace to accept whatever happens.

Where Were You?

FOR VETERANS who sincerely question God because of what they saw in Vietnam, the biblical story of Job provides a powerful insight. While suffering unspeakable hardships, Job also questioned God. Even though he was a "blameless and upright" man, he lost everything through a series of inexplicable (to Job) catastrophes. His children were killed, and all his possessions carried off. Job himself was afflicted with sores that covered his entire body. Through his long journey of despair he questioned not only his physical suffering but also the character of God himself. Over and over he pleaded for an answer.

When God did finally answer Job, it was not in the way Job expected. God didn't explain Job's suffering, but instead gave him an amazing insight into his own divine nature, recorded in one of the greatest biblical passages:

> Then the LORD answered Job out of the storm. He said: "Who is this that darkens my counsel with words without knowledge? Brace yourself like a man; I will question you, and you shall answer me. Where were you when I laid the earth's foundation? Tell me, if you understand. Who marked off its dimensions? Surely you know! Who stretched a measuring line across it? On what were its footings set, or who laid its cornerstone—while the morning stars sang together and all the angels shouted for joy?
> ~Job 38:1–7

Overwhelmed by God's presence and power, Job forgot his questions. He could only say, *"Surely I spoke of things I did not understand, things too wonderful for me to know . . . My ears had heard of you but now my eyes have seen you"* (Job 42:3, 5). Directly experiencing God for the first time, Job finally had a glimmer of understanding about God's nature and his own. Instead of questioning God's motives, he surrendered to him in faith and humility.

In his book *Out of the Night*, Bill Mahedy came to a remarkable conclusion about the questions directed at God by Vietnam veterans:

There is a certain irony in the question asked of God, "Where were you in Vietnam?" The question comes full circle when one allows God to ask in return, "Where were *you* in Vietnam?" When this kind of dialogue with God is possible, one is already underway in the journey out of the night.[494]

THE VIETNAM VETERAN

I HAVE ALWAYS been proud of my service in Vietnam and have felt a special bond with other veterans who did their duty in that dangerous and faraway place. Most of the ones I have known are also proud of their service, but have since moved on with their lives and in no way feel defined by their experience in the war.

On certain occasions, however, I have met a different kind of veteran, who seems more connected to the past. They often have beards and wear an assortment of camouflaged fatigues and jeans, with an array of unit patches and medals. I always enjoy the company of these men, although I have also felt a little sense of distance. Amazingly, these are the vets I have seen most often photographed and interviewed for newspaper articles and television specials about Vietnam. I have great respect for these men, but have wondered how they came to epitomize the war I fought in.

In researching this book and talking with a wider range of Vietnam veterans than I had known before, I think I may have found an answer to that question. In his insightful book, *Stolen Valor*, B. G. Burkett traced the efforts of the Vietnam antiwar movement after the war to continue painting the Vietnam War as an American atrocity. The large numbers of these former protesters in academia and the press corps have given them an influential voice in shaping opinion to their point of view. Their storyline is best supported by portraying the Vietnam veteran as a victim of an unjust war. The guy in fatigues fits this picture better than the businessman in a suit, even though the two may have seen combat together.

In saying this, I don't mean to diminish the fact that there are many veterans with physical and mental wounds who, after their combat experience, struggled to readjust to a normal life. For some, a normal life was never again possible. Post-traumatic stress disorder is a real problem, requiring medical resources and careful treatment. It is my firm belief, however, that these problems are not representative of this war's veterans.

During the Vietnam era, between 1964 and 1972, 27,000,000 men reached draft age. More than 8,000,000 went into the military during this time, and 2,700,000 served in Vietnam. About one-third of those were drafted, compared with 67 percent during World War II.[495] The vast majority of men serving in Vietnam manned the extensive complex of bases, ports, and airfields, considered "rear areas" by troops in the field, even though all were at risk of rocket or mortar attack at one time or another. In comparison, relatively few were committed to active combat, although the action for them was often intense. The mortality rate for those serving in Vietnam was less than half that of World War II or Korea, thanks to improved medical procedures and the helicopter.[496]

A *Washington Post*/ABC News survey released in 1985 found that 91 percent of Vietnam veterans were *"glad they served their country."*[497] A 1988 study by the U.S. Centers for Disease Control (CDC) found that 90 percent of Vietnam veterans were employed and felt satisfied with their current personal relationships. A CDC epidemiologist said, *"We're not trying to minimize the importance or severity of psychological problems, but in the vast majority of cases, the facts do not support the stereotypes."*[498]

I believe the truly stereotypical Vietnam veteran is a normal citizen with a family and a successful career. He does not dwell on his military service but is nevertheless extremely proud of it. Among his many noteworthy achievements, he and his fellow veterans have been influential in reshaping public opinion to ensure today's men and women in uniform are honored in every positive and appropriate way.

Sweating the Small Stuff

VIETNAM AFFECTED the people who fought there in different ways. Many were proud of their service and felt good about their contribution to a worthwhile cause. Some were traumatized by their experience and had to fight to regain equilibrium afterward. There was one small change in attitude, however, common to almost every person who saw combat. One veteran described it thoughtfully:

> "I consider my life worth nothing to me, if only I may finish the race and complete the task the Lord Jesus has given me—the task of testifying to the gospel of God's grace." ~Acts 20:24

It's easy to pick out Vietnam veterans in a crowd whenever a helicopter flies overhead. It's those 50- or 60-year-old guys looking up and just staring into a time gone by. My wife says she can always pick a veteran out by the look of distant fires in their eyes—they are the gentle souls, just happy to be where they are, who find almost everything around them somewhat amusing. I guess it comes from not sweating the small stuff.[499]

Since Vietnam, I've felt this description applied to me, and have taken a lot of secret satisfaction in feeling "above" many situations that have completely agitated others around me—at home and at work. At times this serenity has been helpful in finding a rational solution in the midst of a heated controversy. At other times it has been simply annoying to others who feel I either don't want to understand the problem or don't want to get involved in solving it.

As a Christian I have tried to be more careful when I occupy that peaceful place where everything is somewhat amusing, especially others' concerns. Another person's problem is never amusing to that person. There are also times when I even need to take a problem of my own more seriously. When something is wrong in my family, it *is* my problem and deserves a serious and involved effort to confront it. The same is true in my church. There are no small obstacles to progress in spiritual growth. There are small efforts to overcome them. Not sweating the *small* stuff is all right unless it leads to not sweating the *big* stuff.

399

Survivor Guilt

I OFTEN THINK of fellow Marines who didn't come home from Vietnam. Some were close friends. All were idealistic young men trying to do their duty under difficult conditions. One veteran eloquently verbalized the questions many of us have as survivors:

> If we confess our sins, he is faithful and just and will forgive us our sins and purify us from all unrighteousness. ~1 John 1:9
>
> "Their sins and lawless acts I will remember no more." And where these have been forgiven, there is no longer any sacrifice for sin. ~Hebrews 10:17, 18

> *Not unlike a lot of other Vietnam veterans . . . I have Survivor's Guilt. For me it's intense . . . Why did I survive? Have I lived an honorable life? Have I minimized my mistakes and corrected those which I could? Have I made the most of the opportunities I've been given that others never had: Have I done right by the memories of my fallen comrades? Would they be proud of what I've accomplished with the time they never had? They're unanswerable questions. We live with them. We don't whine or complain . . . We just go about life and do the best we can.*[500]

I have asked these questions and have also concluded there are no definitive answers. We owe a debt we can't repay to our fallen comrades. We do the best we can, realizing there will always be some element of guilt over the apparent randomness of events that spared us and took them.

Fortunately, there is a way to resolve this guilt and every other form of anxiety that plagues our hearts. Freedom from past wrongs, real and imagined, has already been won for us by our Savior, Jesus Christ. When we take our guilt and worries to him and ask for forgiveness, he gives us a clean slate. We can be thankful not only for our physical survival on the battlefields of life, but also for a chance to start life anew every day with a clear conscience. We pray that our fallen comrades rest in peace and that somehow each had an opportunity to know and accept what was accomplished for them and for all of us by our Lord and Savior.

The Unknown Boots

THE BOOTS appeared on the monument ten days before Memorial Day. For ten years a pair of jungle boots with a small American flag stuck inside them have been placed anonymously on the old stone pillar marking the entrance to a Macon, Georgia, neighborhood. While other public events, parades, and gun salutes remembered the service of veterans, this silent but powerful tribute continued with little notice.

> If only you would set me a time and then remember me! If a man dies, will he live again? All the days of my hard service I will wait for my renewal to come. You will call and I will answer you; you will long for the creature your hands have made.
> ~Job 14:13–15

It was recently discovered that the Memorial Day boots were placed by a man named Jack Cartwright, a resident of the neighborhood. He did it to honor five of his high school classmates from his home town of Bristol, Tennessee: Jimmy Farmer, Lonnie Burchett, Charles Duty, Charles Buchanan, and Michael Charles. Each of these young men had gone into the Marines after high school, and all had died in Vietnam.

Jack had served in the Army himself after attending college at Washington and Lee, although he did not go to Vietnam. He was one of the few in Bristol able to go to college, and so was granted a student deferment. His friends, however, were drafted. Jack felt sorrow for what happened to his friends, and gratitude for their heroic service. He also admitted, *"There is some guilt there, too."*[501] His deferment had caused him to miss the war, whereas others were not so fortunate.

I hold my own silent memorial service in a church sanctuary every year for fallen comrades, especially remembering my close friends, Joe Loughran, Jud Spainhour, Brad Collins, and J. J. Carroll. I consider this my duty, to make sure these men are not forgotten. This act also does something for me. I feel that Jack Cartwright and I are reaching out to our friends so they won't forget *us.* We will see them again. I pray that our nation never forgets the sacrifice of these young men and the countless others who have given their lives for ours.

Sermons on Wheels

RELIGIOUS FREEDOM does not exist in present-day Vietnam. According to the U.S. State Department Report on International Religious Freedom,

The Government [of Vietnam] maintained supervisory control of the recognized religions, in part because the Communist Party fears that not only organized religion but any organized group outside its control or supervision may weaken its authority and influence by serving as political, social, and spiritual alternatives to the authority of the Government.[502]

> Now a man crippled from birth was being carried to the temple gate . . . When he saw Peter and John about to enter, he asked them for money . . . Then Peter said, "Silver or gold I do not have, but what I have I give you. In the name of Jesus Christ of Nazareth, walk." ~Acts 3:2, 3, 6

This governmental control includes strict prohibition of evangelizing within the country. These restrictions have not prevented a small group of Christians traveling to Vietnam to serve others and to carry the gospel in a unique way. Mark Richard, a member of Harvest Covenant Church in Sioux Falls, South Dakota, developed a program, working through the state prisons, to refurbish wheelchairs. Through his church, he began a wheelchair ministry to change the lives of Vietnamese people who, due to handicaps, move by hand along the ground. After traveling there to witness the results, his minister commented:

> *We gave wheelchairs to people who were relegated to the back room of a hut and it moved me to tears to see some of these people. The wheelchairs gave these people dignity. You can't preach the sermon (legally) in Vietnam, but there are 3,000 people in this country who are sermons on wheels. And just on one trip alone, 750 sermons were delivered.*[503]

This ministry is a unique and obviously effective way of carrying the gospel to people in need. It should be an inspiration to every Christian. We are not all called to preach. Most of us present Jesus to the world every day by the way we live and by the way we serve others. Our actions are our "sermons."

Twenty Years Old

CRAIG TOURTE enjoyed listening to his college-student son's stories of friends and girls, and the good times he was having at school. One day as he listened, Craig couldn't help remembering himself at age twenty—he was in the middle of the siege of Khe Sanh:

I heard what sounded like a jet plane scream over the top of my head . . . Upon hearing the first explosion I immediately knew the base was under attack. The rockets and other incoming continued . . . The ammo dump had blown and we dodged hot, deadly shrapnel from our own ammunition along with those from the enemy guns the rest of the day and night.[504]

As the former Marine contemplated these memories he was filled with gratitude his son did not have to share experiences such as these. He was thankful a life of promise and hope lay before the young man.

I am sure he was thinking all of the things that twenty-year-old men should be thinking. I was glad he would never have to think that his hole was not deep enough, pray that he ran fast enough, and that at any time it could be him.[505]

No combat veteran would wish the experience of war on a son or daughter. Every instinct of a parent is to protect his or her children. Yet we know the time will come we have to let them go. Eventually, they must have the freedom to find their own way in life.

Our heavenly Father has a similar relationship to us, *his* children. He gives us the freedom to find our own way, knowing we have the potential to make good or bad choices. It is up to us to use all our resources to discern which are the good paths we are meant to take. Paradoxically, when we use the freedom God gives us to make the wrong choices, we become bound to things of this world that are much more dangerous than artillery or rocket attacks.

> Jesus replied, "I tell you the truth, everyone who sins is a slave to sin. Now a slave has no permanent place in the family, but a son belongs to it forever. So if the Son sets you free, you will be free indeed.
> ~John 8:34–36

Orders Home

FORMER ARMY Chaplain Bill Mahedy described a troubled young soldier who returned from Vietnam an angry man, with no patience for a society preoccupied with trivial interests. Hooked on action and violence, he became a policeman. As time passed the man became more and more troubled about his violent nature. He began talking to other veterans and slowly began to deal with many unresolved moral and religious questions from the war that had affected his behavior. One day he felt ready to take a final step to put the past behind him. He formally relieved himself from combat duty:

> The gifts and sacrifices being offered were not able to clear the conscience of the worshiper... How much more, then, will the blood of Christ, who through the eternal Spirit offered himself unblemished to God, cleanse our consciences from acts that lead to death, so that we may serve the living God!
> ~Hebrews 9:9, 14

(He) decisively, symbolically, and very effectively made his DEROS (date eligible to return from overseas) from Vietnam complete. He "cut a set of orders" for himself on his own typewriter. These orders contained all the correct military jargon with name, rank, service number, unit. He simply relieved himself from duty in Vietnam . . . from the responsibility of staying awake nights, waiting for the next combat action . . . (He) has posted his orders on the wall of his bedroom and looks at them often. He's now back in the world.[506]

There are times we can each free ourselves of baggage from the past by consciously thinking of it and simply letting go. Sometimes, however, a more significant effort is required. When we realize the extent of our weaknesses and all the things we have done to disappoint our loved ones, not to mention God, we find there is too much to put aside on our own. We need help. At these times we need to take whatever is weighing us down to our Savior, Jesus Christ, who waits to lift these burdens from us. He stands ready to issue our orders home, to the place of true peace in this life and in the next: God's eternal kingdom.

I Care

FORMER MARINE Steve Wiese rarely talks about his Vietnam experiences. Recently, however, he was having dinner with his wife and friends on a day that happened to be the anniversary of a battle fought by his old unit. He felt moved to offer a toast to the men who didn't return home. Unexpectedly, his "friend" blurted out, *"It's been over 30 years, nobody cares, just forget about it and get over it."*[507]

Taken aback, Wiese composed himself and replied quietly but firmly, *"I care."* That was his only response, although his wife added, *"He's spent over 30 years trying to forget about it. There are some things you just don't forget."*[508]

After this incident, Wiese thought a lot about the men who fought in Vietnam and the question, *"Who cares?"* He concluded in a thoughtful article for other veterans,

> *I believe the people that loved them care, their families care, the men that knew them that stood shoulder to shoulder in combat with them care. It is our responsibility to remember. So every year I will continue to make a toast to these men, the ones that made it back, and the ones that did not.*[509]

The need for others to care about the good things we do is not peculiar to veterans. Unfortunately, appreciation from others is often in short supply in just about every aspect of everyday life. Rather than resenting that fact, we can simply try to do better ourselves in showing appreciation to others. A friendly comment or thoughtful question to anyone we meet or someone who serves us in some way can make it clear we *care* about them. The important people in our lives deserve even more. We pray God will always give us the urge and the ability to assure every one of our family members we love and care deeply for them.

> Love must be sincere. Hate what is evil; cling to what is good. Be devoted to one another in brotherly love. Honor one another above yourselves. ~Romans 12:9, 10

Soaring to Heaven

IT WAS a mystical day for Bill McDonald. Nui Ba Den, locally known as "Black Virgin Mountain," stood like a silent sentinel, still guarding the approaches to Saigon. He had flown over this terrain countless times during the war and had fought many battles on its slopes. Now, visiting this sacred site as a tourist, his mind was filled with old memories and new sensations.

After taking a cable car and climbing a series of rock steps he found a temple near the summit. A nearby monk struck a gong, sending chills down his spine. He sat on the floor for a long while, praying and meditating. It was an emotionally moving experience.

Outside the temple, a young man approached with a cage filled with little birds. He was giving people a chance to pay for a bird's release back into the wild. When a bird was released with a prayer for someone special, it was considered good luck and a spiritual gesture. McDonald described what he did:

> I decided to release two birds, one for each of my children. I offered a prayer for each one as I released the little birds from my opened hands. They quickly soared skyward, racing with my prayer, no doubt, to heaven. I watched the birds flying away with my prayers across the same skies from which only 35 years before I had fired machine gun bullets onto this mountain. I was hit with the symbolism of it all. I stood absorbed in the moment.[510]

The image of bullets going down and prayers going up is powerful. Bullets are taken down by gravity, along with every other physical object of this world. Prayers, however, defy that downward force as they rise up to God. I believe that God honors any technique we devise to make this image more real to ourselves—even the release of birds. The ultimate aid to our prayer life, however, comes from God himself, as Jesus promised, *"The Holy Spirit will teach you at that time what you should say"* (Luke 12:12).

> We do not know what we ought to pray for, but the Spirit himself intercedes for us with groans that words cannot express. And he who searches our hearts knows the mind of the Spirit, because the Spirit intercedes for the saints in accordance with God's will.
> ~Romans 8:26, 27

You Are Important

SPEAKING TO a group of 11th Armored Cavalry Regiment veterans, Chaplain Larry Haworth tried to give his fellow veterans some reassurance about their true importance:

> "Love the Lord your God with all your heart and with all your soul and with all your strength and with all your mind."
> ~Luke 10:27

> *Your importance isn't dependent on how you feel about it. I remember some years ago when I was in a real funk. I was going through a hard time and I really felt down and very unimportant to anyone . . . Then, a friend, who I'll never forget, said to me, "Larry, if you knew how others feel about you, you wouldn't feel that way about yourself." That was well over thirty years ago. I assure you that the same applies to you. You are important. You are important in and of yourself. You are important just because you're you. You're important because someone loves you.*
>
> *Finally, let me remind you that you are important because God made you and He says you are important. You are not an accident. You were planned by God and you are loved by God. Whether you feel it or not, you are loved and you are important.*

Each of us is important to God. Jesus himself compared our standing with him to that of the sparrows: *"Yet not one of them will fall to the ground apart from the will of your Father. And even the very hairs of your head are all numbered. So don't be afraid; you are worth more than many sparrows"* (Matthew 10:29–31).

This knowledge of God's love is deeply gratifying and should, in turn, affect how we feel about others. The significant people in our lives need to know how important they are to us. We can each do better at demonstrating our affection toward those who make our lives worthwhile.

We should also be better at returning the love given us so freely by our heavenly Father. We know we are important to him, but do we show him how important he is to us? I'm sure he appreciates seeing us in church on Sunday. But he also sees how we spend our time, our talents, and our money the other six days. Do our total lives show him how important *he* is to *us?*

Won Over without Words

I FOUND JESUS CHRIST thanks to my wife, Lani. Her life's journey after the death of her mother was difficult for her and the rest of our family. As the light seemed to go out of her, a kind of darkness also descended on the rest of us. For a long time she and I went through the motions emotionally, having no spiritual resources to help each other or ourselves.

> Wives, in the same way be submissive to your husbands so that, if any of them do not believe the word, they may be won over without words by the behavior of their wives, when they see the purity and reverence of your lives.
> ~1 Peter 3:1, 2

The light at the end of this tunnel finally appeared from an unexpected direction. A friend invited Lani to a women's Bible study. Over a period of months, with the help of other caring women, she started learning new things and finding answers to her troubling questions. Meanwhile, at home, a new light seemed turned on and gradually grew brighter. Since our marriage up to that time had been firmly grounded on religious skepticism, she was careful not to talk too much about the spiritual nature of her recovery. She just allowed herself to change, loving those around her and evangelizing her family through her actions.

These memories about Lani's role in my spiritual awakening were rekindled recently by a letter from a fellow Vietnam veteran and good friend, Ron Rayner. He was extolling the childhood sweetheart he married soon after returning from Vietnam. During their life together, Ron was able to overcome a skepticism that had always kept him from full participation in the church. He gave Cathy the credit, saying, *"In later years I would tell people that only God could have arranged for someone like me to marry such a good person as my wife. And as it turned out, that is what happened."*[511]

I tell stories like these to encourage other Christian wives with skeptical husbands. You not only have a great opportunity to change your husband's life and the life of your family, but you have a biblical responsibility as well.

Freedom

JIM MELANSON was a proud former Marine and Vietnam veteran. He died in 2007 when he was only 61. His son, Tony, gave a moving eulogy describing his father as a complex man who loved the outdoors, art, and poetry but who also struggled with a drinking problem. His father also had a special sense of humor that prevailed even as he succumbed to liver disease. Tony particularly focused on this man's great love of freedom:

> *My Dad was captivated by this thing called freedom. He fought for freedom. He hoped for freedom as he began a new life with Donna after his tour in Vietnam. He lived it out through his love for the outdoors.*
>
> *Ironically, he is more free now than he ever was while here on earth . . . True freedom is everlasting, breaks bonds and lets you discard the baggage of life. That's what my father wanted more than anything—to drop his own baggage and live a life of freedom.*
>
> *What does true freedom—the kind from God himself—what does that look like in our lives? Where does our freedom come from? Can you count on it? Is it infallible? Because my father made a profession of faith in Jesus and chose to believe in Him, our hope rests in God's promise that he is now experiencing true and complete freedom in eternity.*[512]

The freedom Jesus offers does not usually pertain to our physical circumstances. When he comes into our lives we aren't necessarily freed from sickness, poverty, or the countless other conditions that make our lives difficult. He came with one purpose: to restore our way to God. He enables us to stand before the Father with complete forgiveness and acceptance. When we place him

> It is for freedom that Christ has set us free. Stand firm, then, and do not let yourselves be burdened again by a yoke of slavery.
> ~Galatians 5:1

at the center of our lives, we finally have freedom in our hearts. As King David said, *"I run in the path of your commands, for you have set my heart free"* (Psalm 119:32). In Jesus Christ our hearts are made free of guilt from the past and anxiety about the future, even the future beyond this life.

Whom Were You With?

WILLIAM MILLER served with the Marines in Vietnam. A few years ago he and his wife attended an outdoor festival in a small Kansas town. He was wearing his red ball cap with a Marine emblem on the front. As they walked along in the crowd, he noticed a man in a similar hat approaching. As they were about to pass, the two men stopped and looked at each other. The man asked Miller, *"Who were you with?"* An interesting exchange followed:

> *"1st Marine Aircraft Wing, MASS Duce, Dong Ha on the DMZ, '68–'69. You?"*

> *"2/5, Hue City, Tet '68."*

> *"Semper Fi."*[513]

With that, the two men moved along in the crowd, leaving Miller to reflect on the brief encounter. There had been many like it over the years. He was often the one asking the question, *"Who were you with?"* He always got an answer. No one ever said, *"What do you mean?"* He was amazed at the enduring strength of this bond with fellow Marines.

I have been privileged to share this bond with Marines and other veterans. I have also been blessed later in life to share an even greater bond. When I say to someone, *"God bless you,"* I often get a nervous glance in return. Frequently, however, I make contact with a brother or sister in Christ. When this happens outside the church, I am always uplifted by the knowledge that the Christian community is strong and active in the world. This community cuts across denominational lines, and these bonds are eternal.

> Instead, speaking the truth in love, we will in all things grow up into him who is the Head, that is, Christ. From him the whole body, joined and held together by every supporting ligament, grows and builds itself up in love, as each part does its work.
> ~Ephesians 4:15

The Salute

RAYMOND CRUZ was driving in heavy traffic between Fort Lewis and Tacoma, Washington. His Seabee and Khe Sanh decals were proudly on display along the rear bumper of his 1990 Ford F-150 pickup truck. In his rear view mirror he observed a motorcycle coming up behind him in the lane to his left. As the bike came alongside, he noticed that it was a black Harley with "USMC" on the tank in gold lettering. The rider wore a leather jacket and black helmet, both with "Semper Fi" in red letters. Cruz noticed long hair coming out of the helmet and could tell the rider was too young to be a Vietnam vet. He guessed he was about the age to have been in the Gulf War.

> Give everyone what you owe him: If you owe taxes, pay taxes; if revenue, then revenue; if respect, then respect; if honor, then honor.
> ~Romans 13:7

As the biker's lane slowed, he dropped back a little, and Cruz could see him looking at the bumper stickers on his pickup truck. What happened next took him by surprise:

> *In my mirror I see the leather clad ex-Grunt intensely looking at the stickers, then suddenly he looks forward and guns the bike in and between other vehicles to pull up alongside again. This time he looks directly at me, stands on the pedals of the bike, while still moving in traffic. He faces me and gives me one of the most perfect Marine salutes, nods his head at me, and roars off.* [514]

The former Navy Seabee was overwhelmed by this impromptu display of respect. In a brief moment a young Marine showed his knowledge and appreciation of the Navy Construction Battalions who have worked so closely with Marines in every war, and of the special service of this man at Khe Sanh.

The amazing thing about this story is that it took so little to make so profound a gesture. We see many people every day that in some way deserve our respect: our ministers, our teachers, policemen, firemen, servicemen—the list could go on. Don't just pass them by. There is always time for a "thank you," an encouraging word—or a salute.

Looking at the Past

TIM SCANLON has spent his life trying to forget. He flew more than fifty missions as a Huey door gunner in Vietnam, many of them into hot landing zones. As he thought about the many times he had to pour machine gun fire into enemy formations, he said, *"I could never see them face-to-face, but I knew I was killing them. And killing people causes you to lose the core of your soul."*[515] His soul was under assault again years later when his mother and brother were murdered in their home by the random and senseless act of a cocaine addict.

Tim Scanlon

Scanlon grew up in a strong Catholic family; he attended parochial schools and served faithfully for years as an altar boy. As a young person he took his religion seriously. Like many others, however, he came home from the war with a sense of futility. After what he had experienced, church seemed irrelevant, and he never went back. The loss of his mother and brother confirmed his apathy toward religion. Years later, however, he did one thing that seemed out of character. He sent his children to parochial school. When questioned about this apparent anomaly, he stated, *"I wanted them to have faith. You have to have something."*[516]

Tim Scanlon has led a very productive and successful life as a father, husband, and professional accountant. Still, he continues to be introspective and troubled about his past. His story is not finished, and won't be until he finds something that will make sense of his combat experience and other tragedies he is still not able to fully understand. I pray that someday he will rediscover a faith that will give him the answers he needs.

> They did not receive the things promised; they only saw them and welcomed them from a distance. And they admitted that they were aliens and strangers on earth. People who say such things show that they are looking for a country of their own . . . They were longing for a better country—a heavenly one.
> ~Hebrews 11:13, 14, 16

To Look Forward

IN 1967 Hal Kushner's helicopter crashed near Chu Lai. With painful burns and several broken bones, he was then shot and captured by a VC patrol. After walking at night for thirty days, his festering wounds were finally cauterized by a Vietnamese woman using a red hot rifle rod and no anesthesia. For three years he survived the most horrible conditions imaginable in a series of primitive jungle prison camps. In 1971 he traveled by foot and train to Hanoi, where he ended up in the Hanoi Hilton until the end of the war.

> Praise be to the Lord,
> to God our Savior,
> who daily bears our burdens . . . Our God is a
> God who saves; from the
> Sovereign LORD comes
> escape from death.
> ~Psalm 68:19, 20

Kushner has a truly amazing story, but he never likes to dwell on the past. He reluctantly agreed to speak to a reunion of his Vietnam unit, the 1st Cavalry Division, in 1999. He told his story, but prefaced it with these comments:

> I want you to know that I don't do this often. I was captured 2 December 1967, and returned to American control on 16 May 1973. For those of you good at arithmetic—1931 days. I have given a lot of talks about medicine (and) ophthalmology. But not about my captivity. I don't ride in parades; I don't open shopping centers: I don't give interviews and talks about it. I have tried very hard NOT to be a professional POW. My philosophy has always been to look forward, not backward, to consider the future rather than the past.[517]

It took Hal Kushner a long time to recover from the effects of his imprisonment and to regain his health. But when it was over, he didn't look back. He went on to a very successful medical practice in Florida, where he focused all his energy on his family and community. He said, "I'm thankful for my life and I have no bitterness."[518]

When Jesus said, "Who of you by worrying can add a single hour to his life?" (Luke 12:25), he was not just referring to our outlook on the future. It is equally pointless to be consumed with either longing or bitterness about the past. God is pleased when we look forward with the attitude of thankfulness for what we have and for hope in the future.

Becoming More Fragile

EARL CLARK didn't expect his own reaction to learning about the death of one of his friends. Head in his hands, tears falling, he said to himself, *"What happened to us, what happened to us?"* He and "Doc" had stayed in touch since their time together in Vietnam with the 26th Marines, and now his friend was dead. Clark was overcome with an unexpected sense of loneliness. In an open letter to other veterans, he said:

> There are some things that are just difficult for my mind and heart to process, my buddies dying too soon is one of them. I know why I'm writing this message. I'm feeling my own mortality. I suppose some, most, if not all of us, are thinking about it at this time in our lives.
>
> I'm sure of one thing, and that is I had the privilege of serving with some of the bravest Marines, FMF Corpsmen, airmen, and soldiers on the face of the earth. I think when we all joined the Marines we thought we were invincible. But I wonder if something happened to us in Nam and at Khe Sanh. I wonder if somehow we became vulnerable in a way, that perhaps we became more "fragile" in our later years . . .
>
> God only knows for sure.[519]

Thoughts of mortality creep into my consciousness, too. A few years ago I finally acknowledged I was not in control of everything in my life, especially the amount of time I have left to live. This realization actually turned into a blessing and the key to the most important event in my life. With a newfound sense of my own weakness and vulnerability, I asked Jesus Christ into my heart and asked him to take control of my life. As my life changed completely, I came to view my fragile nature as my greatest strength—a constant reminder it is not in my control to be reconciled with God. I need the One who has already accomplished this for me—my Savior, Jesus Christ.

> This is what the sovereign LORD, the Holy One of Israel says: "In repentance and rest is your salvation, in quietness and trust is your strength" . . . For the LORD is a God of justice. Blessed are all who wait for him! ~Isaiah 30:15, 18

Young at Heart

RON RAYNER is the chaplain of the Khe Sanh Veterans and writes an inspirational column for the association's *Red Clay* magazine. He recently observed that all veterans of the Siege are now close to sixty years old, and that most seem to be taking full advantage of the "extra" forty-plus years given them by virtue of their survival of the ordeal. To provide even more encouragement, he republished an essay from another era:

> I write to you, young men, because you are strong, and the word of God lives in you.
> ~1 John 2:14

> *Youth*
> *Youth is not a time of life; it is a state of mind; it is not a matter of rosy cheeks, red lips and supple knees; it is a matter of the will, a quality of the imagination, a vigor of the emotions; it is the freshness of the deep springs of life . . . Nobody grows old merely by a number of years. We grow old by deserting our ideals.*
>
> *Years may wrinkle the skin, but to give up enthusiasm wrinkles the soul. Worry, fear, self-distrust bows the heart and turns the spirit back to dust . . . In the center of your heart and my heart there is a wireless station; so long as it receives messages of beauty, hope, cheer, courage and power from men and from the infinite, so long are you young.*
>
> *When the aerials are down, and your spirit is covered with snows of cynicism and the ice of pessimism, then you are grown old, even at twenty, but as long as your aerials are up, to catch the waves of optimism, there is hope you may die young at eighty.*[520]

Those of us who now belong to the "Old Corps" should take careful heed of these words. We need to beware of a creeping cynicism that tends to give us a jaded outlook on current events. When I find myself slipping, I try to remember the prayer learned in my youth as a Citadel cadet, asking Almighty God to help me keep him at the center of my life by granting: *"A humble heart, a steadfast purpose, and a joyful hope."*[521] God doesn't guarantee us healthy bodies, but he does assure us the optimism of youth as long as we claim it.

Death to Life

URING HIS seventeen months in combat Roger Wilson went from being a small town boy to a worldly-wise soldier. To cope with the fears and frustrations of combat, he started drinking to excess whenever he had a chance. Later in his tour, he was promoted to sergeant and took command of a twelve-man squad. Shortly after, he was totally devastated by the loss of five of his men. His views on Vietnam and the war were summed up when he said, *"I hated the country, and I hated the Vietnamese people."*[522] After coming home from the war, Wilson's life appeared to go smoothly, on the surface. On the inside, however, he boiled with anger and hate, as alcoholism took him on an ever-descending path. At one point, his wife became so depressed with their lives she attempted suicide.

> Therefore, if anyone is in Christ, he is a new creation; the old has gone, the new has come! All this is from God, who reconciled us to himself through Christ and gave us the ministry of reconciliation.
> ~2 Corinthians 5:17, 18

A change in Wilson began one day when he was scuba diving with his family and suddenly encountered trouble with his air supply while sixty feet below the surface. Blacking out from lack of oxygen, he was struck by a nightmarish picture of his own life and a frightening encounter with God. As his life flashed in front of him, a voice, or thought, accused him mercilessly: *"Failure!"*

Suddenly, he found himself on the surface, gasping for air, convinced that God had spoken to him. He was shaken to the core to think that his whole life might have been in vain—that he might indeed be a failure. He wrestled with these accusations, and, even though he had ignored God all his life, finally responded to him in desperation: *"God, I'm a worthless no-good. I know it's not much, but I give You my life—what's left of it."*[523]

He didn't know it then, but, in that moment of prayer, Roger Wilson went from being dead to being alive spiritually. His life changed completely as the desire for alcohol disappeared. He eventually turned to the church and the Bible. In 2 Corinthians he found the explanation for the new life that had opened up to him.

Memorial Day salute. (U. S. Marine Corps)

Remembering a friend at The Wall (U. S. Air Force)

Let Him Do the Healing

AS A new Christian Roger Wilson longed to do more for God to make up for his past mistakes. He prayed, *"Lord, if there's ever a place you want to use me, I'm willing. I don't feel qualified to do anything special, but I'll do whatever you ask."*[524]

Soon after, he was asked to go back to Vietnam to help a group of Vietnamese Christian pastors. He was apprehensive about making such a trip, but when he discerned that this had to be God's answer to his prayer, he agreed to go. During the long flight, he grew increasingly nervous. He remembered his earlier hatred for Vietnam and his vow to never return. He remembered his friends who were killed during the war. The closer he came to his destination, the more apprehensive he became.

> Praise the LORD. How good it is to sing praises to our God . . . He heals the brokenhearted and binds up their wounds.
> ~Psalm 147:1, 3

As the airplane came to a stop, Wilson was almost a nervous wreck. He was trembling and choking back tears as he stepped onto the ramp, where he was hit with the long-remembered heat and smell. The death and destruction that had plagued his dreams flooded back. He closed his eyes and cried out, *"God, you've got to take over. I cannot do this."*[525]

God did take over, as Wilson somehow found the resolve to continue on his mission and meet the people he was supposed to help. In the past he had known only hatred for the Vietnamese, and was totally amazed to discover a growing love in his heart for these brave people who were risking their lives for God's kingdom. He realized that the love within him represented the conclusion of a long and tortured journey. He said, *"The only path to healing is allowing God to be God in your life. Let him do the healing. We can't do it; we're incapable. We can't change what happens in war, but God can change what war does to us."*[526]

It's About Friendship

IN July 2009 a golf tournament was held at Richmond Country Club near Westerly, Rhode Island, to raise funds for college scholarships. The event was named in honor of Lieutenant Carl Myllymaki, USMC, a former football player at Westerly High School. The tournament was organized by Dick Smith, a former classmate of the deceased Marine.

> A friend loves at all times, and a brother is born for adversity.
> ~Proverbs 17:17

In October 1968, Myllymaki was the commanding officer of a reconnaissance company in Vietnam and near the end of his combat tour. Leading his unit on a patrol, he was tragically killed by a land mine, leaving behind his young wife, Jan, and many friends back in Rhode Island. One friend in particular would not forget him and would make sure others didn't forget him, either.

Dick Smith was close to Myllymaki (called "Bud" by his friends) through elementary and high school and played football with him. Within a month after his friend's death he initiated the Myllymaki Award and started raising money to endow scholarships for Westerly High students to attend the University of Rhode Island. For more than forty years Smith has faithfully kept up this effort with raffles, golf tournaments, and matching contributions from local companies. He has funded an endowment of $120,000, which now awards several scholarships every year in honor of his friend.

During the 2009 golf tournament, Jan said, *"For everyone to show up 41 years later to honor and respect Bud, that's quite a tribute to who he was as a person. And for Dick Smith to have done what he's done, something hit him in the heart."*[527] A close friend of Smith also commented, *"He lost a friend and it bothered him. This all has been his way of giving back. Why has he done it? To keep Buddy's spirit alive. Basically the whole thing is about friendship."*[528] This is a story not only about friendship, but also about loyalty and commitment to a friend over a lifetime.

The Things I've Done

MAC GOBER returned from Vietnam in 1967. The hostility directed at veterans caused him to become disillusioned with the war and himself. He became convinced he had served for nothing and, worse still, that his buddies had died useless deaths. In time, he managed to find a sense of belonging again—this time in drugs and a motorcycle gang.

Gober soon earned a reputation for being the toughest member of the gang. The others feared him. Filled with hate, there wasn't anything he wouldn't do. All this time, however, he suffered the pain of loneliness and a gnawing sense of guilt.

When someone handed him a gospel tract one day, he looked at it briefly before throwing it away. Even after this brief episode, however, a few of Jesus' words kept coming back to his mind. Then, one day he found a single page from a similar tract lying on the floor. Something led him to read and reread that page and the gospel message on it. As he read and thought more intently about Christ he came to a pivotal moment:

> Get rid of all bitterness, rage and anger, brawling and slander, along with every form of malice. Be kind and compassionate to one another, forgiving each other, just as in Christ God forgave you.
> ~Ephesians 4:31, 32

> *I hurt so bad inside and had nowhere else to go, so one day I simply prayed and turned my life over to Christ. I didn't think anyone could love me. But I discovered that God did. And he proved it by sending his only Son, Jesus, to die for me and take away my sin. When I realized that, all the hate and bitterness I felt inside—for my father, for the inhumanity I saw in Vietnam, for the rejection I experienced when I came home—was released. It was incredible! Overnight I became a different person.*[529]

Mac Gober has a moving testimony meant specifically for other veterans suffering the kind of anger and guilt that once imprisoned him: *"Looking back, I know that only God knows some of the things I've done. I'm not proud of them, but I do know that God has forgiven me completely and given me another chance. If he can do that for this 'tough guy,' he can do it for you too."*[530]

Point Man

BILL LANDRETH was the son of a World War II Corsair pilot, born while his father was imprisoned in a Japanese concentration camp. Bill himself became a lieutenant in the U.S. Army and served as a platoon leader with the Americal Division in Vietnam. Severely wounded in action, he was miraculously rescued by a helicopter pilot who spotted him helpless on the ground and pulled him out to safety. He always felt that God had saved him for a reason.

> If we claim to be without sin, we deceive ourselves and the truth is not in us. If we confess our sins, he is faithful and just and will forgive us our sins and purify us from all unrighteousness. ~1 John 1:8, 9

In 1984 Landreth started a Christ-centered organization called Point Man Ministries to help other veterans recover from combat-related emotional problems. Another leader of the ministry explained the essence of the Point Man approach:

> *Like all Bible-based support ministries, the key to success in helping veterans lies in the area of confession. Perhaps you immediately think of confession as telling someone, such as a jury or police officer, about the wrong you have done. This kind of confessing gets you locked up, punished, and ridiculed publicly. Nobody wants that. But there is another kind of confessing.*
>
> *Like physical wounds, psychological and emotional wounds have to be cleaned out before they can heal. And you clean these kinds of wounds by dumping, letting it out, confessing the pain, hurt, anger, sorrow, terror, and remorse. A Point Man outpost meeting provides the safest environment in which to do this. You can finally talk about the horrible things you witnessed, did or failed to stop while in Vietnam. No one will judge you. They will help you cleanse the wound.*[531]

Every person can learn a lesson from the Point Man ministry: You will never solve a problem until you admit you have the problem. Jesus did not come into the world to help people who "have it all together." He came to redeem those who humbly admit their flaws and needs. Within the body of Christ there are priests, ministers, and fellow Christians ready to listen and to help anyone with this kind of need. We have to open our wounds to Jesus before he can cleanse and heal them.

Silent Night

JUST BEFORE sunrise a torrential rain soaked the Marines and half-filled their foxholes with water. During the day temperatures soared above one hundred degrees, subjecting the men to a tropical steam bath and unremitting heat. As the sun set that evening, Navy corpsman Bob Dirr thought to himself this was a heck of a way to spend Christmas Eve. He was on watch, leaning against the back of a muddy foxhole, trying to keep his feet out of the water. Arrayed around him were his medical bag, M-16, and three hundred rounds of ammo.

> And there were shepherds living out in the fields nearby, keeping watch over their flocks at night. And an angel of the Lord appeared to them, and the glory of the Lord shone around them. ~Luke 2:8, 9

As he gazed at the North Star, he thought of another star long ago and of other Christmases from his past. His heart ached with loneliness as he thought of home and loved ones, and contemplated the desolation around him—no presents, no decorations—only doubts about whether he would see another Christmas at home.

As he stared idly into the darkness, a green flare streaked across the sky, fired from a distant fire support base. Quickly, another flare went up, and then another. As he watched, the sky above the horizon was crisscrossed with red, blue, yellow, and green flares. Dirr glanced at the luminous dial on his watch. It was one minute after midnight—it was Christmas. Faintly at first, he heard singing in the distance. It grew louder as men along the line picked up the familiar melody. Soon, the hills resounded with the quiet but firm voices of hundreds of men. As tears ran down his face, the young corpsman joined the chorus:[532]

Silent night, holy night
All is calm, all is bright
Round yon virgin mother and child.
Holy Infant, so tender and mild,
Sleep in heavenly peace.
Sleep in heavenly peace.[533]

Christmas Mission

IT DIDN'T seem like Christmas Eve. The Huey pilots were in a somber mood as they sat around in T-shirts, sweltering from the heat. Everyone's thoughts turned to places far from the base at Phan Thiet. To dispel the gloom, Jim Schueckler and several other airmen decided to stir up a little Christmas spirit. They would take up a collection for the Project Concern hospital at Dam Pao. They had recently flown a Vietnamese child to the sparsely equipped, one-story, tin roof facility and were amazed by what they had seen there. Volunteers from the United States, England, and Australia manned the little hospital, working in a dangerous place with few resources. They might appreciate a little help.

> For you know the grace of our Lord Jesus Christ, that though he was rich, yet for your sakes he became poor, so that you through his poverty might become rich ... Whoever sows generously will also reap generously.
> ~2 Corinthians 8:9; 9:6

After getting the CO's permission to use a helicopter the next day, they began asking for money. On the first stop, they found a poker game, where one of the pilots gave them all his winnings, saying, *"Here—take it! I'd just lose it back to these guys anyway. Merry Christmas!"*[534] Encouraged, they continued their rounds:

> *Similar responses began to fill our ammo can with money of all denominations as we roamed among hooches and tents, collecting money from young men whose generosity made me believe in the Christmas spirit again. As we left one hooch, the men inside started singing "Deck the Halls," and soon those in other buildings were competing. Christmas Eve had arrived in this tropical land of heat and snakes and death!*[535]

As the little group went around the base, they also collected food. The cooks in the mess halls had plenty. They had to borrow a truck to get it all to the helo-pad. Finally, Schueckler and his friends got all their booty loaded into their Huey for the next day's mission, returned the truck, and started walking back to their tent. One looked at his watch and said, *"Hey, guys! It's midnight. Merry Christmas!"*[536]

Christmas at Khe Sanh

THERE IS no good place to be when you're away from home at Christmas. A hill outside the perimeter of the Khe Sanh combat base would surely rank among the worst. On Christmas Day 1967, Sergeant James Oyster stood duty on this faraway outpost. A helicopter took away three friends rotating back to the States, after a sad farewell for those left behind. An airplane flew overhead playing Christmas carols. When the Marines heard "I'll Be Home for Christmas," several joked they should shoot the plane down. Sergeant Oyster noted his thoughts about all this in his diary:

> The angel said to them, "Do not be afraid. I bring you good news of great joy that will be for all the people. Today in the town of David a Savior has been born to you; he is Christ the Lord. This will be a sign to you: You will find a baby wrapped in cloths and lying in a manger." Suddenly a great company of the heavenly host appeared with the angel, praising God and saying, "Glory to God in the highest, and on earth peace to men on whom his favor rests." ~Luke 2:10–14

We've been outside all day just kind of messing around and we had a spotter plane fly over playing Christmas carols. Sitting there listening to that was kind of sad: kind of melancholy I think. You know that back home the family is opening the Christmas presents and I hope they are thinking of me. But it is just not the same. This is not the first Christmas I have spent away from home. This is the first Christmas that I was in a position I couldn't at least get on the phone and call them. But I'm sure they are thinking of me. I hope that they are praying for me, too.[537]

I spent a Christmas day in Vietnam at the Phu Bai combat base with a lot more amenities than those enjoyed by Sergeant Oyster. On Christmas days now, I am surrounded by friends and family with all the comforts of home. For all of us in safe and secure places, it is a time to remember those not so blessed. At this moment there are men and women on alert at lonely outposts far from home. Some are in danger. All are lonely. All are missing their families and other loved ones. They deserve our thoughts and prayers.

We Went, We Suffered

ALLEN CLARK lost both legs below the knee during a mortar attack on the Special Forces camp at Dak To in June 1967. While learning to walk on prosthetic legs, he earned an MBA degree and worked in a series of private sector jobs. He then entered a distinguished career in public service to veterans, culminating in his nomination by President George H. W. Bush to the post of Assistant Secretary for Veterans Liaison and Program Coordination at the U.S. Department of Veterans Affairs. He was also twice appointed and confirmed by the Senate as the Director of the National Cemetery System.

> Once you were alienated from God and were enemies in your minds because of your evil behavior. But now he has reconciled you by Christ's physical body through death to present you holy in his sight, without blemish and free from accusation.
> ~Colossians 1:21, 22

In his "retirement" Clark has continued a ministry to veterans who are experiencing emotional and spiritual difficulties recovering from their wartime experiences. His ministry is based on the one sure way wounds can be healed and forgiveness received:

> *Our errors on the battlefield are not always even close to being sins. Many times they were due to circumstances beyond our control, misjudgments in the fog of war, or faulty choices under pressure. When this is the case, we need to forgive ourselves. If what we did was legally or morally wrong, we must confess it as a sin, and we will be forgiven . . . Uncle Sam needed us, we went, we suffered, we returned with huge losses to our bodies, souls, and spirits. Now we need something. Jesus took the penalty on the cross at Calvary for anything we ever did or did not do. He is the answer to what we need to heal the hurts of our wars.*[538]

Clark points out that accepting Jesus Christ may not in itself bring complete healing from the ravages of war. However, he has found this step toward spiritual renewal the most important in the healing process. To go from spiritual alienation to reconciliation, we need a power greater than we have ourselves, a power found only in Jesus Christ.

A Prayer for Families

Father

Provide for and protect the families of our armed forces. Preserve marriages; cause the hearts of the parents to turn toward their children and the hearts of the children to turn toward the fathers and mothers. We plead the blood of Jesus over our troops and their families. Provide a support system to undergird, uplift, and edify those who have been left to raise children by themselves. Jesus has been made unto these parents wisdom, righteousness, and sanctification. Through Your Holy Spirit, comfort the lonely and strengthen the weary.

Father, we are looking forward to that day when the whole earth shall be filled with the knowledge of the Lord as the waters cover the sea. In Jesus' name, amen.[539]

I N HER book titled *Prayers That Avail Much*, Germaine Copeland has written prayers for members of the Armed Forces, including this special prayer for the families who have to be separated from their loved ones. Every war exacts a heavy toll on families. Mothers, fathers, wives, and husbands of the Vietnam era identify with the stresses of military life today. Even those who are spared the grief of wounds and death must suffer the trials of long separation and continuous anxiety. Spouses on the home front have to assume responsibilities to which they are unaccustomed for every aspect of family life, including the constant care of children. This twenty-four-hours-a-day, seven-days-a-week task goes on without physical or emotional relief. When the spouse does return, another major adjustment has to occur, with another period of anxious stress.

The author of this prayer introduces the best and surest source of comfort available to those facing the pressure of wartime service. When we live in Jesus Christ and immerse ourselves in his body, the church, we are never alone. Physical and emotional relief is there for us at all times, as well as the spiritual assurance that can only come from him.

> "Come to me, all you who are weary and burdened, and I will give you rest. Take my yoke upon you and learn from me, for I am gentle and humble in heart, and you will find rest for your souls. For my yoke is easy and my burden is light."
> ~Matthew 11:28–30

Declaration of Support

A FTER THE terrorist attacks of September 11, 2001, a group of Vietnam veterans issued a Declaration of Support to a new generation of young men and women, about to fight a new and deadly war:

> Be ye doers of the word, and not hearers only.
> ~James 1:22 (KJV)

> We combat veterans of the 11th Armored Cavalry Regiment (Blackhorse), fought for the United States of America in Vietnam and Cambodia.
>
> As our nation now prepares for a long struggle against a new enemy, our freedom and way of life are threatened . . .
>
> On September 11, 2001, our fallen caretakers of freedom welcomed new heroes—those valiant and heroic victims who perished on American soil in New York, Virginia, and Pennsylvania. As a nation, we grieved our loss, mobilized to again defend our country and pledged to lead the world against the threat of terrorism. We, a nation of diverse religions and cultures, turned our collective eyes to the Lady in the Harbor who welcomed those tired and poor; those yearning to be free who stood unified as one people, Americans!
>
> Now we, combat veterans of another generation, are once again stirred by the hallowed words of General Douglas MacArthur: "Duty, Honor, Country."
>
> We solemnly offer our unqualified Declaration of Support to our President, our civilian and military leadership and the valiant men and women of our armed forces. We ask all Americans, regardless of race, religion or creed, to do nothing less.
>
> May God bless the United States of America and all freedom-loving nations of the world.[540]

The men behind this declaration had fought a war with little apparent public support. Even though many Americans were behind the war effort in Vietnam, radical voices against the war dominated the media. These veterans of the 11th Cavalry Regiment understood that *feeling* support is not enough. They knew that it has to be made tangible and effective. Likewise, *every* American citizen should do something tangible and specific in support of our men and women in harm's way today. These brave young Americans need this support, and they deserve it.

For Those Fighting Today

DURING THE present-day conflicts in the Middle East, there is considerable support for the men and women doing the fighting. However, just like Vietnam, the wars in Iraq and Afghanistan do not directly touch the American population in any significant way. We see violence in the news and read about increases in the national debt, but life goes on as usual for all but the servicemen and servicewomen themselves and their families. Before our young men and women are committed to battle, a stronger national consensus must be forged by our political leaders. There should be a sense of unity and shared sacrifice before any of our own citizens are sent to war.

To rally support for the soldiers of today, a Vietnam veteran named Ed Pippin made an appeal to his fellow veterans from America's previous conflicts:

> *Let us veterans who truly know the score keep these young soldiers in our prayers every day, and multiple times a day. American support seems to be lacking in its concern about the war, and with that naturally too often they forget the soldiers engaged in conflict. We should never forget that, since we know what they are going through. "Pray without ceasing" (1 Thessalonians 5:17 KJV).*
>
> *My prayer is we will always be . . . faithful to God, country and, especially, all of our service men and women. God bless you all.*[541]

There are countless ways to support our nation and our troops, but none more meaningful or powerful than prayer. Every soldier needs God at his side, just as this nation needs God at its helm. Every prayer is important and effective. Pippin also said in his letter, *"I have . . . learned that the grace of an almighty God is sufficient."*[542] When the apostle Paul complained to God about his own difficulties and lack of support, God responded with the classic assurance that applies to all soldiers and civilians alike:

> But he said to me, "My grace is sufficient for you, for my power is made perfect in weakness." Therefore I will boast all the more gladly about my weaknesses, so that Christ's power may rest on me. That is why, for Christ's sake, I delight in weaknesses, in insults, in hardships, in persecutions, in difficulties. For when I am weak, then I am strong. ~2 Corinthians 12:9, 10

Hound of Heaven

> *I fled Him, down the nights and down the days;*
> *I fled Him, down the arches of the years;*
> *I fled Him, down the labyrinthine ways*
> *Of my own mind; and in the mist of tears*
> *... But with unhurrying chase,*
> *And unperturbed pace,*
> *Deliberate speed, majestic instancy,*
> *They beat—and a voice beat*
> *More instant than the Feet—*
> *"All things betray thee, who betrayest Me."*[543]

IN HIS most enduring work, the poet Francis Thompson (1859–1907) depicted God as a patient but relentless pursuer. He even suggested there are times when God deprives us of what we need so we will have to turn to him to find it:

> *"All which I took from thee I did but take,*
> *not for thy harms,*
> *but just that thou might'st seek*
> *it in My arms."*[544]

He is patient with you, not wanting anyone to perish, but everyone to come to repentance.
~2 Peter 3:9

Former Army chaplain Bill Mahedy used the same imagery in his words to troubled Vietnam veterans:

> *Vets and others whose neat notions of God, self, and the world have been shattered by evil of great magnitude have been thrust unwillingly into the same condition of spiritual darkness that mystics know is the prerequisite for the deepest knowledge of God possible in this life. The first voluntary step in the journey out of night is to cease the frantic efforts to escape from the darkness, realizing that one already has begun to grasp God in a very different way—this is true even though one wants nothing further to do with God. The painful and haunting presence of God, even among vets who have attempted for years to dismiss him, is a fair indication of God's tenacity. The poet Francis Thompson likened God to a hound who pursues a person "down the nights and down the days." Escape and evasion tactics—at which many vets are expert—do not work against God. One must first stop running in the darkness and allow the "hound of heaven" to catch his quarry.*[545]

The Rest of Your Life

A YOUNG AIRBORNE trainee listened intently to the instructor's lecture on the various items of equipment necessary for jumping out of an airplane. The main parachute, with its canopy, static line, suspension cords, quick release buckle, and straps, was explained in detail. After describing all the things that could go wrong during a jump, the instructor then explained and demonstrated the reserve chute with its D ring for manual deployment. The trainee asked the instructor, *"If the main chute fails to open, how long do I have to open the reserve?"* The instructor replied, *"Son, you have the rest of your life to deploy that reserve."*

Paratrooper with reserve chute.

On the day I became a Christian, a man explained to me there has to be a point in your life when you make a decision about Jesus Christ. He is obviously one of the most important figures in history; any person should have an opinion about who and what he was. A little study will reveal he declared himself to be the Son of God, sent into the world to save mankind. There are many other facts that can be learned about him through more intensive study. But you can't go on studying and weighing the pros and cons about this person forever. At some point, you have to decide either he was who he said he was, or he was the biggest hoax in history. We also have to realize that ignoring the question or not deciding is a decision.

So, if there is a decision we each must make, what is that "point" where we have to make it? How long do we have? I believe the airborne instructor had it right: "Son, you have the rest of your life." Do you know if the rest of your life will be measured in years, or in hours? You wouldn't wait to pull your reserve chute, and you shouldn't wait to make the most important decision of your life.

> "Let no one on the roof of his house go down to take anything out of his house. Let no one in the field go back to get his cloak . . . He will send his angels with a loud trumpet call, and they will gather his elect from the four winds, from one end of the heavens to the other."
> ~Matthew 24:17, 18, 31

Bibliography

Adler, Bill, ed. *Letters from Vietnam*. New York: E. P. Dutton, 1967.

Appy, Christian G. *Working-Class War: American Combat Soldiers and Vietnam*. Chapel Hill, NC: The University of North Carolina Press, 1993.

Baker, Mark. *Nam: The Vietnam War in the Words of the Men and Women Who Fought There*. New York: William Morrow, 1981.

Beesley, Eddie R. *Lucky Enough*. Branson West, MO: River Road Press, 2006.

Bergen, Doris L., ed. *The Sword of the Lord: Military Chaplains from the First to the Twenty-First Century*. Notre Dame, IN: University of Notre Dame Press, 2004.

Bergsma, Herbert L. *Chaplains with Marines in Vietnam: 1962–1971*. Washington, DC: History and Museums Division, Headquarters, U.S. Marine Corps, 1985.

Bird, Annette, and Tim Prouty. *So Proudly He Served: The Sam Bird Story*. Wichita, KS: Okarche Books, 1993.

Blehm, John L. Sr., and Karen Blehm. *Angel of Death*. New York: iUniverse Inc., 2008.

Bonhoeffer, Dietrich. *Ethics*. New York: The MacMillan Company, 1965.

Boykin, William G., with Lynn Vincent. *Never Surrender*. New York: Faith Words, 2008.

Broughton, Jack. *Thud Ridge: F-105 Thunderchief Missions over Vietnam*. Philadelphia and New York: J. B. Lippincott Co., 1969.

Bunzel, John H., ed. *Political Passages: Journeys of Change through Two Decades, 1968–1988*. New York and London: The Free Press, a Division of Macmillan Inc., 1988.

Burkett, B. G., and Glenna Whitely. *Stolen Valor: How the Vietnam Generation Was Robbed of Its Heroes and Its History*. Dallas: Verity Press, 1998.

Cadwalader, George. *Castaways: The Penikese Island Experiment*. Chelsea, VT: Chelsea Green Publishing, 1988.

Camp, Colonel R. D., with Eric Hammel. *Lima-6: A Marine Company Commander in Vietnam*. New York: Pocket Books, 1989.

Carroll, Andrew, ed. *Grace under Fire: Letters of Faith in Times of War*. New York: Doubleday, 2007.

Certain, Robert G. *Unchained Eagle: From Prisoner of War to Prisoner of Christ*. Palm Springs, CA: ETC Publications, 2003.

Chambers, Larry. *Recondo: LRRPs in the 101st Airborne*. New York: Ivy Books, 1992.

Chambers, Oswald. *My Utmost for His Highest*. Grand Rapids, MI: Discovery House Publishers, 1992.

Chapman, Gary. *The Five Love Languages*. Chicago: Northfield Publishing, 1992.

Clark, Allen. *Wounded Soldier, Healing Warrior*. St. Paul, MN: Zenith Press, 2007.

Conroy, Pat. *My Losing Season*. New York: Bantam Books, 2002. Copeland, Germaine. *Prayers That Avail Much*. Tulsa, OK: Harrison House, 2008.

Dean, Chuck. *Nam Vet: Making Peace with Your Past*. Seattle: Wordsmith Publishing, 2000.

Downer, Phil et al. *Peace for the Vietnam Vet*. Colorado Springs: International Bible Society,1984.

Downs, Frederick. *The Killing Zone: My Life in the Vietnam War*. New York: W. W. Norton, 1978.

Edelman, Bernard, ed. *Dear America: Letters Home from Vietnam*. New York: W. W. Norton, 1985.

Eldredge, John. *Wild at Heart*. Nashville: Thomas Nelson Publishers, 2001.

Esper, George and the Associated Press. *The Eyewitness History of the Vietnam War, 1961–1975*. New York: Ballantine Books, 1983.

Fall, Bernard B. *Street without Joy*. London and Dunmow, UK: Pall Mall Press, 1965.

Franks, Tommy. *American Soldier*. New York: ReganBooks, 2005.

Gaither, Ralph with Steve Henry. *With God in a P.O.W. Camp*. Nashville: Broadman Press, 1973.

Greenberg, Martin H., and Augustus Richard Norton, eds. *Touring Nam: The Vietnam War Reader*. New York: William Morrow, 1985.

Hamilton, Michael P., ed. *The Vietnam War: Christian Perspectives*. Grand Rapids, MI: William B. Eerdmans Publishing, 1967.

Harvey, Frank. *Air War: Vietnam*. New York: Bantam Books, 1967.

Hildreth, Ray, and Charles Sasser. *Hill 488*. New York: Pocket Books, 2003.

Hutchens, James M. *Beyond Combat*. Chicago: Moody Press, 1968.

Hybels, Bill. *Just Walk Across the Room*. Grand Rapids, Michigan: Zondervan, 2006.

Kueter, Dale. *Vietnam Sons: For Some, the War Never Ended*. Bloomington, IN: Author House, 2007.

Lehrack, Otto J. *No Shining Armor: The Marines at War in Vietnam*. Lawrence, KS: University Press of Kansas, 1992.

Lind, Michael. *Vietnam: The Necessary War*. New York: Touchstone Books, 1999.

Mahedy, William P. *Out of the Night: The Spiritual Journey of Vietnam Vets*. Cleveland: StressPress, 1996.

McClary, Clebe. *Living Proof*. Pawleys Island, SC: Clebe McClary, 1987.

McDonald, W. H. Jr. *A Spiritual Warrior's Journey*. Bloomington, IN: W. H. McDonald Jr., 2003.

Miller, John Grider. *The Bridge at Dong Ha*. Annapolis, MD: Naval Institute Press, 1989.

Miller, Zell. *Corps Values*. Marietta, GA: Longstreet Press, 1996.

Norman, Michael. *These Good Men: Friendships Forged from War*. New York: Crown Publishers, 1989.

O'Brien, Tim. *If I Die in a Combat Zone: Box Me Up and Send Me Home*. New York: Delacorte Press, 1973.

O'Rourke, P. J. *Give War a Chance*. New York: The Atlantic Monthly Press, 1992.

Palmer, Laura. *Shrapnel in the Heart: Letters and Remembrances from the Vietnam Memorial*. New York: Vintage Books, 1987.

Prados, John, and Ray W. Stubbe. *Valley of Decision: The Siege of Khe Sanh*. New York: Dell Publishing Group, 1991.

Reed, David. *Up Front in Vietnam*. New York: Funk & Wagnalls, 1967.

Santoli, Al. *Everything We Had: An Oral History of the Vietnam War by Thirty-Three American Soldiers Who Fought It*. New York: Ballantine Books, 1981.

Sasser, Charles W. *God in the Foxhole: Inspiring True Stories of Miracles on the Battlefield*. New York: Threshold Editions, 2008.

Schulzinger, Robert D. *A Time for War: The United States and Vietnam, 1941–1975*. New York and Oxford: Oxford University Press, 1997.

Schwarzkopf, Norman H. *It Doesn't Take a Hero*. New York: Bantam Books, 1993.

Scruggs, Jan C., and Joel L. Swerdlow. *To Heal a Nation: The Vietnam Veterans Memorial*. New York: Harper Perennial, 1985.Sofarelli, Michael. *Letters on the Wall*. New York: Smithsonian Books with HarperCollins Publishers, 2006.

Sorley, Lewis. *A Better War: The Unexamined Victories and Final Tragedy of America's Last Years in Vietnam*. New York: Harcourt, 1999.

Spainhour, Jud. *Carolina Marine*. Charlotte, NC: Heritage Printers, 1967.

Terry, Wallace. *Bloods: Black Veterans of the Vietnam War: An Oral History*. New York: Random House, 1985.

Venzke, Roger R. *Confidence in Battle, Inspiration in Peace: The United States Army Chaplaincy, 1945–1975*. Washington, DC: Department of the Army, 1977.

Vietnam Veterans Bible. Wheaton, IL: Tyndale House Publishers, 1990.

Wallace, Mike, and Gary Paul Gates. *Close Encounters: Mike Wallace's Own Story*. New York: William Morrow, 1984.

Webb, James. *Fields of Fire*. New York: Bantam Books, 1985.

Welch, Bobby. *You, the Warrior Leader*. Nashville: Broadman & Holman Publishers, 2004.

Index of Names

Topical Index

440

Notes

1. Michael Lind, *Vietnam: The Necessary War*, 152.
2. W. D. Ehrhart, "The Volunteer," *American Experience: Reflections on a War*, www.pbs.org
3. Ibid.
4. Bernard B. Fall, *Street without Joy*, 271.
5. Ibid., 273–74.
6. Zell Miller, *Corps Values*, 59–65. Admittedly, this is a heavily sanitized version of Zell Miller's story.
7. Michael P. Hamilton ed., *The Vietnam War: Christian Perspectives*, 105, "Vietnam and World Peace," by Canon Jean-Marie Aubert.
8. Ibid., 108.
9. Ibid., 110–11.
10. David Horowitz, "Letter to a Political Friend," *Political Passages*, John H. Bunzel, ed., 194.
11. Frank Harvey, *Air War: Vietnam*, 98.
12. J. B. An Dang, "Defaming sisters of Vinh Long to turn their orphanage into a hotel," December 20, 2008, www.AsiaNews.it (search by "An Dang")
13. Author unknown, "Bonds Between Soldiers," Bravo Company, 2nd Battalion, 8th Cavalry, www.eagerarms.com/bondsbetweensoldiers.html
14. Hamilton, *The Vietnam War*, 136, "Ecumenism and Peace," address given on April 26, 1967, by The Reverend Eugene Carson Blake.
15. Dietrich Bonhoeffer, *Ethics*, 355–57.
16. Hamilton, *The Vietnam War*, 98, "Fear and Faith," by The Right Reverend Ronald O. Hall, 1966.
17. Ibid., 101, quoting Simone Weil in *A Fellowship of Love*, by Jacques Cabaud, 323.
18. George Cadwalader, *Castaways: The Penikese Island Experiment*, 24.
19. Ibid., 21.
20. Michael Murphy, "Shoes," www.vietvet.org/mmurphy.htm.
21. Ibid.
22. Anonymous, "Murphy's List Continues to Grow," *NamVet Newsletter*, November 12, 1994, www.vietvet.org/nvethew.htm. (page 12)
23. Arthur W. Myatt, "Vietnamese Dolls Surprise GIs," *Allons*, 1st Edition, August 1967, www.landscaper.net/articles.htm#ALLONS.
24. Nguyen Ba Chung, "The Vietnam War and Vietnam," *American Experience: Reflections on a War*, www.pbs.org
25. Ibid.
26. Dr. Martin Luther King, "Beyond Vietnam," address given on April 4, 1967, regarding African-American involvement in the Vietnam War, www.aavw.org
27. Ibid.

28. Richard Souto, "Medic's Concern Saves Life," *The Steadfast and Loyal,* August 31, 1969, http://1-22infantry.org

29. Author unknown, "Pope and the Paratrooper," www.173rdairborne.com

30. Don Poss, "Heaven's Gates: Vietnam War Stories," www.war-stories.com

31. Ibid.

32. Excerpts from the inaugural address of President John F. Kennedy, January 20, 1961, John F. Kennedy Presidential Library and Museum, www.jfklibrary.org

33. Robert Conover, "A Shot to the Heart," December 1968, Vietnam Helicopter Pilots Association, www.vhpa.org

34. Ibid.

35. James M. Hutchens, *Beyond Combat,* 15–16.

36. Ibid.

37. Ibid.

38. Ibid., 88–89.

39. Ibid., 202.

40. Ibid., 203–7.

41. Ibid., 275.

42. Ibid. Although the Clarks would eventually divorce, they were able to maintain a warm and cordial relationship, and share the lives of their daughters.

43. Ibid., 309.

44. Teresa of Avila (1515–82), www.journeywithjesus.net

45. William G. Boykin with Lynn Vincent, *Never Surrender: A Soldier's Journey to the Crossroads of Faith and Freedom,* 46.

46. Ibid., 47.

47. Ibid., 59.

48. Ibid., 60.

49. http://thinkexist.com

50. Jason C. Redman, "The Gift," *On Patrol, The Magazine of the USO,* Vol. 1, Number 4, Winter 2009–10.

51. Lind, *Vietnam,* 10, quoting a 1995 *China Quarterly* article.

52. Robert D. Schulzinger, *A Time for War: The United States and Vietnam, 1941–1975,* 152.

53. Frank Cavestani, "Duc Co," *Allons,* 5th Edition, January 5, 1968, www.landscaper.net

54. Lady Borton, "Still in Hiding," *American Experience: Reflections on a War,* www.pbs.org

55. Otto J. Lehrack, *No Shining Armor: The Marines at War in Vietnam,* 14.

56. Bill Adler, ed., *Letters from Vietnam,* 171, letter by Carl D. Rogers.

57. Mike Malsbary, "Vietnam: Day 1," www.3rdMarines.net

58. Ibid., 42.

59. H. L. Bergsma, *Chaplains with Marines in Vietnam, 1962-1971,* 40–41, report of March 14, 1966, by Chaplain (Commander) Peter J. Bakker.

60. Ibid.

61. Ibid.

62. Ibid., 43–44, report by Commander William Hollis, July 1966.

63. Rudyard Kipling (1865–1936), "The Ballad of East and West."

64. Tony Blake, "A Grunt's View," www.gruntsview.org

65. Ibid.

66. Bob Neener, "Hand Grenade Incident," www.3rdMarines.net

67. Ibid.

68. Bergsma, *Chaplains*, 53, quoting Max E. Dunks report of November 19, 1966.

69. John Eldredge, *Wild at Heart*, 175–76.

70. Ibid., 141.

71. Tom Collins, letter to his brother, Rupert, June 16, 1966.

72. "The History of Valentine's Day," www.history.com

73. Eddie R. Beesley, *Lucky Enough*, 43.

74. Ibid., 45.

75. Bergsma, *Chaplains*, 109, report by Lieutenant John T. Collins, May 17, 1967.

76. Ibid.

77. Ray Bows, "The Naming of Camp Radcliff," 1st Battalion, 22nd Infantry, http://1-22infantry.org

78. David Grant, "A Father's Prayer," vietnamexp.com

79. Dean Norland, "Soldiers' Precious Cargo Delivered Daily by APO," *Southern Cross*, Vol. 1, No. 9, October 1968, www.americal.org

80. "Lone Footprint Discloses Mine," *Southern Cross*, Vol. 1, No. 8, September 1968, www.americal.org

81. Carolyn Carty, "Footprints in the Sand," different versions also attributed to Mary Stevenson and Margaret Fishback Powers, www.wowzone.com

82. This story is of unknown origin, given me by my friend and Chaplain to the Khe Sanh Veterans Association, Ron Rayner.

83. Ibid.

84. Bergsma, *Chaplains*, 11, quoting Lieutenant Commander Paul Lindemann in a letter dated April 24, 1967.

85. Albert French, "The Time (I remember): Chu Lia, Vietnam, 1965," *American Experience: Reflections on a War*, www.pbs.org

86. Ibid.

87. Hutchens, *Beyond Combat*, 71.

88. Ibid., 73–74.

89. Bernard Edelman, ed., *Dear America: Letters Home from Vietnam*, 185–86.

90. Bergsma, *Chaplains*, 55, quoting James E. Seim report of February 25, 1967.

91. Colonel R. D. Camp with Eric Hammel, *Lima-6: A Marine Company Commander in Vietnam*, 197–98.

92. Lehrack, *No Shining Armor*, 90.

93. Michael Combs, "Maggie," *NamVet Newsletter*, Vol. 7, No. 1, November 12, 1994. http://www.vietvet.org/nvetnew.htm (page 8)

94. Ibid.

95. Lieutenant Walter Judson "Jud" Spainhour, *Carolina Marine*, August 31, 1966.

96. Adler, *Letters from Vietnam*, 133–34, March 14, 1966, letter by James C. Kline.

97. Robert Baird, "Charlie Ridge," www.vietvet.org

98. David Reed, *Up Front in Vietnam*, 33–34.

99. Al Santoli, *Everything We Had: An Oral History of the Vietnam War by Thirty-Three American Soldiers Who Fought It*, 52–56.

100. Bergsma, *Chaplains*, 100, quoting Lieutenant General Victor Krulak letter of March 23, 1966.

101. Tim O'Brien, *If I Die in a Combat Zone: Box Me Up and Send Me Home*, 153.

102. Rodger R. Venzke, *Confidence in Battle, Inspiration in Peace: The United States Army Chaplaincy 1945–1975*, 151–52.

103. C. T. Anthony, "A Combat Story," *Red Clay*, Issue 70, Spring 2008.

104. Adler, *Letters from Vietnam*, 172, letter by Hiram D. Strictland.

105. Ibid.

106. Hutchens, *Beyond Combat*, 95.

107. Ibid., 96.

108. Blake, "A Grunt's View," www.gruntsview.org

109. Oswald Chambers, *My Utmost for His Highest*, October 11 entry.

110. Author unknown, "A Fighting Man's Prayer," contributed by Sergeant Stephen Stultz, *Allons*, 1st Edition, August 1967, www.landscaper.net

111. Robert Buzogany, "Bomb Problem? Call EOD PDQ," *Southern Cross*, Vol. 1, No. 6, August 1968, www.americal.org

112. Ibid.

113. Author unknown, "The Things They Carried," www.11thcavnam.com. The content of this article bears some resemblance to Tim O'Brien's book by the same title.

114. Ibid.

115. Ibid.

116. Lieutenant Clebe McClary, *Living Proof*, 135.

117. Ibid., 155.

118. Ibid.

119. Chuck Dean, *Nam Vet: Making Peace with Your Past*, 129–30.

120. Ibid., 130–31.

121. Bergsma, *Chaplains*, 200–1.

122. Edelman, *Dear America*, 157–58.

123. Adler, *Letters from Vietnam*, 164, letter by Carl D. Rogers.

124. Ibid., 164–65.

125. Interview with the author, April 8, 2010.

126. Author unknown, "Don't Quit," contributed by Kenneth Drayton, *Allons*, 4th Edition, October 1967, www.landscaper.net

127. Marine Corps Rifleman's Creed, www.usmcpress.com

128. Craig Tourte, "My M-14," *Red Clay*, Issue 63, Winter 2005.

129. Ibid.

130. Marion Lee Kempner, letter to his aunt, October 22, 1966, New York Vietnam Veterans Memorial, www.nyvietnamveteransmemorial.org

131. Ibid.

132. George Esper, *The Eyewitness History of the Vietnam War 1961–1975*, 70.

133. Ibid., 93.

134. Camp, *Lima-6*, 157.

135. Dale Kueter, *Vietnam Sons: For Some, the War Never Ended*, 24–25.

136. Phil Downer et al., *Peace for the Vietnam Vet*.

137. John Prados and Ray W. Stubbe, *Valley of Decision: The Siege of Khe Sanh*, 167.

138. Tommy Franks, *American Soldier*, 94.

139. Richard Goodwin, *Red Clay*, Spring 2006.

140. Medal of Honor Citation, Chaplain (Major) Charles Joseph Watters, www.173rdAirborne.com

141. Frank D'Orsi, interview, October 15, 2009.

142. Ibid.

143. Ibid., 112.

144. Ibid., 110, quoting John T. Collins report of May 17, 1967.

145. Venzke, *The U.S. Army Chaplaincy*, 172, quoting Wendall Danielson.

146. Irving Berlin, copyright 1939, by www.scoutsongs.com. Berlin dedicated royalties to the God Bless America fund for the Boy Scouts and Girl Scouts of the USA.

147. Annette Bird, *So Proudly He Served: The Sam Bird Story*, 148–49.

148. Navy Cross Citation, Andrew D. DeBona, www.legionofvalor.com

149. Camp, *Lima-6*, 160.

150. Edelman, *Dear America*, 133.

151. Frank D'Orsi, interview, October 15, 2009.

152. Ibid.

153. Ray Hildreth and Charles W. Sasser, *Hill 488*, 28.

154. "Twice 'Dead' Medic Shocks His Friends," *Southern Cross*, Vol. 1, No. 4, August 1968, www.americal.org

155. Ibid.

156. Ron Rayner, "My Road to Becoming a Christian," personal letter to the author, January 2010.

157. Author unknown, "Great Comeback," http://usmilitary.about.com

158. Dean, *Nam Vet*, 142.

159. Michael Sofarelli, *Letters on the Wall: Offerings and Remembrances from the Vietnam Veterans Memorial*, xvi.

160. Ibid. The team was later rescued by a large force after three days of heavy fighting.

161. Joe Moring, "What Semper Fi Means to Me," *Red Clay*, Issue 63, Winter 2005.

162. "Thomas J. Kerr USMC HMM-164, 1947–2007," *Red Clay*, Issue 68, Spring 2007.

163. Robert Clark, "I Was There Just Last Night," *NamVet Newsletter*, Vol. 7, No. 1, November 12, 1994, www.vietvet.org/nvetnew.htm (page 17)

164. Author unknown, "What's Special about a Marine?" www.leatherneck.com

165. Esper, *The Eyewitness History of the Vietnam War*, 108.

166. Schulzinger, *A Time for War*, 259.

167. Ibid., 260.

168. James Dalto, "My Khe Sanh Experiences," *Red Clay,* Issue 69, Fall/Winter 2007.

169. Ibid.

170. An Army experimental lab discovered that perspiring men produce ammonia, which can be detected by its reaction with other chemicals. This 'electronic nose' was used in back-pack form and in helicopters.

171. Ray Stubbe, "Presentation to 8th Air Force Historians, Mitchell Field, Milwaukee, December 1, 2009.

172. Steven Wiese, "A Proud Moment," *Red Clay,* Issue 64, Spring 2006.

173. Jim Eckl, "Memories of a 4/42 FA Forward Observer," http://1-22infantry.org

174. Stubbe, "Presentation," December 1, 2009.

175. Andrew Carroll, *Grace under Fire: Letters of Faith in Times of War,* 93.

176. Ibid., 101.

177. "Children's Hands Hold Key to Understanding," *Southern Cross,* Vol. 1, No. 2, June 1968, www.americal.org

178. Jerome Howell, "A Day at Khe Sanh with A Company 3rd Shore Party Battalion," *Red Clay,* Issue 66, Fall 2006.

179. Tet Offensive 40th Anniversary Remembrance Month, Proclamations Archive, http://gov.state.ak.us

180. Stanley Homiski, "A Letter to My Wife," www.vietvet.org

181. Homiski, e-mail to the author, November 10, 2009

182. Jack Stoddard, "Hey Wait a Minute," www.m11thcav.com

183. David Stafford, "Rest and Relaxation," *Dave's Scrapbook,* 1995, about.com 20th Century History, www.history1900s.about.com

184. Prados, *Valley of Decision,* 169.

185. Stubbe, letter to the author, December 30, 2009.

186. Sam Messer, used by permission.

187. Francis Lewis, "Joy of Discovery," *Southern Cross,* Vol. 1, No. 1, May 1968, www.americal.org

188. Letter of August 10, 1969, www.lettershome.net

189. Author unknown, www.tiffincompassionatefriends.org

190. Doris L. Bergen, ed., *The Sword of the Lord: Military Chaplains from the First to the Twenty-First Century,* 221–22.

191. Ibid.

192. Mac Dorsey, "The Story of Ruby," vietvet.org

193. W. M. McMillan, "Letter from Home," *Southern Cross,* Vol. 1, No. 3, July 1968, www.americal.org

194. Dennis Eilers, "Determined Villagers Stop Vicious Enemy," *Southern Cross,* Vol. 1, No. 2, June 1968, www.americal.org

195. Jack Randles, "Link at a Time," *Southern Cross,* Vol. 1, No. 6, Aug. 30, 1968, www.americal.org.

196. Jack C. Randles, "Frog on the Burner," *Southern Cross,* Vol. 1, No. 9, October 11, 1968.

197. Stubbe, letter to the author, December 30, 2009.

198. Craig Torte, "Mini Reunion," *Red Clay,* Issue 64, Spring 2006.

199. Dennis Mannion, "First Visit after Boot Camp," *Red Clay,* Issue 66, Fall 2006.

200. Ibid.

201. Ryan Blaich, "General Pace 2nd Platoon Reunited," I Marine Expeditionary Force, September 13, 2007, www.i-mef.usmc.mil

202. Ibid.

203. Ibid.

204. *Khe Sanh Veterans 2008 Membership Directory.*

205. Ibid.

206. Ibid.

207. David Stafford, "A Day at Luc Giang," *Dave's Scrapbook,* 1995, About.com 20th Century History, www.history1900s.about.com

208. Sam Messer, "Why . . ." written at Khe Sanh, 1967, reprinted with permission.

209. Lewis Sorley, *A Better War: The Unexamined Victories and Final Tragedy of America's Last Years in Vietnam,* 31.

210. Ibid., 64.

211. Adler, *Letters from Vietnam,* 57–58, August 13, 1966, letter by John N. Norwood, Jr.

212. Franks, *American Soldier,* 66.

213. William P. Mahedy, *Out of the Night: The Spiritual Journey of Vietnam Vets,* 68.

214. Reed, *Up Front in Vietnam,* 48.

215. Ibid., 211–12.

216. Ibid., 214.

217. Author unknown, "Vietnam Diary," www.skytroopers.org

218. Bergsma, *Chaplains,* 182, report by Lieutenant Bryant R. Nobles, September 1, 1970.

219. Ibid.

220. Mark Baker, *NAM: The Vietnam War in the Words of the Men and Women Who Fought There,* 90.

221. Martin H. Greenberg and Augustus Richard Norton, eds., *Touring Nam: The Vietnam War Reader,* 211–12, passage derived from a fictional account by Tom Suddick.

222. "A Solo Charge," Bravo Co., 2nd Battalion, 8th Cavalry Regiment, www.eagerarms.com/asolocharge.html

223. James Henderson, "Hunger Hill," 1st Battalion, 22nd Infantry, http://1-22infantry.org

224. M. C. Brown Jr., "Moments with the Maker," *Southern Cross,* Vol. 1, No. 2, June 1968, www.americal.org

225. Ibid.

226. Eckl, "Memories of a 4/42 FA Forward Observer," http://1-22infantry.org

227. "Glider Watches Birds," 1st Battalion, 22nd Infantry, news article, Vietnam, 1967, http://1-22infantry.org

228. Mike Nicastro, "Sleeping on Watch," 1st Battalion, 22nd Infantry, news article, October 5, 1969, http://1-22infantry.org

229. David Holman, "The Artist's Touch," *On Patrol, The Magazine of the USO,* Vol. 1, No. 4, Winter 2009–10.

230. Ibid.

231. "NVA Has Good Aim with Dud," 1st Battalion, 22nd Infantry, news article, http://1-22infantry.org

232. Ibid.

233. Joe Cardone, *War Letters: Rochester Writes Home, June 25, 1969,* www.wxxi.org/warletters

234. Alan Cutter, "The Warrior's Pledge," National Conference of Vietnam Veteran Ministers, www.vietnamveteranministers.org

235. Roger Helle, "A Killing Machine," Vietnam Veterans Bible.

236. Ibid.

237. Ibid.

238. John L. Blehm Sr. and Karen Blehm, *Angel of Death,* 20.

239. Ibid., 22–23.

240. Ibid., 73–75.

241. Blehm, *Angel of Death,* 79.

242. Francis Thompson (1859–1907), "Hound of Heaven," www.bartleby.com/236/239.html.

243. Blehm, *Angel of Death,* 107.

244. Ibid., 110.

245. Tom Robison, interview, March 1, 2010.

246. Laura Palmer, *Shrapnel in the Heart: Letters and Remembrances from the Vietnam Memorial,* 38.

247. Ibid.

248. Frederick Downs, *The Killing Zone: My Life in the Vietnam War,* 40.

249. Michael Norman, *These Good Men: Friendships Forged from War,* 162.

250. Otis Carey, "Vietnam KIA Bronze Star/Purple Heart," www.11thcavnam.com

251. Sorley, *A Better War,* 107, quoting President Nixon on NBC's *Meet the Press,* April 10, 1988.

252. Ibid., quoting William Saffire, *Before the Fall,* 368.

253. Ibid., quoting Lieutenant General John Tolson, *Airmobility, 1961–71,* 227–33.

254. Carl Ekmark, "Forward Observer Has Tough Job," *Artillery Review,* March 25, 1971, www.landscaper.net

255. Kevin Howe, "Last Look Around," *Southern Cross,* Vol. 1, No. 3, July 1968, www.americal.org

256. Hildreth, *Hill 488,* 94.

257. Medal of Honor Citation, 1st Lieutenant Loren Douglas Hagen, www.arlingtoncemetery.net/ldhagen.htm

258. Baker, *Nam,* 32.

259. William Wordsworth (1770–1850), "Lines Composed a Few Miles above Tintern Abbey," www.bartleby.com

260. Reed, *Up Front in Vietnam,* 215–16.

261. Ibid.

262. Ron Main, "Coming Home: 'Hansen Decontamination,'" *Red Clay*, Issue 72, Spring 2009.

263. From the hymn *O God Our Help in Ages Past*, by Isaac Watts and William Croft. This song was sung at Winston Churchill's funeral in 1965.

264. James Webb, *Fields of Fire*, 213.

265. Larry Chambers, *Recondo: LRRPs in the 101st Airborne*, 179.

266. Ibid.

267. Reed, *Up Front in Vietnam*, 57–58.

268. Ray Bono, "Remember Our Dogs?" www.eagerarms.com

269. Robert Baird, "Observation Post Ba Na," www.vietvet.org

270. Author unknown, "The Military Wife," *The Trooper*, Issue 3, April 2008, 8th U.S. Cavalry Regiment, www.8cavalry.org

271. Bergsma, *Chaplains*, 63, quoting Allen B. Craven report of November 1965.

272. Wallace Terry, *Bloods: Black Veterans of the Vietnam War: An Oral History*, 73.

273. Ibid., 78.

274. Jack Cunningham, "Surrender Was Not an Option," www.capveterans.com

275. Ibid.

276. Ibid.

277. Ibid.

278. Jack Randles, "Step by Step," *Southern Cross*, Vol. 1, No. 8, September 1968, www.americal.org

279. King George VI Christmas Day broadcast, www.royal.gov.uk. The poem was written by Minnie Louise Haskins in 1908 and was a favorite of Queen Elizabeth.

280. Cary S. Sklaren, "Friendship Takes Work," *Southern Cross*, Vol. 1, No. 10, October 1968, www.americal.org

281. Henry Veldman, "LZ to Korea," *The Ivy Leaf*, 1969, http://1-22infantry.org

282. "Rugged 'Regulars' Unveil Memorial," *Ivy Leaf*, October 1969, http://1-22infantry.org

283. Mike Maattala, "Detached Violence," *Typhoon*, 1969, www.landscaper.net

284. "Unique Force Guards Southern II Corps," *Uptight*, Summer 1969, www.landscaper.net

285. Ibid.

286. Sorley, *A Better War*, 180.

287. Palmer, *Shrapnel in the Heart*, 73.

288. Ibid., 60.

289. Ty Dodge, "The Battle for Buttons," I Troop, 3rd Squadron, 11th Armored Cavalry Regiment, www.itrp3-11acr.com

290. Steve and Rosie Williams, "Hill 474," story provided to the author on April 2, 2010.

291. Williams, "Angels in Disguise," story provided to the author on May 20, 2010.

292. Ibid.

293. Lehrack, *No Shining Armor,* 267.

294. George Goodson, "A Burial at Sea: Remembrances of a Casualty Notification Officer," *Marine Corps Gazette,* September 2007.

295. Ibid.

296. Ibid.

297. John Grider Miller, *The Bridge at Dong Ha,* 173.

298. Chaplain Devine, "The Grunt," *Ivy Leaf,* 4th Infantry Division, 1970, http://1-22infantry.org

299. Terry, *Bloods,* 33–34.

300. Baker, *Nam,* 92.

301. B. G. Burkett and Glenna Whitley, *Stolen Valor: How the Vietnam Generation Was Robbed of Its Heroes and Its History,* 24–25.

302. Miller, *The Bridge at Dong Ha,* 60.

303. Wiseman himself apparently quoted the King James Version, saying, "We have a house not made with hands, eternal in the heavens."

304. Bobby Cox, interview with the author, March 10, 2010.

305. Reed, *Up Front in Vietnam,* 181.

306. Ibid., 182.

307. Burkett, *Stolen Valor,* 475.

308. Ibid., 13.

309. Ibid., 14.

310. Ryan Blaich, "General Pace 2nd Platoon Reunited," I Marine Expeditionary Force, September 13, 2007, www.i-mef.usmc.mil

311. Edelman, *Dear America,* 52.

312. Ibid., 159.

313. Bobby Welch, *You, the Warrior Leader,* 211.

314. Ibid.

315. Ibid., 227.

316. Ibid., 230.

317 .Ibid., 231.

318. "Too Short for Bad Luck," *Southern Cross,* Vol. 1, No. 2, June 1968, www.americal.org

319. Ibid.

320. Grant, "Corky Went Home," www.vietnamexp.com

321. Ibid.

322. "Two Brothers Stretch Idea Bit Too Far," *Southern Cross,* Vol. 1, No. 1, May 1968, www.americal.org

323. Bergsma, *Chaplains,* 96, quoting Robert L. Reiner report of September 1965.

324. W. H. McDonald Jr., *A Spiritual Warrior's Journey: The Inspiring Life Story of a Mystical Warrior,* 312–19.

325. David Rosenthal, "January 24, 1969," www.vietvet.org

326. Ibid.

327. Ibid.

328. Terry, *Bloods,* 32.

329. Charles W. Sasser, *God in the Foxhole: Inspiring True Stories of Miracles on the Battlefield*, 191–92.

330. Ibid., 193.

331. Ibid.

332. Baker, *Nam*, 67.

333. Author unknown, "A Soldier's Story," *The Trooper*, Issue 2, May 2009, 8th U.S. Cavalry Regiment, www.8cavalry.com

334. Reed, *Upfront in Vietnam*, 131–32.

335. Ibid.

336. Reed, *Up Front in Vietnam*, 77.

337. Bergsma, *Chaplains*, 33–34, quoting Ronald G. DeBock report of August 12, 1966.

338. Lehrack, *No Shining Armor*, 334.

339. Ed Blanco, "Welcome Home, Soldier," *Pieces: Recollection of a Rifleman*, vietnamdiary.com

340. Ibid.

341. Sorley, *A Better War*, 372, quoting the *History of the People's Army of Vietnam*.

342. Carroll, *Grace under Fire*, 102.

343. Interview with the author, April 12, 2010.

344. Bergsma, *Chaplains*, 47.

345. Baker, *Nam*, 75.

346. George Graves, interview with the author, April 28, 2010.

347. Carol Oates Brown, "History of the POW/MIA Bracelets," www.miafacts.org

348. Pam Scott, "Loveletters," November 6, 2008, www.pownetwork.org

349. Colonel Roger D. Ingvalson, "Veteran of the Quarter," Presbyterian Church in America, Mission to North America, Chaplain Ministries, www.pca-mna.org

350. Ralph Gaither with Steve Henry, *With God in a P.O.W. Camp*, 42.

351. Ibid., 19.

352. Ibid.

353. Ibid., 37.

354. Ibid., 38.

355. Ibid., 75.

356. Ibid., 105.

357. Leo Thorsness, "Honoring the American Flag," www.11thcavnam.com

358. Gaither, *With God in a P.O.W. Camp*, 30.

359. Ibid., 31.

360. Adam Rossi, quoting Barry Bridger, "Former Vietnam POW to share experiences with local residents," *Saratoga News*, May 29, 2009, www.saratoga.com

361. Ibid.

362. Prayer of St. Francis de Sales, www.catholic.org

363. Gaither, *With God in a P.O.W. Camp*, 58.

364. Ibid., 42, 60.

365. Robert G. Certain, *Unchained Eagle: From Prisoner of War to Prisoner of Christ,* 84.

366. Gaither, *With God in a P.O.W. Camp,* 129–30.

367. Dean, *Nam Vet,* 160.

368. Ibid., 161–62.

369. Adler, *Letters from Vietnam,* 80, July 18, 1966, letter by Pat Brantley.

370. P. J. O'Rourke, *Give War a Chance,* 90.

371. Ibid., 95.

372. Ibid., 97.

373. *The Declaration of Independence.*

374. Stubbe, letter to the author, December 30, 2009.

375. U. T. Nguyen, interview with the author, April 18, 2010.

376. Ibid.

377. "Birthday Tribute, My Dad, Forgotten Hero, No More!" *Red Clay,* Issue 63, Winter 2005.

378. Ibid.

379. Courtney Robinson, "The Quiet Women," *On Patrol, The Magazine of the USO,* Vol. 1, No. 4, Winter 2009–10.

380. Ibid.

381. Franks, *American Soldier,* xv.

382. Sasser, *God in the Foxhole,* 198.

383. Colonel William Benedict Nolde, United States Army, www.arlington-cemetery.net/wbnolde.htm

384. Sorley, *A Better War,* 83.

385. Battlefield: Vietnam, www.pbs.org/battlefieldvietnam/air

386. Jack Broughton, *Thud Ridge: F-105 Thunderchief Missions over Vietnam,* 36.

387. "Helicopters at War," U.S. Centennial of Flight Commission, www.centennialofflight.gov

388. "Helicopter Losses During the Vietnam War," www.vhpa.org

389. Denell Burke, "Welcome Home, 'Operation Homecoming,'" Travis Air Museum, jimmydoolittlemuseum.org/html/vietnam.html#homecoming

390. Richard Dworsky, "Memories," *Red Clay,* Issue 70, Spring 2008.

391. Bergsma, *Chaplains,* 47.

392. John F. Kennedy, First Inaugural Address, 1961.

393. Harvey, *Air War: Vietnam,* 103.

394. Reed, *Up Front in Vietnam,* 129–30.

395. Ibid.

396. Ibid.

397. Michael Ryerson, "The Man in the Doorway," www.vhpa.org/stories/doorway.pdf

398. Arthur Hugh Clough (1819–61), "Say Not the Struggle Nought Availeth," originally published in 1855.

399. John Galkiewicz, "The Longest Night in My Life," http://www.angelfire.com/ga3/galkie/indexmoments.html

400. Mike Vaughn, "Two Down," www.vhpa.org/stories/twodown.pdf

401. Ibid.

402. Gary Roush, "Chinook Crash," http://www.angelfire.com/mo/242sdASHC/crash.html

403. Christian G. Appy, *Working-Class War: American Combat Soldiers and Vietnam,* 176.

404. McDonald, *A Spiritual Warrior's Journey,* 90, and an interview with Bill McDonald, October 10, 2009.

405. Ibid.

406. Ibid.

407. McDonald, *A Spiritual Warrior's Journey,* 114.

408. Ibid., 117.

409. Ibid., 118.

410. Vice Adm. Gerald E. Miller, "Training for Combat," *The Hook,* Summer 1999, www.tailhook.org

411. Rear Adm. Paul T. Gillcrist (Ret.), "The Keystone Cops in a Skyraider," *The Hook,* Winter 2000, www.tailhook.org

412. Medal of Honor Citation, Lieutenant Colonel Joe M. Jackson, www.homeofheroes.com/wings/jackson.html.

413. www.homeofheroes.com/moh/citations_living/vn_af_jackson.html.

414. "'Copter Gives Cupid a Lift," *Pacific Stars and Stripes,* July 17, 1968, www.25thaviation.org/id288.htm.

415. Mike Kelsey, "Wedding Bells and Chopper Pads for Couple," *Southern Cross,* Vol. 1, No. 4, August 1968, www.americal.org

416. Ibid.

417. Galkiewicz, "The Miracle Rocket," http://www.angelfire.com/ga3/galkie/indexmoments.html

418. Ibid.

419. John Tuthill, "Why Me?" manuscript given to the author, February 4, 2010.

420. Ibid.

421. Ibid.

422. Ibid.

423. Ibid.

424. Tuthill, "Testimony: Ironside for Veterans," manuscript given to the author, February 4, 2010.

425. Ibid.

426. Ibid.

427. Tuthill, e-mail, February 4, 2010.

428. Pancho Pasqualicchio, interview with the author, May 3, 2010.

429. Ibid.

430. Murphy, "Ridley," vietvet.org

431. Certain, *Unchained Eagle,* 18.

432. Ibid., 11.

433. John Stuart Mill, "Contest in America," *Harper's New Monthly Magazine,* Vol. 24, Issue 143, April 1862, http://digital.library.cornell.edu

434. Lieutenant Commander William Shivell, U.S. Navy, "Remembering 'Bug,'" www.tailhook.org

435. Prayer written by Commander John "Bug" Roach, www.tailhook.org

436. Navy Cross Citation, Captain (then Commander) Paul Lloyd Milius, U.S. Navy.

437. VO-67 Association, www.vo-67.org

438. Certain, *Unchained Eagle,* 33.

439. Ibid., 37.

440. Gillchrist, "Three's a Crowd," *The Hook,* Summer 2000, www.tailhook .org

441. Harvey, *Air War: Vietnam,* 5.

442. Burkett, *Stolen Valor,* 53, quoting Tom Wolfe in "Art Disputes War," *Washington Post*, October 13, 1982.

443. Andrew Glass, "Carter Pardons Draft Dodgers, January 21, 1977," *Politico,* January 21, 2008, www.politico.com/news/stories/0108/7974.html.

444. Jan C. Scruggs and Joel L. Swerdlow, *To Heal a Nation: The Vietnam Veterans Memorial,* 159.

445. Ibid., 72.

446. Gustav Niebuhr, "Veterans Day at the Wall," *New York Times*, November 11, 1994; *NamVet Newsletter,* Vol. 7, No. 1, November 12, 1994, www .vietvet.org/nvetnew.htm. (page 21).

447. Scruggs, *To Heal a Nation,* 152.

448. Ibid., 7.

449. Ibid.

450. Ibid., 80.

451. Ibid., 97.

452. Ibid., 88–89.

453. Rosenthal, "Meet Me at the Wall," May 1992, www.vietvet.org

454. James M. Griffiths, "A Tale of Two Walls," http://11acr.com

455. Ma Van Khang, "Know How to Read a Great Book," *American Experience: Reflections on a War,* www.pbs.org

456. Palmer, *Shrapnel in the Heart,* 93–94.

457. Ibid.

458. Jim Schueckler, "I came to see to see my son's name," www.vietnamexp.com

459. Ibid.

460. "A Forest for Those Who Fell in Vietnam," *Red Clay,* Issue 70, Spring 2008.

461. "Last-Minute Gifts Save a Vietnam Memorial," AP, January 5, 1989, www.nytimes.com

462. Ibid.

463. Ron Rayner, "Chaplain's Corner," *Red Clay,* Issue 71, Fall–Winter 2008.

464. "How do I get over depression?" Vietnam Veterans Bible.

465. "Why do I feel so guilty?" Vietnam Veterans Bible.

466. "Can I be forgiven?" Vietnam Veterans Bible.

467. Mike Wallace and Gary Paul Gates, *Close Encounters: Mike Wallace's Own Story,* 240.

468. Ibid., 241.

469. Santoli, *Everything We Had,* 79.

470. William Crapser, "Returning from Vietnam," *Red Clay*, Volume 73, Summer 2009.

471. Sam Hodges, "Church Evangelizing with Service, Not Sermons," *Dallas Morning News,* July 26, 2007.

472. Ibid.

473. Richard Bernstein, "A Vietnam War Project in Cowboy Country," *New York Times,* March 25, 2007, www.nytimes.com

474. Pham Tien Duat, "Remember in Order to Forget," *American Experience: Reflections on a War,* www.pbs.org

475. Julie Weaver, 11thcavnam.com, iwvpa.net, capveterans.com, warstories.com, dmzdustoff.org, ivydragoons.org, plus others.

476. J. Carole, "It Is Still With You!" www.m11thcav.com

477. Tuthill, "Testimony: Ironside for Veterans," manuscript given to the author, February 4, 2010.

478. Ibid.

479. Ibid.

480. Oscar Wilkie, "Proper Perspective!" *DAV Magazine,* Vol. 32, Issue 5, reprinted in *NamVet Newsletter,* Vol. 7, No. 1, November 12, 1994.

481. Ibid.

482. Pat Conroy, *My Losing Season,* 375–76.

483. Ibid., 371.

484. McDonald, *A Spiritual Warrior's Journey,* 284–85.

485. Mike Fishbaugh, "MIA/Air Force Brought Home," *Red Clay,* Issue 70, Spring 2008.

486. Mark Mueller, "Remains Identified as NJ Pilot Shot Down during Vietnam War," *The (NJ) Star Ledger,* November 27, 2007, www.nj.com.

487. Fishbaugh, "MIA/Air Force-Brought Home."

488. Jack Randles, "Our Day of Thanks," *Southern Cross,* Vol. 1, No. 12, November 1968, www.americal.org

489. Charles M. Gettys, "This Thanksgiving," *Southern Cross,* Vol. 1, No. 12, November 1968, www.americal.org

490. Eric Bray, "Ash and Trash Missions," www.vhpa.org

491. Ibid.

492. Mahedy, *Out of the Night,* 155–56.

493. "Where was God in Vietnam?" Vietnam Veterans Bible.

494. Mahedy, *Out of the Night,* 218.

495. Burkett, *Stolen Valor,* 51–52.

496. Ibid., 64.

497. Ibid., 73, quoting a *Washington Post* article of April 11, 1985, by Barry Sussman and Kenneth John.

498. Ibid., quoting the Vietnam Experience Study, "Health Status of Vietnam Veterans: Psychosocial Characteristics," *Journal of the American Medical Association*, Vol. 259, No. 18, May 13, 1988.

499. Pasqual Gutierrez, "Alpha Troop Stories," http://atrooperoes.com

500. Sam Messer, "When You Leave the Job," *Red Clay,* Issue 71, Fall–Winter 2008.

501. Ed Grisamore, "The Story of the Unknown Boots," *Red Clay*, Spring 2009 (from an article in the *Macon Telegraph*).

502. U.S. State Department, Bureau of Democracy, Human Rights, and Labor, Report on International Religious Freedom, 2004.

503. Craig Pinley, Covenant News Service, "Wheelchair Ministry," June 10, 2000, www.covchurch.org

504. Tourte, "Twenty Years Old," *Red Clay*, Issue 64, Spring 2006.

505. Ibid.

506. Mahedy, *Out of the Night*, 118.

507. Steven Wiese, "I Care," *Red Clay*, Issue 68, Spring 2007, 85.

508. Ibid.

509. Ibid.

510. McDonald, *A Spiritual Warrior's Journey*, 293.

511. Ron Rayner, "My Road to Becoming a Christian," personal letter to the author, January 2010.

512. Tony Melanson, "Obit, Jim Melanson, B Co. 1/26," *Red Clay*, Issue 70, Spring 2008.

513. William R. Miller, *Red Clay*, Issue 72, Spring 2009. MASS Duce is Marine Air Support Squadron 2, 2/5 is 2nd Battalion, 5th Marine Regiment.

514. Raymond Cruz, "The Salute," *Red Clay*, Issue 74, Fall 2009.

515. Tim Scanlon, interview, October 18, 2009.

516. Ibid.

517. Hal Kushner, "Personal Story," www.war-stories.com

518. Ibid.

519. Earl Clark, "To My Friends, Thank You," *Red Clay*, Issue 73, Summer 2009.

520. Rayner, "Chaplain's Corner," *Red Clay*, Issue 73, Summer 2009, essay by Samuel Ullman, 1920.

521. Cadet Prayer, The Citadel, by Bishop Albert S. Thomas, Class of 1892.

522. Downer, *Peace for the Vietnam Vet*.

523. Ibid.

524. Ibid.

525. Ibid.

526. Ibid.

527. Doug Champion, "Remembering a Hero," *The Westerly (RI) Sun*, July 25, 2009, www.thewesterlysun.com

528. Ibid.

529. Mac Gober, "Tough Guy," Vietnam Veterans Bible.

530. Ibid.

531. Dean, *Nam Vet*, 137–38. Learn more about Point Man International Ministries at www.pmim.org

532. Sasser, *God in the Foxhole*, 203–4.

533. Hymn by Joseph Mohr, circa 1816–18, music by Franz X. Gruber, circa 1820.

534. Schueckler, "The Day It Snowed in Vietnam," www.virtualwall.org

535. Ibid.

536. Ibid.

537. James C. Oyster, "Christmas in Vietnam," *Marion (OH) Star,* November 10, 2008, www.marionstar.com

538. Allen Clark, "PTSD from All America's Wars," www.combatfaith.com. Clark can be contacted at allenbclark@aol.com

539. Germaine Copeland, *Prayers That Avail Much,* 485.

540. Ollie Pickral, President, 11th Armored Cavalry Veterans of Vietnam and Cambodia, October 1, 2001, www.11thcavnam.com

541. Ed Pippin, *The Ivy Dragoons Dispatch,* Vol. XII, Fall 2008, www.ivy-dragoons.org

542. Ibid.0

543. Thompson, "The Hound of Heaven," www.cs.drexel.edu

544. Ibid.

545. Mahedy, *Out of the Night,* 204–5.

About the Author

LARKIN SPIVEY is a decorated veteran of the Vietnam War and a retired Marine Corps officer. He commanded Kilo Company, 3rd Battalion, 3rd Marines, and Bravo Company, 3rd Reconnaissance Battalion, in combat. He also served as Executive Officer of 1st Battalion, 9th Marines, at sea in support of Vietnamese Marine units in-country. He was trained in parachute, submarine, and Special Forces operations. He was with the blockade force during the Cuban Missile Crisis and served President Nixon in the White House. As a faculty member at The Citadel, he taught courses in U.S. military history, a subject of lifelong personal and professional interest. He now writes full-time and resides in Myrtle Beach, South Carolina, with his wife, Lani, and their four children. He is a lay eucharistic minister of the Episcopal Church and has been actively involved in the Cursillo Christian renewal movement and the Luis Palau Evangelistic Association. He has made numerous television and radio appearances nationwide and speaks frequently to church, veteran, and other groups with his patriotic and spiritual message.

Then . . .

. . . and now.

For more information about the author, his other books, and speaking engagements, visit:

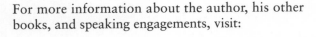

www.larkinspivey.com